OXFORD & CAMBRIDGE

OXFORD

*The book which is
always open at the same page*

CAMBRIDGE

*The book which is
never opened*

OXFORD & CAMBRIDGE
An Uncommon History

Peter Sager

with 63 illustrations, 46 in color

 Thames & Hudson

For Elle & Laura

Translated from the German by David H. Wilson

The publication of this work was supported
by a grant from the Goethe-Institut.

OXFORD & CAMBRIDGE by Peter Sager
© 2003 Schöffling & Co. Verlagsbuchhandlung GmbH, Frankfurt am Main
This edition © 2005 Thames & Hudson Ltd, London

First published in 2006 in hardcover in the United States of America by
Thames & Hudson Inc., 500 Fifth Avenue, New York, New York 10110

thamesandhudsonusa.com

Library of Congress Catalog Card Number 2005923410

ISBN-13: 978-0-500-51249-4
ISBN-10: 0-500-51249-3

Printed and bound in Germany by Bercker

Contents

Cambridge: History and Culture

Preface

There are about 30 Oxfords and 25 Cambridges in the world. This book is about the original prototypes, and tells the story of two cities that became the embodiment of elitism and gave birth to a cultural myth whose patina is as unmistakeable as its enduring potency.

While I was writing it, the Oxford graduate Tony Blair became British Prime Minister for the second time. His Conservative challenger, William Hague, was also an Oxonian, as was the former American President Bill Clinton and the first German Minister of Culture Michael Naumann. While this English edition was being prepared, Blair won his third election, this time beating a Cantabrigian, Michael Howard. The Oxbridge network even extends to the pages of the *Frankfurter Allgemeine Zeitung*, one of whose editors, Frank Schirrmacher, studied in Cambridge, while the arts and culture editor Patrick Bahners, a well-known Donaldist (an expert on the world of Donald Duck), graduated from Oxford. It is in fact amazing how many Germans have enjoyed (or perhaps not enjoyed) the Oxbridge experience, ranging from Theodor W. Adorno to Peter Zadek.

Oxford and Cambridge are not merely educational standard-bearers – they are capital cities of knowledge and all forms of intellectual life, and they have been reaffirming and revitalizing themselves since the Middle Ages, flowing sometimes with but often against the tide of the times. As you wander through the pages of this twin-town pen-portrait, you will visit colleges and you will meet dons and students, but you will not be offered a university guidebook. There is only one thing that I want to convey, and that is the endless fascination of these two cities.

If you want to see the sights for yourself, alas things are no longer quite as straightforward as they were, say, in Victorian times. In those days one of the sights of Oxford was Benjamin Jowett, Master of Balliol College. The guide would stop outside his lodgings in Broad Street, and point at the window behind which the famous professor would be working. Then the guide would bend down, throw a few pebbles at the window, and announce to his group: 'Here is the Great Man himself!'

The historian Hugh Trevor-Roper, who spent most of his life in Oxford and Cambridge as student, lecturer, professor and Master of Peterhouse, Cambridge, made the following comment: 'Who can really know any Cambridge (or Oxford) college? There are depths below depths, caves within caves…. Nothing, in those learned little societies, is quite what it seems.' For the fact that I, as an outsider, was able to explore at least some of the corridors in this academic labyrinth I must thank numerous people and institutions: in Oxford, Dr Norma Aubertin-Potter (The Codrington Library, All Souls College), C. J. Buckley (Oxford Union Society), Lord Ralf Dahrendorf (St Antony's College), Michael Heaney (Bodleian Library), Ann Pasternak Slater (St Anne's College), Dr Benjamin Thompson (Somerville College) and Colin Dexter; in Cambridge, G. C. Cannell (Parker Library, Corpus Christi College), Dr H. Dixon (King's College), Jonathan Harrison (St John's College Library), David J. Hall (Cambridge University Library), Dr Richard Luckett (Pepys Library, Magdalene College), A. P. Simm, CBE (Trinity College), Dr David McKitterick (Trinity College Library), Dr Tessa Stone (Newnham College), Dr David Watkin (Peterhouse), Brian Human (Cambridge City Council).

I would like particularly to thank two Oxbridge friends: the writer and translator David Henry Wilson for various items of information and, once again, for giving an English shape to my German thoughts; and Ted East, former Marshal of Oxford University and retired Superintendent of Thames Valley Police, who skilfully guided me through the problems (and pubs) of town and gown.

I received all kinds of help from my friends in Southwold, Eleanor P. Bray and John O. Veitch (Sidney Sussex, Cambridge), Dr Winfried Knoch (Bonn) and Dr Elke R. Wawers (Staats- und Universitätsbibliothek Hamburg).

I am delighted to have found in Jamie Camplin a publisher who has committed himself so enthusiastically to this project, and am immensely grateful to Thames & Hudson for their meticulous editorial work.

This book is dedicated to my wife, Else Maria, who opened my eyes to some of the most unusual aspects of Oxbridge, and to our daughter Laura, who nevertheless decided, at least for the time being, to go and study in Austin at the University of Texas.

Peter Sager
Hamburg, Spring 2005

Oxbridge:
The Non-Identical Twins

'Future Prime Ministers aren't educated at Durham,' he informed his mother. 'How about Cambridge?' she enquired, continuing to wipe the dishes. 'No political tradition,' replied Simon. 'But if there is no chance of being offered a place at Oxford, surely – ?'
Jeffrey Archer, *First Among Equals*, 1984

Oxbridge is a world in itself, and Oxford and Cambridge are worlds apart. They're about 65 miles away from each other, and yet they're talked of in the same breath and indeed in a single word: Oxbridge. On the intellectual map of the nation, this lies somewhere in the clouds above Middle England – an island above the island, elitist and yet so popular that every year millions of viewers switch on to watch two universities – to whom they are otherwise totally indifferent – jump into boats and row the hell out of each other.

There are some places that have become forever linked with their products, like Sheffield steel or Cheddar cheese, but the Oxford–Cambridge link is made of different stuff. They are like Castor and Pollux, the heavenly twins, shining down from their academic heights, and there is nothing else like them, with the possible exception of their transatlantic cousins Harvard and Yale. Thus it is, writes the novelist Javier Marías, 'that the Oxonians, who react with spontaneous contempt to the graduates of any other university in the world, show selective respect (which can well be the expression of a deeply rooted hatred) to the Cantabrigians, as if they could only feel comfortable in the company of those with whom they must share their uniqueness.'

By comparison with the ages of Oxford and Cambridge, Oxbridge is a youngster. William Thackeray was the first to circulate this synthetic product, in his novel *Pendennis* (1849). The hero, Arthur Pendennis, studies (and fails) at 'St Boniface, Oxbridge'. It was not, however, until the middle of the 20th century that this made-up word (and not Thackeray's variant 'Camford') entered into common usage. The name Oxbridge and the spread of such a 'disrespectful term' signalled the end of a myth, as the Reverend Eric William Heaton, Senior Tutor at St John's Oxford, wrote in 1970: 'Once people went to Oxford or Cambridge, but today

Oxbridge is an alternative to the dozens of other universities that we now have in England.' The universities that sprang up in London and the provinces from the beginning of the 19th century challenged the monopoly of Oxford and Cambridge, offering alternatives of mind and material: first brick, and later concrete and glass. Now there are even new buildings of red brick and plate glass in Oxbridge as well, perhaps to the chagrin of the 'happy few' within the old college walls.

For centuries, these twins were England's only universities. Their origins go back to the Middle Ages and the world of the monasteries. Latin was the equivalent of the Internet for European scholars from Paris to Oxford, from Padua to Cambridge, while Greek philosophy and Christian morality were their spiritual basis. After the Reformation, the colleges managed to survive the dissolution of the monasteries thanks to their status as private foundations. Their autonomy was guaranteed by royal decrees and acts of parliament. Thus Oxbridge played an ambivalent role between Church and Crown, and enjoyed its privileges as a republic of the mind and a refuge of the Establishment.

Through the Church of England, which became the church of the State, the Crown ensured that the two universities would remain loyal and peaceful. After the turbulence of the Civil War, the Act of Uniformity (1662) banned Catholics, Jews, and Nonconformists of all kinds from the colleges, and this continued more or less unabated until the middle of the 19th century. In Oxford every student had to swear an oath on matriculation that he would abide by the Thirty-Nine Articles of the Church of England, whereas in Cambridge this took place on graduation, which at least allowed some dissenters to study, even if they could not end up with a degree.

No other private institutions have had a greater influence on England's history than these two universities. They have provided Church and State with veritable hosts of officials, priests and teachers, who have in turn gone on to spread their language and their culture throughout the land, not to say the world. They are a homogeneous elite, whose sense of duty is exceeded only by their self-confidence – classic preconditions for those offices of leadership associated with kingdom and with empire. But Oxford and Cambridge have always been far more than elitist training grounds for the nation. Alongside the Prime Ministers the colleges also sent out the cleverest spies that Communism could recruit, and next to the Archbishops stood the great heretics and reformers: John Wyclif, John Wesley, Cardinal Newman; there were the rebellious geniuses of literature, from Lord Byron to Salman Rushdie, and large numbers of the lateral thinkers and eccentrics to whom English culture owes its glorious abundance. And so even a radical left-winger like Bertrand Russell would always defend the social and intellectual elitism of Oxford and Cambridge: 'They are wonderfully suited to *first-class people*; the security that they give is, however, damaging to second-class people, who only feel isolated and idiotic.'

In the Middle Ages Oxbridge was the stronghold of scholasticism, and from the Tudor Age onwards, it produced the finest administrators in the realm. What about today? Even now its influence is striking within the corridors of power. Both critics and apologists seem to enjoy nothing more than the social game that constitutes the great Oxbridge race: who has risen from which college to the highest position? The present director of the National Gallery in London, Charles Saumarez Smith, is a Cambridge graduate, as is the present director of the National Theatre, Nicholas Hytner, and at the head of the British Museum stands a Scotsman from Oxford, Neil MacGregor. The British Ambassador in Berlin, Sir Peter Torry, is an Oxonian, and at the beginning of the 1990s, out of 370 Conservative MPs in the House of Commons, no less than 166 were from Oxford or Cambridge. Margaret Thatcher (Oxford) had nine Cambridge ministers in her cabinet of twenty-two. Her successor, John Major – the second non-graduate prime minister since 1945 (after Jim Callaghan) – made up for this handicap by appointing ten Oxonians and six Cantabrigians. As it turned out, this may not have been the ideal safety net for the son of a former trapeze artist. His successor, Tony Blair, was made in Oxford, while the latter's former spin doctor Alastair Campbell first wove his magic in Cambridge, as did the Leader of the Opposition, Michael Howard. Even after the triumph of New Labour, every sixth MP was still an Oxonian.

More than half the senior officials in Whitehall are Oxbridge graduates. The mandarins of the Civil Service, and especially the Foreign Office, turn instinctively to Oxbridge to spawn their new generations, for as a rule no less than 40 to 50 per cent of the most coveted vacancies go to the high fliers with light or dark blue wings. At the bar, the percentage is even higher. Whether it is in Whitehall or Fleet Street, the BBC or the banks of the City, you will hear the same story. The myth perpetuates itself through an excellence that has persisted down through the centuries. 'Everyone thinks we're good,' said Sian Griffiths, President of the Cambridge Student Union. 'It may not be true, but so long as people believe it, it works.' On the other hand, though, the old school tie has long since ceased to guarantee a top job, in spite of the online recruitment agency Oxbridgelife.com.

Six unemployed arts graduates from Oxford came together in London. In order not to starve, they drew lots. Whoever drew the shortest straw was to kill himself, and the two who drew the next shortest straws were to sell his body for scientific research. No sooner said than done. With their dead friend draped over a wheel-barrow, off they went. When they returned several hours later, they still had the body with them. 'Hopeless,' they moaned. 'People only want scientists from Cambridge.' This story, emanating from the circles of the academic unemployed, is not, of course, about the labour market in London, but about the rivalry between the two universities, which goes back to even before the Boat Race, and is more complicated than the laws of cricket. 'If Oxford were not the finest thing in England,' wrote Henry James, 'the case would be clearer for Cambridge.' Are they really so very different? Or are they even more different than they think they are?

Both cities lie on rivers: the Cam and the Isis. Both had fords and bridges and developed quickly into trading centres, holding their own markets and fairs. Oxford had the more favourable situation, in the heart of England, in the urban Thames Valley within smelling distance of the Court. Cambridge remained more isolated in the wilderness of the Fens, a quiet little country town, which in many respects it still is. Oxford is not. It has grown into a large industrial city. There is no physical link between the two – not even a proper road – and if it were not for the universities there would be no link at all. The locals didn't even need these, but once the colleges were there, they had to come to terms with the new reality, which they did with great reluctance and in very different ways: Oxford became a town with a university, and Cambridge became a university with a town.

Even though the two have always gone their own way, Oxford and Cambridge belong together like Adam and Eve. Perhaps feminists no longer grimace when they hear the tale of Eve being made from Adam's rib, but just try telling a Cantabrigian that his or her university was founded by an Oxford scholar. The year: 1209. The reason: obscure, but maybe murder. Not the most enlightening of stories. Cambridge, an Oxford colony. It started as a secession, almost a hundred years after teaching had begun at Oxford. You can never make up for such a late start – anyone with older brothers and sisters can tell you that. You are always the late-comer even if you catch up – or overtake, which is often the case. But this little defect of birth, if such it was, brought about a rivalry that has fuelled the fires of fantasy and given the world some of its finest contests: scientific, academic, sporting, political, artistic, rhetorical, to the level of utter absurdity.

'Oxford for arts, Cambridge for science' – such slogans may please the masses, but they come nowhere near the truth. Oxford has a scientific tradition that goes all the way back to Roger Bacon, even if theology remained dominant there for longer than it did at the university of Newton and Darwin. If one of Cambridge's strengths lies in mathematics, certainly the most imaginative of mathematicians belonged to Oxford: Lewis Carroll, who took his Alice to a Wonderland far beyond the bounds of calculability. Nonetheless, the more prosaic folk of Cambridge set up a Science Park with profitable hi-tech firms some thirty years before their Oxford counterparts.

Cambridge has more Nobel laureates, but Oxford has more prime ministers: Attlee, Eden, Macmillan, Douglas-Home, Wilson, Heath, Thatcher, Blair – all Oxford men (except, of course, Thatcher, who is generally believed to have been a woman), making No. 10 into a kind of Oxford annexe. This, however, never made much of an impression on the serene folk of Cambridge. Oxford people think they rule the world, whereas Cambridge people don't care who rules the world. Since the 1930s, in fact since Stanley Baldwin, Cambridge has produced not one British prime minister. But it has sent forth a remarkable number of spies: Anthony Blunt, Donald MacLean, Guy Burgess, and Graham Greene's 'Third Man', Kim Philby, were all notorious Soviet spies from the murky corridors of left-wing Cambridge. No one in Oxford disputes Cambridge's supremacy in this field, although they also had a Communist spy network there, but it was never uncovered because it never really came out and flaunted itself. Thus the treason of the 1930s was solely a Cambridge phenomenon. It was an Oxford historian, however, who made the most provocative claim – namely, that in the quest for absolute moral truth, Cambridge people tend to consult gurus, while in sceptical Oxford all dogmas and authorities come under far closer scrutiny. 'This intellectual difference,' wrote Hugh Trevor-Roper, 'seems to me to explain why Cambridge rather than Oxford was more susceptible to absolute certainties and hence to the temptations offered by the recruiting agents of Communist Russia.'

The roots of this different morality reach far back into the history of nonconformist Cambridge. Among its students were Thomas Cranmer, Hugh Latimer, Nicholas Ridley – all promoters and martyrs of the English Reformation, concerning whom the (Cambridge) historian Thomas Macaulay wrote: 'Cambridge had the honour of educating those celebrated Protestant Bishops whom Oxford had the honour of burning.' An example of symbiosis *par excellence*. Oliver Cromwell and John Milton studied in Cambridge, which was the university of the Puritans and provided a stronghold of support for parliamentary troops during the Civil War. Oxford was the bastion of the Catholics, became the headquarters of Charles I, and a mouthpiece for the Royalists. When the House of Hanover acceded to the throne, Cambridge demonstrated its loyalty, and George I presented to this university of the Whigs a lavish gift of books. To Oxford, however, in the very same year of 1715, he sent a regiment of cavalry because it was rumoured that at this university of the Tories there were still substantial Catholic and Jacobite sympathies.

Anyone who has lived long enough with such tales will end up believing that in Oxford even now he can sense the Anglo-Catholic, Baroque heritage, and a carefree, relaxed attitude towards life, whereas Cambridge still labours under the severe, often pedantic spirit of the Purists and the Puritans. Even the rain, they say, is drier there than in Oxford. 'In Oxford things are more brilliantly formulated, in Cambridge things are more seriously thought through,' suggests Benjamin Thompson, a Fellow of Somerville who has taught at both universities. Cambridge has a reputation for taking everything seriously – especially itself – but Oxford cultivates the style of effortless superiority, with a weakness for extremes, for eccentrics, and for lost causes. For those seeking to understand these differences of mentality, a great aid is the Monty Python Test. England's classic comedy sextet came with one exception from Oxbridge, and in accordance with their respective origins, they can be clearly distinguished by their style and their personalities. The Oxford men (Michael Palin and Terry Jones) radiate absurdity, visual imagination and warm-heartedness; the Cambridge men (John Cleese, Graham Chapman, Eric Idle) are logical, sarcastic, unscrupulous. Monty Python is a prime example of how well Oxford and Cambridge go together – as contradictory and as complementary as Yin and Yang.

Each likes to call its rival 'the other place', rather like the inhabitants of heaven. The former President of the Federal Republic of Germany, Richard von Weizsäcker, having already received an honorary doctorate from Oxford, was given the same honour by Cambridge in 1994. The fact that Oxford had got there first was dismissed in Cambridge with the observation: 'Never mind, there is always a chance in life to improve oneself.'

An Oxbridge postgraduate will show just whose spiritual child he or she is by means of the title: a D.Phil is from Oxford and a Ph.D. from Cambridge. Academic trivia? Far from it, for these differences are cultivated down to the last letter. An Oxford encyclopaedia has one more letter than a Cambridge encyclopedia, and do not confuse Oxford's Magdalen with Cambridge's Magdalene, or Oxford's St Catherine's with Cambridge's St Catharine's. Watch out too for Oxford's Queen's, which is different from Cambridge's Queens'. The latter was founded by two queens, whereas the former only had one. Even when colleges share the same name, they don't share the same patron saint: St John's in Oxford is named after John the Baptist, whereas the Cambridge St John is the Evangelist.

Oxford and Cambridge are a sort of Tweedledum and Tweedledee but, as they would say themselves, 'contrariwise'. 'It was all Looking-Glassy,' observed Robert Graves when he went from Oxford to visit Cambridge in 1923: 'everything was so much the same and yet so disturbingly different.' Oxford students go for a tutorial, and Cambridge students have supervision; Oxford colleges have quads, and Cambridge colleges have courts; students relax in common rooms (Oxford) and combination rooms (Cambridge); the second term is called Hilary in Oxford and Lent in Cambridge, and classical philologists have an exam called Greats (Oxford) and Mays (Cambridge). Even the Anglophile American Henry James had trouble distinguishing between the two: 'When I say Oxford I mean Cambridge, for a stray savage is not the least obliged to know the difference.' And yet it's all as logical as the apostrophe in Queens'. In Oxford the yearly regatta is called Eights, and in Cambridge it's called Mays, though of course it doesn't take place in May but in June.

Punting is equally popular on the Cam and on the Cherwell, but the style is as different as heads and tails: in Cambridge you stand at the back and use the pole to go forwards, whereas your Oxford man 'punts from the bow and goes stern first.' Which of the two positions is better gave rise to passionate arguments until 1967, when a new type of punt appeared on the Cam – with a square end fore and aft.

They compete on land and on water, for trophies, Nobel Prizes, research grants, academic prestige and political influence. Oxford has the older university, Cambridge the older university press, but Oxford now publishes four times as much as its rival. Even *The Cambridge Quarterly* is published by Oxford – the only Quarterly to appear three times a year.

They don't like to admit that there are more similarities than differences. For the Revised Version of the Bible in the reign of James I, in the 'laboratories' of the Cavendish and Clarendon, Oxford and Cambridge scholars worked happily together. The finest scientists and scholars have taught at both places, like George Steiner, the classic Oxbridge man. Corpus Christi College has a foot in both camps, and so does the historian David Stone, who in 1999 became the first Oxbridge don appointed to teach in both colleges alternately, two years here and two years there.

Finally, as if to prove that the best of rivals can also be the best of friends, there is the United Oxford and Cambridge University Club. Founded in 1817, its home is a classical palazzo in Pall Mall, one of the most exclusive addresses in London's Clubland. Some 4,000 members come from all over the world to enjoy the magnificent billiard and bridge rooms, squash courts, 45 bedrooms, restaurant, library (with 22,000 books) and wine cellar (with double that number of bottles). It used to be the last and noblest male stronghold. Women were not even allowed to use the main staircase, library or bar. It was not until 1996 that the last barriers fell.

Bluestockings and Black October:
Women in Oxbridge

'The great point of Oxford, in fact the whole point of Oxford, is that there are no girls.'
Compton Mackenzie, *Sinister Street*, 1914

On 10 October 1986, fluttering above the porter's lodge of Magdalene College, Cambridge, was a black flag. Many of the students were wearing black or mauve ties and black armbands. Had one of their fellow students died, or a famous don, or perhaps even the Master? No, something far worse had happened, at least in the eyes of the Magdalene macho men: the last male bastion of Oxbridge had just made the decision to admit women – for the first time in 444 years. During that same month, a group of students founded a new club which they called Black October, its purpose being to indulge in a suitably exclusive yearly commemoration of this disaster.

A few years later, in 1992, there was uproar in Oxford. The windows of Somerville College were bedecked with stickers and posters announcing a red NO or a red YES. A vote for university reform, for the Labour Party, against England adopting the euro? No, of course not, for once again this was something far more important: the admission of male students 113 years after the foundation of this all-women's college. 'Somerville's got enough balls' proclaimed the T-shirts of the protesting young ladies, and 'We don't need to go mixed'. The dispute went on for two years, and then the first men moved in.

The history of equal rights for women at Oxbridge is full of strange incidents. Today, female students wander in and out of the colleges as if they had done so for ever. But if you take a glance into the great halls, you will see that the walls are covered with portraits of the famous alumni and the outstanding dons, and they are all men. In this constellation of academic stars, women remain in a tiny minority. All the old statutes specified that women could not be members of the college, and until 1877 the general rule for Fellows was that they must not be married. Even the so-called scouts, who served and waited on the students, had to be men. Colleges were monastic institutions, celibate, inhabited by scribes, scholars and choirboys, Masters and Bachelors, Etonians and gentlemen – closed-off miniature Vaticans. Of this 'patriarchal machinery' Virginia Woolf wrote: 'Every one of our male relations was shot into that machine and came out of the other end, at the age of sixty or so, a Headmaster, an Admiral, a Cabinet Minister, a Judge.'

Nevertheless, some of the oldest colleges in Oxbridge were founded by women. Balliol, for example, named after a somewhat uncouth 13th-century knight, would never have been built had it not been for the enterprise of his widow Dervorguilla, just as Oxford's Wadham College is forever indebted to Dorothy Wadham. It was thanks to her prudence that the library was constructed over the kitchen, thereby keeping the books dry. Six of the oldest colleges in Cambridge were founded by women, but there was not a single college *for* women until the second half of the 19th century.

In England as elsewhere, men wanted their women to be bright and beautiful rather than brainy. Around 1750, with Mrs Montagu's salon in London, the 'blue-stockings' came to prominence (although originally it was the men who wore them), and this somewhat derogatory image clung to the first residential college in England to provide a university education for women: Girton College, Cambridge, founded in 1869. Its founder, Emily Davies, accommodated her girls in Girton, a village on the outskirts of the city, at a safe distance from the men's colleges. The young ladies then had to go some three kilometres to attend lectures. It took eighty years for them finally to achieve recognition as full members of the university. (It was not until 1900 that women were allowed to study at the universities of Freiburg and Heidelberg.)

The second women's college, Newnham, was also set up in Cambridge in 1875, and that must have given the final push to conservative Oxford. The Association for the Education of Women proceeded to lay the foundations for Lady Margaret Hall (or LMH), in 1878, swiftly followed by Somerville College in 1879. While it took Cambridge until 1950 to add two more women's colleges, New Hall and Lucy Cavendish, Oxford fairly raced ahead, and by the end of the 19th century had founded three more – St Hugh's, St Anne's and St Hilda's.

The first lesson for all newcomers is not to be shy of Oxbridge, and for the female pioneers that must have been the hardest task of all. Everything around them reeked of the dominant academic male: the aura of history, the architecture, the bursting libraries, the gardens, the sportsfields – the whole mighty mass of centuries-old scholarship, masculine comfort and exclusivity constituted something that the ladies knew their colleges could never compete with. And so they were all the more determined to pursue the end that they *could* achieve: the same education with the same academic rights.

Only gradually did their student residences develop into colleges with their own tutors and lecturers. Even though some male colleagues were quite liberally minded, the official policy of the university remained extremely restrictive for a long period. There were repeated campaigns and demonstrations, and in May 1897 these reached such a peak that all the university members who were entitled to vote (i.e. the men) were summoned to Cambridge to decide whether women should be allowed to take degrees. A large majority voted against, and celebrated their victory in the marketplace until late in the night. With biblical self-assurance, Dean J. W. Burgon preached a sermon to the female students of Oxford in 1884: 'Inferior to us God made you, and inferior to the end of time you will remain.' In the mid-1930s the writer Nigel Nicolson recalled a history professor at Hertford College, Oxford, informing the girls who had come to listen to him: 'I do not lecture to *undergraduettes.*'

After 1881, women in Cambridge were allowed to take exams, but they were still not awarded degrees. This time it was 'the other place' that led the way: in 1920, two years after England's women earned the right to vote, Oxford University awarded its female students the same degrees as their male counterparts. Cambridge did not follow suit until 1948. In the same year, Girton and Newnham were accepted as colleges with the same rights as all the others. Since then, women have also had the right to a seat and a vote in the Senate, and in 2003, for the second time in its 800-year-old history, the University of Cambridge appointed a woman Vice-Chancellor, Alison Richard, Professor of Anthropology and former Provost of Yale.

Lady Antonia Fraser's account of the house rules in Lady Margaret Hall at the beginning of the 1950s might have come from another century: 'No men were admitted to the college before lunch-time, and they had to leave by supper at seven. There were no locks on the doors. I was told that my Aunt Julia's generation at Somerville had been compelled to put the bed out in their corridor when entertaining a gentleman to tea. We did not exactly have to do that.'

Step by step, in all domains, Oxbridge women have fought for and obtained their rights. In 1908, just forty years after the arrival of the first undergraduettes, the Oxford Union decided to admit women – although only as silent auditors to hear the men debate. 'If the sanctum of the Union were to be profaned by the cackle and pernicious perfume of tea-drinking ladies,' thundered one of the great national newspapers of the 1930s, it would mean 'the end of the art of debating.' Indeed it took until 1964 for the Oxford Union to admit women as full members. In 1977 an undergraduette from Lady Margaret Hall became President of the Union. Her name was Benazir Bhutto, later to become Prime Minister of Pakistan. When in 1993 Pauline Neville-Jones became Chairman of the Joint Intelligence Committee, the old boys' network was at least able to claim that she was 'one of us' – an Oxonian from LMH.

For a long time, there seemed to be a fear that the universities might be overrun by such talents. In 1927 the Congregation in Oxford voted that a limit should be set on the number of places available to women. Each of the five women's colleges was given a quota, and in total they were not allowed to take more than 780 students. Not until 1956 was this quota officially abolished in Oxford, and it took Cambridge four more years to follow suit. Such restrictions helped to keep the women's colleges comparatively poor, and many very gifted women were excluded from studying at Oxbridge. Gradually, however, the picture changed. In 1973, out of 10,331 students in Oxford, 2,094 were women. One year later, the dam broke. Oxford's colleges went mixed.

In Tom Sharpe's *Porterhouse Blue* (1974), the extent of the shock can be gauged from the dialogue between the Master and the porter: 'Women in College too.' – 'What? Living in College?' – 'That's it. Living in College.' – 'That's unnatural, Mr Skullion. Unnatural.'

Brasenose, Hertford, Jesus, St Catherine's and Wadham were the first five men's colleges to admit women. After the Sex Discrimination Act, others also felt themselves constrained to change their statutes – in most cases against the will of the majority of students. When the first girls moved into Christ Church in 1981, they were confronted in the quad by an Oxford-style Full Monty: the male students did a striptease that was a mixture of war dance and fertility rite. The 'Christ Church Rain Dance' did not, however, give rise to a new tradition. More than ever, Oxbridge women knew just what was expected of them: it was not enough to be brilliant; they must be better than the best of the men. In the 1950s, recalls the writer Lady Antonia Fraser, 'all the girls of my generation had to write two essays a week, in contrast to the men who only wrote one.' As time went by, however, competition between the sexes became normalized, but then a new discrepancy emerged from the statistics. In 1973, a year before coeducation had begun, 12 per cent of male and female students achieved first-class honours in Oxford; in 1996, 23 per cent of the men got firsts, and only 14 per cent of the women. Were they not brainy enough, or were they unable to cope with the stresses and strains of Oxford life?

In the meantime, the women's colleges had undergone radical changes. Long gone are the days when the only man to be seen on the premises was the gardener. Girton, the oldest of them all, was the first to admit male students in 1979, and St Hugh's celebrated its 100th birthday in 1986 by doing the same. 'No, we never will!' cried the girls of Somerville. Since their male counterparts were already allowed to spend the night, what was the point in having them living there as well? This logic made less of an impression on the head of the college than the statistics of the Norrington Table. This is the league table of exam results, within which Somerville occupied the number one spot until the men's colleges started taking in women, whereupon Somerville plummeted into the lower depths. It was the same story at Newnham and New Hall in Cambridge. Why? Because the best A-Level girls tended to prefer mixed colleges to single-sex.

In 2003, for the first time the intake of female students in Cambridge exceeded that of men, although Girton and St Hugh's, the original pioneers of female education, now have more men than women. 'They got swamped by the men they let in and lost their sex appeal,' say the 'Hildabeasts', those valiant members of the dying species of women-only colleges. The proportion of female students at Oxbridge has now risen to more than 40 per cent, as it is at most other British universities. This increase is, however, in stark contrast to the static number of female Fellows. Only 19 per cent of Oxford professors are women, and the number is even lower in Cambridge (though even there, the figures are better than in Germany). This seems to be a reverse trend in coeducation, for the former men's colleges continue to take on mainly male dons, and the former women's colleges are doing precisely the same. Even in Somerville, three-quarters of the Fellows are now men – a truly ironic development. In the 1990s, to the outrage of protesting female academics, 95 per cent of appointments and promotions in Oxford went to men. It smacks of sexism, though Oxbridge women themselves are still very wary of any proposals for a quota system.

There can be no doubt that women have won their right to equal opportunities in education, and in particular they have been successful as readers and lecturers, as well as occasionally occupying top positions in the colleges. However, anyone observing high tables or faculty meetings will have to question whether women have been able to take full advantage of these newly acquired rights. At its heart, Oxbridge remains a man's world, the intellectual playground for the old boys' network, with just a whiff of Chanel in the common rooms. Sometimes it can even get overly macho, as when posters appear at the beginning of the term with the slogan 'It's fuck-a-fresher week!' The pressure on women to be both academically successful and at the same time sexy is all the more intense on this continuous intellectual catwalk.

Newnham therefore sticks unyieldingly to its statute that 'All Fellows must be women'. It was at this women's college that in 1997 there arose a quite extraordinary and grotesque controversy. A female astrophysicist who several years earlier had undergone a sex change was outed by her colleague, the radical feminist Germaine Greer, as a transsexual. By law she therefore counted as a man, and so should not remain a Fellow at Newnham.

Another incident made a rather happier impression. May Day is the traditional festival time for students in Oxford, and one of its highlights is when the daring young men fling themselves off Magdalen Bridge. On 1 May 1995, a girl from St Hilda's named Jocelyn Witchard jumped naked from the bridge into the Cherwell, 'striking a blow for feminism and equal opportunities'. Since then, the students of Oxford have respectfully rechristened her college St Thrillda's.

Out of the Blues:
Rugby, Bumps and the Boat Race

'As a seat of learning, it is doomed, as a third-class
watering-place, it has a great future.'
Ben Latham, Master of Trinity Hall, 19th century

According to an old colonial joke, at the peak of Britain's dominance as a world power, Africa was 'a country of blacks ruled by Blues'. Blues are the sporting stars of Oxbridge, recognizable from the colour of their jerseys: dark blues for Oxford, light blues for Cambridge. Winning a Blue is a major achievement, almost on a par with getting a First, but you can only attain this honour by representing your university at one of the sports played between the two great rivals. Victory or defeat makes no difference; you will get your Blue even if you only come second.

Oxford and Cambridge chromatics differs from everyone else's, for you must distinguish not only between light and dark, but also between Full and Half (though neither of these should be confused with Oxford Blue, a deliciously spicy cheese). Full Blues are not awarded for all sports, however. Badminton, archery and table-tennis, for instance, have only achieved Half Blue status, whereas since 1997 squash and basketball and even ballroom dancing have risen to a full height, along with boxing, cricket, football and athletics. But the two glamour sports for the muscle men are undoubtedly rugby and rowing. Aesthetes like Stephen Spender were never much at ease in these sporting circles, and Oscar Wilde felt himself to be out of place when rowing for the Magdalen eight: 'I don't see the use of going down backwards to Iffley every evening.' One day Wilde's son Vyvyan Holland, a student at Trinity Hall, Cambridge, met his friend Ronald Firbank, a prime specimen of Edwardian dandyism. Firbank was on his way back to college in shorts and jersey. Holland asked him what he'd been doing. 'Football,' came the reply. 'Rugger or soccer?' 'Oh, I don't remember.' 'Well, was the ball round or egg-shaped?' 'Oh, I was never near enough to it to see that!'

In the 19th century, before college sports became organized and serious, students indulged mainly in boating, hunting, shooting and fishing – the normal leisure pursuits of young gentlemen. Today there are annual competitions in almost all sports: 'Cuppers' between the colleges, and Varsity matches between Oxford and Cambridge. The rugby match takes place on the first Tuesday in December, and is played at Twickenham, the headquarters of the sport. It is a national event, covered by television, and the list of players who have gone on to represent their country is long and distinguished, though it has been markedly reduced since the game went professional.

These intervarsity sporting duels began in 1827, not with the Boat Race but with cricket. Although the players are all amateurs, they nevertheless enjoy first-class status and play against some of the Counties. Since 2001, however, they have joined up with four other University Centres of Cricketing Excellence to form a league. The one-day Oxford vs Cambridge match is played at Lord's, but the four-day battle now alternates between The Parks and Fenner's. These two grounds are still the only ones where you can watch a first-class county free of charge, and in April it is always touching at the beginning of the season to see the fans with anoraks and thermos flasks taking part in the annual rituals, which for a continental European are as arcane as a Zulu fertility dance.

Some of them might go and thaw out at The Cricketer's Arms in Oxford, where perhaps they will drink a toast to the memory of Charles Burgess Fry. C. B. Fry won a triple Blue for athletics, cricket and soccer (representing England in all three), and in 1893, while still a student at Wadham, set a world record in the long jump, allegedly between two puffs on his cigar. As a batsman he became an English cricketing legend, and he played for Sussex in company with Prince

Ranjitsinhji – another national hero who began his cricketing career in Cambridge, beautifully described in Ian Buruma's novel *Playing the Game*. In more modern times, Oxbridge has spawned many outstanding England captains such as Ted Dexter, Peter May, Colin Cowdrey, Mike Brearley, and more recently Mike Atherton, but not even they could achieve the superstar status of C. B. Fry. His portrait, complete with a patriarchal Victorian beard (though according to Buruma he looked like 'a Greek god with a bat') is among the icons to be found at Vincent's in Oxford.

Of all the sports clubs in the two universities, this is the most famous. Its membership is limited to 150 students who are chosen for their all-round talents, 'social, physical and intellectual qualities being duly considered', according to the statutes of 1863. Even today, women are not allowed in, except as dinner guests. Of all the anachronisms at Oxbridge, Vincent's certainly leads the way. The walls of the premises in King Edward Street are hung with photographs of prominent members, including two former prime ministers (Harold Macmillan and Sir Alec Douglas-Home, the latter having been the only British prime minister to have played first-class cricket), two kings (Edward VIII and Olaf of Norway), a viceroy of India and several archbishops. Anyone qualified to wear the club tie – three crowns on a dark blue background – will have a head start in the careers race, particularly in the City of London.

Former presidents of Vincent's include the neurologist Sir Roger Bannister. On 6 May 1954 he was the first man to run the mile in under four minutes, which he did on the Iffley Road track in Oxford. That was also the training ground for Lord Porritt, who later became George VI's personal physician and who in 1924, while still a student at Magdalen College, won a bronze medal for New Zealand in the 100 metres at the Paris Olympics. Films like *Chariots of Fire*, which immortalized the story behind that race, have contributed as much to the myth of the Oxford Blue as more modern celebrities such as Imran Khan, the glamorous Pakistan cricketer turned politician, and Earl Snowdon, who left Cambridge without a degree but with a coveted Blue for being in the triumphant Cambridge eight of 1950. It was essential, he said, to hate one's opponents as if they were one's enemies, which in the post-war period meant: 'You thought of Oxford as Germans.' Exactly a hundred years before, the Victorian author and 'muscular Christian' Charles Kingsley, in his novel *Alton Locke*, described a regatta in Cambridge as the embodiment of imperial 'Englishness': 'The true English stuff came out there …the stuff which has held Gibraltar and conquered at Waterloo – which has created a Birmingham and a Manchester, and colonised every quarter of the globe –

that grim, earnest, stubborn energy, which, since the days of the old Romans, the English possess alone of all the nations of the earth.'

Rowing is recorded as far back as 1793 as one of the main activities of the students. Anyone wandering round the colleges today and seeing the graffiti might think that Oxbridge was nothing but a rowing academy, for daubed all over the walls in fresh or faded paint are crossed oars with dates, lots of names, and the cryptic caption 'Head of the River'. This is the emblem granted to any college whose crew is victorious in Bumps. These take place in Eights Week, known as May Week in Cambridge, or the fifth week of the Trinity Term, which in actual fact is the beginning of June. This regatta marks the end of the academic year, and is one long celebration of balls and concerts.

In Bumps the college crews start at a certain distance from one another, and the whole point is to bump the boat in front of you and knock it out of the race. The collisions go on for four days, at the end of which the leading boat is declared 'Head of the River'. This very special form of watersport developed in Oxford, beyond Iffley Lock, where the Isis gets too narrow to hold several boats rowing abreast, and records go back to 1815, when Brasenose were the first winners. But the race that caught the nation's imagination was not Bumps. It was the annual Boat Race between Oxford and Cambridge.

The Boat Race is far more than a mere sporting event. The time was, and in some cases still is, when it split whole families and even the country as a whole into light blues and dark blues. In 1979, at the traditional celebratory dinner held at the London Savoy, Harold Macmillan told the audience: 'My father was at Cambridge, so as a child we were Cambridge. Nanny was violently for Oxford.' The novelist Colin Dexter told me that he had now been living in Oxford for more than thirty years, 'but I still want Cambridge to win the Boat Race'. Over 400 million viewers tune in every year to watch it, although the oarsmen are not even the best in England, let alone in the world – an obsessive fascination that is as irrational as the appeal of Oxbridge itself.

The first race took place on 10 June 1829, along the Thames near Henley, and Oxford won. The present course, between Putney and Mortlake, goes back to 1845, and the race has been rowed annually since 1856, generally on the last Saturday in March, when the weather is at its most unpredictable. The course measures four miles and 374 yards – seven kilometres, which is more than three times as long as the furthest Olympic event. Oxbridge rowers do not have the luxury of still waters – the Thames is a moody tidal river, which doesn't even run in a straight line, but curves in a great S-bend. The Cambridge crew sank in 1859 and 1978, and the Oxford crew in 1925 and 1951, while 1912 was the roughest year of all because both of them sank. To date, no crew has ever been disqualified.

The oarsmen train six hours a day, six days a week, six months of the year, and training is as much of a torture as the race itself. Cambridge train on the Ouse, and Oxford on the Isis (actually part of the Thames), and nowadays it's rare for any crew to be without a hunk of imported American muscle; indeed the respective club presidents tend to recruit the best rowers from Berkeley, Boston or Harvard. Every so often there are Germans in the boat as well, and the winning Cambridge crew of 1998 contained two German world champions in Marc Weber and Stefan Forster. In 1981 the first woman cox, Susan Brown from Wadham College, steered the Oxford boat to victory.

Cambridge hold the course record of 16 minutes 19 seconds (1998) as well as having the slowest winning time of 26 minutes 5 seconds (1860). But for all this endeavour, and in spite of the fact that sponsors are more than welcome when it comes to financing the boats and the training, there is no money involved for the rowers themselves. This is amateur sport at its purest – dash without cash. The winners' trophy, donated by a liqueur company and usually presented by a member of the Royal Family, is a relatively new addition. Up until 2005, Cambridge had won 78 times, and Oxford 72, with one dead heat in 1877: 'Oxford won, Cambridge too' (*Punch*).

The eternal losers when it comes to the Boat Race are the London University crew. The purples have not been beaten for years, but of course they can't take part in *the* Boat Race. The 1991 challenge thrown down by the London trainer Marty Aitken ('The Boat Race is a pretty boring event') was regarded as poor form by Oxford: 'It is a private race between England's two oldest universities. London taking part would spoil the whole event'. The Cambridge trainer added a further dimension to the debate: 'Marty is Australian and does not understand the culture.' Clearly there is more to the Boat Race than merely finding out which crew is the faster!

Speed is also a secondary consideration for the competitors in the annual Tortoise Race. For more than thirty years this race between Balliol and Corpus Christi has been one of the most spectacularly unspectacular sporting events in the calendar. It is the apotheosis of slowness, drawn straight from the nonsense world of Lewis Carroll. The grand finale of 1993 was truly unforgettable, when the Balliol tortoise, the glamorous Rosa Luxemburg, beat her Corpus Christi rival Thomasina by inches in an astonishing sprint-crawl finish.

Student Societies:
Fat Bastards and Tiddlywinkers

'Clubs. Join the Carlton now and the Grid at the beginning of your second year.
If you want to run for the Union...make your reputation *outside* first, at the Canning
or the Chatham, and begin by speaking on the paper.'
Evelyn Waugh, *Brideshead Revisited*, 1945

Anyone walking down the High Street in Oxford at the beginning of the
Michaelmas Term, i.e. in early October, when the academic year gets under-
way, will come upon 'Freshers' Fair' in the Examination Schools. Here the
different student societies display their wares in an attempt to attract new members: there are clubs for fans of King Arthur, *Doctor Who*, the Mad Hatters, Bell
Ringers, Arcadian Singers, a Chinese Debating Society, a Lesbian Gay and Bisexual Society, and a Tiddlywinks Society.

Some of these sound more eccentric than they really are, but many are more
eccentric than they really sound. The Oxford Guild of Assassins is a non-violent
drinking club, named after a Persian secret society. The Pooh Sticks Society meets
for comic debates, presided over by Winnie the Pooh, and they all go together to
Magdalen Bridge and throw sticks into the Cherwell, resulting in races far more
passionate than the Boat Race itself.

Oxford students have a choice of more than 200 societies, not counting the innumerable sports clubs. Cambridge boasts the same rich variety. There are political,
religious, literary and musical societies, theatre groups, hiking groups, ethnic
groups, and clubs for the oddest subjects and the weirdest hobbies. If someone has
an interest that isn't catered for, in no time there will be a new society. Nowhere in
the world is there such a vast variety of associations in such a confined space, and
they are all magnificent vehicles for self-expression, for the nurturing of talent, for
eccentricity, friendship and social intercourse.

Mountaineering, for example, has been a competitive sport among the Oxford
elite since the 19th century. The Mountaineering Club attracts especially intellectual climbers, whose exploits might include such peaks of achievement as planting
a chamber pot on the dome of the Radcliffe Camera. Apart from the conventional
sports, there are such associations as Oxford's Dangerous Sports Club, whose
members are obliged, for instance, to jump from the Golden Gate Bridge in San
Francisco. Less heroic souls might prefer the initiation rites of the Cambridge

Claudians – a dining society which is named after a particularly gluttonous Roman emperor, and whose novitiates must introduce themselves with an ode to drunkenness in Latin.

The Oxbridge love of strange rituals finds its most inventive expression in these societies. Anyone wishing to join the Fat Bastards in Oxford must, in the course of one evening, devour a shepherd's pie, a cream cake, an apple crumble with custard, and in total one stone (6.35 kg) of goodies. It appears that there is no great rush of applicants, which of course guarantees exclusivity. But the really exclusive clubs are as hermetic as Freemasons' lodges, and they do not even try to recruit people at the Freshers' Fair. Among the most recondite is Cambridge's Metaphysics Club, which according to its constitution cannot have any club officers and is not allowed to indulge in any activity. Such pure contemplation is not the hallmark of most Oxbridge societies.

There have always been a few dining and drinking societies that have burnished the elitist image of Oxbridge. The rituals, ideals, vanities and class-consciousness of these male bastions were described by Evelyn Waugh in his first novel *Decline and Fall* (1928): 'At the last dinner, three years ago, a fox had been brought in in a cage and stoned to death with champagne bottles. What an evening that had been!' He was at Hertford College during the 1920s, and friendships and 'serious clubbing' were of considerably more importance to him than examinations – which he scraped through with the lowest possible grade. His favourite club was the Bullingdon, known as the Bollinger, and it is still one of the most socially prestigious (otherwise called snobbish) addresses in Oxford, along with the Gridiron Club – the Grid – which was founded in 1884 and whose members have included crown princes, top politicians, and writers such as John Le Carré ('I played the classy guy'). The actor Hugh Grant was among the handsome young men to be drawn to the Piers Gaveston – a club named after Edward II's favourite which, like its Cambridge counterpart the Adonians, only accepts male members. The female equivalent at St Catharine's College is called the Alley Catz, and one of its initiation rites is the consumption of a Mars Bar out of a pair of men's underpants (with or without the man inside them).

Clubs and societies in the modern sense of the terms have existed in Oxford since the middle of the 17th century. There were regular musical gatherings in the house of the St John's College organist, while the Warden of Wadham used to invite his top scientists for social get-togethers, and as far back as 1694 friends of the arts and of the Celts used to meet in the Red Herring Club. By the middle of the 18th century, there were more than forty such societies in Oxford, including the Free Cynics, the Arcadian Society, the Jellybag Club and the Nonsense Club. 'Those little Nocturnal assemblies' Joseph Addison called them, and as social networks they were to play a not insignificant role in the political life of the nation. Political societies per se, however, did not come into being until relatively late: the Canning Club was founded in 1861, and the Oxford Conservative Association in 1869. It was there, in 1945, that a chemistry student named Margaret Roberts began her career. Soon afterwards, she got married and became Mrs Margaret Thatcher. The real training ground for future prime ministers, however, was the only Oxford club to have been founded in the Regency period and still to be in existence today: the biggest and most famous of all, the Oxford Union (see p. 152).

Oxford
History and Culture

Uproar at the Ford for Oxen:
A Short History of Oxford

'God, these bloody English. Bursting with money and indigestion.
Because he comes from Oxford. You know, Dedalus,
you have the real Oxford manner.'
James Joyce, *Ulysses*, 1922

L ong before I first visited Oxford, I had felt its special, bittersweet taste on my tongue. It was in 1874 that Frank Cooper's Oxford Marmalade first found its way onto the nation's palate, and it then proceeded to spread itself on breakfast toast all over the British Empire. But it was not only marmalade that had made Oxford into a familiar name. The Oxford Movement, Oxford shoes and Oxford bags (flannel trousers) all took their name from the city, as did the colours Oxford blue and Oxford grey, and the Victorian Oxford picture-frame, and even the artificial Oxford knee for those who needed a new joint. And what student has not heard of the exemplary form of the language, Oxford English, or its affected echo, the Oxford accent?

You approach it from Elsfield or down Boar's Hill, and there you see it – the famous view of Oxford with all its 'dreaming spires'. The city lies in a dip, though everyone who studies there goes *up* to Oxford. This little preposition bears all the weight of the superiority that adheres to Oxford like Frank Cooper's marmalade mixing with the butter. There is even a bed shop here with the Pepysian name 'And So To Bed'.

Oxford's patron saint is Frideswide, an early 8th-century Anglo-Saxon princess. She fled from an importunate suitor as far as the Isis, which she is said to have crossed on the back of an ox, and on the opposite bank she founded a nunnery and performed various miracles. Christ Church Cathedral now stands on the site of her convent, and the town grew up around it. This is one of those virginal foundation myths so beloved of the Middle Ages, and the story of the saint is told in shining colours by an Edward Burne-Jones window in the Cathedral.

The etymology of Oxford is thus made clear, but where was the first ford? Was it at Magdalen Bridge, or Hinksey Ferry? The latest excavations suggest that it was near the present-day Folly Bridge, in the south of the city. The name 'Oxnaforda' is first mentioned in the Anglo-Saxon Chronicle of 912, and the settlement was established at a spot where it was easy to drive the cattle across the river, at an intersection of ancient trade routes running from north to south and from east to west, virtually in the middle of central England. The gravel banks between the Isis and the Cherwell offered solid, dry foundations, and the rivers themselves provided natural protection on all sides. But it was the Anglo-Saxons who first settled here, as the ancient Romans avoided building in such marshlands.

Oxford is still surrounded by meadows except in the north, and it is very much a green city whose fields bear such poetic names as Music Meadow, Angel Meadow and Magdalen Grove. These fields are often flooded, though not so much today as in the past. The climate is wet and misty, which is ideal only for gardeners and melancholics like Robert Burton. The biographies of famous Oxonians are full of headcolds, depressions and indefinable neuroses. The American novelist Herman Melville, who did a grand tour of Europe, remarked in his journal in May 1857: 'Catching rheumatism in Oxford cloisters different from catching it in Rome. Contagion in Pamfili Doria but wholesome beauty in Oxford'. The real Oxford disease, however, apart from the permanent snuffles, has been described by Colin Dexter as 'that tragic malady that deludes its victims into believing they can never be wrong in any matter of knowledge or opinion.'

In the Domesday Book of 1086, Oxford is listed as having 1,018 houses, which made it the sixth largest town in England after London, York, Norwich, Lincoln and Winchester. The walls enclosed a rectangle of some 50 hectares. Today only names like Westgate Shopping Centre and Eastgate Hotel recall these long since demolished ramparts, and even Beaumont Palace, the royal residence, has left little trace other than the name of Beaumont Street. At the western end of this stood Henry I's palace, in which his grandson Richard the Lionheart was born – more or less on the spot where the bus station is now situated. Oxford in those days was an expanding market town, at the centre of the Cotswolds' textile and wool industry. Weavers and tanners had organized themselves into guilds, and their businesses on Cornmarket Street were flourishing. The charter which Henry II bestowed on Oxford in 1155 endowed these guilds with certain trading privileges and gave the citizens the self-confidence of belonging to a city that was far older than its university. For it was only around this time, though no one knows exactly why or when, that the first academics appeared at the ford for oxen.

They came from Paris, various English masters and scholars either on their travels or driven out of the university there, perhaps summoned home by Henry II after he had quarrelled with Philip Augustus, and the University of Paris became closed to Englishmen. This happened in 1167, but the beginnings remain somewhat obscure, and certainly there are no royal or papal seals to formalize the foundation, as there were with many continental universities. In the search for suitable founding fathers, there has been much imaginative speculation: King Alfred was one candidate, and the Roman Brutus another, while several Greek philosophers are said to have thought their great thoughts around 'Oxina'. But why Oxford anyway? Why did the university rise up here in the provinces and not in the great metropolis? Nobody has yet come up with a satisfactory answer.

Even before the first charter of the *Universitas Oxoniensis* (1214), there had been informal lectures and courses of study, based mainly in monastic schools. Augustinians, Benedictines, Cistercians, Carmelites, and later Black Friars, Grey Friars and all the major religious orders had establishments in Oxford, and the first-known Chancellor of the University (*c.* 1224) was Robert Grosseteste, who later became Bishop of Lincoln. He was a great scholar and theologian who developed a methodology that combined Aristotelian logic with Catholic Orthodoxy but also incorporated optics, physics and astronomy into a teaching programme that extended far beyond the confines of metaphysics. Grosseteste was the first in a long line of great Franciscan scholars in Oxford that included Roger Bacon, John Duns Scotus and William of Ockham. It was these and a number of mathematically orientated philosophers from Merton College who were predominantly responsible for Oxford's rapid rise to become one of the leading universities in Europe. 'Study as if you were to live for ever: live as if you were to die tomorrow.' This was the advice that St Edmund of Abingdon gave to his students. He led the life of an ascetic, became Archbishop of Canterbury, and was canonized in 1247 – an Oxford icon.

Initially, the majority of the students lived in so-called halls, the predecessors of the present-day colleges. These *hospitia* or hostels were private lodgings rented by individual teachers in the town to accommodate their students and provide rooms for teaching. It was only when various bishops and courtiers began to found the colleges that these became proper institutions with their own statutes. Unlike the hostels they were possessed of permanent endowments, which were conditional upon the obligation to pray for the soul of the founder. This symbiosis of learning and remembrance of the dead gave the colleges autonomous powers and increasing influence over university politics. The halls, of which at one time there were more than 120, were gradually swallowed up by the colleges, and today St Edmund Hall is the only survivor without an endowment.

Towards the end of the 12th century the various scholastic and residential communities linked up to form a university, which initially constituted nothing but an
universitas magistrorum et scholarium – a combination of teachers and students
who organized themselves as a kind of academic guild which, like other guilds,
gave its members legal protection and privileges, including rent control. Along
with Paris and Bologna, Oxford was one of the first three European universities.
Prague did not follow until 1348, while the earliest German university was Heidelberg in 1386. Oxford, however, developed its own constitution which was quite
different from those of its continental counterparts. The Oxonians insisted on
electing their own Chancellor, which gave the university relative independence
from Church and State and was only limited by the autonomy of the individual
colleges. This federal collegiate structure, which prevents centralization, is common to Oxford and Cambridge even today, and matriculation for instance is done
by the colleges and not by the university.

Oxford's growing reputation soon attracted students and teachers from all over
Europe. They lived mainly in the north and east of the old city, in the vicinity of
the University Church of St Mary. This became the so-called Latin Quarter, where
Latin was spoken and the academic gown was worn. The town with its commerce
was concentrated in the west, in the Cornmarket area, and this division between
town and gown is still apparent.

And so it all began. The migrants had arrived, initially as tenants but then as
their numbers increased, so they settled in, spread themselves out, constructed
their own premises and indulged in their own strange rituals. The townsfolk looked
on suspiciously, as if the university was a cuckoo that had landed in their nest.
Nevertheless, they profited from these unpopular newcomers – the landlords as
well as the businessmen, bakers, shoemakers, tailors, stonemasons, service indus-
tries, all of whom grew fatter as the colleges grew bigger. But of course there were
also constant tensions between town and gown, with resentments and conflicts
never far below the surface. It all came to a head in 1355 on St Scholastica's Day.

It was Tuesday 10 February, and a group of students in the Swyndlestock Tavern
complained that the wine was bad. Jugs were thrown, and the pub brawl developed into a street battle. Even this was not exactly unusual, but during the next
two days the townsfolk ran riot, and ransacked the student quarters, looting and
killing. In the end, 63 students lay dead in pools of their own blood. The King
imposed a fine on the town, to be paid in instalments over the next 500 years. After
that, every year on St Scholastica's Day, Oxford's mayor together with 62 citizens
had to eat humble pie. At a memorial service in St Mary's they would hand over

the requisite amount to the Vice-Chancellor of the university: one silver penny for every dead student. Not until 1825 was this symbolic penance lifted. On 10 February 1955 there was a further gesture of reconciliation: the Mayor was made an honorary doctor of the university, and the Vice-Chancellor received the honorary freedom of the city.

Right from the start, however, it was the privileges of the gown that upset the town. The charter of 1214 had granted the university certain rights in relation to the town: the academic teachers, then all clerics, were not subject to civil authority but only to that of the Church. The Chancellor, or *cancellarius scolarium Oxonie*, was not slow to exercise his powers, for as the highest authority he was not responsible simply for the discipline of the students. During the Middle Ages his Chancellor's Court endowed the university with legal powers that could cost the miscreant not just an arm and a leg, but his head as well. As recently as the 18th century, a college servant was condemned to death because he had stolen some wine from Brasenose. The university had the right to control market trading and to license theatrical performances within a twenty-mile radius, and it did not officially give up its legal sovereignty until 1977.

Oxford University was a monastic-style institution, just as Cambridge was. Its medieval scholarship was derived from this background, but the ecclesiastical, monastic roots of the colleges have only survived in peripheral matters like the black gowns, Latin rituals and titles, and names like Jesus College, Trinity, All Souls and Corpus Christi. Magdalen's foundation stone is immured in the chapel altar, a fixed symbol from the distant past. While early Italian universities flourished in the fields of medicine and law, it was the *doctrina sacra*, the School of Divinity, that dominated the Oxford scene. It was not for nothing that John Wyclif called Oxford 'the Vineyard of the Lord'. A theologian and vehement critic of the Church, Wyclif taught at Oxford until 1381, when he was banned from teaching. By translating the Bible into English, he made it directly accessible to everyone, but this and his critical writings were viewed as heresy. In the 14th century no less than six Archbishops of Canterbury came from Merton College, and the present incumbent, Rowan Williams, did his doctorate and taught at Oxford. There were more episcopal college foundations in Oxford than in Cambridge, and the number of bishops and deacons was also far greater. But the theological seminars also spawned political power, for the Crown often plucked its chancellors and ministers from the higher ranks of the clergy. Thus Oxford became a national institution, producing a long line of brilliant church and state dignitaries, and the history of the university became a mirror of the history of England.

In the early 16th century, Oxford had a population of about 3,000. It was still a small town which during the Renaissance grew into a centre of intellectual life, on a par with such universities as Paris, Padua and Salamanca. The humanist Erasmus of Rotterdam sensed this spirit when he visited Oxford in 1499. He stayed there for three months, enjoyed the discussions and the college feasts, but was disturbed by 'that sordid and superstitious crowd of divines, who think nothing of any learning but their own', and he was conscious of 'the jealousy of so many men' – in other words, the same old problem of academic arrogance. Later he settled in Cambridge, although he always preferred Oxford, or so the Oxonians like to believe. The humanistic ideal of educating the whole person helped to secularize the colleges, from the libraries through to the curriculum. Now, instead of the medieval divinities, it was the humanities that were generally focused upon, and instead of the scholastic canon, students were given a more linguistic and literary training, based on study of the ancient classics. From this emerged the Faculty of the *Litterae Humaniores*, which are now known as Greats. Philology and History became the central subjects, and for generations of students Greek and Latin became the passport to success in Africa, India and the rest of the world. Anyone who knew about the Roman Empire was considered basically qualified to run the British Empire.

The Reformation bit deep into Oxford. St Frideswide's Priory, Osney Abbey, Godstow, Rewley – the monasteries had circled the city like a rosary since the Middle Ages, but now they crumbled into dust. However, when the Protestant reformers also wanted to dissolve the colleges and plunder their riches, Henry VIII put his foot down: 'I tell you, sirs, that I judge no land in England better bestowed than that which is given to our universities, for by their maintenance our realm shall be well governed when we be dead and rotten.' And so although the religious orders lost their colleges, the colleges themselves were not lost: Gloucester Hall turned into Worcester Hall. Durham College into Trinity, but the biggest of them all, Wolsey's Cardinal College, which was then still under construction, was newly founded by the King himself after the fall of Wolsey, then was extended and took on the new identity of Christ Church, and in 1546 it became the centre of the new bishopric of Oxford. At the same time Henry VIII also founded Trinity in Cambridge – a clear demonstration of the importance he attached to the college system at the two universities. Of course, he expected the theologians to help him establish the Church of England. When soon afterwards his daughter Mary came to the throne and wanted the country to return to Catholicism, Oxford's theologians played a leading, if not altogether laudable role.

In 1555 two major figures of the Reformation were sent from the Tower to Oxford. It was here and not in London that Bishops Hugh Latimer and Nicholas Ridley were made to appear before an orthodox ecclesiastical court, to face the charge of heresy. The Disputation took place in the School of Divinity, a classic show trial, and the heretics were burned at the stake opposite Balliol College. 'Be of good comfort, Master Ridley, and play the man; we shall this day light such a candle, by God's grace, in England as I trust shall never be put out.' Latimer's last words are among the most heroic to have come down to us from the Reformation. He died a swift death. The powder that had been hung round his neck exploded, whereas Ridley's stake merely smouldered ('I cannot burn!' he cried). Barely six months later, Mary the all-too-Catholic also sent the Archbishop of Canterbury, Thomas Cranmer, to the stake in Oxford.

Elizabeth I played her part too in university politics, with rather more moderation than her half-sister, though with no less resolve. Oxford and Cambridge had now had the monopoly of Anglican education for quite some time, but this strength was also their weakness: Catholics, Jews, Quakers, Baptists, atheists and Nonconformists of all kinds generally remained excluded from studying there until well into the 19th century. Every student was made to swear on the Thirty-Nine Articles of 1571, affirming his Anglican beliefs – at Oxford when he registered, and at Cambridge before he took his examinations. Not until 1854 was this dubious test of conscience abolished, but until 1871 dissenters were still excluded from all academic positions and professorships.

During the Civil War, the old conflict between town and gown reached another and somewhat unusual crisis point. The university remained loyal to the King, while the town sided with Parliament. For four years, Oxford was the Royalist capital, and in autumn 1642 Charles I, having been driven out of London, moved his court and his army to his academic headquarters. He requisitioned some of the colleges, and had their silver melted down in order to finance his war effort. New College became his arms depot, and University Parks his artillery base. Dons and students alike were forced to spend one day a week digging trenches. King Charles himself lived at Christ Church, and Queen Henrietta Maria at Merton. Between the two lay Corpus Christi. In order to facilitate access between King and Queen, a wooden gate was made in the garden wall – King Charles Gate which, I was assured by David Leake, the anti-Royalist gardener at Corpus Christi, 'has never been opened since'.

On 24 June 1646, Oxford fell to the parliamentary forces, although the King, disguised with a false beard as a servant, had already fled the city in April. Two years after his execution, the university elected Oliver Cromwell to be its Chancellor. But once more Oxford, 'home of lost causes', had put its eggs in the wrong basket, for the monarchy then made its comeback. Just like his father, Charles II resided at Christ Church when he came to Oxford, took his King Charles spaniels for walkies in University Parks, and put his mistress Lady Castlemaine in Merton. The fact that in 1665 she bore him a son in this very college was not part of the plan, but it was still a great deal more welcome than the plague, which killed 70,000 people in London alone. Oxford, as the King's second home, hosted two sessions of the English parliament, the 1681 session being the last to be held outside Westminster.

Of all the dynasties, it was the Stuarts who were most closely tied to Oxford. Nevertheless, in 1687 there arose a power struggle between the university and the Crown. In defiance of the colleges' autonomy, James II installed a Catholic as President of Magdalen, with the intention of making Oxford subservient to Rome and bringing England back on the path of the true religion. But he could not get the Fellows of Magdalen to toe his line, and he could not intimidate them either, and even when he dismissed them, the college still rejected his choice. He came to Oxford in person, but still to no avail, and two months before his own downfall he finally gave way. There were jubilant scenes at Magdalen, and the bells were rung. The celebrations have gone on ever since, and every year the reinstatement of the Fellows is marked by a Restoration Dinner on 25 October.

Right from the start, the university sought the protection of the Crown. Oriel was the first college to have a royal patron, Edward II. Regius Professorships – established by a monarch and officially appointed by the current monarch – have always been highly coveted, but despite all this proximity to and even dependence on outside authority, the university has never allowed any impingement on its autonomy. Elizabeth I twice visited her 'dear Oxford' ('God bless thee and increase thy sons in number, holiness and virtue'), and James I praised it as the 'holiest temple of Mnemosyne', mother of the Muses. Only Queen Victoria seems to have disliked 'that old monkish place which I have a horror of'. It did not, however, stop her from sending her eldest son Prince Edward to study at Christ Church. 'Bertie' found Oxford boring, and preferred Cambridge. Prince Charles's elder son William, on the other hand, couldn't be bothered with either of them, and went off to St Andrews instead.

It is not only the British Royal Family that likes to inject a bit of dark or light blue blood into the veins of its issue. King Olaf V of Norway sent his daughter to Lady Margaret Hall and his son to Balliol (where he had studied himself). The first member of the Japanese Royal Family to be educated outside his own country was

Crown Prince Naruhito, who took his degree in history at Merton College in 1988, writing a thesis on the role of the Thames as a transport route during the 18th century. His wife Masako and brother Aya also studied there, and since then the Japanese elite have regarded an Oxford degree with the same veneration as the very best designer labels.

There has been one constant source of annoyance in Oxford: the traffic. 'Oxford city is sheer hell. Compared with New York, it's five times as crowded and the noise of the traffic is six times louder.' (W. H. Auden) The 56-mile journey to London used to take two days, until express coaches like Bew's Flying Machine cut the travelling time to a single day after 1669. With the increasing number of coaches towards the end of the 18th century, it became necessary to demolish the last two city gates. There were a hundred stagecoaches a day at that time, which shows just how relative 'sheer hell' can be.

A far more pleasing form of progress had meanwhile emanated from one of the colleges. In 1637 a new and wonderful aroma wafted its way through the corridors of Balliol: the heavenly smell of coffee. A student from Greece named Nathanael Konopios 'was the first I ever saw drink Coffé,' his contemporary John Evelyn recorded in his diary.

England's first coffee house opened in Oxford in 1651: The Angel on the High Street, more or less where the Grand Café is situated today. Nearby, at Tillyard's, young Christopher Wren drank his coffee, read the latest newspapers from London, and discussed life and the world with his friends from the Chemical Club, later to be the firebrands of the Royal Society. The second half of the 17th century was a golden age not only for the coffee houses, which were known as 'penny universities' because a cup of coffee cost a penny, but also for the academic world, for Oxford boasted a whole host of famous names, ranging from John Locke the philosopher to Robert Hooke the physicist. It was at this time too that the colleges gradually began to change into a mixture of club and high-class residence.

The rich sons of the upper classes, who since the Restoration had made their way in increasing numbers to both Oxford and Cambridge, extended the curriculum in their own inimitable way to embrace drinking, gambling and whoring – pursuits far better geared to the needs of young bloods than the study of Greek or Hebrew. The historian Edward Gibbon spent 14 months in 1752–53 as a student at Magdalen College, and rated them as 'the most idle and unprofitable of my whole life', for the professors had long since 'given up altogether the pretence of teaching', or if they did do any teaching, it was clerical and reactionary. Gibbon had to leave the university anyway, as he was a self-confessed Catholic. Dr Johnson, the great lexicographer, also left Oxford after just a year in 1729, 'depressed by poverty', as his friend Boswell explained. Even a clever brain requires soles on his shoes. 'Our Universities are impoverished of learning, by the penury of their provisions. I wish there were many places of a thousand a-year at Oxford, to keep first-rate men of learning from quitting the University.'

In the 18th century, the university was a microcosm of the class society outside. The poorer scholars were part of the social hierarchy, financing their studies as 'servitors', waiting on the 'gentlemen commoners', the privileged members of the college club for whom Christ Church had already built apartments of their own by 1600. In such an atmosphere, the Wesley brothers and their friends stood out a mile. They came together in 1729 at Lincoln College, where John was a Fellow and Charles a student, and on weekdays they read the classics together, on Sundays the Bible, but in addition they visited prisons, attended the sick, and did a great deal of social work. Their contemporaries dubbed them the 'Holy Club', or 'Bible Moths', or – because they lived and worshipped so methodically in accordance with their convictions – 'Methodists'. Methodism, which was meant initially as a term of ridicule, was to turn into a worldwide religious movement.

Oxford was always a town of thinkers and seekers, of famous sceptics and fanatical reformers, from John Wyclif in the 14th century to John Wesley and a long line of successors. Those present at the Assize Sermon in St Mary's on 14 July 1833 could say that they had seen the beginning of the Oxford Movement. The preacher was John Keble, Professor of Poetry, and his subject was the nation's departure from the true faith. The immediate spur was the oppression of certain Irish dioceses, and the wider problem was the independence of the Church from the State and its return to its Catholic roots. In the years that followed, radical ideas were to spread from Oxford all through the country, sparking off one of the great controversies of the time, and exercising a great deal of influence on the cultural life.

The Oxford Movement is said to have been born in the Common Room at Oriel. This was the meeting place of the three dons who were the spearhead of the movement: John Keble, later a country parson and popular hymn-writer; Edward Pusey, a professor of Hebrew and canon of Christ Church; and John Henry Newman, vicar of St Mary's. In sermons and a total of ninety *Tracts for the Times*, they propagated their reforms: one must go back to the teaching of the Fathers of the Church, to the old liturgy, to the mysteries of the Sacraments, one must care for the poor in the cities, and not only for their souls. This was an attempt to find a middle course between Rome and the Church of England – a new, Anglo-Catholic form of piety.

John Henry Newman became the emblematic figure of the Oxford Movement. His sermons filled St Mary's and divided Oxford. 'Who could resist the charm of that spiritual apparition, gliding in the dim afternoon light through the aisles of St Mary's, rising into the pulpit, and then, in the most entrancing of voices, breaking the silence with words and thoughts which were a religious music – subtle, sweet, mournful?' This description of the great preacher comes from Matthew Arnold, who was a student at the time. The 'Newmaniacs' copied their hero in language and dress, fasted when he did and, to the intense irritation of their opponents, were inveterate cigar smokers. In 1845 Newman converted to Catholicism, which came as a great shock to his disciples, and then he left Oxford. Many years later, the Pre-Raphaelite painter John Everett Millais portrayed him as a pale, ascetic, charismatic figure in the scarlet robe of a Cardinal.

Keble College, Pusey House: at its place of origin the Oxford Movement seems more tangible than anywhere else, even if its reformist zeal has long since been dissipated by the Anglican establishment. All that remains are the incense-burning High Masses at St Mary Magdalen, the traditional High Church liturgies with their Catholic leanings. And by the canal in the part of the town known as Jericho lies the former flagship of the Oxford Movement, St Barnabas Church, neo-Romanesque, neo-Byzantine, with its shining golden apse. A 19th-century cartoon depicts the church as a Victorian railway station: 'St Barnabas, all change for Rome!'

The anti-papal mood had a long tradition. Catholics were once regarded as fifth columnists, in the service of Spain and France, England's great enemies. Catholicism was a deadly political sin. And then this happened – a movement which resulted in the numbers of Catholics in England more than doubling between 1840 and 1850 to around 846,000.

Even in more recent times, many prominent converts have come from Oxford: writers like Graham Greene and Evelyn Waugh, the fervent poet and Jesuit Gerard Manley Hopkins, the Anglo-Catholic apologist C. S. Lewis, fans of whose Narnia books included even Pope John Paul II. The Master of Balliol, where Greene studied during the 1920s, was the first Catholic since the Reformation to have been appointed as a Fellow: 'Sligger' Urquhart, one of those legendary dons whose alleged vices so incensed Greene's friend Evelyn Waugh that he went out into the college quadrangle one night and shouted, 'The Dean of Balliol sleeps with men!' In Waugh's *Brideshead Revisited*, Jasper gives his cousin Charles the following advice: 'Beware of the Anglo-Catholics – they're all sodomites with unpleasant accents.'

Not until 1854 were Catholics, Jews and other Nonconformists officially admitted to the university. The abolition of the Thirty-Nine Articles of the Church of England was due in no small measure to the Oxford Movement.

Another kind of movement also came to Oxford: the railway. But as has often been the case in England, it arrived late. Until 1844 the dons refused to let it in. Stagecoaches then took only six hours to get to London – why should the students be given even swifter access to the temptations of the capital? The university also vehemently opposed the establishment of a Great Western Railway carriage factory in Oxford, and so in 1865 this industrial plum went to Swindon. It seemed that the Industrial Revolution had no chance of making its way into the city of dreaming spires. It is true, though, that in 1790 Oxford, like every other self-respecting town in England, had allowed itself to be penetrated by a canal. This linked the town to Coventry and the coal mines of the Midlands – an important economic factor, even if the dons didn't like it – and this was the first major instance of cooperation between town and gown since the tragedy of St Scholastica's Day.

Oxford's wealth in the Middle Ages derived mainly from the cloth makers. When eventually they left for the rural regions, it was only the colleges that gained from this loss of business, because now they were in a position to buy the prime sites in the city centre. By the middle of the 19th century, more than half the inner city, over 30 hectares, belonged to the university. The locals lived in the narrow lanes off the High Street, or in the unhealthy suburbs. There were frequent cholera epidemics, also in the slums of St Ebbe's, in the midst of which stood Christ Church. Between 1801 and 1851 the population doubled to more than 25,000, and in the working-class districts poverty and disease were rife. During the 19th century there was only one notable industry in Oxford, and that was books – the biggest employer, with a staff of 750, being the University Press.

Oxford University Press. There is something majestic about the name and about the coat of arms of its owner: an open book between three crowns, with seven seals and the motto Dominus illuminatio mea – 'The Lord is my light' (Psalms 27: 1). The Word of the Lord meant good business, as Archbishop Laud discovered in 1636. That was when he acquired the exclusive right for his university to distribute the Authorized Version of the Bible, as well as the royal privilege of being allowed to print books of all kinds. Bibles and prayer books were OUP's best-sellers in the 19th century, and were shipped by the ton to America and all corners of the British Empire. Then came text books, anthologies, encyclopedias and dictionaries, above all the legendary Oxford English Dictionary. Thus Oxford Books became famous, and the Press became the largest university publishing firm in the world.

What were conditions like for the workers? In 1830 the Press moved to a magnificent new building in the suburb of Jericho, and in addition to its specialists, it employed hundreds of children. The factory laws did not apply to presses. Ten-year-old typesetters worked twelve hours a day, and were paid five shillings a week or less. They were known as 'printer's devils'. When they reached the age of sixteen they were fired so that the Press did not have to pay them adult wages. It was no better in other Victorian presses. Today, however, Oxford books are printed all over the world – except in Oxford. The university closed its own press in 1989, as it was no longer competitive.

From the early 19th century, after the writer William Cobbett's visit to Oxford in 1822, when he wrote scornfully of the colleges, ' the drones that they contain and the wasps they send forth', criticism of the academic ivory towers became sharper. The university reforms of 1854 modernized both the administration and the curriculum, which now included the natural sciences. There was also improved access for poor students, and twenty-five years later the first female students were admitted. Other restrictions, including the ban on Fellows getting married, were lifted in 1877, and it was really only now that Oxford emerged from the Middle Ages.

By 1900 Oxford had almost 50,000 inhabitants, and the town had far outgrown the university. There were some 2,500 teachers and students – and all of them were cyclists. Out of this somewhat different Oxford Movement grew the University Cycling Club, the oldest in Britain, founded in 1877. The highest density of cycles in England can be pin-pointed with absolute accuracy: at the King's Arms on the crossroads at the end of Broad Street. Only in Hanoi will you find more cycles than in Oxford.

At the end of the 19th century, an enterprising young townie took note of this transport phenomenon. At the age of fourteen he started repairing cycles for students, and in 1901 he opened his own cycle shop in the High Street. His name was William Richard Morris, later to become Lord Nuffield – England's most successful car manufacturer. At 21 Longwall Street, opposite Magdalen's deer park, stand the old Morris Garages, birthplace of the MG.

The first Morris Oxford left the works in Cowley in 1913. It was a small, cheap, snub-nosed car that became immensely popular. Soon there were over 100,000 a year coming off the production line. Another William Morris had, after his Oxford studies, revolutionized the Arts and Crafts movement at the end of the 19th century and had also preached Socialism, but it was his 20th-century namesake who brought full employment and fair wages to the people of Oxford. By 1936 Morris was the biggest car manufacturer outside America. After 1945 two more highly successful cars came out of Oxford: the Morris Minor, which became a symbol of the post-war era, and the Austin Mini, which all the stars of the Swinging Sixties loved to drive, from Twiggy to Lord Snowdon. At its peak, the car and steel works in Cowley had some 30,000 employees, but then competition from abroad inevitably took its toll, and after several mergers, the numbers had dwindled to a few thousand when BMW took over the remnants from Rover. October 2000 saw the last of 5,387,862 Minis leave the factory. However, its successor, the new Mini, is once more being manufactured in Cowley and has proved to be the best-selling British car in Japan.

In the boom period, town and gown had been joined by a third Oxford, which John Betjeman called 'Motopolis'. It was almost as if Oxford had become Cowley's Latin Quarter, with the university a mere appendix to the great industrial city. It was a world within a world, observed the student Stephen Spender. 'The part of the town known as Oxford to members of the University was a little archipelago of colleges, churches, halls and a few old buildings, surrounded by the flooding red-brick tide of industrial Oxford, on which lorries and cars floated like the craft of a new era among Greek islands.' Within thirty years the population doubled to almost 100,000 (1939), with a large influx of people from Wales and the Midlands. But the university expanded too, from 1,300 students in 1850 to 4,600 in 1931. By the end of the century, that number had more than tripled. The growing number of female students, undergraduates from state schools, natural scientists and postgraduates all contributed to this rapid growth.

In October 1934 a young philosopher from Frankfurt embarked on the heroic enterprise of getting the tough guys of Merton College to 'think in contradictions'. Theodor Wiesengrund Adorno, as he was then known, was one of the German emigrants to have found refuge in Oxford from Hitler's Nazi Germany. Others included the Austrian winner of the Nobel Prize for physics Erwin Schrödinger and his colleague Nicholas Kurti from Berlin, who as one of the leading experimental physicists at the Clarendon Laboratory later worked on the development of the British atom bomb. From Heidelberg came the philosopher Raymond Klibansky; from Vienna the art historian Otto Pächt, and a pupil of Schönberg's, Egon Wellesz, later to be a specialist at Lincoln College on Byzantine music; from Hamburg Ernst Cassirer; from Prague the anthropologist and poet Franz Baermann Steiner; and from Freiburg Eduard Fraenkel – the first foreigner to occupy the Chair for Classical Philology. Little wonder that after this influx of so many prominent German scholars Oxford was regarded as 'the best German university in Europe'. The poet and essayist Michael Hamburger fled from Berlin as a child along with his family in 1933, and survived his years on the 'Gothic rack' of Christ Church to become a great champion of German literature in the English-speaking world through his translations of Hölderlin, Celan, Grass and others. The fact that the Bodleian Library has one of the most extensive archives of Felix Mendelssohn-Bartholdy is also due to a German emigrant – a Fellow of Balliol, Albrecht Mendelssohn-Bartholdy, a direct descendant of the composer.

Oxford today has forty colleges, but you still get American tourists stopping you on the street to ask, 'Where's the university?' The name also casts its lustre on a vast number and variety of other educational institutions: prep schools, second-ary schools, a polytechnic, secretarial colleges ('seccies' to the students), language schools by the dozen, summer schools, academies, private colleges – all of them marketing themselves with the famous Oxford label. And then there are the 'crammers', like Edward Greene's Tutorial Establishment, where would-be undergraduates (or their parents) pay horrendous fees to hone their academic tal-ents to the required sharpness. Since the decline of the motor industry, education has become Oxford's biggest earner alongside tourism, which is booming and keeps a good 10,000 people in employment.

Oxford is a city of books, and is the second largest publishing centre in the country after London. The hospitals, too, which are as highly specialized as the colleges, are among the traditional pillars of the economy. Then there are hi-tech firms and an expanding service sector in which over three-quarters of the working population now earn their living. During a trip to Oxford in the summer of 1996, I saw between the sightseeing buses (which really ought to be kept out of the over-crowded streets) the very first pedicabs – cycle rickshaws – a new tourist service devised by some enterprising students. In that same year, the city engaged its first director of tourism, having been content until then just to have a tourist office without lowering itself to actual marketing ('never wanted it, never needed it'). Oxford receives about five million visitors a year, half of them on day-trips going to and from London and Stratford-upon-Avon. Along with Venice, Florence, Salzburg, Bruges and Aix-en-Provence, it counts as one of the six most chroni-cally overcrowded cultural centres in Europe. If UNESCO had its way, during the high season we would only be able to visit the city with an entrance ticket, strictly timed as if it were a Vermeer exhibition.

Beyond the realm of the colleges and their hordes of tourists lies the other Oxford – the barren concrete wastes of Barton and Blackbird Leys, the fringe estates where the fringe people live – the social cases, the unemployed, the single parents, the pensioners, the ethnic minorities...though even in the prosperous heart of the city, you can't avoid seeing the losers and the lost. 'One gets the impression that there are nearly as many beggars as there are students. The latter are the main reason for the proliferation of the former,' writes Javier Marías in his novel *All Souls*. Oxford, one of the richest cities in England, has the largest number of homeless people per head of the population anywhere except in London – a vast collection of down-and-out drifters. Oxford seems to draw them like a magnet, as indeed it has done since the Middle Ages, when beggars and migrant workers could always be sure of alms and a bed for the night thanks to all the monks and philanthropists congregated here. This tradition continues today through the work of Oxford Night Shelter and other charities.

Oxford has been called the 'begging bowl capital of Britain', and the more hopeless the project, the more enthusiastically it will be embraced, as if Oxford owed it to itself to maintain its reputation as the 'home of lost causes'. On 5 October 1942 a group of Oxford citizens gathered in the Old Library of St Mary's to organize food aid to the war zones, and in particular for the people of Greece. Town and gown joined forces for this initiative, which was the brainchild of a Quaker lady. At that time there were a lot of similar organizations, but only one – the Oxford Committee for Famine Relief – became world-famous, and of course it is now known by its abbreviated name Oxfam. It has more than 30,000 volunteer workers and almost 900 charity shops throughout Britain, and is the country's most important charity for countries of the Third World. It is also the richest, with a yearly income of around £100 million.

The 1990s saw local inhabitants among the homeless for the first time. The shortage of accommodation is worse than in comparable areas of London. Large housing blocks in the centre belong to the colleges, and they rent these out to the students, but other accommodation remains sparse and expensive. There are several thousand families on the waiting list for the City Council's social housing, and hundreds of them are now in temporary lodgings or mobile homes on the edge of the town. Those who can afford it move to North Oxford, Old Headington or Cumnor Hill, but in the meantime even the modest houses of the former working-class suburb Jericho have become both trendy and expensive. By comparison, eastern Oxford, Cowley, Botley and Osney remain relatively cheap.

What about the old conflict between town and gown? From 1604 onwards, the university was allowed to send its own MP to Parliament, independently of the city and elected by all Oxford graduates, no matter where they lived. This academic privilege, which James I also granted to Cambridge, was finally abolished by the Labour Government in 1945.

Similarly in 1974 Parliament took away the university's right to representation on the City Council. And so after 600 years, Oxonians became ordinary citizens. Today there are no more major battles in the streets, and at worst there are disputes over planning matters and the occasional skirmish between students and townies.

The accommodation crisis, however, crime and other social problems are no less rife than in other large towns, although they may be less obvious to the tourist. The Oxfords of the All Souls dons and of the Cowley Pakistanis, of Balliol and of Blackbird Leys, are worlds apart. 'Oxford is not an easy place to settle into,' said Richard Harries, Bishop of Oxford. 'Whereas I didn't feel nervous. I had all the social assurance of a person who was a Cambridge graduate!' It is a city of barriers and rifts: between town and gown, university and polytechnic, the different districts, colleges, schools of thought, between academic and other staff, and between insiders and outsiders. The city lives on these contrasts and even seems to foster them, and it thrives too on the irony and the humour that they engender, with an eccentric love of language such as permeated all of Alice's adventures in Wonderland.

From Geoffrey Chaucer to Javier Marías:
Literary Oxford

'The clever men at Oxford
Know all that there is to be knowed.
But they none of them know half as much
As intelligent Mr Toad.'
Kenneth Grahame, *The Wind in the Willows*, 1908

The first Oxford student you will find in English literature is a seducer. He sings, plays the psaltery, and smells 'as sweete as is the roote of lycorys'. We don't learn a great deal about his studies, but we are treated to a detailed account of his love life. In *The Miller's Tale* (c. 1395) Geoffrey Chaucer tells the story of Nicholas the student, who has lodgings in the house of a carpenter. He seduces the latter's young wife Alison, and he does this most charmingly and most cleverly, thereby exemplifying all the advantages of an Oxford education. 'A clerk hadde litherly biset his whyle, / But if he koude a carpenter bigyle' (in other words, his studies have been wasted if he can't cheat a carpenter). Naughty Nicholas is the prototype of the academic *roué*. Centuries later, in the days of Brideshead, his equivalent would leave college with a teddy bear in his arms.

Chaucer presents another scholar in his *Canterbury Tales*: the noble 'Clerk of Oxenford', who is hollow-cheeked, melancholy, rather shy, devoted to Aristotle rather than to fine clothes, a true scholar – ' gladly wolde he lerne and gladly teche' – who, for all his learning, had remained as poor as the proverbial church mouse. He rode forth upon his ancient nag, the first of the Oxford Dons, to be followed hundreds of years later by the hollow-cheeked, melancholy Aristotelians in their ancient Morris Minors.

Since Chaucer's 14th-century saga, Oxford has always been one of those places as rich in fiction as it is in real life – like Venice, or maybe Atlantis. You can get to know the town, the people, the houses, the smells, the strange ideas without even going there. It is a place to be thought about rather than seen, and its spirit speaks more to readers than to tourists. Apart from London, there is no other city in England, and no other university in the world, that has had so much written about it. For 600 years authors have been writing stories, essays, poems, memoirs, guidebooks, diaries, anthologies, biographies and hundreds and hundreds of novels. Oxford is a fiction, and the city named Oxford is just its suburb.

The true foundations for Oxford's many-sided literary myth were laid above all by two authors: William Camden and Matthew Arnold – an Elizabethan historian and a Victorian poet and critic. In his *Britannia* (1586) William Camden, a humanist and a patriot, showered Oxford with praise: 'our most noble Athens, the seat of the English Muses…the very soul of the nation'. Oxford University could never have mounted a finer advertising campaign than this prolonged piece of trumpet-blowing. A graduate of Christ Church, Camden described it as 'the most celebrated fountain of wisdom and learning, from whence Religion, Letters and Good Manners are happily diffused thro' the whole kingdom'.

But if you want to know what Oxford was really like in the 17th century, read John Aubrey's *Brief Lives* – an absolute joy for any reader. At Trinity College he had 'the greatest felicity of my life', and got to know many of the heroes whom he describes in such inimitable fashion – these worthy Fellows and their favourite subjects: drinking, gambling, whoring and even walking 58 miles to London and back again, just to win a bet.

And so Oxford became the 'seat of the Muses' and the Olympus of learning. Defying even its periods of academic drought, Camden's literary topos was taken up, with many variations, by all the elite of England, until John Ruskin and all the Victorians actually believed that Oxford was the hub of the academic world. The echoes even resounded from Cambridge, with much-quoted praise ranging from Samuel Pepys ('Mighty fine place!') to John Dryden. One of the best of all Oxford poems was written by a Cambridge man, William Wordsworth: 'O ye spires of Oxford! domes and towers! / Gardens and groves! your presence overpowers / The soberness of reason....'

What the Romantic Wordsworth felt during his visit on 30 May 1820 became a byword to rank with Matthew Arnold's 'dreaming spires'. This is Oxford *par excellence*, the picture postcard view that we all have in our mind's eye. Arnold's magical expression combines imagination and reason, beautiful architecture, and a sense of some lofty, noble truth. This is stone turned into the dream of reason.

The man who coined the image was a schools inspector for thirty-five years, and one of the most influential literary and cultural critics of his time. In 1857, Matthew Arnold returned to his place of study as Professor of Poetry, and he proved equally popular as a poet and a teacher. With *The Scholar Gipsy* and *Thyrsis*, two elegiac Oxford poems, he wrote his way into the hearts of the Victorians. These are the pastoral works of an intellectual who, despite the onward march of the sciences and industrialization, maintained his love of the countryside. In the wide bend of the Isis between the mouth of the Windrush and the Cherwell lay his favourite, then still unspoilt haunts of Ilsley Down and Hinksey, Bagley and Cumnor Hill, the latter with its classic view of Oxford celebrated in the immortal line from 'Thyrsis' (1867): 'that sweet city with her dreaming spires'. A tree still stands in solitary isolation on the hill, the 'signal-elm' – except that literary sleuths scouring 'Arnold Country' soon discovered that it was not an elm but an oak. Those 'dreaming spires', however, became beacons for generations of Oxford-lovers. The emotions of the graduates, the memories of the alumni, ambition, pride, disappointment – everything led to this one great image before time downgraded it to the level of cliché.

The other scarcely less popular image of Oxford is also derived from Arnold: 'home of lost causes'. It is in the preface to his *Essays in Criticism* of 1865 – a eulogy but at the same time an elegy to his spiritual home: 'Beautiful city! so venerable, so lovely, so unravaged by the fierce intellectual life of our century, so serene!' This is the enthusiastic beginning of the most famous, most quoted description of Oxford in English literature – a veritable Moonlight Sonata that conjures up all the magic of the city and its history more perfectly than 'all the science of Tübingen' – that aura of golden youth in a medieval setting, and that melancholy but heroic 'home of lost causes, and forsaken beliefs, and unpopular names, and impossible loyalties!' Again and again Oxford had proved to be just that – forever on the losing side, in matters of faith and in the Civil War, loyal indeed to the point of absurdity. Soon Arnold's contemporaries would see another lost cause in the classicism of which Oxford had become a bastion. The 'dreaming spires' and the 'home of lost causes' now sound like advertising slogans – much in the vein of 'Guinness is good for you' (the invention of another Oxford graduate, Dorothy L. Sayers). But like no other writer, Matthew Arnold had given form to the sentimental idealization of Oxford at that time, and it lasted until well into the 20th century. When Cecil Rhodes lay on his deathbed far away in Africa, he did not want a passage from the Bible read to him, but the Oxford passages from Arnold's book.

Oxford was never a place of dreams, and yet the romantic image lived on, and a Victorian children's book turned it into a wonderland. Its author was a mathematician named Charles Lutwidge Dodgson, who for a pseudonym turned his Lutwidge into Lewis and his Charles into Carroll. His heroine was a little girl he had met at the college: Alice Liddell, daughter of the Dean of Christ Church. The shy bachelor told his finest stories to her and her two sisters as they rowed along the Isis, and the stories became *Alice's Adventures in Wonderland* (1865).

After she has fallen down a rabbit-hole, and subsequently in the land *Through The Looking-Glass*, Alice goes through a whole series of strange experiences and absurd encounters, just as in real life, only crazier. Readers all over the world can identify with the topography of her childhood, for this was also their own. At the same time, however, a whole industry of interpretation has evolved, one strand of which makes Oxford itself the location of the adventures. The grotesque gargoyles on the college walls, the bizarre rituals of the dons, Lewis Carroll's contemporaries, Alice's environment – everything becomes a fantastic puzzle and an equally fantastic solution, with Wonderland nothing else but an Oxford bestiary. It has been explored more thoroughly than China, from the rabbit-hole to the branch on which the Cheshire Cat sat smiling. But if one takes the story literally, one will see that there is one setting that stands out above all others, and that is language.

'If it was so, it might be; and if it were so, it would be; but as it isn't, it ain't. That's logic.' Playfully Lewis Carroll, this great wizard of words, undermines the rules of language and logic, and as perspectives constantly switch, so the conventions of the adult world are turned upside down, nonsense reigns, and the everyday world turns into a wonderland. 'Do let's pretend....' In a world of such possibilities, Alice is constantly playing new roles and trying out new forms of expression as she searches for her own identity. Thus her adventures may also be read as a series of verbal tests and professorial parodies, from the egg-headed Humpty-Dumpty to the Caterpillar lecturing to Alice from his mushroom podium – a very special sort of tutorial. Incidentally, the Oxford-born thriller writer P. D. James was desperate to know as a child whether Humpty-Dumpty had indeed fallen from the wall or was pushed. Thus began her life in crime.

Lewis Carroll made Oxford the capital of nonsense and fantasy, and it was from here, a hundred years later, that J. R. R. Tolkien's hobbits went out into the world, while C. S. Lewis took us through a wardrobe into the world of Narnia. These exotic flowers of professorial fantasy were also flights from the academic realm into that of myth, the unconscious, and childhood. And the latest flight of Oxford fancy comes from the children's author Philip Pullman, a graduate of Exeter College. *Northern Lights*, the first volume in his trilogy *His Dark Materials*, is set partly in an imaginary Oxford, in Jordan College, which has been spreading its branches both above and below ground since the Middle Ages.

In spring 1879, a young priest and poet named Gerard Manley Hopkins went upriver from Oxford to Godstow. He had already gone on this classic walk along the Isis when he was a student, as so many had done before him. He was therefore all the more upset by the sight of fallen trees on the riverbank. On his return home, he wrote an elegy on the poplars of Binsey, with a passionate grief crying out through every syllable: 'My aspens dear, whose airy cages quelled / Quelled or quenched in leaves the leaping sun, / All felled, felled, are all felled....' As a Jesuit in the anti-Catholic atmosphere of Oxford, Hopkins, who at the time was curate at St Aloysius (built in 1875 as the first new Catholic church in Oxford since the Reformation), felt as isolated as had his famous theological predecessor Duns Scotus. Hopkins dedicated a sonnet to him and to the 'grey beauty' of the city – one of the subtlest of all Oxford poems, whose first lines seem to vibrate with the sound of the bells and the birds: 'Towery city and branchy between towers; / Cuckoo-echoing, bell-swarmed, lark-charmed, rook-racked, river-rounded....'

The call of Oxford was like a siren's song, echoing far across the Atlantic. After Washington Irving received an honorary doctorate from the university in 1831, almost all the most famous 19th-century American writers went to Oxford (and to Stratford) on their European Grand Tour. Ralph Waldo Emerson, Nathaniel Hawthorne, Herman Melville, Mark Twain and Henry James came and sang its praises. 'Old reef washed by waves & showing detached parts – so Oxford,' noted Melville in May 1857, and he enthused over the lawns ('Grass smooth as green baize of billiard table') and the college Fellows: 'Improvement upon the monkish. As Knights Templar were mixture of monk & soldier, so these of monk & gentleman'. Oxford was seen as a pastoral seat of learning, and college life was like living on a country estate. For authors from the New World, this was the very epitome of European culture. It was not Bill Clinton but an earlier president, Woodrow Wilson, who wrote home enthusiastically after his visit in July 1896: 'A mere glance at Oxford is enough to take one's heart by storm.' It is true that Emerson viewed the colleges as 'finishing schools for the upper classes, and not for the poor', but that was as integral to the England of the time as the monarchy. Reacting to this growing Oxford-worship by American students and tourists, Max Beerbohm wrote: 'While Americans have a right to exist, they should refrain from exercising that right in Oxford.' Such silliness did not prevent F. Scott Fitzgerald from endowing his Great Gatsby with the glamour of an Oxford education.

Henry James was the prototype of the Anglophile American, and his depiction of his compatriots' love for Oxford is second to none. Here they found a unique combination of learning and emotion, of ambition and high spirits, for 'Oxford lends sweetness to labour and dignity to leisure'. In an early short story, *A Passionate Pilgrim* (1871), he describes a dying American named Searle returning for the last time to his Alma Mater: 'No other spot in Europe, I imagine, extorts from our barbarous hearts so passionate an admiration,' says Searle to the friend who is accompanying him through Oxford. The college gardens were 'the fairest things in England and the ripest and sweetest fruits of the English system...they seem places to lie down on the grass for ever, in the happy faith that life is all a vast old English garden, and time an endless English afternoon.' But just before he dies, while still in Oxford, he asks a leading question: 'Isn't it all a delightful lie?'

In Holywell is a graveyard where the fictional Searle gazes at fine English soil from down below, but here too lies the real American science-fiction author James Blish, who was buried in 1975. Like Henry James, he had settled in England, and he is best known for his work on the *Star Trek* series. In 1964, this Oxford fan from New Jersey wrote a biographical novel about Roger Bacon, *Doctor Mirabilis*. It is said that the 13th-century Franciscan scholar had a laboratory in the gatehouse that once stood on Folly Bridge, and his experiments caused a sensation throughout Europe, for they anticipated the invention of gunpowder and flying machines. He was a real-life science-fiction hero of the Middle Ages.

In 1895 there appeared a novel that shook the Oxford myth to the core: Thomas Hardy's *Jude the Obscure*. It is the story of an outsider, Jude Fawley, who longs to come into the light, into the 'paradise of the learned'. He comes from a simple provincial background to Christminster (= Oxford), in order to study theology. But he is rejected by all the colleges, including Biblioll (= Balliol). He is 'a man with a passion for learning, but no money', and such a man at such a time had no chance of access to this upper-class university. Ironically, he finds employment as a stonemason, working on the very walls that bar him from study. And it is as a stonemason that he meets his early death.

This is a *Bildungsroman* with a working-class hero who dies in poverty – in Oxford! It was an affront to late Victorian society, and the critics were outraged. *Jude the Obscure* shattered a national myth, and it was not until many years later, after the university reforms, that Hardy was finally recognized in Oxford with the award of an honorary doctorate in 1920. Today there is a pub in Jericho named after Jude, for that was there he had his lodgings, and in 1996 Michael Winterbottom's *Jude*, a film version of the novel starring Kate Winslet, caused quite a stir.

The so-called 'Oxford novel' became a popular genre in its own right during the 19th century. Generally the central figure was a student facing a series of spiritual and moral challenges that tended to be more along the lines of a Rake's Progress than a Pilgrim's. Oxford and its colleges were the background to a curriculum consisting predominantly of wine, women and gambling debts, and the embodiment of all such heroes was undoubtedly William Makepeace Thackeray's Arthur Pendennis, the eponymous hero of *Pendennis* (1849). A failure at his college, St Boniface (= Pembroke), he is nevertheless a fine figure of a snob who, 'after meeting certain men of a very low set in hall', finds himself bathing in perfume.

Readers loved such insights into the fascinating world of the social elite, particularly at a time when Oxbridge was very much the domain of the privileged upper classes. They enjoyed reading about the club-cum-country-house atmosphere of the colleges, with all its eccentricities, initiation rites, fashions and secret codes. It was like reading accounts of expeditions to far-flung territories and exotic tribes. According to a study from 1989, there are 533 known novels that are set wholly or partly in Oxford, and this ever-popular genre stretches from Edward Bradley's *The Adventures of Mr Verdant Green* (1853–57) through Evelyn Waugh's *Brideshead Revisited* (1945) to Colin Dexter's Inspector Morse novels and beyond. Julian Barnes's appeal for a twenty-year ban on novels set in Oxford or Cambridge continues to fall on deaf ears.

No Oxford novel, however, has ever been as dazzling or as complex as the real-life story of Oscar Wilde. What others merely wrote about, he lived with every fibre of his being. As a student at Magdalen, he stylized himself into a human artwork, the aesthete par excellence. His college rooms were full of peacock feathers, lilies and Greek figurines from Tanagra. 'I find it harder and harder every day to live up to my blue china,' was one of his student witticisms, which immediately found its way into *Punch*. He was a master of the greatest virtue in Oxford, which was to be amusing, and his whole oeuvre is basically a variation on this theme.

During his four years at college, Wilde cultivated his aphorisms, his artist's pose, his wit, his charm and, with apparent ease, a classical education. His hero was Walter Pater, a Fellow of Brasenose and a friend of the Pre-Raphaelites. Pater's Renaissance studies were the Bible of aestheticism for Wilde's generation, summed up by the famous conclusion to his *Studies in the History of the Renaissance* (1873): 'To burn always with this hard, gemlike flame, to maintain this ecstasy, is success in life.... Of this wisdom, the poetic passion, the desire of beauty, the love of art for art's sake, has most.' But Pater also recommended that his students read Plato, and there they found the apparent justification of all their dreams – thoughts on an ideal state, an apologia for manly beauty, love of boys as a source of inspiration. 'His left leg is a Greek poem,' gushed Wilde as he watched a long-distance runner. But this carefree attitude to classical and personal homoeroticism aroused some suspicion among his peers. One of the young Oxonians whom he met on a later visit to Magdalen, 'so Greek and graceful', was to become his nemesis: Lord Alfred Douglas, known as Bosie. Bosie's poetry was even worse than his character, but one line became famous and was quoted during Wilde's trial: 'I am the Love that dare not speak its name.' Wilde's speech in his own defence at the Old Bailey in 1895 drew public attention to the link between Hellenism and homosexuality in Victorian Oxford. Two years later, in *De Profundis*, he looked back bitterly on the consequences of this link: 'The two great turning-points of my life were when my father sent me to Oxford, and when society sent me to prison.'

Oscar Wilde was a role model for Max Beerbohm, who also studied classical philology, though he never subjected himself to the rigours of an exam. Oxford, he complained as soon as he got there in 1890, was like 'a bit of Manchester through which Apollo had once passed' – full of 'the hideous trains and the brand-new bricks', 'the tumult of my disillusioning'. 'The incomparable Max' (Shaw) devoted the rest of his long life to being a dandy and looking like he had just stepped out of a hatbox. 'I was a modest, good-humoured boy. It is Oxford that has made me insufferable.' He also drew some 2,000 caricatures, wrote essays and stories, and penned one overrated novel, *Zuleika Dobson* (1911), the Oxford best-seller of its day.

Zuleika comes to Oxford to visit her grandfather, the Warden of Judas College (Christ Church). This femme fatale is so stunningly beautiful that even the stone busts in front of the Sheldonian break out in a sweat at the sight of her. All the students fall head over heels in love with her, including the arrogant Duke of Dorset, and as she yields to none of them, they all jump into the river during Bumps, performing a collective, lovelorn suicide. It is a parody and an ironic swansong to the *fin de siècle* cult of the dandy. Beerbohm's flowery prose has gathered a great deal of dust since then, and its Edwardian kitsch is accurately reflected by Osbert Lancaster's Zuleika illustrations in the Randolph Hotel.

'You have come to Oxford, some of you to hunt foxes, some of you to wear very large and very unusual overcoats, some of you to row for your college, and a few of you to work.' This is the welcoming speech delivered to the freshers by the head of their college in Compton Mackenzie's novel *Sinister Street* (1913–14), the third part of which takes place in Oxford. There is a seamless connection between the Oxford cult and English patriotism. Mackenzie's student hero Michael Fane is convinced 'that the best of Oxford is the best of England, and that the best of England is the best of humanity.' Mackenzie had studied at Magdalen, Oscar Wilde's college, and it was here too that in 1925 John Betjeman, later to become Poet Laureate, took up residence in a set of beautifully panelled rooms.

There were two species of student at that time: the hearties and the aesthetes. The hearties went rowing, drank beer, wore college ties, and made a lot of noise. Betjeman and his ilk read books, wore exotic silk ties, had long hair, and 'never found out where the college sportsfields were situated'. Sir Isaiah Berlin recalled a fellow student from the camp of the aesthetes being asked which college he was at. The response was: 'My dear, I simply can't remember.' The aesthetes would meet for sherry in the rooms of a tutor for Spanish named George Alfred Kolkhorst. On a string around the neck of the Colonel, as he was known, hung a lump of sugar, 'to sweeten his conversation', and he also wore a small ear trumpet 'for catching good remarks'. In his verse memoirs *Summoned by Bells* (1960), one of the most popular works of 20th-century English poetry, Sir John Betjeman described Oxford's 'golden twenties', its young literary lions, its ageing dandies and its endless parties: 'And who in those days thought it odd / To liven breakfast with champagne / And watch, in Canterbury Quad, / Pale undergraduates in the rain? / For, while we ate Virginia hams, / Contemporaries passed exams.'

One member of the aesthetic circle grouped around Betjeman was the millionaire patron of the arts Edward James, nicknamed Ganymede after the beautiful youth who served Zeus as cup-bearer. James had painted the ceiling of his suite in Christ Church black, and he had draped the walls with silver silk. In the next quad, and at the same time, the poet W. H. Auden was practising the art of serious entertaining: in darkened rooms (he hated daylight) he received his poet friends Stephen Spender, Louis MacNeice and Cecil Day-Lewis, all of whom were then studying in Oxford, and together they laid the foundations for a worldwide Marxist revolution while he read his poems to them, dressed in an oversized frock coat. In 1956, the head of the Auden Gang returned to Oxford as Professor of Poetry.

None of Auden's cronies, however, could exceed Harold Acton when it came to eccentricity. 'Back to mahogany!' was his battle cry. His room was painted lemon yellow, and from his balcony he would use a megaphone to declaim T. S. Eliot's *The Waste Land* and his own poetry across the green fields of Christ Church. In those days, anyone with any self-respect wore Oxford bags – baggy trousers with pleats, which Acton himself had designed. According to *Who's Who*, his favourite occupation was 'hunting the philistines'. He was a snob and a connoisseur, the last of the great English aesthetes, and a good deal more eccentric than Anthony Blanche, the flamboyant character in *Brideshead* whom Evelyn Waugh modelled on him. Incidentally, the fact that *Brideshead*'s hero Sebastian always goes out with his teddy bear had its own real-life counterpart, as John Betjeman's teddy Archibald Ormsby-Gore accompanied him wherever he went in Oxford.

The Brideshead style, this world of academic peacocks and turtledoves, was anathema to the 'hearties' and almost everyone else. In 1929 D. H. Lawrence wrote a sarcastic poem entitled *The Oxford Voice*, satirizing the Oxford accent – that trademark of the elite upper classes: 'And oh, so seductively superior, so seductively / self-effacingly / deprecatingly / superior – / We wouldn't insist on it for a moment / but we are / we are / you admit we are / superior.' He had heard all too much of this affected, idly superior tone in the salon of Lady Ottoline Morrell, on whose country estate at Garsington the London 'Bloomsberries' and the Oxford 'bright young things' would congregate. They were birds of a feather, and not even Stephen Spender was of quite the same plumage, though he was studying at the very source of the 'Oxford Voice'. 'A community dominated above all by the consciousness of class' was how he described the university in his autobiography *World Within World* (1951). Coming from the right family, a public school education and money – these were the vital factors, and anyone who didn't have them 'was to be excluded at Oxford from Oxford'. But what struck Spender even more than his own position as an outsider was the isolation of the university itself, its complete detachment from everything that seemed important to the writers of his generation: social conflict, the political upheavals that rocked Europe during the 1930s. 'We were the Divided Generation of Hamlets who found the world out of joint and failed to set it right.'

In 1945, this world lay in ruins and the old Oxford had disappeared, but that was the year in which Evelyn Waugh's *Brideshead Revisited* was first published. It was a nostalgic look back at the Arcadia of Waugh's youth, the very same university of the 1920s that Stephen Spender had criticized so savagely. It is a glamorous college romance, telling the story of two friends, Charles Ryder and Sebastian Flyte, and an aristocratic Catholic family. Oxford, the aristocracy and picnics with strawber-ries – with this mixture Evelyn Waugh wrote what Nancy Mitford called his 'G.E.C.', or Great English Classic. The weaknesses that he saw for himself some-how only added to the appeal of this romantic historical painting, which enjoyed even more success when it was made into a TV serial starring Jeremy Irons (1981).

No novel has had a greater impact on present-day Oxford than *Brideshead Revisited*. The city now swarms with even more tourists and even more teddy bears. The university has fewer problems with these best-selling consequences than it does with its Brideshead image. In summer 1986, a girl student died from an overdose of alcohol and heroin after an examinations party, and her death hit the headlines. She was no ordinary student, but Olivia Channon, the daughter of a government minister, and she was found in the Christ Church rooms of an aristocrat friend, Count Gottfried von Bismarck. It was a perverted version of *Brideshead* – the fatal reverse side of the myth. Excess is as much a part of Oxford life as asceticism, and whenever the smart set is hit by a scandal involving sex or drugs, the Brideshead syndrome raises its head, as if life were confirming art.

After the Second World War, Evelyn Waugh's novel marked the last goodbye to Oxford as the 'English Athens'. Its special academic status and its belletristic aura were gone for ever. This does not mean, however, that it has ceased to play a dom-inant role in the literary life of the land: literary historians such as John Carey, Peter Conrad, Terry Eagleton and Hermione Lee, the poet and English specialist Tom Paulin, the author and publisher Michael Schmidt, satirists such as Richard Ingrams and John Wells, the journalist and former Thatcher adviser Paul Johnson, writers and celebrities like James Fenton, A. N. Wilson, Ian Hislop, Christopher Hitchens, Peter Stothard, Ferdinand Mount, Anthony Thwaite, Marina Warner, Melvyn Bragg – all of them are so pre-eminent in the various media that one might almost suspect that there is an Oxford literary mafia. Many of the finest 20th-century English authors were or are Oxford graduates: winners of the Nobel Prize for literature William Golding and V. S. Naipaul, John Buchan, Graham Greene, Philip Larkin, Kingsley Amis and his son Martin, Christopher Hampton, Will Self, Julian Barnes, Adam Thirlwell, Jeanette Winterson – but it cannot be said that their inspiration came from the city itself. One of the few exceptions is the Man Booker Prizewinner of 2004, Alan Hollinghurst (Magdalen), whose novel *The Line of Beauty* tells the story of Nick Guest, a gay Oxford graduate. Ian McEwan is another writer writer who lived in Oxford until 2002. For one particular scene in his novel *The Innocent* (which is set in Berlin), he consulted a pathology tutor at Merton College. That is certainly a major advantage of living here – within a single

square mile you will find specialists on virtually every subject. But the novel itself
has nothing to do with Oxford.

Iris Murdoch was an exceptional person in every respect, and she studied, taught
and lived in Oxford all her adult life, and knew the place and the people as well as
anyone could. Her novels reflect the city as a kind of spiritual life force. Self-
awareness, liberty, determinism, sexuality, morality – her work constantly
grapples with these basic philosophical and existential problems. She regarded
novels as 'halls of reflection', and there is an aura of the Senior Common Room
about many of her characters. Her great novel of ideas *The Book and the Brotherhood* (1987) tells the story of a group of friends who meet again at a college ball
thirty years after their exams. It is a tale of passions, ideological conflicts and disil-
lusionment ('we were all Marxists once') – a veritable panorama of lost causes.

The only internationally successful Oxford novel after *Brideshead* was written
by a Spaniard: Javier Marías. *All Souls* (*Todas las almas*, 1989) plays around with the
clichés of the city and of the genre. It is almost a postmodern sequel to *Zuleika
Dobson* and narrates the tale of the twofold havoc caused by love and by Oxford.
A young Spaniard comes to the university as a guest lecturer, and falls in love with
the wife of a colleague. What this Don Juan sees among the Oxford dons provides
us with the delightful inside stories of an outsider, as witty as Wilde himself. With
splendid irony, Javier Marías deconstructs the Oxford myth, satirizing everything, and yet somehow the magic persists as it does in the circus, and over a
decade later it resurfaces in a sequel: *Your Face Tomorrow* (*Tu rostro mañana*, 2002).

'Anyone who's not a scandalmonger or, at the very least, malicious is doomed to
live as marginal and discredited an existence as someone unfortunate enough to
have graduated from a university other than Cambridge or Oxford itself.' Marías
finds the Oxford gift for scandal and espionage quite remarkable. It was from here
that John Le Carré set forth into the world of the latter. In his novel *A Perfect Spy*
(1986), he describes the career of a double agent, Magnus Pym, who while still a
student at Oxford spies on Socialists and Marxists, just as Le Carré himself had
done when he was at Lincoln College in the 1950s. But it was Cambridge not
Oxford that was the true home of espionage, and Oxford's speciality is the detective story and not the spy story.

The classic campus detective story is Dorothy L. Sayers' *Gaudy Night* (1935).
The heroine, Harriet Vane – who writes detective novels – returns to Oxford for a
college reunion, but apart from the crime itself, this is the first literary work to deal
with the problems of women students. Somerville – where Sayers herself studied –
was the model for Shrewsbury College, and at the time it was for women only.

Murder was the chief preoccupation of this Anglican vicar's daughter, who enjoyed the intellectual challenge (and the royalties) associated with solving mysteries, while guilt and atonement mattered more to her than action. Her first novel, *Whose Body?* (1923), introduced her aristocratic amateur detective Lord Peter Wimsey – a Balliol graduate – and twelve novels later in *Busman's Honeymoon* he married Harriet Vane, in Oxford of course. Sayers broke off her last Wimsey novel, *Thrones, Dominations*, in 1936 after six chapters, but it was published in 1998, having been completed by Jill Paton Walsh, a writer who had been so enamoured of *Gaudy Night* as a schoolgirl that she set her heart on studying at Oxford.

During the 20th century the campus thriller developed into a highly productive variation on the Oxford novel. *Death at the President's Lodging* (1936) was another classic of its type, written by J. I. M. Stewart, who later became a professor at Christ Church. Apart from his studies on Shakespeare, Joyce and many others, this versatile don wrote nearly fifty thrillers – many of them set in Oxford – under the pseudonym of Michael Innes. His detective, Inspector Appleby, is as sophisticated as only an Oxonian could possibly be. The poet Cecil Day-Lewis, Oxford Professor of Poetry and Poet Laureate (despite his earlier leanings towards Communism), published twenty thrillers under the pseudonym of Nicholas Blake. His best-known novel, *The Beast Must Die*, was filmed by Claude Chabrol in 1969. And who would have thought that the organist at St John's, Bruce Montgomery, would also turn out to be a spare-time thriller writer, under the name of Edmund Crispin? His amateur detective Gervase Fen is an Oxford professor of English Literature – the perfect product of the 'donnish school of detection'.

Sophisticated crime, scheming dons, well-read detectives – these are only to be found in Oxford thrillers, in this environment of murderous intelligence. These may take place in the 13th century (Ian Morson) or in Bill Clinton's late 1960s (Aaron H. Barken), though certainly the most esoteric of all these scholarly crimes was set in 1663 at New College: the Oxonian Iain Pears's *Judgement* (1997). Every year there seem to be new blossoms on the Oxford branch of the thriller industry: among the most recent are Charlotte Mendelson's debut novel *Daughters of Jerusalem* (2004) and the Argentine author Guillermo Martínez's *The Oxford Murders* (2004). The scene has also long since been enlivened by lady detectives: Lady Antonia Fraser's *Oxford Blood* (1985) features her famous Jemima Shore, and Veronica Stallwood has written several Oxford thrillers. Meanwhile, anyone wishing to make a closer study of the academic criminal world should attend the yearly conference 'Mystery and Crime' held at St Hilda's, which incidentally is the thriller writer Val McDermid's college.

The most popular of all the Oxford detectives, however, was created by a Cambridge man: Colin Dexter. He has been living in Oxford since 1966, and sat for many years on the university's Examinations Board, into whose workings we are given a degree of insight in his novel *The Silent World of Nicholas Quinn*. Quinn is poisoned with potassium cyanide in his sherry, because he is going to expose the lucrative racket in divulging examination questions. Dexter's labyrinthine plots are best-sellers, and the TV series have been shown all over the world, with John Thaw starring as the fascinating character of Inspector Morse. The everyday life of the city – a far cry from that of *Brideshead* – plays its part, from the surrounding districts and pubs and backstreets to Woodstock, all of them engendering a new form of tourism: the scene of the crime. 'That's an Oxford crime, it needs an Oxford man to solve it.' Dexter has been responsible for 81 murders in and around Oxford, including three college Masters, and it was with a certain degree of repentance that he confessed to me: 'I managed single-handedly I think to make Oxford the murder capital of Europe.' But in reality, statistics show that in the last forty years, only two murders have taken place in the colleges of Oxford.

We must not leave the subject of literature without casting a glance at that magnificent institution the Oxford Professorship of Poetry. The incumbent can be a poet or a critic, and sometimes both (or neither). The post lasts for five years, though in former times it was for ten, and carries an emolument of £5,457 per annum – considerably more than that given to the Poet Laureate. The duties comprise one public lecture a term, adjudicating a literary competition for students, the Newdigate Prize, and above all promoting the art of poetry. 'When Auden did the job,' says James Fenton, himself a former Professor of Poetry, 'he let it be known that he would be in a tea room at a certain time every afternoon, so people could come and show him their poems or talk about poetry. He turned it into a kind of creative writing fellowship.'

The Professor of Poetry is the only one in Oxford to be elected and not nominated. All graduates are entitled to vote, but they must come to Oxford in person, though they need no longer wear their gowns. If the ritual has now lost some of its pomp and circumstance, its prestige remains undiluted. Among the illustrious holders of this office have been Matthew Arnold, Robert Graves, Roy Fuller, Peter Levi, Seamus Heaney and Paul Muldoon. Since 2004, the 43rd occupant of the Chair has been a connoisseur rather than a practitioner of the art: Christopher Ricks, graduate of Balliol, Boston professor, and an avid fan of Bob Dylan.

This remarkable institution goes back to 1708 and the last will and testament of a certain Henry Birkhead from Berkshire. He was fed up with his wife, cut her off with a symbolic shilling, and left the rest of his fortune to the university with the proviso that if possible there should be a Professor of Poetry at Oxford in perpetuity. The fact that in 300 years the post has never been occupied by a woman should not be blamed on Henry Birkhead.

Where *The Light of the World* Always Shines: Art in Oxford

'I was in Oxford today, where all the Lords and little Indian princes acquire their knowledge.... An immense museum specially for schoolchildren, so that one would like to stay here for a year in order to enjoy the pleasure of studying all the antiquities.'
Oskar Kokoschka, 1928

Oxford is a city of books, words, dictionaries, concepts and abstractions. Initially I thought that pictures played more of a metaphorical part in this cerebral setting – as secondary as the shadows in Plato's cave. Of course there was the Ashmolean Museum, an enclave of visual delights, but the rest, it seemed to me, was architecture, albeit in massive abundance. But then I began to look round the colleges – their libraries, dining-halls, chapels – and everywhere I found pictures, busts, statues, sculptures in marble and bronze, stained glass, wood carvings. It was as if every college was itself a museum.

From the medieval illuminations in the Bodleian to Ronald B. Kitaj's portrait of Clinton in University College, Oxford is indeed a place of pictures. They are scattered all over the city, hidden in Senior Common Rooms and other inaccessible places, but they are there if you know where to look. So let us begin in places that *are* accessible, for instance Exeter College. In the Victorian glow of the Chapel shines *The Star of Bethlehem*, a tapestry of Pre-Raphaelite splendour designed in 1887 by Edward Burne-Jones. Three weavers worked for more than two years on this monumental *Adoration*, whose solemn and elongated figures stand between lilies, roses and narcissi like some vast flowered tapestry from the early Florentine Renaissance. This was the first major weaving commission for the firm of Morris & Co, and it became their most popular wall-hanging. There are now ten versions, of which this is the first.

William Morris and Edward Burne-Jones had got to know each other at Exeter College, where both of them enrolled as theology students in 1853. They wanted to become priests, and were followers of the Oxford Movement. But Morris, known as Topsy – 'a rather rough and unpolished youth who exhibited no special literary tastes or capacity' according to his tutor – was more concerned with Ruskin's apotheosis of the Gothic than with the reforms of Cardinal Newman. Similarly his friend from Birmingham, Burne-Jones, had his first taste in Oxford of the mysteries of the Middle Ages that would henceforth inspire his paintings. 'All by the river's side I came back in a delirium of joy...and in my mind pictures of the old days – the abbey, and long processions of the faithful, banners of the cross, copes and crosiers, gay knights and ladies by the river bank, hawking-parties and all the pageantry of the golden age.... I never remember having such an unutterable ecstasy, it was quite painful with intensity, as if my forehead would burst,' wrote Burne-Jones in 1854, after seeing the ruins of Godstow Abbey. In the window of a gallery on the High Street the two friends saw a picture that perfectly combined their aesthetic and religious ideals: it was John Everett Millais's *The Return of the Dove to the Ark*. The painting belonged to the director of the University Press, Thomas Combe, and in his collection they also saw works by William Holman Hunt, Dante Gabriel Rossetti and other members of the Pre-Raphaelite Brotherhood. Two years later, after meeting Rossetti, they were completely converted to the cause. Morris became the driving force behind the Arts and Crafts Movement, and Burne-Jones became the great Romantic Symbolist.

In 1857, he and Morris returned to Oxford, where Rossetti had proposed a cycle of wall paintings for the new Debating Hall at the Union; he wanted to do this free of charge together with his artist friends. The paintings were to be scenes from the legend of King Arthur, the heroic and patriotic heart of Victorian courtly romance. But this communal work of the Pre-Raphaelites, painted with more enthusiasm than experience, swiftly faded into a beautiful spectre on the poorly prepared surface of the brick walls. Morris's later floral paintings were unable to conceal this debacle by the amateur fresco-painters, as indeed were more recent attempts at restoration.

In the same year, Rossetti and Burne-Jones met a young woman at the theatre. Of her deathly beauty, Shaw wrote: 'the effect was as if she had walked out of an Egyptian tomb at Luxor.' Her name was Jane Burden, and she was the daughter of a stablehand, but she was the ideal model for the Pre-Raphaelites. Rossetti became her neurotic lover, William Morris her unloved husband. When they got married at St Michael's, Oxford, in 1858, Burne-Jones gave them a cupboard which he had painted with scenes from Chaucer's *Prioress's Tale*. Jane posed for the figure of Mary, and the angels too are *femmes fatales* in pious disguise. In the bottom right-hand corner of the cupboard is a portrait of Chaucer, whose work was a lifelong preoccupation of the two friends, from their reading him together at Exeter College to the Kelmscott edition of 1896, which Burne-Jones illustrated and Morris printed on his hand press – one of the loveliest illustrated books of the 19th century.

The wedding cupboard is now a prize exhibit in the Pre-Raphaelite room at the Ashmolean, surrounded by paintings from the collection of Thomas Combe, the university printer. He was not only a follower of the Oxford Movement but also an enthusiastic supporter of the Pre-Raphaelites. The brand new painting that he acquired in 1853 must have seemed to him like an aesthetic revelation from the new religious movement: it was Holman Hunt's *The Light of the World* – Christ with a lantern at daybreak, knocking on a closed door with weeds growing all around it. Hunt's painting was reproduced a million times, and was an integral part of the Victorian's spiritual treasure chest, an icon of the age, full of symbols, emotions, ultra-realistic details, as sweet and as heavy as plum pudding. I can still remember this painting from Holy Communion in my childhood, and in later years I used to come across it in junk shops as an oleograph in an old-looking frame. But the original is in Oxford. Combe's widow gave it to Keble College, and for this, the High Church's most popular devotional picture, the college built a special side-chapel next to the main chapel. But since the college was short of cash, it proceeded to charge visitors sixpence a look, which so infuriated Holman Hunt that in 1900 he painted a replica and gave it to St Paul's Cathedral. Thus Oxford lost its monopoly on this particular light of the world.

In the college chapels, the art-religion of the Pre-Raphaelites really found its identity. Nowhere can one trace the development of their glass painting more vividly than in Oxford. In 1858, Burne-Jones designed his first church window for Christ Church Cathedral: sixteen scenes from the life of St Frideswide – a glowing, medieval-style mosaic of crowded, animated figures, not as statuesque as his later figures, which became simpler and more stylized, with clearer forms and fewer colours. Burne-Jones created five windows altogether for Christ Church Cathedral, the last in 1878 – St Catherine of Alexandria, who has the features of Edith Liddell (the sister of Lewis Carroll's Alice), who died very young. Opposite her is St Cecilia, patron of music; Burne-Jones's cartoons of her accompanying angels were sold off at Christie's during the 1940s at £5 a piece.

When William Morris set up his firm in London in 1861, Burne-Jones worked together with his friend, and their first window was in the chapel at St Edmund

Hall – a crucifixion (1865). Their last joint undertaking in Oxford was the windows of Manchester College Chapel (1893–96), which brought a real ray of sunshine into the conventional architecture of the Victorians. On the southern wall are the Christian virtues, a series of allegorical figures, and opposite these are *The Six Days of Creation*: angels in ruby-coloured robes with the blue planet in their hands, and the magic spheres of Creation with the Diderot motto '*Élargissez Dieu*' [Make God greater]. The model for the angels was May Morris, William's daughter. No other firm in England or indeed in Europe produced such brilliant stained glass as that of Morris & Co. They were lucky, for the best possible lessons in technique and in the spirit of the material itself were already to be had in Oxford: the Thomas Becket window (*c.* 1340) in Christ Church Cathedral, the lilies window in St Michael's (15th century) and, above all, the stained glass of Merton Chapel (1289 onwards).

One does not have to be an expert to appreciate the delights of such windows, and there is nowhere more conducive to this than Oxford. One need only consider the works painted between 1622 and 1641: superb biblical narratives, influenced by the Mannerism of Flemish art, and executed by two master glaziers from Emden, Bernard and Abraham van Linge. The elder, Bernard, worked in the chapels at Wadham and Lincoln, while his brother – or possibly cousin – Abraham was responsible for windows at Queen's, Balliol, University and Christ Church. My own personal favourite is in the Cathedral at Christ Church: the monumental Jonah window, with Nineveh in the background.

Before the Civil War, when Cromwell's Puritans decided that visual beauty should have no place in the House of God, a London goldsmith named Richard Greenbury created a series of grisaille windows around 1632 for Magdalen College, with full-length figures of saints, kings and bishops. The sepia tones fill the anteroom of the Chapel with a warm, coffee-coloured light. The largest of the windows, the western one, which depicts the Last Judgment, was taken away in 1939 just before the war to a place of safety, and it was not reinstalled until 1996. There is a descent into Hell, an ascension to Heaven, angels blowing trumpets, Christ on a rainbow, and underneath all this a brass plaque commemorating a love affair that started here. Two former students, Minnie and John McMillan from California, financed the restoration of this window 'in gratitude for a marriage that began in this Chapel on Midsummer's Day 1975'. For all their fragility, both love and glass have a wonderful capacity to survive.

Oxford is not so well endowed with modern stained glass. There is not a single Chagall, but there are some John Pipers. He designed five abstract compositions

(1961) for the chapel in the attic storey of Nuffield College, though you will find his finest work in the Norman church at Iffley. Here a group of animals announce the birth of Christ, with Latin bubbles coming out of their mouths: 'Christus natus est,' crows the cock from the top of the Tree of Life. 'Quando, quando?' quacks the duck. 'In hac nocte,' answers the crow from the next branch. 'Ubi, ubi?' asks the owl. 'Bethlem! Bethlem!' bleats the sheep at the bottom of the tree. This glass menagerie is as onomatopoeic as it is colourful, and it is the most poetic and most cheering Nativity that I know. Piper designed it in 1982, and it was painted after his death by David Wasley in 1995.

Artists were always drawn to Oxford, long before its dreaming spires were downgraded to picture postcards. In 1669 an artist from Danzig named David Loggan was appointed engraver to the university. His book *Oxonia illustrata* (1675) shows the city and its colleges with all the pre-photography precision of a veduta. Genre painters and caricaturists found a host of subjects in Oxford, from coachmen to dons – as Thomas Rowlandson, for instance, sketched them in the midst of the intoxication and fornication that constituted Georgian academic life. The ubiquitous J. M. W. Turner left behind no less than seventy oil paintings, watercolours and engravings of Oxford.

University towns like Oxford have always offered lucrative commissions to artists. Colleges had to be built and decorated, and so did chapels, libraries, dining halls and rooms for teaching and accommodation. Founders and benefactors wanted to be honoured with statues, Masters wanted portraits of themselves, and so did dons and famous alumni and generous donors; at the very latest these things might wait until they were dead, but then it was essential to put a monument or at least a plaque in the chapel, the hall, the corridor. In the Bodleian Library, the Examination Schools and the various colleges there are hundreds of portraits, from Gainsborough and Reynolds right through to David Hockney's portrait of the Principal of Hertford College.

There are also lots of statues, particularly from the 18th and 19th centuries. In the entrance hall of Christ Church Library alone, between the file-card boxes and the computers, is an extraordinary collection of sculpted celebrities: there are busts of Louis François Roubiliac, John Bacon, Francis Chantrey, Jacob Epstein and, tucked away in a niche, the full-length marble figure of the great philosopher John Locke, a masterpiece by Michael Rysbrack (1757). In almost every college chapel there is an art-historical surprise, and often more than one: in Lady Margaret Hall, for instance, is an early triptych by Edward Burne-Jones (1862), in St Edmund Hall an altarpiece by the Welsh painter Ceri Richards (*Christ at Emmaus*, 1957), and in

New College Chapel there is not only an El Greco (*St James, c.* 1610) but also a window by Joshua Reynolds (1777) and Jacob Epstein's *Lazarus* (1948), freeing himself from his burial bindings – a limestone figure that expresses the full pathos of the post-war era and its crisis of faith.

No one knows precisely what art treasures lie hidden in these Oxford colleges. As private institutions – and also for security reasons – they are reluctant to divulge the details. It's more than likely that many of them don't even know themselves what has been accumulated over the centuries. In Lady Margaret Hall and St Anne's there are collections of 20th-century British paintings (Stanley Spencer, Paul Nash, David Jones, Christopher Wood and more), Worcester College has a special collection of architectural drawings ranging from Inigo Jones to William Burges, Campion Hall has religious art from the Middle Ages to modern times, Pembroke has a collection of post-war British art that includes Lynn Chadwick, Elisabeth Frink, Patrick Heron, Tom Phillips: the list goes on and on. Generally these works are not accessible to the public, although Christ Church is a notable exception. This is by far the biggest and most important of all the college collections, and since 1968 it has been on exhibition in a purpose-built picture gallery. The Ashmolean is a university museum of international rank, independent of the city and of the state, and on a par with the Fitzwilliam in Cambridge and the Courtauld Institute in London.

In 1944, during the blitz, the Slade School of Art was evacuated from London to Oxford's Ruskin School of Drawing, and with it went a young Scotsman named Eduardo Paolozzi. His study fees were waived, and in return he worked as a fire watcher in the Ashmolean Museum, where he also slept at night. In his spare time he copied the Dürers and Rembrandts and the other old masters he found there.

When the American painter Ronald B. Kitaj saw the collection of Raphael and Michelangelo drawings at the Ashmolean, he pronounced himself 'stunned for life'. Towards the end of the 1950s, when he was a student at the Ruskin School of Drawing, he went there nearly every day to attend life-drawing classes (as did his fellow countryman John Updike). This school, which is now situated in the High Street, was established in 1871 by Ruskin in the University Galleries, as the Ashmolean was then called. Ruskin gave part of his art collection – which he also used as teaching material – to the university, including about 150 of his own drawings, 77 pieces by J. M. W. Turner, and a large number of works by the Pre-Raphaelites, whom he championed from very early on. Ruskin taught at Oxford for nearly fifteen years, and he was the first Slade Professor of Fine Art. The Slade Lectures are still a major event today, thanks to such eminent art historians as Kenneth Clark,

Ernst Gombrich, Francis Haskell and Charles Hope, the current director of the Warburg Institute and a graduate of Balliol College. The present head of the Ruskin School is the sculptor Richard Wentworth.

With all the abundance of classical art in Oxford, it is greatly to the city's credit that there is also a museum of modern art. It was here and not in London that the first British solo exhibitions of artists such as Joseph Beuys, Carl André and other pioneers of the avant-garde were staged. Modern Art Oxford does not have a collection of its own, but since its foundation in 1965 it has continually organized ground-breaking exhibitions and discussions, embracing art from Eastern Europe, from outside Europe, and in all visual media. All this, with a modest subsidy from the city itself, is housed in a former brewery in Pembroke Street.

Honeycombs and Fan Vaults: Architecture in Oxford

> 'Mainly architectural, the beauties of Oxford.'
> Max Beerbohm, *Zuleika Dobson*, 1911

The past envelops Oxford like an invisible dome, as if the city were one huge monument, a tomb of ideas that have been laid to rest century after century. I stood on the tower of St Mary's, face to face with the Gothic gargoyles, and looked down on Radcliffe Square, and the grey roofs and the green quads of the colleges, the warren of lanes and the endless phalanx of towers, cupolas, chimneys and pinnacles. As I gazed over this panorama, I felt like Thomas Hardy's stonemason Jude Fawley when he first arrived in Christminster: 'The numberless architectural pages around him he read, naturally.'

Within the narrowest confines, Oxford offers a complete history of English architecture, from Norman religious buildings right through to postmodern shopping centres. Gothic, Renaissance, neo-Gothic, Georgian, Victorian – all the periods are amply represented here, as are the great architects: Christopher Wren, Nicholas Hawksmoor and James Gibbs, William Butterfield, Edwin Lutyens, James Stirling – every one of them left his mark on the city as if it were a second capital. It is said that Hitler gave orders for Oxford to be spared from the Baedeker raids because when he had achieved his final victory, he intended to establish the centre of Nazi administration there for the government of occupied England. However, in the absence of any documentary evidence, perhaps we should accept the popular version, which is that he didn't bomb Oxford because after the war he hoped to get an honorary doctorate.

Over the last seven hundred years, since the Middle Ages, college architecture in both Oxford and Cambridge has developed with astonishing density and variety. Their high walls protect these fortresses of learning from the outside world, and they can turn their backs on the bustling streets beyond, gazing inwards in quiet contemplation. Emblematic of the symbiosis between learning and architecture is the typical, fortified gatehouse, with a tiny door in its massive portal, like the eye of a needle through which one passes into a different world. Here you are absorbed by the college community – and by yourself.

It was not the private halls but the colleges that first developed their own style of architecture, and this became almost a corporate identity. The prototype of the autonomous, medieval academic fortress was Merton, founded in 1264, the mother of all the colleges. The dining hall, the Warden's house, the chapel are all grouped round a central quadrangle, like that of a monastery. The stalls of the chapel are arranged opposite one another like the Government and Opposition benches in the House of Commons – echoing the choir stalls in monastic churches and cathedrals. The 'staircase' idea in the Mob Quad is also typical: the rooms are not linked by corridors, but each staircase is a unit in itself. Oxford's students live vertically and not horizontally. This arrangement fosters peace and privacy, and it set the example for all the later colleges. Not until 1870 did Keble change the staircase principle, with rooms placed on corridors, and the women's colleges followed suit.

A century after Bishop Walter de Merton's pioneering foundation, William of Wykeham founded what was then architecturally the most impressive college in all England: New College (1379). For the first time, all the main buildings were designed as a unit, with a ground plan as coherent as that of a monastery. The refectory and the chapel stand back to back on the north side of a quadrangle that is almost four times the size of Merton's Mob Quad. The dining hall on the first floor has a hammer-beam roof like the hall of a typical medieval manor house, and where the lord of the manor and his family would dine on a dais at the end of the room, the Fellows and their guests sit at High Table. The latter plays a significant role in college mythology, but its origin is simply the fact that it is situated on a higher level than the rest of the tables, rather than, as Javier Marías remarks, 'because of any unusually high standard of cuisine or conversation'.

When the Prussian architect Karl Friedrich Schinkel came to England, he stopped very briefly in Oxford and was less than enthusiastic. The colleges seemed to him 'very strange and rich...but everywhere the architecture repeats itself.' He got it wrong. His verdict overlooked the fact that certain repetitions were inevitable in the building of a college: chapel and hall, gatehouse and library, quadrangles and gardens – these were all essential elements, but within this framework there are as many variations as in a fugue by Bach.

Beyond the basic pattern, the colleges have in common a deep distrust of all fashions, both intellectual and architectural. The Renaissance motifs of Hampton Court, Cardinal Wolsey's palace, are not to be found in his Oxford college: Christ Church is strictly Gothic – so strict that even in 1640 the hall staircase was given a Gothic fan vault, a grandiose anachronism if ever there was one. Similar fan vaults are to be found in the gatehouses of Wadham and Oriel (1620–22), and in Brasenose Chapel (as late as 1665); there are even Gothic-style windows and Gothic hammer-beam roofs in the halls at Exeter, Wadham and Oriel. Whether all this constituted Gothic Survival, Posthumous Gothic or Gothic Revival is open to speculation.

According to the architectural historian Nikolaus Pevsner, this 'curious behaviour' was more widespread in Oxford than anywhere else in England, where generally neo-Gothic was more common than on the Continent. 'It stands for antiquarian leanings, but it also stands for a dislike of radical changes.' By going back to medieval architecture, the colleges were symbolically establishing their institutional continuity. This could be seen as Oxford's strength, continuity being more important than any stylistic innovation, but also as Oxford's weakness – a relapse into mere traditionalism.

The Bodleian Library presents its façade to the world like a medieval pattern book, with its late Gothic blind arcades, pure Perpendicular, dating from 1612. Oxford's first non-Gothic, classical chapel was at Trinity (1691), with its unique wood carvings by Grinling Gibbons. Renaissance motifs occur late and only sporadically in the colleges, most strikingly in the Canterbury Quad at St John's, curiously intermingled with elements of Gothic and Baroque (1631–36). The general dislike of the Italian Renaissance is 'especially puzzling', says Pevsner, 'since Oxford played such an important part in English late C15 humanism.'

The major ceremonies take place in the Sheldonian Theatre. This was designed in 1663 by a thirty-one-year-old professor of astronomy named Christopher Wren – 'that miracle of a Youth', as his friend John Evelyn described him. The Sheldonian was his first public commission, along with Pembroke Chapel in Cambridge, both of them the work of an amateur who was also a genius. England's greatest architect was not an architect at all but a scientist. While he was still a student at Wadham, Wren was already designing useful things like a barometer and a language for the deaf. His interest in solving technical problems of construction first revealed itself in the huge, unsupported span of the Sheldonian ceiling. This classical building set the standard for the rest of Oxford. After the Great Fire of London (1666), Wren was appointed Surveyor-General, and was chosen to be the architect for the new St Paul's Cathedral – a turning point in his career. Years later, long after he had been knighted and had executed countless major projects including buildings for the Royal Family, he was still designing buildings for Oxford. In 1681–82 he completed the main Tudor gateway at Christ Church with the great Tom Tower, but my own favourite is an early work of his: the sundial at All Souls (1659), on the southern wall of the Library, showing the passing hours in all its Baroque splendour – 'Pereunt et imputantur' [they perish and are brought to reckoning].

England is a land of sundials, and this ancient gnomonic art is particularly popular in Oxford. One might think that those who live in the shadows of the college walls want not only to do their solar calculations, but also to conjure up the sun itself with their ornamental fantasies, their astronomical ingenuity, and their magical Latin incantations. 'Floribus Anna tuis faveat sol / Luce perenni,' says the sundial that the Fellows of St Hugh's erected in 1937 in memory of their gardener Anne Rogers: 'May the sun be kind to your flowers, Anne, with everlasting light.' In the front quadrangle of Corpus Christi is a pillar surmounted by a pelican, and this contains no less than twenty-seven different sundials – a triumphal totem pole of Christian astronomy erected in 1579. There are sundials everywhere – on the walls of Merton, Brasenose, Christ Church, in college quads and gardens, and there is even a glass dial on a staircase window at University College. Along with gargoyles, sundials are the most popular architectural appendages in Oxford.

Let us return to All Souls, where at one time Christopher Wren was a Fellow whose main duties were to calculate the course of the stars and the course of the college finances. His London assistant Nicholas Hawksmoor designed the twin towers (1716–36), a bizarre Gothic echo, and indeed he dreamed of reconstructing the whole city in a Roman-Baroque style, but unlike Wren in London he was not given the support of a Great Fire, and his ideas were far too eccentric for his Oxford clients. All they allowed him to construct was the Clarendon Building plus a few bits of All Souls. Hawksmoor's boldest design was the round library known as the Radcliffe Camera (1737–48), which was built after his death by his Scottish architect colleague James Gibbs. With its imposing dome, this is the most elegant book depository in England – a mixture of Wren's Baroque and the classicism of Rome, where Gibbs had studied. He was a Catholic and a Jacobite, and this was the only masterpiece that he built in Oxford.

There were two amateurs who contributed a great deal to Oxford's architectural golden age in the early 18th century. Henry Aldrich, Dean of Christ Church, extended his college with a new residential quarter, Peckwater Quad (1705–14), the wings of which surround the inner quad like the façades of an Italian Renaissance palace. The southern range – the Library with its Corinthian columns – was designed in 1717 by George Clarke, Fellow of All Souls, who was also an amateur architect. All Saints Church (1706–8), which is now used as a college library, is attributed to Dean Aldrich, a classical scholar and *bon vivant*, while Henry Keene, a champion of Rococo-Gothic, designed the Radcliffe Observatory, which was completed in 1794 by James Wyatt with an octagonal tower modelled on the Tower of the Winds in Athens – the most unusual observatory of its time in Europe.

Almost every prominent English architect of the 19th century left behind major or minor buildings in Oxford: museums, villas, churches, cricket pavilions – a complete anthology of Victorian styles ranging from Greek Revival (Ashmolean Museum) to the street lamps by Giles Gilbert Scott. If you find William Butterfield's monumental Keble College a bit too overpowering, then I recommend Worcester Chapel: a virtuoso interior by William Burges (1864–66), a High Victorian pot-pourri of art and the story of Creation right down to the carved dodo in the pews. The dodo, Oxford's unofficial heraldic emblem, has been given an even more splendid cage – a veritable cathedral of glass and cast iron: the University Museum (1855–60). With this edifice, the Gothic men of Oxford ventured on their first excursion into the Industrial Age.

During the 19th century, there was plenty of work for masons such as Hardy's Jude Fawley in this city of crumbling towers. The smoke from the coal fires had seeped so deep into the college walls that major restoration became essential. The local stone, especially from Headington, was considerably less resistant than the coral rag that can still be found in some of Oxford's oldest buildings, in parts of the city walls and in the tower of St Michael's. The first great wave of college restorations began around 1825, initially using honey-coloured Bath stone, but then later with pale cream Clipsham limestone from Lincolnshire. The work done on the façades was so drastic, for instance in Jesus College, that William Morris described the result as 'ruined by fakement various'. Today more and more use is being made of French limestone, which is cheaper and, according to the purists, even worse.

Oxford's conservative love of stylistic echoes predominated throughout the 20th century as well. A striking example is Nuffield College, which was designed in 1939 and completed in 1960 with the country house look of the Cotswolds. The International Style of the 1930s did not manage to reach Oxford until thirty years later, when Michael Powers built a student hall of residence for St John's, with hexagonal rooms in a honeycomb design: the façade is a polygonal zigzag, with large glass windows in metal frames – the first glimpse of modernity on the banks of the Isis. But then all of a sudden, 20th-century architecture arrived in full force with St Catherine's (1960–64), a whole college designed by Arne Jacobsen, complete with furniture and fittings. A few years later, Sir James Stirling designed a student hall of residence for Queen's, the Florey Building on the Cherwell, a pretty monstrous specimen of functionalist architecture.

The Science Area appears to have grown up higgledy-piggledy north of South Parks Road, and is crammed with architecturally boring science buildings and laboratories. The only notable building, on the fringe of this area, is by Sir Leslie Martin and Colin St John Wilson: the Law Library (1961–64), whose long bands of windows and cubes of sand-coloured brick are reminiscent of the Bauhaus.

Towards the end of the 20th century the university experienced one of the biggest building booms in its history. With the increase in the number of students, the colleges needed new living and teaching quarters. One ten-million-pound project was Richard MacCormac's Garden Quad for St John's – a very successful combination of old and new (1993). Most of the other additions, however, are consistently dull – neo-Georgian, postmodern, and not a spark of originality. A good example is the Grove Buildings at Magdalen (1994–99), designed by Demetri Porphyrios: pale neo-Classicism with workmanship of top quality. These backward-looking buildings with their comfortable interiors are meant not only to accommodate the students but also to cater for another clientele that has become increasingly important: the business and conference people who fill the university's coffers during the long vacations. The turn of the century also galvanized the university into commissioning a number of 'millennium buildings', including Sir Norman Foster's Economics Department (Manor Road) and the Saïd Business School (near the station) by Jeremy Dixon and Edward Jones.

As far as non-university buildings go, Oxford's efforts have led to the ugliness that characterizes nearly all the city centres of contemporary England. Into one of the oldest areas around Queen Street they piled not one but two shopping centres: Westgate (1972) and the Clarendon Centre (1984), with the customary postmodern ornamentalism and reflecting glass. The new station (1990) is also in supermarket style, described by *The Observer* as 'Oxford's terminal disaster'. William Morris would have been appalled. Back in 1885 he was already objecting to the demolition of old houses and incompetent town planning. Oxford's culture was 'steeped to the lips in the commercialism of to-day.' 'Need I speak to you of the degradation that has so speedily befallen this city, still the most beautiful of them all, a city which with its surrounding world, if we had a grain of common sense, would have been treated like a perfect jewel, whose beauty was to be preserved at any cost.'

Not until 1968 was part of North Oxford put under a preservation order, though in the meantime there are now more than a dozen such conservation areas. Why did it take so long? The Oxford Preservation Trust came into existence as long ago as 1927. Its original aim was to preserve the classical view of the city of dreaming spires, and it actually purchased part of Boar's Hill and other sites in order to prevent uncontrolled building. It was a worthy cause, but it didn't go far enough. For decades the colleges themselves, as the biggest landowners, had been buying up land, and they at least share the guilt for the developments which they are the first to complain about. The erosion of the countryside around Oxford was only halted after 1947 with a Green Belt policy that imposed strict limitations on building within a twelve-mile radius of Carfax. Beyond this protected zone the villages proceeded to expand, and places like Witney and Woodstock became dormitory towns for Greater Oxford. We do, however, still have the same unspoilt view of Christ Church Meadow that J. M. W. Turner painted in watercolours around 1800, looking towards the towers from St Aldgate's to St Mary's – a skyline that has scarcely changed in 200 years. Through these very meadows, however, the City Council wanted to build a road in order to relieve the congestion on the High Street. In the Battle of Merton Mall, the old town versus gown conflict flared up again, and there were countless public hearings, protest marches, planning commissions, until finally it was acknowledged that it would be better to build a road across the moon than across Christ Church Meadow. Some 60,000 cars a day drive through Oxford. Pedestrian zones in the centre have simply increased the number of buses, and the signs, street markings and barriers add to the ugliness. To solve Oxford's notorious traffic problems, the simplest thing to do would be to divert the Isis down the High Street, suggested John Sparrow, the eccentric Warden of All Souls, who because of his homosexual leanings was dubbed 'Warden of All Holes'.

The middle of the 1980s brought another Oxford uprising. Environmental groups protested against the extension of the A40, the ring road around the north of the city. Today, however, the M40 sends its six lanes hurtling through Cherwell Valley, a savage slash into a classical landscape which Lady Bullock, wife of the prominent historian, was unable to prevent, despite her threat to throw herself in front of the bulldozers.

John Betjeman called Oxford 'an unplanned muddle'. For centuries the city and the university practised a kind of architectural apartheid policy, each for itself and often in conflict with the other. Today, cooperation is something that has long been taken for granted, although that does not prevent controversy. Plans for the Science Park, which began life on the edge of Port Meadow in 1985, and construction of the Oxford Centre for Islamic Studies in New Marston (2001–) are two cases in point. The Islamic Centre, the largest in England, was designed by the Egyptian Abdel Wahed Al-Wakil, and has the ground plan of a typical Oxford college, with its quads half-Alhambra, half-medieval cloister, in a mixture of Gothic and Islam, west and east, crowned with a minaret and a mosque cupola – perhaps one last exotic addition to the dreaming spires.

Choirboys and Rattling Balls: Music in Oxford

'As the train proceeded towards what he had once with an eye to
its plethora of music described as the City of Screaming Choirs,
Nicholas sipped cheerfully at a flask of whisky.'
Edmund Crispin, *The Case of the Gilded Fly*, 1971

On the edge of Magdalen Meadow, beneath the boughs of a wild cherry tree, sit two students playing their violins – Irish folksongs. 'If it's not raining, we always practise out here,' says one of them. At lunchtime in Wadham Chapel, up in the organ loft, a girl is singing Schubert's *Ave Maria*, alone with her teacher. In every college, when you walk across the quadrangle and go into the gardens, you will always hear someone playing the piano.

Oxford is a city of music. When you arrive, the first thing you hear above the noise of the traffic is the bells: the bells of Magdalen, of Merton, of New College, of St Mary's, Lincoln, Christ Church, and accompanying the bells of the colleges are the bells of the seven inner-city parish churches. There are bells everywhere, some high, some low, some light, some heavy, and the sound is heavenly. When Evelyn Waugh's Brideshead student Charles Ryder walks from the Broad to his college on the last Sunday of the academic year, 'through a world of piety', he finds himself surrounded by churchgoers and the sound of church bells. The piety has long since faded, but the churches remain – some sixty-five Anglican churches and college chapels. Outside London, nowhere in England will you find such a concentration of bells. From early on in Oxford's history, they summoned not only the faithful but also the bell-ringers, for shortly after the Reformation campanology became very fashionable for young 'gentlemen-ringers'. The rules were laid down by a Cambridge campanologist named Fabian Stedman. In his *Tintinnalogia* of 1668, he developed the art of change ringing just as it is practised today – such a virtuoso technique that Georg Friedrich Handel thought the bell must be England's national instrument.

Change ringing is a ritual that is mathematically calculated and can go on for hours – a mixture of Zen and cricket up in the bell-tower. In the colleges too this team sport still has its devotees. Members of the Oxford University Society of Change Ringers, founded in 1872, practise regularly in St Mary Magdalen and St Thomas-the-Martyr, and sometimes also in St Cross, St Ebbe's and the parish church of Old Marston. Here such Oxford specialities as Magdalen Bob and Nuffield Bob were first introduced, and here in 1958 a world record was set: 12,600 changes in 6 hours and 20 minutes. One prominent member of this society was John Betjeman. After his student days in Magdalen, bells accompanied him through his life, even as far as the title of his memoirs in verse: *Summoned by Bells*.

If you follow the call of the bells, you will often find yourself listening to some of the finest music that Oxford has to offer, and you needn't pay a penny: church music in the great English choral tradition, ranging from William Byrd to Benjamin Britten. This institution is called evensong, and is the purest relic of the monastic origins of the colleges. Generally it is only sung during term-time, but not all the colleges have a choir of students. Only Christ Church, Magdalen and New College have their own choir schools, and it follows that they also have the best choirs. For many years they have organized tours all over the world – the stars of a genre of music that remains as popular as ever. In 1996, New College Choir sang its way not only to the top of the classical charts, but even into the pop charts as well.

'Praise the Lord, O my soul.' Vespers in New College Chapel, and sixteen choirboys are singing their hearts out, the youngest of them scarcely able to peep over the stalls. Their heads are haloed in high lace collars, and behind them are fourteen older singers dressed in black and white surplices. They are all singing Psalm 104 to their lord and master, who in this case – apart from God himself – is Edward Higginbottom. He is the choirmaster, a man with long, thin El Greco hands which he waves like a snake charmer over his sopranos, tenors and basses, until the thirty voices are woven to a single texture – preferably a cappella – of pure, clear sound, perfectly balanced between the parts. Each of his fingers modulates the tone, and he also conducts with his eyebrows, as if the winged angels high above on the beams of the roof are expected to join in. Then for a moment the hands hover motionless in the air until the last, barely audible note has faded away – an 'Amen' of extraordinary beauty that you would like to last forever, and it very nearly does. Sometimes, at Halloween, on the eve of All Saints Day, his seraphic singers smuggle a devil's mask into the choir stalls.

These wonderful voices bring out all the beauty of the Gregorian chant and the complex polyphony of later church music – Farinelli voices, countertenors, human angels under threat of the broken voice or the demands of the examiners, replaced year by year, century by century. They have been singing like this in New College since 1379, as was stipulated by William of Wykeham in the deeds of the foundation. In Christ Church Cathedral, the choristers still wear the flat Tudor caps from the time of Cardinal Wolsey, and in Magdalen the choirboys have been wearing red robes with white surplices since they first trooped into their candle-lit chapel for evensong in 1458. A remarkable force emanates from the college choirs, from their simplicity and their vocal purity – an inner harmony that transcends ritual and faith. If you are lucky enough to hear Allegri's *Miserere* on an Ash Wednesday in Magdalen, you will never forget it.

The choirs are as different as the colleges, even when it comes to the timing of the vespers. In Magdalen College evensong begins at six o'clock, in New College at 6.15 pm, and in Christ Church at precisely 6.05 pm. And of course the Magdalen *informator choristarum* has a different title from his counterparts as well as a different style. What does link the three great choirs, however, apart from the liturgies, is their love of church music from Tudor times – which is shared by their Cambridge rivals at King's and St John's. The repertoire extends from Tudor composers like William Byrd, Thomas Tallis and Orlando Gibbons to Palestrina, Monteverdi and Orlando di Lasso, from Renaissance motets to Baroque chorales and cantatas. In a single week you might hear Handel, Bach and Purcell together with Penderecki and Stravinsky, followed perhaps by Bruckner and Britten, and English classical composers like Elgar, Vaughan Williams, Tippett, right up to the latest works by John Tavener.

One of the choristers' all-time favourites is Orlando Gibbons. He was one of them – a Cambridge choirboy who was born in Oxford and made his name as a composer in London. He played the virginal at the court of King James I, was organist at Westminster Abbey, and because of his virtuosity on keyboard instruments was referred to as 'the greatest finger of that age'. One of his best-known anthems is 'O clap your hands', a contrapuntal tour de force, and in his birthplace there is no more brilliant interpreter of it than Edward Higginbottom, the maestro of the long Amen. William Walton also began as a choirboy at Christ Church, in 1916. At the age of fourteen he wrote the litany 'Drop, drop slow tears' for his choir – the first of his works to have been preserved. Henry Purcell's brother Daniel was cantor at Magdalen, and was such a witty man that he was called the 'Punmaster General'. As for singers, the countertenors James Bowman and Robert Hollingworth began their international concert careers in the chapel at New College, and another singer from the same college, Jeremy Summerly, is currently in charge of Oxford's 'Schola Cantorum', one of the finest choirs in Britain.

'The sound of a choir of men and trebles is utterly different from that of a mixed choir. It is the sound many composers wrote for, including Handel.... This is our tradition, but I do wish that we also had the equivalent in Oxford of Trinity's or Clare's mixed choir in Cambridge,' said Edward Higginbottom in 1993. Since then, Exeter, Oriel and various other Oxford colleges have opened their choirs up to women students.

Daily attendance at vespers was for centuries as much a part of college tradition as the wearing of gowns. Today, though, there are more tourists than students at evensong, and sometimes in winter the choir outnumbers the congregation. Then they sing just for the people in stone – the prophets, apostles and saints that are gathered in the dark niches around the altar. But even if the pews are empty, the choir will still sing with the same dedication as at the big festivals, when the chapel is full to bursting. The fact is, they do not need an audience. Did they not sing in the olden days purely for the glory of God and for the salvation of their Founder? Such duties have now been supplemented by other engagements that bring a different kind of glory: international concert tours, CDs, appearances at the Proms, television, the next film set in Oxford. But there is no sound studio, however digitally sophisticated it may be, that can match the magic of evensong in chapel. The harmony between the architecture and the sound is an irreplaceable element of church music.

Once a year, on May morning, the choirboys of Magdalen climb the college tower and, at six o'clock in the early light of dawn, they sing the 'Te Deum Patrem Colimus', an ancient Eucharistic hymn. Then the thousands of students, townies and tourists that have gathered in the High Street fall completely silent. May Morning, and the bells of Magdalen ring out to mark the end of Oxford's longest night. Those who have stayed up all night celebrating now troop off for breakfast in the college, the pubs or the cafés, while Morris dancers twirl through the streets, and students wear ivy and garlands in their hair. One of them dances with his teddy bear, and another wears a gigantic papier-mâché penis with rattling testicles and a vagina hoop of red velvet. 'It's pagan, it's vulgar, it's all faintly silly, but it works,' says Jack to Joy in *Shadowlands*, when the Oxford don takes his American friend to Magdalen Tower to hear the May Morning song.

Music is as much a part of college life as theatre and sport. In addition to all the music societies, there are two orchestras which consist almost exclusively of members of the university. There are also chamber orchestras and choirs in which people from the city join the students, and professionals play and sing alongside amateurs. I have seldom seen a more enthusiastic collection of musicians than the Oxford University Orchestra or a more knowledgeable audience than in the Holywell Music Room. 'We went along once to a concert in which they were playing some obscure work by Dvorák,' Colin Dexter told me. 'The organist had been held up, and we waited and waited until the conductor said to the audience: "Is there anybody in the audience who knows this Dvorák Requiem?" And thirteen people put their hands up. This is Oxford – we all here are grossly overqualified.'

Concerts are going on all the time and all over the place, in college chapels and churches, in Freud's Café, in the Jacqueline Du Pré Music Building at St Hilda's, in the Sheldonian Theatre, and in a very unlikely venue in Holywell Street. The Holywell Music Room was inaugurated in 1748 with a Handel Oratorio, and it is one of the oldest concert halls in Europe. It was here that Joseph Haydn conducted his Symphony No. 92 in G sharp, the so-called Oxford Symphony, on 7 July 1791. The following day, the title 'Doctor of Music' was bestowed on him at the Sheldonian. During the 1920s, this was the scene of a rather unusual event: Tom Driberg, later to become a Labour MP, declaimed his poems through a loudspeaker to the accompaniment of a rattling typewriter and, at the grand climax, the flushing of a toilet. A natural progression, perhaps, from poetry to pan to politics.

Oxford is the home not only of the Bate Collection and the Allegri Quartet – a collection of historical musical instruments and the internationally renowned string quartet – but also of the rock bands Radiohead and Supergrass. The Beatles came here too, in 1964, although it was only to attend a charity dinner organized by a Brasenose trickster named Jeffrey Archer. Ringo Starr, on seeing the nimble Archer busily collecting the money, remarked: 'That guy would bottle my pee and sell it for five pounds.'

Brief Lives:
A Galaxy of Oxford Stars

'Oxford always gave her the feeling that she was stupid.
She couldn't stand Oxford.'
Virginia Woolf, *The Years*, 1937

ELIAS ASHMOLE (1617–92)

The son of a saddler, he studied at Brasenose, became a lawyer and a customs officer, married a rich widow and eventually was able to devote himself full-time to
the natural sciences, which were his chief interest. Ashmole was a founder member of the Royal Society, wrote a *History of the Order of the Garter*, became a
Rosicrucian, but above all else was an indefatigable collector. His friend John
Tradescant the Younger, gardener to Charles I, bequeathed his collection of rarities and curiosities to Ashmole, who gave it together with his own collection of
coins and more to the university in 1683. This formed the basis of the Old Ashmolean, the first public museum in England. Like his contemporary Samuel
Pepys, he kept a diary for over fifty years, but it was so encoded that it was not
until 1949 that the Oxford curator Kurt Josten, a German, managed to decipher it.

SIR ISAIAH BERLIN (1909–97)

Historian of ideas and founding President of Wolfson College, intellectual *flâneur*
between Oxford and Washington and between High Society and High Table. As a
Russian Jew in England, he embodied the spirit of Oxford so brilliantly that he
became a cult figure, awarded more than twenty honorary doctorates. Born in
Riga, he was a child when the Tsar was overthrown, and he was an old man when
Communism collapsed. His answer to all totalitarian systems was the freedom of
the individual: 'Liberty is liberty, not equality or fairness or justice or culture or
human happiness or a quiet conscience' (*Two Concepts of Liberty*, 1958). Berlin's
liberalism lays emphasis on the incompatibility of absolute value judgments with
the desirability of pluralism and tolerance as ways of thinking and living. He
wrote about David Hume, Alexander Herzen, Karl Marx, Kant, Herder, Hamann
– the thinkers of the Enlightenment and the Counter-Enlightenment. This was a

history of ideas, always demonstrated through the work of individual thinkers. His preferred form was the biographical essay, which elucidated thought with what T. S. Eliot called 'torrential eloquence'. 'The Paganini of the platform' (*Guardian*) was the first Jewish Fellow in the five-hundred-year history of All Souls, and indeed was only the third Jew ever to be elected Fellow of any Oxford college. He communicated in his own conversation the intellectual pleasure that he found there, and he had a lightness of touch and a goodness of nature that was rarely to be found even among the sages of Oxford.

WILLIAM BUCKLAND (1784–1856)

Geologist, pioneer of palaeontology, canon of Christ Church Cathedral, blessed eccentric. Buckland's lectures in the Old Ashmolean were a big attraction. He would hand out fossils to the audience and, even before Darwin's *Origin of Species*, would explain that Genesis was about God's relation to humanity and not to reptiles, and so scientific corrections must be applied to the story of Creation. He was the first, in 1824, to give a scientific description of a dinosaur, the *Megalosaurus bucklandi*. His family shared their home in Christ Church with snakes, owls, ferrets and Billy, the hyena. So insatiable was the curiosity of this great scholar that at mealtimes there would sometimes be dishes like rhinoceros pie, panther cutlet, or moles. His son, the naturalist Frank Buckland, evidently thrived on this universal upbringing. He kept a tame bear which used to accompany him to parties, dressed in cap and gown. When his father was shown the relics of St Rosalia in Sicily, he remarked, 'They are the bones of a goat.' In Naples he fell to his knees before the bloodstains of St Januarius, tasted them with his tongue, and declared that they were the urine of bats. Many fossils and minerals from Buckland's collection are now in the University Museum.

ROBERT BURTON (1577–1640)

'Paucis notus, paucioribus ignotus, hic jacet Democritus junior, cui vitam dedit, & mortem Melancholia.' This is the Latin inscription on the memorial bust in Christ Church Cathedral: 'Known to few, to fewer unknown / here lies Democritus Junior / to whom Melancholy gave life and death.' In 1621, under the pseudonym of the ancient philosopher, Burton had published the single book that made him famous: *The Anatomy of Melancholy*, a bitter satire on the vanity of humanity's quest for knowledge: 'we lead a contentious, discontent, tumultuous, melancholy, miserable life; insomuch, that if we could foretell what was to come, and it put to our choice, we should rather refuse than accept of this painful life.' Even religion offers no comfort in this universe of futility, which Burton gathers together from a vast array of writers, with a wit and a baroque world-weariness that is far more radical than all the absurdist works of modern times. *The Anatomy of Melancholy* was the only book that Dr Johnson would get up two hours earlier than usual in order to read. Unaffected by his success as a best-selling author Burton, the Christ Church priest and scholar, led the life of a bookworm right to the end. 'I am not poor, I am not rich; ...I have little, I want nothing.' It is said that most of the time he was silent and sad, and yet he could make people laugh. However, the only time he himself would laugh was when he heard the boatmen cursing on the Isis.

LEWIS CARROLL (1832–98)

A parson's son from Cheshire, left-handed, deaf in the right ear. He began his studies at Christ Church in 1851, taught mathematics, and remained at the college until he died. He enchanted little girls and then the whole world with his stories. Charles Lutwidge Dodgson was his real name, and he simply switched his two Christian names round, latinized them to Ludovicus Carolus, and then anglicized them back into Lewis Carroll. Under this pseudonym he wrote *Alice's Adventures in Wonderland* (1865) and *Through the Looking-Glass* (1871), two children's books that made him into the 'Church Father of all modern literature', in the words of James Joyce (for whom 'loose carolleries' were a kind of prototype for *Finnegan's Wake*). Childhood nonsense, with absurd games of logic – these were his refuge and the subversive outlets of a man whose life was filled with inhibitions. His nude photographs of prepubescent girls brought the shy young bachelor under posthumous suspicion of paedophilia, but the latest research suggests that his eye was far more innocent than our own Lolita vision.

RICHARD DAWKINS (BORN 1941)

Ethologist, first holder of the Oxford Chair for the Public Understanding of Science, also known to students as Professor of Public Misunderstanding. His thesis that the 'selfish gene' is the real driving force behind evolution brought him acclaim from far and wide. A brilliant popularizer and best-selling author, his books include *The Selfish Gene* (1976), *The Blind Watchmaker* (1986), *River Out of Eden* (1995), *Unweaving the Rainbow* (1999), and most recently *The Ancestor's Tale* (2004). He calls himself an orthodox neo-Darwinist and 'the devil's chaplain'.

TIMOTHY GARTON ASH (BORN 1955)

Historian in the tradition of the English adventurer, Fellow of St Antony's College, Director of the Centre for European Studies since 2001. He wrote an eyewitness account of the downfall of Communism in Eastern Europe (*We the People: The Revolution of '89 witnessed in Warsaw, Budapest, Berlin and Prague*, 1990), analysed the German Ostpolitik (*In Europe's Name: Germany and the Divided Continent*, 1993) and his own Stasi file (*The File: A Personal History*, 1997), as well as the precarious relationship between Europe and the USA (*Free World: Why a Crisis of the West Reveals the Opportunity of Our Time*, 2004). He combines exemplary journalistic skills with scholarly archival research. When the *Frankfurter Allgemeine Zeitung* asked him his favourite colour, he replied in true Oxford style, 'The colour of Magdalen Tower.'

DOROTHY MARY HODGKIN (1910–94)

Chemist, crystallographer and molecular biologist, initially at the Cavendish Laboratory in Cambridge, but from 1936 worked in Oxford. She did pioneering work on the structure of penicillin and insulin, and was only the third woman to receive the Nobel Prize for chemistry (1964) for her research into the structure of vitamin B12. During the 1960s, Dorothy Mary Hodgkin was prominent in the anti-nuclear movement. Her best-known student at Somerville was Margaret Thatcher.

BENJAMIN JOWETT (1817–93)

Translator of Plato, Master of Balliol, the personification of Oxford arrogance and the Victorian cult of success: 'First come I, my name is Jowett. / There's no knowledge but I know it. / I am the Master of this College. / What I know not isn't

knowledge' (Student satirical verse, 1881). Jowett said that he had a 'general preju-
dice against all persons who do not succeed in the world.' 'The Jowler' was a small,
owl-like man whose ambition was to make Balliol the intellectual giant of England's colleges, and to 'balliolize' the world. 'I should like to govern the world
through my pupils,' he wrote to Florence Nightingale. In fact four Balliol graduates have become prime ministers, and the first Director General of UNESCO
after 1945, Sir Julian Huxley, was another Balliol man. In 1883, Jowett opened the
Indian Institute, today part of the Bodleian Library, with the largest collection of
Sanskrit manuscripts outside India itself. After he had given a lecture in Glasgow,
a Scottish professor said to Jowett: 'I hope you in Oxford don't think we hate
you.' – 'We don't think of you at all,' was Jowett's reply. As a tutor, he had his own
distinctive style. While out walking with a student he would generally say nothing
until the student spoke, then he would stay silent before suddenly replying, after
they had walked another mile, 'Your last observation was singularly commonplace.'

WILLIAM LAUD (1573–1645)

Son of a clothier from Reading, rose to become Archbishop of Canterbury, was
executed for high treason during the Civil War, is buried in his college chapel at
St John's. As a politicized churchman of the Counter-Reformation he was orthodox, and as Chancellor of Oxford University he was a reformer. He set up a chair
in Arabic and oversaw the university's first written constitution. This 'Laudian
Code' of 1636 regulated every aspect of academic self-administration, from examinations to the length of students' hair. 'No scholars of any condition are to play
foot-ball within the University or its precinct.... They are not to encourage the
growth of curls, or immoderately long hair.'

CLIVE STAPLES LEWIS (1898–1963)

Literature professor, science-fiction author, guru, Oxford's first media don. In
Belfast, the city of his birth, there is a monument to him: a man entering a
wardrobe which leads to Narnia. He became famous largely through his seven
children's books about the land of Narnia and his radio talks on religious subjects.
In 1929, C. S. Lewis was converted from atheism to Catholicism, and in 1954 he left
Magdalen (Oxford) for Magdalene (Cambridge), although he continued to live in

Oxford until he died. A. L. Rowse called him the 'unconsecrated Bishop of Oxford'. He hated Socialists, vegetarians and non-smokers. Pop stars like Liam Gallagher are among his fans, as was Pope John Paul II, and his books have sold over 100 million copies. Even those who have not read his work know about him through the film *Shadowlands*: this tells the story of how, late in his life, the misogynist Jack experienced love and death in Oxford through his American wife Joy.

DESMOND MORRIS (BORN 1928)

Zoologist and best-selling author, did his doctorate at Magdalen College with a thesis on the reproductive behaviour of the stickleback. He successfully applied his methods of observing fish and monkeys to the observation of humans (*The Naked Ape*, 1967), and after years of research expeditions in many different countries, declared: 'Oxford is the perfect city for me. It only has two faults: one is the climate, and the other is the parking.'

WILLIAM R. MORRIS, LORD NUFFIELD (1877–1963)

Son of a farm labourer, left school at fourteen, repaired the bicycles of Oxford students, and became Britain's most famous car manufacturer. He founded the Morris Garages in Cowley in 1912, where two classic family cars rolled off the production line: the Morris Oxford and the Morris Minor. Thus Oxford turned into an industrial centre, and William R. Morris became Lord Nuffield. He hated the unions, did not like employing academics, was a reactionary, a hypochondriac, and a despotic but immensely generous philanthropist. He financed professorships, medical institutions and Nuffield College. His work ethos is as relevant now as it ever was: 'The one object in life of many makers seems to be to make the thing the public cannot buy. The one object of my life is to make the thing they can buy.'

INSPECTOR E. MORSE (1932–99)

Oxford's most famous detective, son of a taxi driver, studied classical philology at St John's. After an unhappy love affair, failed his examinations and ended up in the police force. Continually gets on the nerves of Sergeant Lewis by quoting Aristotle and insisting on correct spelling. Has a human side: 'Nearest pub, Lewis. We need to think a little.' Chief Inspector Morse, who tries to keep quiet about his first name (Endeavour), is a conservative outsider, a fan of Wagner and crossword puzzles, a bachelor, and a melancholic in the Oxford tradition of Robert Burton. He cannot stand the sight of blood, and loves the poems of A. E. Housman, real ale, Fauré's *Requiem*, and women with nicely rounded breasts. After his first public appearance (in *Last Bus to Woodstock*, 1975) gained international fame as the hero of novels and a TV series. Morse lived in North Oxford until he himself was killed – by his author and alter ego Colin Dexter in the fourteenth Morse novel, *The Remorseful Day* (1999).

DAME IRIS MURDOCH (1919–99)

The grande dame of English Literature was both a philosopher and a novelist. Born in Dublin, grew up in London, found her spiritual home in Oxford. She taught philosophy at St Anne's for fifteen years. Her first book, about Sartre, was published in 1953, and the following year saw the publication of her first novel *Under the Net*. After that she wrote twenty-seven novels, several plays, poems and a large number of philosophical works. For her, art was a 'moral discipline', metaphysics was a guide to morality, and Plato was her true God. She admired Tolstoy, Dostoyevsky and the novelists of the 19th century, in whose tradition she stood. Her best novels (*The Bell*, *The Black Prince*) combine moral reflection, exciting action and an instinct for dramatic dialogue. Her final years were overshadowed by Alzheimer's disease, and were described by her husband, the Oxford don and novelist John Bayley, in his *Elegy for Iris*, one of the great love stories of our time (and made into the film *Iris* starring Judi Dench). The extraordinary magnetism of her personality shines through in the portrait of her that Tom Phillips painted for the National Portrait Gallery.

SIR JAMES MURRAY (1837–1915)

Son of a Scottish village tailor, teacher, philologist, lexicographer. Spent some thirty years of his life in the corrugated iron garden shed at his home in Oxford, surrounded by millions of notes. The dream behind the notes was to collate every English word since 1150, and ascertain its derivation, its earliest usage and the history of its meanings. The first volume of the legendary *Oxford English Dictionary* (originally called the *New English Dictionary*) appeared in 1884, and the last in 1928, long after Murray had died. Photos show him in black tails, with a flowing, patriarchal beard. His maxim was: 'Know everything about something and something about everything.' He had twelve children, nine honorary doctorates, and a murderer as his most productive colleague: Dr W. C. Minor, a psychopathic word-lover who for twenty years sent him lexical contributions from Broadmoor.

JOHN HENRY NEWMAN (1801–90)

A leading figure in the Anglo-Catholic Oxford Movement, studied at Trinity College, where he wrote that the only qualification necessary was 'Drink, drink, drink.' His explosive sermons from the pulpit of St Mary's sparked off a regular 'Newmania'. A convert to Catholicism, he advanced from don to cardinal, but twice failed in his attempts to found a Catholic college in Oxford. He wrote many influential tracts, hymns that are still sung today (*Lead, Kindly Light*), and a masterpiece of an autobiography, *Apologia pro Vita Sua*. Even James Joyce praised his 'cloistral silver-veined' prose. The intrigues of the Curia in Rome, who feared his liberal reforms, deprived him of much of his influence. Nevertheless, he worked all his life for a rapprochement between the two faiths, and for freedom of scientific study and of conscience. In 1991 the Pope granted him the title of *Venerabilis*, and all that is required for canonization is proof of two miracles.

CRAIG RAINE (BORN 1944)

Son of a fairground boxer, poet, librettist, full-bearded latter-day hippie and Fellow in English Literature at New College. Apparently prepared to risk falling off bicycle in order to look under girls' skirts. Occasionally surprises friends with silly questions like: 'Do you think insects fart?' Also shocks people with poems like 'Arsehole' or *The Way It Was*, an erotic elegy on the death from Aids of a former girlfriend. Raine's volume of poetry *A Martian Sends a Postcard Home* (1979) pointed the way for the so-called Martian School of Literature. The surreal universe of objects and its everyday magic is one of his pet themes: 'I will bring you the beauty of facts' (*Clay. Whereabouts Unknown*, 1996). Editor of the literary magazine *Areté*, Raine is married to the English don Ann Pasternak Slater, a

granddaughter of the painter Leonid Pasternak, who died as an Oxford exile in
1945. The story of both families, from the Russian Revolution until the present, is
the subject of Raine's verse epic *History: The Home Movie* (1994).

ALFRED LESLIE ROWSE (1903–97)

Son of a Cornish miner, was the first working-class Fellow to break into the
upper-class society of All Souls. Historian, Tudor specialist, notorious egotist and
know-all: 'Partly I enjoy hating people for their folly and rubbing their noses in it;
partly I am acting a part, I suppose.' He said that if his critics were too stupid to
understand that he knew more than anyone else about the Elizabethan age, then he
had no qualms about pointing it out to them. He wrote so many popular books
that he was dubbed the Barbara Cartland of history. His most controversial claim
was to have identified the 'Dark Lady' of Shakespeare's sonnets, which he did with
some ingenious speculation. He was a lifelong bachelor, a self-confessed bisexual,
and had a special affection for the Oxford student Adam von Trott zu Solz: 'I felt
here is the one I have always hoped to find; someone beautiful in all ways, mind
and body. No woman or man I had ever come across was this that I longed for.'
When he was a visiting professor in California, he used to phone his home in
Cornwall in order to hear his cat purring. From 1925 onwards he kept a diary, only
selections from which have been published – a little academic time bomb waiting
to explode.

JOHN RUSKIN (1819–1900)

Son of a wine merchant and a Puritan, most influential art critic of his time, champion of J. M. W. Turner and the Pre-Raphaelites, prophet of the Arts and Crafts
Movement. While he was still an undergraduate at Christ Church, he started on
his magnum opus *Modern Painters*, which grew into a polemic against the industrial destruction of the countryside, the pollution of the rivers, and the
architectural ruination of the towns. Without Ruskin, there would never have
been a National Trust. As the first Slade Professor of Fine Art, he founded the
Ruskin School of Drawing and Fine Art in 1871, and donated a dazzling selection
of pictures (by himself and others): 'To see clearly is poetry, prophecy, and religion
– all in one'. Later, he was at odds with the university, which mistrusted the

extended concept of art advanced by this dedicated reformer. For him, art and design were inextricably linked to morality, religion, the environment and social conditions. To put his 'gospel of labour' into practice, he took a group of students to resurface a road in the village of North Hinksey, much to the derision of the Oxford eggheads. In protest against the university's decision to allow vivisection, he resigned his professorship in 1885 and never returned to Oxford. He spent his last years fading quietly away in the Lake District. The centre of Ruskin research with the largest collection is now the Ruskin Library at the University of Lancaster.

DOROTHY LEIGH SAYERS (1893–1957)

Born in Oxford, like her fellow thriller writer P. D. James. Her father was a parson and headmaster, and a graduate of Magdalen. When Dorothy was six, he told her: 'I think, my dear, that you are now old enough to begin to learn Latin.' She studied at Somerville College, rode a motorcycle, and was a feminist *avant la lettre*, a medievalist and translator of Dante. 'I am a scholar gone wrong,' she used to say. She only wrote detective stories because she needed the money, and when she had enough to live on, she stopped writing them and devoted herself to the work she really wanted to do: 'higher' literature and religion. All the same, she is regarded as the Virginia Woolf of the detective story. Oxford, 'a city sanctified', is the setting for her penultimate Lord Peter Wimsey novel *Gaudy Night* (1935). Her best-known work, however, was the advertising slogan 'Guinness is good for you'.

WILLIAM ARCHIBALD SPOONER (1844–1930)

The Reverend Spooner was a don who sometimes mixed up the beginnings of words. Thus he announced a hymn in New College Chapel as: 'Kinquering Congs Their Titles Take' When dismissing a student, he famously declared, 'You have deliberately tasted two worms. You have hissed my mystery lectures. You can leave Oxford by the town drain!' Such spoonerisms found their way into anthologies even during his lifetime, and his name entered into the language – a fine example of how creatively Oxonians can handle even a speech disorder. Generations of students have since cultivated the unfortunate mannerism of a don who once, it is said, proposed a toast to 'our dear old Queen' who inadvertently turned into 'our queer old Dean'. In Oxford folklore, he has come to personify the cliché of the doddery don. 'Do come to dinner tonight to meet our new Fellow, Casson.' – 'But Warden, I *am* Casson.' – 'Oh well. Never mind. Come anyway.'

JOHN RONALD REUEL TOLKIEN (1892–1973)

Professor of Anglo-Saxon Literature, philologist, born in South Africa, came to Oxford as a student in 1911 and, with a few interruptions, remained there for the rest of his life. In Oxford 'Tolly', as he was known to his friends, devised the Elvish languages of Sindarin and Quenya, used in the fantasy world of Middle Earth. *The Hobbit* (1937) and *The Lord of the Rings* (1954) became cult books in the 1960s, paving the way for Harry Potter in our time. In Tolkien's mythical world, fantasy reigned supreme. 'Gandalf for President', 'Frodo lives' proclaimed the buttons and T-shirts of the hippie generation. J. R. R. was a word wizard, and his Middle Earth was the counterworld of a Romantic who hated anything more mechanical than a handloom. Thus an arch-Conservative became an icon for the students of 1968 and for the Italian neo-fascists, and his medieval fantasy turned into an ersatz Utopia. Tolkien's books have sold over 100 million copies, quite apart from their adaptations as comics, films, board and computer games. Sometimes a Tolkien fan will stand in Hobbit-green trousers before the grave that Tolkien shares with his wife in Wolvercote, on which are chiselled the names Beren and Luthien – heroes and lovers from his posthumous *Silmarillion*. In its three-part film adaptation (2001–3), *The Lord of the Rings* (starring Sir Ian McKellen as the wizard Gandalf) has once again conquered the world and transported millions of people into the dark and mysterious depths of Middle Earth.

HUGH TREVOR-ROPER, LORD DACRE (1914–2003)

Regius Professor of Modern History in Oxford, 1957–80; Master of Peterhouse in Cambridge, 1980–87. Had the misfortune to be tricked twice: by the double agent Kim Philby, with whom he worked during the war as a Secret Service officer, and by the forged Hitler Diaries which he authenticated in 1983. Like his fellow Oxford historian Alan Bullock, Trevor-Roper became well known through a book on Hitler (*The Last Days of Hitler*, 1947). His real speciality was the intellectual history of early modern times, and his books on Erasmus, Thomas More and Archbishop Laud displayed his impeccable research and stylistic elegance.

South-East of Carfax

'Most interesting spot I have seen in England.
Made tour of all colleges.... Learning lodged like a faun.'
Herman Melville, 1857

Paradise Street and Music Meadow, Divinity Road, Aristotle Lane, Logic Lane – even the names of roads and fields celebrate the *genius loci* of this city. Perhaps we should begin our tour a little more prosaically at Carfax Tower, where Oxford is at its noisiest. Four roads cross here – it's a *quadrifurcus*, if you want to know the Latin, and if you say that often enough in English, you'll find yourself corrupting it to Carfax.

Since the Middle Ages this crossroads has been Oxford's centre. Everyone came from all directions through all the city gates, converging on this one spot – cattle drovers, traders, monks, market women, Chaucer's student and all the rest, on foot, on horseback, in carts and carriages, creating so many traffic jams that even back in 1789 they had to pull down the Baroque fountain that once stood here. It wasn't enough, and so to broaden the road, they demolished St Martin's Church. Only the tower survived – Carfax Tower and its Quarter Boys, two figures dressed as Roman legionnaires, who strike the hours with their battleaxes. Opposite the church there used to be a tavern called Swyndlestock. Where you now pay in or, more likely, take out your savings from the Abbey building society, once upon a time the students and locals waged the bloodiest of battles on St Scholastica's Day (see p. 36). Carfax is still the point of intersection between town and gown, with the business district west of St Aldate's and Cornmarket Street, and the colleges on the other side. From Carfax, St Aldate's leads down to the river. So long as it flows through Oxford, the Thames is called the Isis (derived from the Latin *Thamesis*), and then it resumes its identity as the Thames. 'Curiouser and curiouser,' says Alice. On a toilet door in an Oxford café I once saw a notice that said 'Necessarium'. Such is the vocabulary of Wonderland.

The point at which Folly Bridge (1825) crosses the Isis is believed to be the spot where once the oxen forded the river, thereby giving the town its name. Ox and waves decorate the coat of arms, a particularly splendid specimen of which is to be seen on the staircase of the Town Hall (1893–97), whose Victorian interiors reflect the civic pride of the period. For decades the Labour Party has had a majority here. On every second Wednesday of the month, in the finest of all these fine stuccoed rooms, a band plays for a very unlaboured *thé dansant* – foxtrots for the old-at-heart. In the neighbouring Museum of Oxford, you can see how town and gown lived in the good old days, thanks to reconstructions of a workroom, a drawing room and a student's room from the 1770s. Objects and documents bring the town's history to life, presented in a manner that is somewhat old-fashioned, but at least more authentic than The Oxford Story in Broad Street, where visitors are sent riding through the centuries on a conveyor belt, accompanied by all sorts of noises and smells in a sort of Disneyland version of history.

Ever since Cliff Richard spiced up the Sunday Service at St Aldate's with a bit of rock 'n' roll, the church opposite Christ Church has enjoyed a reputation for spreading the gospel in less than orthodox fashion. In its own way, that is what Modern Art Oxford (formerly the Museum of Modern Art) – just a few doors down in Pembroke Street – does too. For contemporary art in Britain, there is no more exciting address than this, even though it doesn't have a collection of its own. Through Western avant-garde, East European or non-European art and all kinds of pioneering exhibitions, Modern Art Oxford has become an international forum, ranging from classical modern to the media of the future.

The entrance to Pembroke College lies a little way off the main road, in one corner of a cobbled square that used to be the graveyard of St Aldate's. Pembroke is one of the smaller, poorer colleges, founded in 1624, architecturally unobtrusive, and permanently in the shadow of its overbearing neighbour Christ Church. However, even if the latter can boast of prime ministers, Nobel laureates and other glittering prizes, only Pembroke has Dr Johnson's teapot. It is a blue Worcester china teapot, and it once refreshed the teeming brain of England's most famous lexicographer. When he was a student, he most enjoyed the social life and long discussions laced with port wine: 'Sir, we were a nest of singing-birds.' When he once skipped a lecture, he was fined twopence, which he regarded as gross inflation since the lecture wasn't worth a penny. 'Ah, Sir, I was mad and violent. It was bitterness which they mistook for frolick. I was miserably poor, and I thought to fight my way by my literature and my wit; so I disregarded all power and all authority.' In 1729, after just a year, Samuel Johnson was forced to leave the college simply because he had no money. Nevertheless, he remained attached to Oxford for the rest of his life, and in 1775, when he was a star of the London literary scene, the university gave him an honorary doctorate. If you want to look up at where he looked down, his room is on the second floor, just above the entrance to Pembroke.

Behind Pembroke, a narrow lane branches off from St Aldate's, and here you will notice a building of light-coloured limestone, clearly defined, combining the International style with the Cotswold tradition. This is Campion Hall, designed in 1934 by Sir Edwin Lutyens. This Jesuit college was his only building in Oxford and is a delight – especially the chapel on the first floor: barrel vaulting, with apse, baldachin and a series of woodcuts by Frank Brangwyn (1935) depicting the Way of the Cross. Lutyens also designed some of the interior details, such as the library ladder, the banisters with Indian bell-knobs, and lamps in the form of cardinals' hats. Campion Hall was named after the Elizabethan Jesuit martyr Edmund Campion, whose biography was written in 1935 by the Catholic convert Evelyn Waugh; he dedicated it to the then Master of the college, 'to whom, under God, I owe my faith.'

On the same side of the street as Campion Hall stands the house where writer Dorothy L. Sayers (see p. 90) was born, 1 Brewer Street. At that time, 1893, her father was headmaster of the nearby choir school of Christ Church, 'where it was part of his duty to instruct small demons with angel-voices in the elements of the ancient Roman tongue.'

The House of Christ and the Prime Minister: Christ Church

'We're all mad here. I'm mad. You're mad.' – 'How do you know I'm mad?' said Alice. – 'You must be,' said the Cat, 'or you wouldn't have come here.'
Lewis Carroll, *Alice's Adventures in Wonderland*, 1865

Every evening at five past nine, the bell of Tom Tower rings out 101 times – once for every member of the college at the time when it was founded. Why at five past nine? Oxford, so certain clever people have discovered, lies a little more than one degree west of Greenwich. And so when the clocks of the United Kingdom show five past nine, in Oxford it is actually only nine. That seems logical, at least to Christ Church. This college has not only its own time zone but also its own terminology. The Fellows here are called students, the porters are not porters but custodians, and the college is not called a college but The House (after the Latin

Aedes Christi, House of Christ). 'This is not England, this is Christ Church,' I was told by one of the custodians, who are the only ones in Oxford that still wear bowler hats, which gives them a kind of Magrittean surreality.

'Dear, dear! How queer everything is today!' Christ Church is where Alice Liddell grew up, the Dean's daughter to whom a young maths tutor used to tell the most extraordinary stories. Two world-famous books came out of this college, one about reason and the other about nonsense: John Locke's *Essay Concerning Human Understanding*, and *Alice's Adventures in Wonderland* by Lewis Carroll. One should add a third classic on human sensitivity, for Robert Burton's *Anatomy of Melancholy* also had its roots in Christ Church.

This is the biggest and one of the richest colleges in Oxford, the only one to have a cathedral and an art gallery of its own. Christ Church is regarded as the academic cradle of the British aristocracy, and the high school of statesmanship and eccentricity, its alumni ranging from Sir Philip Sidney, the Elizabethan soldier poet, to Alan Clark, the flamboyant minister and diarist of the Thatcher years. Before they became prime ministers, William Gladstone studied Greek and maths here, and Anthony Eden did Middle Eastern studies. Lord Salisbury, Lord Derby, Portland, Canning, Peel – thirteen British prime ministers and eleven viceroys of India passed through the gates of Christ Church. It's scarcely surprising, then, that this was the first college in Oxford to charge tourists for doing the same.

The calibre of the Fellows here is demonstrated by a story told about the philosopher Alfred J. Ayer. At a party in New York in 1987, 'Freddie' Ayer noticed that the boxer Mike Tyson was making a nuisance of himself with the model Naomi Campbell, and so he told him to leave her alone. 'Dammit, d'you know who I am?' snapped Tyson. 'I'm the heavyweight champion of the world!' Ayer replied, 'And I'm the former Professor of Logic at Oxford University.'

Christ Church is as mighty as its founders, Cardinal Wolsey and Henry VIII. It began under the name of Cardinal College, in 1525. Thomas Wolsey, known as 'the boy bachelor' because he had taken his degree in Oxford at the age of fifteen, planned to build on the site of the dissolved priory of St Frideswide a college that would surpass all others; it was to be as magnificent as his home on the Thames, Hampton Court – a palace of learning, with sixty canons, forty junior canons and a dean at the head (totalling 101 clangs of the bell). But in 1529 Henry VIII's policies concerning marriage and Rome resulted in the ambitious Cardinal's downfall. By this time, only three wings of the Tom Quad, including the dining hall, were complete or under construction. 'Though he had started a college, he had finished an eating-house,' mocked his contemporaries.

Henry VIII confiscated Hampton Court and, for good measure, the college as well, but he extended it and guaranteed it a yearly income, mainly from the estates of the monasteries he had dissolved. In 1546 he linked his college with the new Anglican bishopric of Oxford, and the college chapel became a cathedral church, the *Ecclesia Christi Cathedralis Oxoniensis* – in short, Christ Church. Ever since, the dean of the Cathedral has also been Head of the College and is appointed by the crown, which is a procedure unique to Christ Church. The college tie, however, still features the red hat of the Cardinal.

Wolsey's grandiose plans are reflected by the entrance: Tom Quad at more than 80 metres in length is bigger than any other quadrangle in Oxford. In the middle is a graceful fountain with the figure of Mercury, the messenger of the gods, who has flown in from Florence or, to be precise, from the Medici Fountain by Giovanni da Bologna (1580, copy 1670). The pond, originally put there to provide water for fire-fighting, is surrounded by extensive lawns, and all around are raised terraces. Only by the plinths and the arcading can one see that these were once meant to be a cloister, following the model of Magdalen, where Wolsey had been a student. He employed the best royal stonemasons, who had also worked at Westminster Abbey and Windsor: John Lubbyns and Henry Redman. By the time of his downfall, in 1529, they had completed the south side of the quadrangle, and half the east and west wings. The gatehouse remained unfinished until 1681, when Christopher Wren arrived and crowned Christ Church with a tower which since then has been a landmark on the Oxford skyline.

Tom Tower is generally acknowledged to be one of the most original examples of English Baroque-Gothic – a hybrid, typologically unimaginable without the medieval gatehouses. It was Christopher Wren's first neo-Gothic building. On top of the Tudor base with its two octagonal corner turrets, and a square mezzanine, he placed an octagonal main tower. All three towers are crowned with ogee caps, the shape of which is echoed by the ogee gables of the windows and blind niches. In this way, Wren respected Oxford's conservatism by completing a Gothic building in neo-Gothic style. The weathered gateman above the entrance is Cardinal Wolsey himself – a statue by the Baroque sculptor Francis Bird (1719). High up in the tower hangs Great Tom, weighing in at approximately seven tons – the mighty college bell, which is not named after Thomas Wolsey but after Thomas Becket, for Tom Tower in fact is its third home after Oseney Abbey and St Frideswide's. Sometimes when Alice's parents were not at home, Lewis Carroll took the Liddell children to see Great Tom, and they would climb up the beautiful oak spiral steps – designed by Wren but now blocked off – until they could stand right beside the bell. They were allowed to tickle it gently with a stick, and it would rumble like an old lion. Later, when Alice went through the looking-glass, the process was of course reversed, and the lion spoke 'in a deep hollow tone that sounded like the tolling of a great bell'. Lewis Carroll's rooms in the north-west corner of Tom Quad are now the students' common room.

Typical of Oxford's conservative style is the fan vault that stretches out in cheerful splendour above the staircase leading to the hall, as if it were purest Gothic instead of early Gothic Revival – completed in 1640. A single, central column appears to carry the whole of the ceiling, but this impression is deceptive, because the stone ribs are only decorative and not part of the construction. In two wide and far from medieval flights the staircase leads up to the Great Hall, and this really does date from Wolsey's time and is spanned by a massive hammer-beam roof. It is the largest pre-Victorian hall in Oxford and Cambridge, and was used as the film set for Hogwarts, the school for wizardry in J. K. Rowling's best-selling *Harry Potter and the Philosopher's Stone*.

The giant dining hall of Christ Church never ceases to be polished and gazed at. It smells of beeswax and the sweat of nations. Long oak tables that shine with scrubbing, chairs with neo-Gothic, ogival backs, plates decorated with the college emblem of the Cardinal's hat – this is where the students have breakfast and lunch, cafeteria-style, whereas in the evening there are two shifts, one an informal dinner, the other 'formal hall' with gowns and Latin grace. Presiding at the head of the hall is Henry VIII, full figure, legs astride, a copy of the destroyed Holbein portrait that was in Whitehall. On the walls all around, in fine gold frames, are the portraits of the great and good: John Locke, John Wesley, William Gladstone, W. H. Auden, and all the other stars of Christ Church, painted by Gainsborough, Reynolds, Lawrence, Millais, Sutherland – a miniature National Portrait Gallery, but not your normal college Valhalla. Here you will find scholars, poets, deans, statesmen, church dignitaries, but no women. In this arch-conservative college, women have not yet achieved portrait status, apart from Elizabeths I and II, who are present as Visitors, i.e. royal inspectors.

On the right of the entrance hangs the portrait of Lewis Carroll, painted posthumously and looking a little sad. High above shines the Alice Window, depicting themes from his stories. How tiny and lost Alice must have felt in this gigantic hall, among all the mighty beasts at the table of her father, the Dean, until at last she ate the cake that made her grow and grow – like the ancient brass figures by the fireplace opposite, with their elongated necks – until her head finally hit the ceiling. Three steps lead up to the High Table, where the Dean, the dons and their guests all dine on a podium that looks down on the academic foot soldiers. In the corner is the portrait of Dean Liddell himself, and next to it, barely visible in the panelled wall, is a door. 'That,' I learn from one of the attendants, 'is the rabbit-hole. It leads straight to the Senior Common Room, the dons' own club. They come out of their hide-away, feed themselves, and then disappear again down the hole.' For a few years, Lewis Carroll was curator of the common room, and had to ensure that his colleagues had everything they needed – enough newspapers, writing paper and, above all, tea and wine. He never rose any higher in the Christ Church hierarchy. It was in the Deanery garden that he first met his real-life Alice, on 25 April 1856, when he was photographing the Cathedral. In the garden behind Alice's Gate you can still see the tree on which, apparently, sat the Cheshire Cat which slowly vanished until nothing was left except a grin.

Punctually, at five past six, evensong begins. Choirboys in flat Tudor caps have been singing the vespers since 1525, when Cardinal Wolsey founded the choir of Christ Church. Under the Norman arcades they sing *Gloria tibi Trinitas* by John Taverner, who was their first conductor, or hymns by William Walton, who was once a choirboy here himself. Enchanting church music, intellectual sermons and indeed the whole atmosphere of this cathedral will make even the unbeliever feel that though he may not be in the presence of God, he is certainly in the presence of English history.

This is the smallest cathedral in the country, while at the same time it is the chapel of the largest college in Oxford. Christ Church Cathedral is just 48 metres long – about half the length of King's College Chapel in Cambridge. The first church that stood on this spot has vanished without trace. It was an 8th-century Anglo-Saxon nunnery whose founder was said to have been St Frideswide, Oxford's patron saint. On the foundations of this legend, and in the second half of the 12th century, the Augustinian canons built the church that we see today, or rather the church that Sir George Gilbert Scott restored between 1870 and 1876. The rose window at the eastern end, for instance, is one of his Norman additions.

Medieval churches were usually built from east to west. The architectural rhythm begins in the choir and continues through the nave: late Norman round pillars with budding Gothic crocket capitals, arcades whose double arches incorporate the triforium, making the walls appear higher than they really are. And above the choir – this is the really sensational bit – is a fan vault with pendants and a star pattern that mirrors the sky. Like stone lanterns these hover below the liernes – a piece of late Gothic sophistication executed entirely without reinforced concrete around 1500. We see only the beginnings of the arches, which meet behind

the vaulting and hold the whole thing up. This ingenious construction was probably the work of William Orchard, one of the most brilliant masons of his time. He
also had a hand in the construction of Magdalen College and the Divinity School,
and is actually buried in Christ Church Cathedral.

Every college chapel – and Christ Church is the most opulent of all – is also a
gallery of dead souls, supplementing the portrait gallery in the dining hall. In black
gown, with stony mien and melancholic gaze, the bust of Robert Burton gazes at
us – a portrait from the time of the Stuarts. Another don, the Reverend Pocock,
wears his mortarboard in death as in life, while the philosopher George Berkeley
enjoys an epitaph written by his friend Alexander Pope, and John Ruskin quotes
himself ('There is no wealth but life'). There is a memorial to W. H. Auden in the
Military Chapel, where once he stood as a student in his carpet slippers, attending
the Sunday service at eight in the morning. In the anteroom is a monument to the
most unpopular Dean of Christ Church, though alas it lacks the verse with which
a student once immortalized him: 'I do not love thee, Dr Fell, / The reason why I
cannot tell; / But this I know, and know full well, / I do not love thee, Dr Fell.' Dr
John Fell was a radical Royalist who sent down both the Quaker William Penn
and the philosopher John Locke. The memorial to the latter in the Cathedral
quotes his credo, which is a classic motto for all those whose quest is knowledge: 'I
know there is truth opposite to falsehood that it may be found if people will & is
worth the seeking.'

For medieval pilgrims, however, there was only one thing to see: St Frideswide's
Shrine. It was probably made in 1289, destroyed during the Reformation, recon-
structed in 1889 and placed between the Lady Chapel and the north choir aisle. In
the spandrels of the canopy, amid the naturalistic foliage, the Gothic masons have
hidden tiny heads: 'green women' in a fantasy forest. This is probably a reference
to the same story that Edward Burne-Jones illustrated on the nearby St Frideswide
window in 1859, painted in glowing colours: it tells of the earthly adventures of the
saint, who fled from her lover to the forest and finally ascended to heaven in the
ship of saved souls. This is one of five windows that Burne-Jones painted for
Christ Church Cathedral (see p. 65). Along with Pre-Raphaelite angels and saints,
you will also find medieval and Baroque windows, including the famous murder
in the cathedral (Becket window, c. 1340) and the story of Jonah and the Whale by
Abraham van Linge (1630s).

From the cloister a Norman doorway leads into the Chapter House. Where
once the chapter used to meet, between lancet windows and delicately leafed capitals, Christ Church now sells souvenirs of Lewis Carroll et al. Opposite his

college, at 83 St Aldate's, stands the Old Sheep Shop. This tiny shop is where Alice, in the fifth chapter of *Through the Looking Glass*, meets the knitting sheep. In the meantime, the sheep has changed into a Japanese lady. Yuki Gander now owns Alice's Shop, and in this narrow house with pointed gables she sells all kinds of Wonderland kitsch: Alice chesspieces, Humpty-Dumpty watches, a dodo on a thimble. 'Stuff and nonsense', as Alice would say. But Yuki's sweets are irresistible – the barley sugars that Alice Liddell herself used to buy here.

On the way from the Cathedral to the college art gallery we cross Peckwater Quad, which the students call 'Peck': three residential wings with Ionic columns and a central gable (1705–14), on the south side of which is the college library (1716–72). Within the walls of this noble quadrangle the gentlemen students of the 18th century used to reside as aristocratically as on their Palladian estates, while those from poorer backgrounds would receive the chance of their lives. This was classical educational architecture in two senses, for it was designed by two Oxford scholars (see p. 73). The young John Ruskin, however, was not so impressed. He was fascinated by medieval architecture, and so in his classical quarters he missed 'an oriel window looking out on a Gothic chapel'.

To imagine that there are only books behind the Corinthian columns of Christ Church Library would be an insult to a college of this grandeur. Straight away in the entrance hall you will be surprised by a small but dazzling collection of busts and statues (see p. 67). Between two Venetian windows, and running the whole length of the building, the library itself stretches out along the first floor, which is one of the most beautiful rooms in Oxford: panelling and columns of Norwegian oak, magnificent stucco decorations above the bookshelves (1764), and a collection of some 120,000 books, incunabula, medieval illuminations, Greek manuscripts and early printed music from the 16th and 17th centuries. In a glass cabinet is a prize exhibit: a red hat, reputed to be that of Cardinal Wolsey himself.

Under the roof the librarians have their own kitchenette, an oak-panelled room where once their predecessor Lewis Carroll used to work, looking out onto the Deanery garden where Alice and her sisters would be playing. By comparison with other collections, the stock of Lewis Carroll memorabilia in his own college is pretty meagre: a few letters, photos and first editions. When the Lewis Carroll Society offered its magnificent collection to the Bodleian Library and Christ Church, no one was interested – not even the city of Oxford. Alice Liddell's collection, which for years was in the college on loan from the family, was also allowed to escape, and was auctioned by Sotheby's in 2001. The purchaser, however – a private collector – had the grace to pass it back to the picture gallery on loan. It would appear, though, that the great minds of present-day Oxford still have their suspicions about the genius of nonsense, and friend and photographer of little girls.

There is no college in Oxford, however, that can boast a more important art collection than Christ Church. In 1968 it moved from the library to a gallery of its own in Canterbury Quad, designed by Powell & Moya. The college owes the main part of this collection to two former students, a general and a diplomat. John Guise fought under the Duke of Marlborough and had a weakness for the Renaissance, the great Venetians of the *seicento*. His collection included paintings by Carracci, Tintoretto, Veronese, Domenichino and Bernardo Strozzi. Anthony van Dyck's *Continence of Scipio* was there, as well as his brilliant sketch in oils of a soldier on horseback.

The second part was donated by the diplomat William Fox-Strangways. He was one of the first English collectors of early Italian Renaissance paintings, particularly the Florentines of the 14th and 15th centuries. Madonnas and sibyls by the school of Duccio, Botticelli, Piero della Francesca, the fragment of a *Lamentation* by Hugo van der Goes, Filippino Lippi's enigmatic Centaur, Salvator Rosa's Eremite, and there is also a brilliant late work by Frans Hals: the portrait of an old lady, which is on loan from the Senior Common Room – a discreet storehouse of good things under the supervision of the dons, who every now and then brighten our lives with a bit of gossip or a fine painting.

There are also around 2,000 drawings by old masters, such as Leonardo da Vinci's *Grotesque Bust of a Man*, Hugo van der Goes's *Jacob and Rachel*, a watercolour of a river by Claude Lorrain, and many wonderful pieces by Michelangelo, Titian, Tintoretto, Correggio, Veronese, Rembrandt, Rubens, van Dyck – a collection of the highest quality. The Christ Church drawings, together with those of the Ashmolean, have made Oxford into a centre for the study of drawings by the old masters.

Scenes of everyday life are comparatively rare in ancient art, and so it is all the more surprising to find a subject like *The Butcher's Shop* presented on the scale of a history painting; the artist was Annibale Carracci (*c.* 1583), and we see a sheep being slaughtered and a leg of mutton being weighed and sold. Not until the 17th century do we find Dutch painters tackling such scenes again, though their burlesque realism is very different from Italian Baroque, even if Carracci's sacrificial scene might be read as an allegory for the Last Judgment. This picture, which for me is the most unusual in an already highly unusual collection, once belonged to King Charles I.

A small quad leads from the picture gallery to the way out, which true to the Christ Church style is in the form of a triumphal gateway, designed by James Wyatt as a monumental finish to the Canterbury Quad (1773–83). In order at least partially to ensure academic privacy, the college has transferred the visitors' entrance – and there are some 250,000 of these a year – sideways to the Meadow Buildings. This Venetian-Gothic block was erected in 1862–66 to house the students. Evelyn Waugh's Sebastian Flyte lived there with his teddy bear Aloysius, and the two of them enjoyed themselves immensely. During a sumptuous luncheon party, one of his friends stepped out onto the balcony and declaimed verses from T. S. Eliot's *Waste Land* across the meadows of Christ Church.

For me, the real treasure of this college is not Tom Quad, but Christ Church Meadow. It lies between the Isis and the Cherwell, and in former times it was often flooded. Since the Middle Ages the fields have never been ploughed and never been sprayed with pesticide. Buttercups, moneywort, columbine, lady's mantle and straggly yellow rattle all grow there in a Wonderland for insects, botanists and entomologists. According to the ancient college statutes, every undergraduate has a right to keep a cow here, so that he can have fresh milk every day for breakfast. In these marsh-marigold yellow fields the longhorn cattle graze, and all around there is a path that is more beautiful and more rural than any city path I know.

Paths, walls, benches – everywhere you go, you find quotations, even along this path. Right at the start, in the Christ Church War Memorial Garden, you will find a plaque in the ground which reads: 'My sword I give to him that shall succeed me in my pilgrimage.' It comes from John Bunyan's *Pilgrim's Progress*, and it gives pause for thought. Curving to the right is the New Walk, which Dean Liddell had laid in 1872 – an avenue of poplars leading down to the Isis. Before then, it was just a path along the millstream, and Lewis Carroll often used to walk along it with the Dean's daughters when they were going on a boat ride, as they did on 4 July 1862 when he first told them the story of Alice.

In June, the banks of the Isis are flooded – with people, for in June there is Eights Week. Christ Church Meadow marks the end of the course, and the excitement leads to many a love affair. It was here that all the students hurled themselves into the river for love of Zuleika Dobson, and if you do not believe me, then read Max Beerbohm's novel about her (see p. 56). From the southern end of the meadows the path leads along the banks of the Cherwell, from where one can see the whole panorama of towers and spires, that most classic of Oxford views, unspoilt by the advance of suburbia. Broad Walk takes us back to our starting point, with cows to the left and the sportsfields of Christ Church and Merton to the right. This avenue was created shortly after the Civil War, originally with elms but now with plane trees. It was Oxford's Pall Mall, a rural catwalk of urban fashion, where people promenaded in order to see and be seen, especially on 'Show Sunday' in June, at the end of the academic year.

For locals and for tourists, for generations of undergraduates and dons, Christ Church Meadow was a place of relaxation and inspiration. Samuel Johnson walked here, Cardinal Newman meditated, John Ruskin drew, and John Locke gathered plants. Field Marshal Blücher, who in 1814 was a guest at Christ Church, walked round the meadows to sober up after an overdose of brandy, and the Methodist George Whitefield prayed here beneath the trees. Now and then, you would see a kingfisher taking off. And then, suddenly, the good citizens of Oxford decided to build a road through it. A four-lane road. A four-lane road through Christ Church Meadow. There were howls of protest, demonstrations, campaigns, public inquiries (see p. 75), and finally Christ Church Meadow was saved, and one of the last pastoral paradises of the Middle Ages was allowed to preserve its wonders for the 21st century.

Oriel and Corpus Christi

'I love Oxford, because I love books and Oxford is a book.
One turns from one street into another, just as one turns a page.'
Julien Green, *Des villes*, 1985

'Oriel? Lots of sport, lots of Americans.' This was my Oxford landlady's summing-up of Oriel College. First in rowing, last in women. The latter were not allowed into this male bastion until 1985. This is as much a part of its image as its film-set buildings – the pointed gables of those bright houses on Oriel Square, the shaped gables in the Front Quad with its late Gothic bay-windows, its lanterns, and the capital letters that form a stone balustrade over the porch: *REGNANTE CAROLO*: from the reign of King Charles. When the first quadrangle was built (1620–42), such strapwork arabesques were as popular as the ruffs on a cavalier's shirt; 'openwork lettering' was a fashion that Jacobean masons took over from the French.

In the niches above the porch stand three rather crude statues: next to Charles I is Edward II, who founded the college in 1326, and above is the Virgin Mary, to whom the college is dedicated. 'The House of the Blessed Mary the Virgin in Oxford' was supposed to be the original name, but as New College also incorporated Mary into its name (officially St Mary College of Winchester in Oxford), this was changed to Oriel, after an old college building called La Oriole on account of its *oratoriolum*, which actually means chapel. Another theory is that this original building may have been blessed with particularly fine oriel windows. Only Celtic knots are more tangled than the history of Oxford colleges.

Behind the Gothic tracery of the windows in the Front Quad lie the hall and the chapel (1637–42), and the library is in the Back Quad. James Wyatt designed this building in 1788. It is only seven bays long, rustic on the ground floor, Ionic columns above, with parapets on the roof – grandeur on a small scale. The ground floor comfortably houses a legend, for here lies the Senior Common Room which, according to the Fellows of other colleges, always stank of logic. It is said that the Oxford Movement was born here, and we see no reason to doubt it (see p. 42).

Two contemporary Nobel laureates studied at Oriel: the chemist Sir Alexander Todd and the economist James E. Meade. Rather more ancient celebrities included Sir Walter Raleigh and Sir Thomas More. Beau Brummell, the famous Regency dandy, was also here, though not for very long. Once he decked a jackdaw out in white ribbons and set it running round the quadrangle to parody the gait of the Provost. There is, however, only one former student who made it onto the college façade on the High Street: Cecil Rhodes, a thoroughly mediocre student, a notorious racist, and one of Oxford's greatest benefactors. Together with Rhodesia, his name would already have sunk into the murky past of colonialism if his interests had been confined to his diamond mines and dreams of empire-building. However, he had one other passion in his life: Oxford. And even though his imperial concept of education may seem somewhat twisted to us today, its consequences in the form of the Rhodes scholarships could scarcely have been more felicitous (see p. 181).

From Oriel to Corpus Christi, and I'm taking you first into a garden. Oxford's smallest college is right next to its biggest – Christ Church – and the garden is small too, and most people won't even notice it. No rarities here: campanula, primroses, buddleia, forget-me-nots, blue-green broccoli leaves, mint, sage – all proliferating, straying beyond their allotted beds and over the paths in a cheerful, carefree mess. It's a mixture of cottage garden and gentle anarchy, and it helps to give Corpus Christi a special atmosphere of its very own, which is nowadays in

the capable hands of David Leake, the college gardener. 'Many students take virtually no notice of the flowers, but they take in the scents all the same,' he told me.
'And when they bring their girlfriends into the garden and say, "I love you, and
doesn't it smell lovely", then I'm happy too.' The end of this garden, quite unex-
pectedly, turns out to be the end of the city. From the terrace on the remains of the
city wall you can look far across the countryside over the sportsfields, the meadows, and the enclosed garden of Christ Church with its ancient Oriental plane.

When Richard Fox, Bishop of Winchester, founded Corpus Christi in 1517, he
compared his college to a bee garden in which the scholars would work busily for
the glory of God and for their own benefit. In order 'therein to plant and sow
stocks, herbs and flowers of the choicest', this pious humanist employed 'three
right skilful herbalists': one to cultivate Latin, one for Greek, and the third – the
head gardener in charge of the noblest and most difficult of all plants – for theology. Five hundred years later, the bees in the Bishop's college garden are buzzing
literally and metaphorically. Two students sit there discussing their work with
their tutor. In the idyllic setting of the Fellows' Garden a person can learn, a person can relax, and a person can rest in peace, for over there beneath the
honeysuckle and the buddleia lie the ashes of Elizabeth Donata Rawson. A classical philologist, mistress of the garden, she died at the age of fifty-five, *docta lepida
benigna* – 'a kind and humorous scholar' – as it says on her epitaph.

Corpus Christi has continued to cultivate the classics, although biochemistry
and the Internet are just as much a daily part of life as the ancients whom Erasmus
so admired here in the library. In the chapel nearby there is the scent of cedar
wood, and just a few yards away in the east wing is the hall, for in this cosy little
college everything is close together. Even the endless mysteries of time have their
place here, on the single pillar in the front quadrangle, where astronomical tables, a
perpetual calendar and twenty-seven sundials pass on all the information that can
be gleaned from the heavens. The pillar was designed in 1579 by Charles Turnbull.
At the top, watching over all this knowledge, is a pelican, the emblem of Corpus
Christi. All around the walls of the quadrangle are hollyhocks, wallflowers and
columbine, euphorbia, acanthus, bamboo and busy lizzies, while above the arch of
the gateway a climbing rose – *Rosa banksiae* 'Lutea', to be precise – spreads its
myriad yellow blooms.

The Mother of All Colleges:
Merton

'No persons can be admitted but those who are of good conduct, chaste, peaceable, humble, indigent, of ability for study, and desirous of improvement.'
From the Statutes of Merton College, 1264

I t'll be easy for you to remember your parking code,' says my landlady. '1264, the year when Merton College was founded.' It lies right next door to Corpus Christi, in Oxford's last cobbled street, where you can still feel the remnants of the Middle Ages beneath your feet. The spiritual nature of the world and the time can be seen on the tympanum of the gatehouse (1418): John the Baptist and the Lamb of God in the wilderness, a book with seven seals in the middle, Revelation, and the kneeling Founder, Walter de Merton. He was Bishop of Rochester and Henry III's Lord Chancellor – a man of the Church and of the Crown, whose college was meant to serve both institutions though governed by its *Magisters*. Academic self-government, an endowment, and the size and layout of the buildings – these made Merton into a pioneering college and an example to all others.

On a relatively narrow site between the city walls and Merton Street, 'The House of the Scholars of Merton' developed into one of the richest and most influential colleges in Oxford. The hall and chapel, the centres of college life, dominate the Front Quad. Outside the hall there are magnolias and white hydrangeas. Ornamental branches and spirals cover the Gothic oak door, a magnificent example of late 13th-century wrought ironwork, dating from the same time as the superb tracery of the great east window in the chapel. Walter de Merton planned his chapel along the lines of an abbey church, with a central nave and aisles, but all that was built was the choir (1289–96) and the crossing (c. 1335), the transepts (1367–1424) and the tower (1451), the latter being mighty enough to contain eight bells. Merton Chapel is therefore a fragment, but it is large enough and self-sufficient enough to have served as the prototype of college chapels.

William Morris and his friends loved this chapel, especially its medieval windows. Many of Merton's Fellows are buried here, with monuments of brass or stone, some very stylized, others splendidly Baroque, like that of Sir Thomas Bodley. The female figures clustered round this classical philologist and diplomat are allegories of music, arithmetic, grammar and rhetoric, and the pilasters are piles of books – the perfect frame for the founder of the Bodleian Library. This wall monument of marble and alabaster (1615) is by Nicholas Stone, one of the finest English sculptors of his time. A plaque in the entrance hall of the chapel lists the names of all the Wardens of Merton. In 1994 the Fellows elected Jessica Rawson to the post – the first female Warden in 730 years.

South of the chapel is Mob Quad. With four ranges of more or less the same size, this is Oxford's earliest complete quadrangle, built between 1290 and 1378. Beneath the high stone saddle roof in the north-eastern corner, the college silver and archives used to be kept in the Treasury. The Fellows' rooms were on the ground floor, and were accessible from the quadrangle by way of ogival doorways that led to separate staircases. The scholars used to sleep four to a room, but they each had their own separate cell to study in, lit by a tiny window. To read the classics, they would go one floor up to the college library.

Merton's Upper Library is one of the oldest medieval libraries in England still being used. The light is dim, and there's a permanent smell of wood and leather. Here more than anywhere else you can feel the atmosphere of the old Oxford. The first catalogue from the year 1300 has a list of twelve titles: a psalter, the Book of Job, Aristotle, Thomas Aquinas, Bonaventura, Augustine and other Fathers of the Church. By the middle of the 16th century, the collection had risen to about 500 volumes. When the number of printed books began to increase on a large scale, Merton introduced the space-saving box system which the Canterbury Cathedral Library had already begun to use around 1260. The bookcases were placed at right angles to the walls, and desks and benches were put between them, so that people sat as if in boxes left and right of the central aisle. This arrangement was later taken over by all the other college libraries. The Renaissance decor and the oak bookcases in the Upper Library date from 1589–90. Valuable books used to be chained to the desk, and this practice continued to a degree until 1792. The prototype of such 'chained libraries' is believed to be the Sorbonne in Paris, which was the most important university library of the 13th century. While the students had to absorb this chained knowledge on the spot, the dons were allowed to borrow some of the rarest volumes from the Merton 'loan chest'. This treasure chest, dating from before the time when the library was actually built (1371–79), had three locks which could only be opened in the presence of all three key-holders. Merton has more than 350 illuminated manuscripts from the Middle Ages, the oldest being the *Chronicle* of Eusebios, which dates from the 9th century. With its collection of over 60,000 volumes, the library has long since expanded to fill the rooms below, where once the Fellows used to live. There is an Epstein bust of T. S. Eliot, who in 1914 came to Merton as an American student after doing a summer course at

Marburg University in Germany. He left there just before war broke out, and did his doctoral dissertation here on the Welsh philosopher F. H. Bradley.

When the number of students increased, Merton built its third and largest quadrangle, Fellows' Quad (1608–10), which was the first three-storey college building in Oxford. It had additional attics, called 'cocklofts', for the servants. This perfectly symmetrical quadrangle, with the façade's classical order of columns, was financed by the same man who had refurbished the Old Library: Sir Henry Savile, a many-sided scholar and Warden of Merton for nearly forty years. In 1619 he established the Savilian Chairs for geometry and astronomy – an outstanding contribution to the scientific revolution in England. Back in the 14th century Merton was already a European centre for astronomy, as it was for theology. At that time a group of philosophers became famous as the 'Merton Calculators', because they analysed everything – and not just physical problems – using mathematical methods. They even tried to make precise calculations about such imponderables as sin and redemption. It is therefore not totally out of keeping that Logic Lane branches off from Merton Street, though for Theodor W. Adorno it proved to be a cul-de-sac.

For nearly four years this Jewish philosopher, musicologist and sociologist from Frankfurt, who had been banned from teaching by the Nazis, tried to get a footing in Oxford. In autumn 1934 he moved into his lodgings at Merton, downgraded from 'private tutor' to 'advanced student'. 'I'm living here now in indescribable peace and quiet and under very pleasant external working conditions; but of course there are difficulties with the subject matter, because trying to make my actual philosophical ideas comprehensible to the English is one of the impossibilities, and to a certain degree I have to simplify my work down to children's level in order to be understood.' He wrote about Edmund Husserl's phenomenology, began preparatory work on the *Dialectic of Enlightenment*, but then made himself a complete outsider by publishing the study *On Jazz* – unheard of for a philosopher. Oxford's positivistic school of thought was as foreign to Adorno as the college environment of Merton. The university's charmed circle remained closed to him, as did the Bodley Club (a discussion circle), but he regularly took part in concerts at the Holywell Music Room and played at the Musical Club. When his hopes for a university career in England were finally dashed, he emigrated to America in 1938.

One of the few things in Oxford that gave Adorno undiluted pleasure was the Fellows' Garden at Merton, with its magnificent view over Christ Church Meadow. I went there myself late one Saturday afternoon, when the bells of Magdalen Tower were starting their change ringing. The glorious sounds rose and fell

like a sea of sound, washing over the roofs and trees and down to the lawns of
Merton. The hibiscus bloomed white and blue against the college walls, and the
wide borders teemed with wallflowers, lady's mantle, white tradescantia and red-
hot pokers, while the sycamore of 1705 watched over them all – the favourite tree
of J. R. R. Tolkien, who was a Fellow here.

From Deadman's Walk to Sweety:
The Botanic Garden

'The English also have their Fascism:
In Oxford there was and still is anti-semitism.'
Thomas Bernhard, *Heldenplatz*, 1988

D eadman's Walk is the name of the path that leads past the foot of the city
wall at Merton to the Botanic Garden. This was the route of the funeral
cortege from St Aldate's to the Jewish cemetery outside the city. Since the early
12th century, Jews had lived in the Great Jewry between Carfax and Folly Bridge –
a small and prosperous community of around 200 families. Their synagogue was
more or less on the spot where Tom Tower now stands. Jewish scholars were also
attracted to Oxford, but they were not allowed to become members of the university, could only offer accommodation and lend money, and from 1218 onwards
were forced to wear yellow badges. Then in 1290, after years of increasing repres-
sion, Edward I drove the Jews out of England altogether.

Deadman's Walk. Not until the 17th century, when Cromwell allowed them
back in, did the Jews slowly begin to return. From the Levant they brought a new
drinking custom: in 1651 Jacob the Jew opened a coffee house in the High Street –
the first in England. Although Hebrew was taught from at least 1312, and there was
even a Regius Chair of Hebrew established in 1540, still no self-confessed Jew was
allowed to study in Oxford (or Cambridge) until the university reforms of 1854. In
1882, the first Jew to be made an Oxford Fellow was the philosopher Samuel
Alexander of Lincoln College. But it was still no picnic to be a Jew at Oxford, as
the philosopher Alfred J. Ayer discovered: 'You are a fraud. You got into Eton and
to Christ Church, you were an officer in the Welsh Guards, you became Wyke-

ham Professor at Oxford and you secured a knighthood. But underneath you are just a dirty little Jew-boy.'

With the influx of refugees, Oxford's Jewish community was about 3,000 strong by the end of the Hitler era. Today this has dwindled to around 250. Their synagogue is situated on the edge of Jericho, and their cemetery is in Wolvercote. At the end of Deadman's Walk you will now find the Botanic Garden.

As you step through the Baroque, barrel-vaulted gateways by Nicholas Stone (1632), you leave behind the noise of the High Street and enter into an oasis of calm beauty. This is the oldest Botanic Garden in Britain. It was founded in 1621 by the Earl of Danby, who gave 500 pounds for the purpose – the equivalent of well over £3 million today. In order to protect this swampy land against flooding from the Cherwell, some 4,000 cartloads of 'Mucke and Dunge' were heaped around it, gathered from the cesspits of the colleges. No Botanic Garden could have a more fundamentally academic basis than this. According to the original deeds, the garden had a dual purpose: 'for the furtherance of knowledge and the glorification of the works of God'. And that, says the superintendent Timothy Walker, hasn't changed.

Initially it was called the Physic Garden, and it served mainly to help train medical students – just like its equivalent at Padua University, which was the very first of its kind (founded in 1545). Fennel, St John's wort, melissa, wormwood, calendula, Sweet Cicely, and along with the medicinal herbs a host of other plants that are of interest to botanists – they all grow here in Family Beds that are divided up and neatly classified according to genera. The first gardener employed by the university was an ex-mercenary from Brunswick, Jacob Bobart. He had settled in the city as the landlord of an inn, and used to wander through Oxford with a goat from whose beard he would hang jingling pieces of silver on festive occasions. He designed the main body of the garden, which he protected with high walls, and near the south wall he built a greenhouse, which was one of the first in England. In 1653, the gardening enthusiast John Evelyn wrote that 'we went to the Physick Garden, where the Sensitive plant was shewed us for a greate wonder' – namely, the recently introduced tropical *Mimosa pudica*, whose leaves roll up the moment they are touched.

Not until the 18th century was botany officially recognized as a science in its own right. Then the university gardens grew in importance as a teaching resource – a living inventory of nature. One of the many plant-hunters who made England's gardens into a flourishing reflection of the Empire was the Oxford scholar John Sibthorp, Professor of Botany and also *horti praefectus*, as the director is called even today. In thirty-six years he only gave one lecture. He had other things on his mind. Time and again he would travel to the Aegean in order to identify the 600 plants that the Greek physician Dioscorides had described in the first century AD. Chinese lantern, box-leaved holly, germander, garden rocket, blechnum – Sibthorp found nearly all of them, planted most of them in the Botanic Garden, and left behind as his life's work ten volumes of *Flora Graeca Sibthorpiana*, the most lavish florilegium imaginable, and published posthumously in a print run of just twenty-five copies (1806–40).

It was in the Botanic Garden that Isaiah Berlin proposed marriage to his beloved Aline, and we may assume that he was neither the first nor the last to pop the question here. One feels that there should be the sound of French horns, as there was when the great Linnaeus discovered a new plant. There are about 8,000 different genera here, with the most important plant families from all over the world. The yellow-green umbels of spurge (euphorbia) swing on their long stems – one of many special collections. The garden has even produced a weed of its very own: *Senecio squalidus*, the Oxford ragwort. People come here again and again, for the show changes almost every day.

Beneath the old black walnut on the bank of the Cherwell sits a lady in her mid-sixties, wearing a white crochet cap and a green jersey. Zoe Peterssen taught economics, but now she is writing poems. Her workplace is a bench, or the greenhouse if it's raining. The birds that visit her on the bank of the Cherwell each have a name: the ducks are Pepe and Sweety, and the white dove is Ignatius.

May Day and Shadowlands:
Magdalen College

'Whatever people may say against Cambridge, it is certainly
the best preparatory school for Oxford that I know.'
Oscar Wilde, 1888

Whether you come into the city from Christ Church Meadow or from Cowley, you will have the great tower of Magdalen before you. It soars above the roofs of the High Street and the trees of the Botanic Garden – four storeys of pure Gothic elegance, crowned with eight pinnacles. Of all Oxford's academic lighthouses, Magdalen Tower shines the brightest – 'the tall lily of towers' (Dorothy L. Sayers). There is even a copy of it in Princeton. The college celebrated the completion of the tower on 1 May 1509 with a party which has gone down in Oxford folklore. What would May Day be without Magdalen, when the choirboys sing from the top of the tower at six o'clock in the morning, and the bells ring out, and a few students try to make their final splash at Oxford by diving from Magdalen Bridge into the Cherwell?

Other colleges might keep a cat, but Magdalen keeps a herd of deer. Another of its little eccentricities is orthography and pronunciation: as they said back in the 15th century, it's pronounced *Mawdlin* not *Magdalin*, and please don't stick an 'e' on the end, as they do in the other place. This is the college of Oscar Wilde, Edward VIII and Princess Diana's brother Charles Spencer, who was known as Charley Boy. Edward Gibbon studied here, as did Desmond Morris, Sir Richard Attenborough and the ex-Tory leader William Hague. Nobel laureates Erwin Schrödinger and Sir John Eccles taught here, and so did C. S. Lewis and A. J. P. Taylor, Oxford's first media dons. If the college now finds it harder and harder every day to live up to its illustrious past, you would scarcely notice it. The buildings stretch out lazily into the green, and everything seems to be perfectly in place. The college covers an area of some 15 hectares – the biggest in Oxford – and in fact the Botanic Garden lies on Magdalen territory. The college was able to expand far beyond the city walls, thanks to the foresight of one of its benefactors .

'Maudeleyne College' was founded in 1458 by William of Waynflete. It is dedicated to Mary Magdalene, patron saint of hairdressers, students and penitent prostitutes, among others. Waynflete was Bishop of Winchester, Henry VI's Lord Chancellor, and a man with an educational mission. He had studied at Wykeham's New College in Oxford, and this was the model on which he based Magdalen. In addition, he founded a school where the future students would learn Latin, and there were scholarships for sixteen choirboys. The college choir is still flourishing today, as is the school, where the philosopher Thomas Hobbes first learned to conjugate his Latin verbs and to think his deep thoughts. In 1928, however, Magdalen College School moved to larger premises on the other side of the bridge, opposite St Hilda's, Oxford's last women's college.

Magdalen's main building was constructed between 1474 and 1510 – Perpendicular Gothic through and through. The master mason William Orchard, who was responsible for the chapel and the cloister, owned the stone quarry in Headington from which Magdalen's limestone came. Unlike the cloister in the older New College, this one is part of the quadrangle (1475–90) and not separate from it. This helps to create the monastic, academic atmosphere that makes Cloister Quad the epitome of medieval college architecture. Wisteria blooms in front of the tracery windows, and on the buttresses is a whole menagerie of grotesque creatures: hippo, camel, greyhound, wrestler and tumbler. Gargoyles ward off the evil spirits.

Magdalen Chapel (1474–80) follows the same T-shaped ground plan as its predecessors at Merton and New College. If I were limited to naming just three of the outstanding features of this rich interior, they would be the sepia-tinted west window with its painting of the Last Judgment (see p. 66), the monumental early copy of Leonardo's *Last Supper*, and – also in the ante-chapel – the misericords of the old choir stalls. Monkeys, owls, foxes and geese are all there, along with a horse lying on its back and, on the fringes of this wood-carved bestiary, a man's head between the open thighs of a woman (it is the first misericord on the left if you dare to look). The nicest event of all in this chapel is evensong, when the choirboys of Magdalen sing their hymns beneath James Wyatt's high neo-Gothic roof of wood and plaster, which is painted like a stone vault (1790). The boys' voices can only be heard on tape in the year 2021, for this is the year of P. D. James's science-fiction thriller *The Children of Men*, whose hero, the historian Theo Faron, is in this chapel when he meets the woman who is about to change his life.

In 1854, the legendary Dr Routh was laid to rest in the chapel of Magdalen College, whose President he had been for sixty-three years. His motto was: 'Always verify your references'. Next to the roll of honour in memory of the war dead, a plaque was erected in 1994 to Ernst Stadler. As a poet, he wrote the Expressionist *Aufbruch* [Awakening], and as a Rhodes scholar he spent 1906 to 1908 in Oxford writing his *Habilitation* [professorial thesis] on Wieland's translation of Shakespeare. Two years later, he returned in order to take his Oxford degree – a young Alsatian poet and literary scholar at the beginning of what should have been a glittering career. Stadler died in Flanders in 1914, killed by a British bomb. 'Poet Scholar Soldier' are the epithets on his memorial, together with the words of the 17th-century poet Angelus Silesius: '*Mensch werde wesentlich*', which means something like 'We humans should get down to basics'.

East of the chapel is the hall: Tudor, linen-fold panelling, silver candlesticks on the High Table and, inserted into the panelling at the top end of the hall, coloured figures in relief depicting themes from the Early Renaissance as well as scenes from the life of Mary Magdalene (c. 1540). At the foot of the kitchen stairs is a sign pointing to the wooden staircase that leads to Oscar Wilde's rooms. He had three different sets of lodgings here between 1874 and 1878, but you can't visit any of them. 'Nothing left of him,' a student tells me. 'Just boring rooms.' When Seamus

Heaney was Professor of Poetry, at the end of his tenure he gave the college – whose guest he was – a bust of his fellow countryman Oscar Wilde. In 1998, it was put up – or perhaps put out of the way – high on a window ledge. The scandal of his life still throws long shadows. 'The infamous St Oscar of Oxford, poet and martyr' was how he later styled himself – and indeed he *was* martyred in those days when gay meant jolly and homosexual marriage meant nothing at all. For him, however, Oxford remained 'the most flower-like time of one's life. One sees the shadow of things in silver mirrors.'

The end of the Cloister Quad marks the end of medieval Magdalen, and beyond it the walled-in academic world suddenly opens out into the green. The view over this broad expanse of lawn across to the New Building is one of those Oxford settings that create the most felicitous combination of architecture and landscape. It was a former Fellow of the college, Edward Holdsworth, who designed this neo-classical residential block in 1733, twenty-seven bays long, with its graceful proportions and no decoration apart from a pediment over the central projection. Colonnades with plaster vaulting set off this minimalist elegance. Above the entrance to each staircase you can still see the old numbers, gold on a black background, but now the doors are equipped with bells and intercoms. The massive plane tree was planted in 1802, to commemorate the Peace of Amiens.

Do you remember the garden party in *Shadowlands*? And Anthony Hopkins and Debra Winger – Jack and Joy, the literature professor's late-flowering love overshadowed by cancer and death? The party took place on the lawn in front of the New Building, part of the college ritual, which was filmed in its original setting by Richard Attenborough who, with this Oxford weepie, returned to the college where he himself had studied. There he had actually seen the hero of his film, the famous C. S. Lewis, Fellow of Magdalen, who as a fantasy writer and charismatic convert to Christianity set off a veritable epidemic of 'Lewismania', especially in America (see p. 85). The Kilns, his house at the foot of Shotover Hill, is now a study centre for a Californian C. S. Lewis Foundation. 'Breezy, tweedy, beer-drinking and jolly' is how John Betjeman, one of his students, described him; later Betjeman dedicated a few ironic lines to his old tutor: 'Objectively, our Common Room / Is like a small Athenian State – / Except for Lewis: he's all right / But do you think he's *quite* first-rate?' In the mid-1920s, Betjeman lived in apple green rooms on the second floor of the New Building. The deer used to graze on the lawn outside, and from the ground floor, students used to feed them on sugar cubes dipped in port wine to get them drunk. The deer park is first mentioned in 1706, and even today the deer add a little welcome variation to the menu.

Magdalen has not earned many awards with its new 20th-century buildings, however. In 1960, on one of the most beautiful sites in Oxford, at the eastern end of Magdalen Bridge, they stuck a box of concrete and brick called the Waynflete Building – 'not exactly pretty' according to the prospectus, though at least it is conveniently situated above Bottoms Up, a liquor store. There are more residences together with an auditorium in ancient odeum style on the edge of the deer park – Grove Buildings by Demetri Porphyrios (1994–99): limestone walls, slate roofs, and a good deal of oak in the interior. Burberry architecture in the spirit of the 17th century.

There is one thing you mustn't miss in Magdalen: Addison's Walk. It is named after the essayist Joseph Addison, who was a fellow here from 1698 until 1711 and greatly enjoyed the 'pleasures of the imagination', which he later developed in his theories about landscape gardening. 'Philander used every morning to take a walk in the neighbouring wood, that stood on the borders of the Isis. It was cut through by an abundance of beautiful alleys, which terminating on the water, looked like so many painted views in a perspective,' he wrote in his *Dialogues upon the Usefulness of Ancient Medals* (c. 1703). Addison's Walk leads between two arms of the Cherwell in a wide curve around the water-meadows of Magdalen. Hundreds of trees line the path: beech and oak, mountain ash, horse-chestnut, willow and whitethorn, mingled with yew, holly, laurel and balsam poplars with their overpowering scent. One can scarcely imagine a more beautiful route to one's ideas.

The great expanse of green in the middle of Addison's Walk is one of Oxford's most sacred meadows because of one single flower: *Fritillaria meleagris*. At the end of April, when this delicate form of lily unfolds its pinkish-violet, porcelain blooms, it is as if the north-eastern half of these meadows were covered with a purple veil. Then Magdalen Meadow becomes the Kaaba of all fritillary pilgrims, who circle around it with awe and admiration. By mid-May the crowds have dwindled to a few persistent souls who train their binoculars on the last pale purple traces of their diva. The beauty with the dark dice pattern has all kinds of names in England: snake's head in Oxfordshire, shy widow in Warwickshire, leper's lily in Somerset (where people thought of the bells announcing the presence of the outcasts). It's also called dead man's bell and sulky lady. Once it could indeed be found all over the country, but there are now fewer and fewer water-meadows, and so the fritillary has become rarer and rarer. Perhaps the largest and certainly the most famous display is that on Magdalen Meadow.

Between High and Broad

'After I got home, I was simply homesick for Oxford – not for college –
but for that curve in the High and Radcliffe Square by moonlight.'
Dorothy L. Sayers, 1913

F rom Magdalen Bridge the High Street makes a long and gentle curve to the
west, into the heart of the city. Every step unfolds new aspects of the urban
panorama – the cupolas of Queen's, the towers of All Souls, St Mary's, All Saints,
until gradually they have all taken their place as if emerging from the wings of a
huge open-air theatre. Oxford's 'High' is one of the world's great streets. It has
everything that a *flâneur* could wish for – shops, churches, cafés, colleges, grand
houses, modest houses, Art Nouveau, Victorian and Georgian shop windows, a
café with Doric columns, façades that echo more elegant times than ours. Some of
the houses (such as nos. 126 and 130) still have their medieval timber-framing. The
University of Oxford Shop, where the university markets its image in the form of
T-shirts, teddy bears and its very own tartan, stands on the rib-vaulted Gothic cellar of what was once Tackley's Inn, an early 14th-century academic hall. If you
want to wear the appropriate garb – a gown and college tie – then the place to go to
is Ede & Ravenscroft, a branch of the London company which since 1689, 'by
Royal Appointment', has served thirteen monarchs and their subjects in a manner
that is truly fitting.

At the top end of the High Street lies one place where town and gown always
mix freely: the Covered Market. Here the locals come to do their shopping, and at
lunchtime the sandwich bars and coffee shops are full of students from the nearby
colleges. These halls, between the High Street and Market Street, were opened in
1774, though the present construction dates mainly from around 1890. You can still
sense Edwardian Oxford here, though, with the cosy little shops that sell fish, vegetables, cheese or books. The butchers wear blue and white striped aprons and
straw hats with a red and black band, and they hang their rabbits, pheasants and
hunks of venison outside their stalls.

The parade of towers along the High Street begins with All Saints. This former
City Church on the corner of Turl Street was built in 1706–8 and probably
designed by the amateur architect Henry Aldrich, Dean of Christ Church. It is

rectangular, has no aisles or chancel, has Corinthian pilasters, a stucco ceiling and tall, arched windows. The tower unfolds itself like a telescope, from its square base to its narrow, elongated colonnaded rotunda right up to its conical spire. Since 1975, All Saints has been the Lincoln College Library, and as such is one of the noblest in Oxford. Lincoln's authors include two who could scarcely have been more different: the Methodist John Wesley (see p. 42) and the thriller-writer John Le Carré, whose tutor, the Reverend Vivian Greene, was the model for the spy George Smiley. Here I must ask your indulgence for a tiny digression: in Bath, Wesley happened to bump into his former fellow student Beau Nash as they were approaching each other along a narrow pavement. 'I never make way for a fool,' said Nash, without budging. 'Don't you?' replied Wesley. 'I always do.' And he stepped aside.

Why is there a mitre on the pub opposite All Saints? When Richard Fleming, Bishop of Lincoln, founded Lincoln College in 1427, he took over not only the living of All Saints but also the profitable inn on the High Street at the corner of the Turl. The stagecoach for London used to leave from here, and anyone with any self-respect stayed at the Mitre Hotel. Guests included the German architect Karl Friedrich Schinkel, Herman Melville and William Thackeray, who in 1857 tried from here to win the vacant parliamentary seat for Oxford, but failed. One summer evening in 1782, a young teacher and preacher from Berlin, Karl Philipp Moritz, was on a walking tour of England ('A pedestrian seems to be a weird and wonderful animal to these people'), and arrived at The Mitre, where he enjoyed the company of the hard-drinking, Bible-thumping Fellows. The next day, after he had sobered up, he went to visit their colleges. 'Oxford seemed to me to have a very sad and melancholy look about it, and I really cannot understand how anyone can consider it to be one of the most beautiful cities in England.' In the meantime, this prestigious hotel has degenerated into a fast-food restaurant. On its upper floors live students from Lincoln College, which still owns the building.

The University Church of St Mary

'There is far too much religion in this University
though and not enough brains.'
Evelyn Waugh, 1922

There is an old mulberry tree, leaning on its crutch and standing outside the portal of St Mary the Virgin. This is the University Church, just a block away from the City Church of All Saints. Every year on St Scholastica's Day, for nearly five hundred years, a delegation of Oxford citizens would come to St Mary's and pay a symbolic fine to the dignitaries of the university, in commemoration of a great battle (see p. 36). The porch (1637) leading into this Perpendicular church of Cotswold stone is a magnificent piece of Flemish Baroque, probably by Nicholas Stone, Inigo Jones's master mason. The twisted columns were an innovation for English architecture. The Madonna above the segmental arch was regarded at the time as a political issue, for Archbishop William Laud, Chancellor of the University, had donated the Virgin's Porch. When he was put on trial in 1644 for supporting King Charles I, the statue of the Virgin was cited as evidence of his papist leanings. The bullet holes were left by Cromwell's soldiers.

In the early 13th century, St Mary's offered the university, which was developing all around it, a common meeting place and a chapel for each faculty. The first academics were members of the clergy, and so it was only natural – even if the arrangement was provisional – that they should come together under the aegis of the Church. Meetings, disputations, examinations, ceremonies took place there, legislation was enacted there, and it was not until around 1320 that the university constructed a 'Congregation House' of its own on the north-eastern side of St Mary's. Oxford's first university library was installed above the assembly room, until Duke Humfrey's Library was built around 1488. The university continued, however, to hold meetings and ceremonies in St Mary's until well into the 17th century. As for the old Congregation House, which from outside appears to be an aisle of this Perpendicular church, it was used as a powder magazine during the Civil War, and later as a school and a lecture room, and more recently as a café. The Chancellor's Throne in Brome Chapel is another reminder of St Mary's academic past, and another institutional link is the fact that at ten o'clock every Sunday morning you can hear the University sermon – no longer in Latin, but often given by prominent guest preachers, and by no means always on religious matters.

It was in St Mary's that John Wesley preached against the irreligiousness of the Fellows, and John Newman for the renewal of faith – sermons that marked the beginnings of Methodism and the Oxford Movement. 'He informed us, 1st that there was not one Christian among all the Heads of Houses, 2ndly that Pride, Gluttony, Avarice, Sensuality, and Drunkenness were the general Characteristics of all Fellows of Colleges who were useless to a proverbial Uselessness. Lastly, that the younger Part of the University were a Generation of Triflers, all of them perjured, and not one of them of any Religion at all.' This was the account given by William Blackstone of John Wesley's last sermon at St Mary's on 24 August 1744.

Here too, Elizabeth I, on her first visit to the university in 1566, gave a much admired speech in Latin. Ten years earlier, Bishops Cranmer, Latimer and Ridley had been tried for heresy here and condemned to death (see p. 137). And one more notable date, from more recent times, was 3 September 1939: this was the day when the British government declared war on Germany, and on this day St Mary's held its first mass in the German language – for the many immigrants who had fled to Oxford during the Nazi era. The German Lutheran Community still congregate here for a service on the first Sunday of every month.

The east window of the southern aisle (c. 1844) is by the Victorian designer Augustus Welby Pugin, and there is a roof boss of Gandhi sitting cross-legged, but otherwise St Mary's has only one truly outstanding feature, and that is the tower. It was begun in the late 13th century, and the spectacular spire was completed around 1325, with unusually long pinnacles and luxuriant Gothic foliage. If you climb the tower, you can get as close to these decorations as the masons who carved them. The view is breathtaking – over the dome of the Radcliffe Camera, the twin towers of All Souls, the roofs of Brasenose, Oriel, Christ Church, and right down into the quadrangles and gardens that form the green soul of the colleges. And you get the glorious feeling that for once you are way above all the great brainboxes of Oxford.

Elite Club with Duck:
All Souls College

'Asquith bets 1 shilling against Malcolm that the
double circumference of his belly is smaller than that
of Malcolm's belly and head put together.'
Bet of 1904, from the All Souls Betting Book

'A novel that is set in Oxford must inevitably be called *All Souls*, regardless of what it is about,' explained Javier Marías, who taught Spanish Literature at Oxford in the mid-1980s. One should not, however, automatically equate his fictional college with the real All Souls. The minimal teaching duties often give the first-person narrator the feeling that he is 'playing a purely decorative role', and so he 'occasionally felt I ought to put on my black gown...with the primary aim of satisfying the many tourists'. These press their noses against Hawksmoor's magnificent wrought iron gates of 1734, through which from Radcliffe Square they can see the impeccable oval lawn of the quadrangle, the sundial and the twin towers which rise up over the glowing Gothic walls like a Fata Morgana.

The gatehouse on the High Street is flanked by the two founding fathers: King Henry VI and his adviser Henry Chichele, Archbishop of Canterbury. The college was founded in 1438, and masses were to be held in perpetuity for those who had fallen in the Hundred Years' War, particularly from the House of Lancaster. In addition to prayers for the souls of the faithful, the founders were concerned above all with the training of future leaders. Chichele was an expert in canon law, and his college was the only one in Oxford where the number of lawyers soon grew to exceed that of theologians. Law has continued to be a speciality at All Souls, and there is a Chichele Chair of International Law. Such specialization apart, the college itself is special – in fact it is more exclusive than the most exclusive London club.

All Souls is a college with no students. But that doesn't even mean that it is a postgraduate college. It has forty Fellows and a Warden, and since Chichele's time they have formed the nucleus here. They are joined only by those who have already achieved something notable or from whom something notable is to be expected – in other words, the crème de la crème. In addition to these scholars, the college elects twenty-two Distinguished Fellows from different areas of public life. About a dozen Visiting Fellows are also invited, mainly to do a year's research. All

Souls is more of an academy than a college, an egalitarian society of first-class minds. There are scarcely any teaching duties, and all that is expected of the members is occasionally to be present and always to be brilliant.

These conditions have been met by a wide variety of people, such as Lord Curzon, Viceroy of India, Sir John Hicks, winner of the Nobel Prize for economics, and the author and adventurer T. E. Lawrence, who wrote part of his *Seven Pillars of Wisdom* here. Not all the Fellows turned out to be high-fliers, however. It was said of John Sparrow, Warden between 1952 and 1977: 'He has a mind that goes at once to the periphery of every question.'

It was at All Souls that the historian A. L. Rowse (see p. 89) reached the peak of his Tudor research and his arrogance, while the Polish philosopher Leszek Kolakowski found ideal conditions here for his work on Marxism and on *Metaphysical Horror* as well as for a life based on the maxim *ama nesciri* [Love to be unknown]. That polyhistorian and *homme du monde* Sir Isaiah Berlin also flourished on this academic Parnassus (see p. 81), and during the 1930s he sharpened up his pragmatic *Sense of Reality* through long discussions with ministers and diplomats in the Common Room at All Souls. 'If you wanted to know how England was governed, All Souls was the place to be.'

The college remained a male stronghold until 1979, when after 541 years the first female Fellows were allowed in. Its comfortable interiors, however, remain – to quote my landlady – 'a closed shop, very closed'. This need not stop us from at least examining the architecture. The Front Quad (1438–43) is still largely in its original state, with the chapel in the north wing. The reredos is one of the most magnificent Perpendicular works in Oxford, but all that is left of the original 1447 reredos is the rich Gothic framework; the sculptures are Victorian copies (1872) – as are the gilded angels in the hammer-beam roof. A mermaid, a bagpipe-player and various other beautifully carved misericords make for a little light entertainment in the stalls.

The chapel was Nicholas Hawksmoor's starting point when he designed the North Quad (1716–33), which is the architectural highlight of All Souls. Two dramatic rectangular towers dominate the quadrangle: the buttresses are tapered, and the top sections seem to have been pulled out of one another like parts of a telescope. These neo-Gothic Baroque twin towers have become a landmark as well as a lasting monument to an architect who did things his own way. He also created an All Souls masterpiece with the Codrington Library (1716–20). This magnificent reading room stretches for some 60 metres through the north wing, like the Long Gallery of some grand manor house. It was the first 18th-century library in

Oxford to depart radically from the medieval box system by setting the bookcases back against the walls, which are more than 12 metres high. In front of these shelves are rows of reading desks with Chippendale chairs. The Venetian windows at either end of the room have classical columns inside and Gothic tracery outside – an ingenious device by a versatile architect.

When I visited the library, I was greeted by a tomblike silence. A dark-suited gentleman was busy polishing the black-and-white marble tiles. Only once a year does this place spring to life, when the University VIPs come across from the Sheldonian after the Encaenia ceremony (see p. 144) to partake of luncheon in the library of All Souls. In the middle of the room, towering over everyone, stands a marble figure dressed like a Roman Emperor, with a pile of books at his feet. This is Christopher Codrington, former Fellow and the man who paid for all this. He made his money out of sugar from Barbados, which is why the Codrington is sometimes called the Sugar Library. When he died in 1710, this bibliophile businessman left his college some 12,000 books. The number has since risen to about 170,000, with law and military history the main specialities. The cornice of the classical, olive-green bookcases is crowned by twenty-four lead busts, dating from 1750–56. Sir Henry Cheere, a sculptor who was very much in fashion, particularly in Oxford, created this gallery of eminent All Souls Fellows, among whom you will find the poet Edward Young, author of *Night Thoughts*, and Christopher Wren, from whose studio the Codrington Library has a collection of some 450 drawings. It was probably while Wren was bursar at the college that he designed the sundial of 1659 – originally meant for the front quadrangle but now on the façade of the library (see p. 72).

Oxford's brainiest college enjoys the most absurd rituals. In the Common Room is a Betting Book, in which the Fellows record their bizarre wagers – occasionally published privately, but otherwise guarded with all the strict secrecy of a Zurich bank account. This, however, is not half as eccentric as their behaviour on Mallard Day. A nocturnal procession of All Souls Fellows wends its way behind a skewered duck, crossing the quadrangle and up to the roof of the library, rather like the famous Monty Python sketch about the Ministry for Silly Walks. As they go, they wave sticks and torches and sing the Mallard Song in honour of the duck that was found during the building of the college in the 15th century. This remarkable ceremony is, however, even rarer than the appearance of Halley's Comet, for it only takes place every hundred years, the next occasion being 14 January 2101. But that need not stop you from practising the Mallard Song next time you have your roast duck:

Therefore let us sing and dance a galliard,
To the remembrance of the Mallard:
And as Mallard dives in pool,
Let us dabble, dive and duck in bowl.
Oh! by the blood of King Edward,
Oh! by the blood of King Edward,
It was a swapping, swapping Mallard.

University College and Queen's

'If you award me a First, I will go to Cambridge. If I receive a Second,
I shall stay in Oxford, so I expect you will give me a First.'
Stephen Hawking to his examiners in Oxford, 1962

I f Oxford was situated on Hollywood Boulevard, the surface of the High Street would now be a mass of glittering brass stars. The street and indeed the city is one vast 'Walk of Fame', full of the ghostly footprints of those who have taught and studied here. Bill Clinton, for instance, though his star may be a little faded now, studied at University College, diagonally opposite All Souls. He was a Rhodes Scholar in 1968–70, diligently practised his fingering on the saxophone and under the skirts, did not do any exams, but made useful contacts and became President of the United States. His daughter Chelsea followed in her father's footsteps.

University College, or 'Univ' for short, would like to be Oxford's oldest college. The deeds relating to its foundation date from 1249, but it was not granted official college status as *Aula Universitatis* until 1280. This means that Merton has older statutes (1264), even though Univ had the first founder: William of Durham. Balliol College, the third competitor in this struggle for academic seniority, claims the longest presence on the same spot (1263).

Architecturally, Univ's history does not begin until 1634, when the old buildings were torn down and it was all rebuilt from scratch, in traditional Gothic style right up to the fan vaulting of the gatehouses. The Front Quad, completed *c.* 1677, is strictly symmetrical, with a rhythmic quartet of curved gables on the attic storey. The hall and chapel, back to back, form a wing together opposite the gatehouse.

Two prime ministers studied here: Clement Attlee and the Australian Bob Hawke, and there have been countless lawyers, ambassadors, writers, and one physicist who acquired worldwide fame when he went to Cambridge: Stephen Hawking. In the hall, below the hammer-beam roof, is a portrait gallery of celebrities, including Clinton – a larger-than-lifesize profile, painted by his compatriot Ronald B. Kitaj.

Next door in the chapel you will find Abraham van Linge's most important contribution to Oxford's art treasures: eight windows, painted in 1641, narrating stories from the Bible with Baroque animation and glorious colours (see p. 66). In the ante-chapel are four monuments designed by John Flaxman, England's great neoclassical sculptor. The quality of his work is especially evident in the relief of the Sanskrit scholar Sir William Jones, who was the first to point out the resemblance between Sanskrit and Latin and Greek, and who codified the Hindu laws, which formed the basis of Britain's colonial rule in India. Much better known, though, is the Shelley Memorial, which can be reached through the west wing of Front Quad. This must be the most spectacular monument ever raised to a student who was sent down from the university. Percy Bysshe Shelley arrived in Oxford in 1810. His room was in the south-west corner of Univ's main quadrangle. He found the first lecture (on mineralogy) so boring that he never went to any more. Instead, he read incessantly, worked on a novel entitled *Leonora*, went pistol-shooting on Shotover Hill, and talked for hours about the tyranny of religion. He was a radical left-winger, and wore a blue coat with a velvet collar. Once, it is said, he startled a young mother on Magdalen Bridge with the question: 'Will your baby tell us anything about pre-existence, madam?'

If his arrival was impressive, his departure was dramatic, and occurred just six months later. He wrote an anonymous pamphlet entitled *The Necessity of Atheism*, and in March 1811 he was sent down. The rest is literary history. There is no trace of Oxford in any of his work, but the myth of the dead Romantic returned in full force to the college. There he lies now, drowned while sailing in the Mediterranean, a lifesize, snow-white marble sculpture borne by two winged, bronze lions, with the Muse of Poetry at his feet. As Edward Onslow Ford's monument was too large for Shelley's grave in the Protestant cemetery in Rome, University College welcomed it in 1893, put it under a blue starred cupola, and thus created a pantheon for its lost son, quoting him in gold letters on a mauve background: 'The One remains, the many change and pass; / Heaven's light forever shines, Earth's shadows fly' (*Adonais*, 1821).

The Poet Laureate Andrew Motion also studied here, as did Stephen Spender (see p. 58) and the winner of the Nobel Prize for literature V. S. Naipaul, though both were as disappointed with Oxford as Shelley had been before them. One thing the Old Etonian Shelley never had to worry about was money, unlike the Trinidadian Naipaul. He came to Univ to study literature (1950–54) and found himself in a 'donkey-trap of learning'. Lack of money and illness drove him to the brink of suicide. He shut himself in his little room and turned the gas tap on, but what saved him was an old English institution: in those days, you had to put money in the gas meter, and he ran out of sixpences.

A bit further down, you will come to the most unpopular building in the High Street: Examination Schools. Behind the Victorian country house façade dwells the Moloch to which all those who last the course must sacrifice themselves. It has been there since 1882. The carvings over the porch already show what is to come. Generations of candidates have filed through these doors into the entrance hall, the *salle des pas perdus*, over marble and mosaic floors into the wood-panelled examination rooms on the first floor. The quad opens out into Merton Street, offering an impressive front, and the overall combination of Elizabethan, Jacobean and other motifs suggests that maybe the architect also wanted to test us passers-by on our knowledge of architecture down through the ages. Sir Thomas Jackson was an Oxford architect who was much in demand, and this is certainly his masterpiece.

The nicest feature of the Examination Schools is the view that you get looking diagonally across the High Street towards the façade of The Queen's College. Between town houses and shops rise a magnificent classical screen, pediments crowned with figures, and an open domed rotunda with Tuscan columns that nestles above the Porter's Lodge like a little round temple. Queen's was founded in 1341 by Robert Eglesfield, chaplain to Queen Philippa, the wife of Edward III. The statue above the main entrance, however, is not of her but of one of the later royal benefactors, Caroline of Ansbach, the generous wife of George II.

The only original building that has survived is the old brewery in the Fellows' Garden, where for nearly 600 years (until 1939) the college brewed its own beer. After the medieval buildings had all been torn down, the new buildings were begun in the 17th century – first the North Quad at the rear (1672–1707), then the front quadrangle (1709–34) with arcades on the ground floor, tall residential wings on both sides, the chapel and hall opposite the entrance – everything classico-baroque, in a unified grandeur that has no equal among Oxford colleges. The architect of Front Quad is believed to have been William Townesend, a local mason, but he probably used and adapted designs by Nicholas Hawksmoor. Whoever designed the Upper Library in North Quad (1692–95) – it may have been

Dean Aldrich – also gave the college something matchless. With its delicate plasterwork and the carved garlands and rocailles on the bookcases this is one of the finest and least altered interiors in Oxford. Among the treasures in this library, which houses some 150,000 books, are landmark works of the history of architecture, like the *Vitruvius Britannicus*, Elizabethan Bibles, and the First Folio copy that belonged to the Shakespearian actor David Garrick.

Every evening at ten past seven a student stands in the Front Quad and blows his trumpet. Ever since the days of Robert Eglesfield, this has been the eagerly awaited announcement that it is dinner time. On Christmas Day, a strange procession makes its way into the high, barrel-vaulted hall: the crowned head of a boar is carried in on a silver tray, adorned with rosemary and mistletoe, and holding an orange between its teeth. The Boar's Head Dinner has been held every year since around 1395 in memory of a Queen's student who survived an attack from a wild boar by throwing his Aristotle into the beast's jaws and crying 'Graecum est!' – 'That's Greek! There is, however, a major threat to this age-old custom: the Provost, Geoffrey Marshall, fears that it may no longer be possible to serve up a boar's head 'because of European food regulations'.

Another 'gaudy night' that is still celebrated at Queen's is the Needle and Thread Dinner. On New Year's Day, the Bursar gives each Fellow a needle and thread, with the words: 'Take this and be thrifty!' The ritual is in fact based on a pun: *aiguille et fil* (needle and thread) corresponding to the Founder's name Eglesfield. With such eccentric customs, it is scarcely surprising that the college has also produced the occasional oddball. The comedian Rowan Atkinson is one, and the utilitarian philosopher Jeremy Bentham another. His clothed skeleton is on public display at University College, London, which he founded. Bentham was a child prodigy: he could read at the age of three, was admitted to Queen's when he was twelve, and complained that at Oxford he learned nothing but 'mendacity and insincerity'. Germany's first Minister of Culture, Michael Naumann, also studied here, and devoted much thought to the *Strukturwandel des Heroismus* [The Changing Structure of Heroism].

Queen's Lane branches off from the High Street, and here one can easily overlook the entrance to St Edmund Hall, which has four Cornish choughs in its coat of arms. Next to the splendour of Queen's, it seems small and modest, and yet it has everything a college should have: chapel and hall, a pocket-sized quadrangle, and even a sundial. The quad at 'Teddy Hall' is like a cosy living-room, with an ancient well, dormer windows and wisteria. The buildings are a bit of a jumble: a north wing with rubble masonry walls (*c.* 1596), a neoclassical chapel (*c.* 1680) and a tiny hall. St Edmund Hall is the only academic hall in Oxford to have survived from the Middle Ages (see p. 35). It was named after St Edmund of Abingdon, who was said to have lived here in the early 13th century. Next to the college and through a cemetery stands the church of St Peter-in-the-East, but don't be misled by its ecclesiastical appearance: apart from its Norman crypt, the whole building is full of books, for this is now the college library. High up on the tower are various Fellows, portrayed in the style of medieval grotesques: the late Principal, Reverend John Kelly, died in 1997 and is shown here with a squash racket; he was a specialist in patristics (the writings of the Fathers of the Church) and a lover of squash; the Reverend Graham Midgley is also here, together with Fred, his Labrador, for whom he wrote the following epitaph: 'Beneath this turf the Dean's dog Fred / Without his master goes to Earth, stone dead. / But on the tower, stone Dean and Fred together / Enjoy the sunshine and endure bad weather.'

If we follow the right-angled bend in Queen's Lane, we shall come to a veritable gallery of grotesque heads and animals carved by the same mason, Michael Groser, at the rear of New College: monkeys, otters, and even a tortoise sitting on its eggs. They are typical of Oxford's bestiary, for on the façades of Magdalen and Brasenose, the tower of Merton Chapel, and in many other places you will find a menagerie of these grotesques and gargoyles which right through to the present have combined medieval tradition with a local love of the absurd – they keep off evil spirits, but they also revel in witty games with secret meanings.

Queen's Lane does another twist before leaving the shadow of its college and, in deference on reaching the gateway of its mighty neighbour, changing its name to New College Lane. Oxford's oldest gatehouse (c. 1380) is now the rear entrance to New College (see p. 149), and nowhere will you get a more vivid impression of an old fortified monastery than here between the high, narrow, soot-blackened walls of this lane. It's therefore all the more surprising when you turn the next corner and find yourself in a Rio di Palazzo, with a Bridge of Sighs spanning the lane. The prisoners used to cross Venice's *Ponte dei Sospiri* to go from the Doge's Palace to the prison, but here in Oxford it's the academics of Hertford College who cross the bridge to go from one quadrangle to another. Sir Thomas Jackson, that brilliant mixer of styles, designed it in 1913 – a picturesque addition to the classical Oxford scene, and an echo of the old bridge over New College Lane. From 1703 until his death in 1742, the astronomer Edmund Halley lived in this lane, and his roof observatory is still preserved. But instead of gazing upwards at comets, we are now about to enter the very heart of the university: the Sheldonian Theatre and the Bodleian Library.

New College: Garden gate with the Mound

High Street: University Church of St Mary

May Day with Bridge of Sighs, Hertford College

The King's Arms

Sheldonian Theatre: Degree Day

Entrance to Bodleian Library with statue of the Earl of Pembroke

Keble College: chapel

Christ Church: Tom Quad with Christopher Wren's Tom Tower

Christ Church Library

Christ Church: Bellringers' chamber in Tom Tower

University College: main quadrangle

Worcester College: hall and chapel

John Ruskin

A. E. Housman

Thomas Hardy

Oscar Wilde with Bosie

John Betjeman

Dorothy L. Sayers

Lewis Carroll

J. R. R. Tolkien

W. H. Auden, Cecil Day-Lewis and Stephen Spender

The Queen's College: chapel and hall

St John's College: Canterbury Quad

St John's College

View of All Souls from Radcliffe Square

High Street: Grand Café

Merton College

Trinity College garden

High Street: St Mary's and The Queen's College

New College: garden and town wall

Magdalen Bridge

Brasenose College with dome of Radcliffe Camera

A World of Books:
Bodleian Library and Radcliffe Camera

'Oxford is willing enough to believe that
the Bodleian is the hub of the scholar's universe.'
Dorothy L. Sayers, *Gaudy Night*, 1935

The way to the University Library leads through the great Schools Quadrangle (1613–24). Latin was the lingua franca of European academics in the Middle Ages, and so the gold capital letters on a blue background above the doors announce the names in Latin of the *scholae*, the different subjects and faculties that were offered to the students of the time. They began with grammar, rhetoric and logic, went on with arithmetic, geometry, music and astronomy, and in all had to study the seven *artes liberales* for a total of seven years. The reward was 'Bachelor of Arts'. But that was just the beginning, because if you wanted to go on and become a 'Master of Arts', you had to walk through the doors marked philosophy, history, classical languages – or, alternatively, cross the quad and go into the faculties of medicine or law, the *scientiae lucrativae*. But the absolute pinnacle, the door of doors, was the Divinity School, the theological faculty at the very head of the quadrangle. However, things have changed slightly since then. If you go through the door marked *Schola Moralis Philosophiae*, for instance, you will come directly to the toilets.

Just as the layout of the Schools Quadrangle reflects the medieval hierarchy of the faculties, so too does the Bodleian façade preserve the stylistic continuity of the *Universitas Oxoniensis*. The Perpendicular Gothic front, with its four rows of densely packed blind arcades (1610–12) echoes the rear of the Divinity School, which is almost two hundred years older. The façade is quite severe, almost as if its lines had been drawn with a ruler, and opposite – on the eastern side of the quad – is the most extravagant of all gatehouses, a showpiece from the pattern book of the Renaissance. The Tower of the Five Orders (1613–19), demonstrating the five orders of columns, celebrates the classical education of those who entered here. Between the twin Corinthian columns on the fourth storey sits James I, gazing at his beloved Bodleian, with the allegorical figure of Fame on his left, and the kneeling Alma Mater on his right, to both of whom he is handing his works. But on the top floor, the true monarch of all he surveys, is the university archivist. When this tower was built, the King James version of the Bible had just been published – the

'Authorized Version' of 1611, on which some fifty scholars from Oxford, Cambridge and London had been working under the patronage of James I, who was described as 'the wisest fool in Christendom'. 'Were I not a king, I would be a university man; and if it were that I must be a prisoner, if I might have my wish, I would have no other prison than this library, and be chained together with these good authors.' Thus said the king when he visited the Bodleian in 1621.

Guarding the entrance to the library, in Field Marshal pose, is the 3rd Earl of Pembroke, Chancellor and benefactor of the university. Pembroke College is named after him, and this bronze statue is attributed to Hubert Le Sueur (c. 1640, based on a portrait by Rubens). Thomas Bodley founded the library for 'the University of Oxford and the Republic of the Lettered', as we are informed by a Latin inscription above the entrance. On the inside of this arch is the Book of Books – an open Bible on a blue background with the words: 'they found him in the temple, sitting in the midst of the doctors' in Greek – a reference to the twelve-year-old Jesus (Luke 2: 46) and an example to all the scholars that are about to enter this temple of books. First, though, we must go through the vestibule shop, the former *proscholium*, into the Divinity School. This was the first large-scale building constructed by the university, but a shortage of money caused constant delays. It was begun in 1424 and not completed until 1483. It was well worth the wait, however. A beautifully constructed, lavishly decorated vault, which Pevsner regards as 'one of the marvels of Oxford': between the four transverse arches the free hanging keystones give the illusion that the vault is fanning out from them, but it is not a fan vault; it is a lierne vault supported by transverse ribs – an original, Late Gothic tour de force. It was probably built by William Orchard, who was one of the master masons that worked in Magdalen College. The heraldic and allegorical keystones shine like stars from the ceiling; there are more than 400 bosses, some with the coats-of-arms of benefactors like Edward IV and the Bishop of London, and others from the Church and the aristocracy. One of these bosses bears the initials WO – William Orchard. Another library was built above this magnificent room in 1488: Duke Humfrey's Library, the very heart of the Bodleian.

Good Duke Humfrey, as the Duke of Gloucester was known, was a brother of King Henry V, a graduate of Balliol College, a war hero (Agincourt), a friend of the Italian humanists, and an avid collector of manuscripts. These he gave to his university, which put them together with the manuscripts from St Mary's to make up a collection of some 600 items. But by the time Duke Humfrey's Library opened, in 1488, it was already out of date because it contained only manuscripts, and this was precisely the time when the printing press began to revolutionize the world of books and hence of libraries. As the university had no money and therefore could not afford the luxury of printed books, it had to close its library around 1550, and paradoxically this was the start of the Bodleian's success story.

The man with whose name it is now forever associated, Sir Thomas Bodley, had taught Greek and Hebrew at Merton before he enjoyed a successful career as a diplomat in the service of Elizabeth I. He paid for the 'greate desolate room' that he had discovered above the Divinity School to be refurbished. It was opened in 1602, with more than 2,000 books, and the coffered ceiling was painted with the coats-of-arms of Bodley and the university. From this single room, the Bodleian has expanded into twelve buildings.

Bodley had been impressed by the continental style of library, and so he was one of the first to introduce this new system in England: in the wing known as the Arts End (1610–12) the bookcases were no longer placed across the room, as they had been in Duke Humfrey's Library, but over the entire surface of the walls – a 'wall system' instead of a 'stall system'. The top shelves are accessible from galleries that rest on delicate Tuscan columns. There is a similar arrangement in Selden End, the west wing (1624–36), which lies above Convocation House and Chancellor's Court. 'The Bod', as most people call it, in fact consists of dozens of libraries – the former private collections of scholars, bishops, lawyers and book-lovers from all walks of life. From Archbishop Laud's collection came hundreds of Arabic and Greek manuscripts; from a senior rabbi in Prague came the Oppenheim Collection of Hebrew manuscripts; the antiquarian Francis Douce donated a priceless collection of incunabula, illuminated manuscripts, emblem books and *danses macabres*. The Opie collection of children's books, comprising some 20,000 volumes, also found its way to the Bodleian in 1989.

The rarest items? The earliest text of *La Chanson de Roland*; the oldest surviving copy of the 'Holy Rule' of St Benedict dating from the 8th century; Marco Polo's *Livre du Grand Chan*; Ferdausi's *Shaname*, the Persian Book of Kings; 'The Gough Map', one of the oldest maps in England (*c.* 1360); The Hebrew Kennicott Bible, a masterpiece of Sephardic book illustration (1476); the manuscript of Mary Shelley's *Frankenstein*; the original typescript of Wittgenstein's *Tractatus logico-philosophicus*...and these are just a few of the pearls from this vast treasure house of books. There are thousands of original musical scores, including Purcell's *Ode for St Cecilia's Day* and Holst's *The Planets*, medieval illuminated manuscripts, many of them from the libraries of monasteries that were dissolved in the Reformation, and Byzantine, Persian and Indian illuminations, plus of course a Gutenberg Bible, along with manuscripts by Aubrey, Shelley, Beckford, Tolkien,

Chandler, and bequests from the estates of countless other authors. The famous black quarto notebooks of Franz Kafka are also here, as are two-thirds of his surviving manuscripts – the basis of the Kafka edition by the late Oxford Germanist Sir Malcolm Pasley.

The Bodleian Library is one of three copyright libraries in England (the others being Cambridge University Library and the British Library). It was Bodley himself who in 1610 negotiated with the Stationers' Company in London that his library should be granted the right to receive one free copy of every book published in England (with the exception of those published in Cambridge). He could have had no idea of the sheer quantity that this privilege would entail. Nowadays, the yearly number of copyright books is in the region of 80,000, which is about twice the number that constituted the original collection in 1714. In response to the inevitable question 'How many books have you got?' Bodley's librarians usually answer: 'Well, about 120 miles.' They are referring, of course, to shelves. If they gave a number today, it would be out of date by tomorrow, but in 2004 the estimate was around 7.5 million. They reckon they expand by about two and a half miles a year, or 130,000 books. They collect almost anything – even telephone books, because 'you never know what's going to be important'. Bodley once bought a bundle of Chinese books, though at the time there was no one in Oxford who could read them. Today such incunabula cannot even be found in China.

The first Bodleian catalogues were regarded as exemplary, but later the system of classification came to be regarded as somewhat eccentric. The titles were listed in folios, and for a long time there were no file-cards. Today, even in this medieval library, electronic cataloguing comes as naturally as reading tables with Internet access. BARD, for example – Bodleian Access to Remote Databases – links the reader electronically with the catalogues of hundreds of specialist libraries all over the world. And yet the Bodleian itself, although its books ceased to be chained in 1757, is still a 'chained library'. Not one book can be borrowed. They must all be read on the spot, in one of the thirty reading rooms. Even King Charles I was refused permission to borrow books, and so was Oliver Cromwell. Instead of sending Cromwell the book he required, the librarian sent him a copy of the statutes, which forbid the lending of any book. The Upper Reading Room, which is for graduates, is decorated by a frieze (c. 1620) containing the portraits of more than 200 famous people, from Aristotle to Luther.

Oxford's world of books is on a seemingly endless course of expansion. The largest of what are now eight branches is the new Bodleian. It was built (1937–40) by Sir Giles Gilbert Scott and has all the charm of an indoor swimming pool. It's connected with the Old Library by a tunnel underneath Broad Street, and a conveyor belt transports the books in boxes from one to the other, like raw diamonds coming out of the Oxford word-mines. Thus about three hours after you've asked for a book, it will arrive. Back at the start of the 20th century, Bodley's moles had already started digging in the opposite direction, with a tunnel under Radcliffe Square to the most beautiful of all the satellites.

The Radcliffe Camera is a St Peter's of books – a round building 'whose dome gathers the surrounding spires and towers together like a hen her chicks'. This was John Betjeman's description of a building that perhaps more than any other has become a symbol of the city – a Baroque masterpiece amid the Gothic towers of St Mary's and All Souls. Once there were dozens of small houses in this square, but they were demolished as part of 18th-century town-planning or, as we would call it today, redevelopment. The idea to build a rotunda came from Hawksmoor, but the plan was not carried out until after his death, by his colleague James Gibbs (1737–49). Round arches on the rusticated ground floor, which originally were open, pairs of Corinthian columns, an attic storey with balustrades and buttresses, and above this, an unusually slender dome with a neat little lantern – the Radcliffe Camera stands on one of the truly great squares of Europe with a grandeur that is almost Florentine.

Above the reading-room on the ground floor of what the students call the 'Rad Cam' is a room of monumental splendour – the domed room with cool white stucco where on 15 June 1814, Tsar Alexander I, the Prussian King Frederick William III, Field Marshal Blücher and the Prince Regent George sat down at a banquet for the victors in the Napoleonic Wars. Halfway up, a gallery runs all round the massive arcades, and the bookcases fill the walls of the covered walk. Dr John Radcliffe could scarcely have wished for a finer mausoleum. He had made his fortune in London as a physician. By all accounts, he was not the greatest of doctors, but he was supposed to have had a good bedside manner comprising the wit, charm and other Oxford qualities necessary for success in high society, particularly among high-society hypochondriacs. Dr Radcliffe was court physician to King William III and also attended Queen Anne, who suffered at least ten miscarriages and had five children, all of whom died young. It is not, then, for his medical achievements that Dr Radcliffe is remembered, but for his gifts to the university and to his old college, University.

Brasenose, Exeter and Jesus

'Although Jesus, of course, did not attend Jesus College,
his father was a Trinity man and read Classics.'
Corny Oxford joke

When Robert Runcie, who later became Archbishop of Canterbury, went to see his tutor at Brasenose College for the first time, an American student was just coming out of the room. 'Boy, when you walk through that door, you meet civilization.'

The prominence of the college's position on Radcliffe Square is matched by the illustriousness of its alumni: the winner of the Nobel Prize for literature William Golding, the author and statesman John Buchan, Field Marshal Douglas Haig, the Monty Python star Michael Palin, and more. Who cares that Brasenose's academic reputation is overshadowed by the prowess of its rowers and rugby players?

The name is believed to derive from 'brazen nose'. The story goes that in the 12th or 13th century there was a door-knocker in the form of a lion's muzzle on the entrance to Brasenose Hall, and if any fugitive from the law managed to grab hold of it, he would be granted asylum. Such were the privileges of academia in the Middle Ages. When the students left Oxford provisionally in 1333, they took their door-knocker with them to Stamford, and it didn't come back to Brasenose until 1890. Since then, it has been hanging over the High Table in the hall beneath the portrait of the founder of the college, William Smyth, Bishop of Lincoln. He founded it on the site of the Hall in 1509, and in that year work started on the Old Quad, now in the magnificent shadow of the Radcliffe Camera. Since 1719, it has been possible to tell the time from the north façade, provided the sun is shining. The chapel in the next quad has a plaster fan vault, which is a fine example of Gothic Revival (c. 1665). One of the memorial plaques in the chapel is dedicated to Walter Pater, the great Victorian aesthete and historian of the Renaissance, whose creed of a cultivated hedonism made a huge impression on the young Oscar Wilde, amongst many others ('There is no Pater but Pater, and I am his prophet'). The bronze relief shows Pater under a willow tree, surrounded by medallions portraying his heroes: Plato, Dante, Leonardo, Michelangelo – a monument that encapsulates the cultural world of the 19th century.

Along Brasenose Lane is a high, rubble masonry wall that is blackened with the soot of the centuries, and behind it towers a tree whose branches reach far across the lane. This is Bishop Heber's Chestnut, planted at the end of the 18th century in the Fellows' Garden of Exeter College. If ever its leaves touch the walls of Brasenose on the other side of the lane, then Exeter's rowers will bump the Brasenose boat in Eights Week. So says the old superstition. Exeter's garden lies behind the front quadrangle, squeezed between walls which protect it from the weather and from sightseers. Four ancient fig trees are growing outside the Fellows' house, and one of them even has a doctorate: Dr Kennicott's Fig, named after a Hebrew scholar who had a predilection for the fruit. The real surprise in this little garden is its terrace, which offers a grandstand view of Radcliffe Square, with the mighty dome of the Rad Cam, the towers of St Mary's and All Souls, and the walls of the Bodleian – as fine a cityscape as you could wish to see.

Since its foundation in 1314, Exeter has always been one of the smaller, poorer colleges, with little of architectural note – especially after the Victorian bits added on by Sir Giles Gilbert Scott, 'who had more work to do than he had talent to carry it out' (John Betjeman). The chapel (1854–60), based on the Sainte-Chapelle in Paris, is far too big for its quadrangle, but all the same it does contain one masterpiece which is well worth a visit: *The Star of Bethlehem*, a tapestry designed by Edward Burne-Jones and woven by the firm of his friend William Morris. They got to know each other in this college, and it was the beginning of a remarkable artistic partnership (see p. 64). A wall hanging by Morris has his 'Bird' design (1878), which was the firm's most popular pattern. 'Topsy's' pipe, inkwell and glasses were given to the college after his death, but they are not on show to the general public; nor are the drawings and weavings by Burne-Jones – Pre-Raphaelite relics in the Morris Room and the library. Students are relatively free to organize their own studies, and compulsory tutorials are minimal, as explained by the novelist and Exeter graduate Martin Amis: 'The unique freedom of Oxford is that you don't have to account for more than, say, ninety minutes a week for eighteen weeks a year. That's about three days out of three years of your life. Conventional ways of filling that time are gone; it is all yours now. It doesn't happen to you before and it never happens to you again.'

Opposite Exeter is Jesus, but they are separated by more than just Turl Street. For centuries Exeter consisted mainly of students from the West Country, while Jesus was the college of the Welsh. The coat of arms over the gate with the ostrich feathers of the Prince of Wales is already a symbol of a link that goes back to the Welsh monk and lawyer Dr Hugh Price. He obtained a Charter from Elizabeth I to found the college in 1571 – the first new foundation since the Reformation, Protestant with a dash of Welsh Nonconformism. The royal Foundress is to be seen in the hall, in the form of a portrait of 1590 and a drinking club named The Elizabethans. The Welsh roots are nourished by the Dafydd ap Gwilym Society, one of whose chairpersons was Ffion Jenkins, the Welsh wife of the former Tory leader William Hague.

In its second quadrangle, Jesus reveals its 17th-century grandeur: slim, round-arched windows, curved gables. The last great adventurer of the British Empire studied at Jesus – the writer T. E. Lawrence. As an archaeology student he obtained a first-class degree in 1910 with his work on the fortresses of the Crusades, but he became world-famous as Lawrence of Arabia, guerrilla leader, translator of *The Odyssey*, and one of the earliest, though most reluctant media stars. There is a monument to him in the chapel – a copy of the marble bust in St Paul's. Among the 'Jesubites' who could later claim to have studied in his room was the Labour Prime Minister Harold Wilson. He came from a middle-class family in Manchester, attended a state school, and then came to little Jesus, not one of the great and glorious colleges like Magdalen or Christ Church. And that, scoffed the smart public school socialists, was why he lacked the social graces. He became a lecturer in economics at Oxford, then went into politics, and was undoubtedly the most brilliant academic of all the post-war British prime ministers.

Jesus, Exeter and Lincoln all lie on Turl Street, right in the centre of the city but in a quiet side street between High and Broad. The crown of a chestnut tree rises luxuriantly over the walls of Jesus, and is echoed at the end of the street by the tower of All Saints Church. The Turl only gets busy at lunchtime, when the students come swarming out of their colleges and head for the Covered Market and the sandwich bars. If you want a new pair of shoes, the address to go to is 6 Turl Street: Ducker & Son, founded in 1898, where you can get handmade shoes and boots, made to measure.

Broad Street:
Between Balliol and Blackwell's

'The moment I heard those arrogant, off-hand,
go-to-blazes tones, I said "Wimsey of Balliol".'
Dorothy L. Sayers, *Gaudy Night*, 1935

B road Street runs parallel to the High Street, is not half as long, but is twice as wide. In the Middle Ages it was called Horsemonger Street. Where the horse market used to be, outside the northern city walls, is now a car park in the middle of the street. The houses are mainly 18th and 19th century, and although there is nothing special about the architecture, there is a pleasing variety of styles. In fact, there is nothing special about the street itself until it spreads itself out at the eastern end, with the Sheldonian Theatre and the Clarendon Building providing a classical view, and the former Indian Institute, with its golden elephant as a weather vane. In the top part of Broad Street, opposite Balliol College, is a cross of stones set in the pavement. It was on this spot that Bishops Nicholas Ridley and Hugh Latimer were burned at the stake as heretics (1555), to be followed six months later by Thomas Cranmer, Archbishop of Canterbury. When this supporter of Henry VIII and co-author of the Common Book of Prayer (the first Anglican prayer book in the vernacular) stood at the stake on 21 March 1556, it is said that he retracted his recantation and thrust his right hand into the flames, crying, 'My hand shall first be punished therefore' – a legendary response to the auto-da-fé.

The Broad is the street of martyrs and bookshops. Between Waterstone's at the beginning and the new Bodleian Library at the end lies a book-lover's paradise, for although Thornton's, Oxford's oldest bookshop, has recently moved to the edge of the city, the more famous Blackwell's is still there, with its various branches. And appropriately when you are tired of reading things in black and white, you can go from Blackwell's to The White Horse, a very conveniently situated pub. Above the bar you will see a photo of four Trinity students 'lawn rowing' in the college garden. No. 6 Broad Street houses The Oxford Story (see p. 94), but I prefer no. 17, which is the first Oxfam shop, opened in 1948 to help the people of war-ravaged Europe, but now dedicated to helping the countries of the Third World.

On the other side of the street is an unobtrusive oak door bearing a brass plate that says 'Balliol College, The Master's Lodgings'. There are few addresses in the academic world that are more sought-after than this. Becoming Master of Balliol was regarded by the American biochemist and Nobel laureate Baruch Blumberg as the pinnacle of his career. Balliol is generally regarded as the intellectual powerhouse of the Oxford elite. Its trademark is 'the tranquil consciousness of an effortless superiority' – a much-quoted phrase coined by one of them, Herbert Asquith, in an after-dinner speech when he became prime minister in 1908. It is an Oxford variation on the Renaissance ideal of the *sprezzatura*, the art of doing the most difficult things with the aristocratic composure of the perfect gentleman. Even in the 1920s, the most obscene examples of lavatory graffiti were still being translated into faultless Latin and Greek.

Balliol has the longest façade of all the Oxford colleges, and it is also the most boring. While you walk along Broad Street and St Giles past the neo-Gothic conglomeration, I suggest you spend the time learning the list of Balliol stars off by heart: Prime Ministers Asquith, Macmillan, Heath, Crown Princess of Japan Masako Owada, King Olaf V of Norway, the writers Robert Southey ('All I learned was a little swimming and a little bathing'), Matthew Arnold, A. C. Swinburne, G. M. Hopkins, Hilaire Belloc, Aldhous Huxley, Graham Greene, Harold and Nigel Nicolson, film directors John Schlesinger and Michael Winterbottom, the Shakespearean scholar A. C. Bradley, Cardinal Manning, Adam Smith, Arnold Toynbee, Richard Dawkins.... By now you will have reached the end of the façade, but the list goes on.

Balliol College is far older than its buildings. It owes its name and its existence to one of the rough, tough barons of the 13th century. John de Balliol kidnapped the Bishop of Durham, and as a penance he was forced to finance the studies of sixteen needy scholars in Oxford. He died in 1269, but his Scottish widow Dervorguilla continued the payments and in 1282 issued a charter. The foundation itself, however, goes back to some time between 1263 and 1268, which one can safely say without hurting the feelings of Merton and University (which also aspire to be the oldest colleges – see p. 124). Balliol is certainly the oldest college whose members have lived on the same spot without interruption. There are, however, only a few traces of the medieval buildings in the Front Quad, and then apart from some Georgian sections, the rest is 19th century. Despite the well-known architects who worked here – William Butterfield, Alfred Waterhouse and Anthony Salvin – the architecture itself is not exactly inspiring. 'We pulled down the good in order to make way for the bad,' complains Lord Peter Wimsey, Dorothy L. Sayers's fictional detective, who studied at Balliol.

The polychrome stripes on the façade of the chapel are like geological strata – a favourite motif of Butterfield's (1857). In this Italian Gothic-style building, a legendary don has his monument: the classical philologist Benjamin Jowett (see p. 84). 'If you do not believe in God by eight tomorrow morning, you will be sent down,' he informed one of his stubborn students. His period as Master was the starting-point of Balliol's golden age in the 19th century. Apart from academic brilliance, the college also fostered character, qualities of leadership and the desire to do great things for Britain. Jowett's purpose in life was to train an elite that should go forth and govern the Empire. It is a fact that by the end of the 19th century, there were more than forty Balliol men in the House of Commons. Between 1878 and 1914, over 200 Balliol graduates served in the colonial administration of India. One of these, Lord Curzon, rose to be Viceroy of India. In more recent times the last governor of Hong Kong and Chancellor of Oxford University, Chris Patten, studied at Jowett's college, and so did his immediate predecessor as Chancellor, the late Labour minister and historiographer Roy Jenkins. It was he who said that Balliol had produced more politically influential figures than all the other colleges put together: 'Life is just one damn Balliol man after another!'

It would be bad form to suppose that all this 'effortless superiority' might be the result of hard work. Colin Lucas, a former Master, explained Balliol's continued success as being a kind of intellectual heritage: 'It's a self-perpetuating atmosphere of the place, bred in the dons and passed on from generation to generation.' In the meantime, however, the politically successful genes seem to have passed on to the now even more influential London School of Economics. Nevertheless, Balliol kept its nose in front of its competitors when in 2001 the Oxford Internet Institute was attached to the college – the very first educational establishment to be devoted exclusively to research on the Internet and its effects on society. It was also in the vanguard for taking in students from state schools and from abroad, and was the first Oxford college to accept black students (which it did before accepting women).

Like many other colleges, Balliol remembers its war dead in the passage leading to the chapel: more than 300, most of them in the flower of their youth. In gold letters you will also see the name of a 'good German', Adam von Trott zu Solz. He was a member of the Kreisau Circle (a group opposed to Hitler), and was hanged on 26 August after the assassination attempt of 20 July 1944. From 1931 to 1933 he was a Rhodes Scholar, and studied philosophy and law at Balliol. Women loved this tall, thin man, and his friends also included David Astor, later to become editor of *The Observer*. The young Trott would go walking at night through the quadrangles of the college reciting Hölderlin, and on his desk next to Hölderlin would be the works of Karl Marx. Later, when he was a diplomat in Berlin, he tried in vain to mobilize his British friends to support the resistance movement against the Nazis. This dichotomous Anglo-German relationship is commemorated by a seminar room in Balliol that is named after him.

A prominent representative of German culture in Balliol today is Rosa Luxemburg. Not the left-wing revolutionary but the college tortoise (whose name is also an indirect tribute to the Marxist historian and former Master, the late Christopher Hill). There is no finer example of Balliol's effortless superiority than Rosie, particularly when she takes part in the annual race with her rivals from Corpus Christi and Keble (see p. 27). I met Rosie in her favourite spot – the shadow of a copper beech in Garden Quad. Nearby are three mulberry trees, the oldest of which is probably one of the James I mulberries, which were planted all over the country at the King's behest in 1608. The royalist gardens of Oxford were particularly keen to oblige. His Majesty's hopes that this would give rise to large-scale breeding of silkworms, and hence a brand new industry, came to nothing, but in some of the colleges the fruit does occasionally find its way into ice cream.

Let us return to the Broad. Right next to Balliol is a splendid, wrought-iron gate dating from 1737 through which one can see lawns and trees that would do credit to the finest country house. This is Trinity College, founded in 1555. The porter sits in one of those picturesque 17th-century cottages that were once so common in Oxford. There are two things you simply have to see in Trinity: the chapel and the garden. The gate tower was built at the same time as the adjacent chapel (1691–94), the latter being the first in Oxford to break with the Gothic tradition. It has round arched windows, a flat plaster ceiling, and a high, narrow interior whose proportions are as perfect as its details. Panelling, stalls, choir screen and reredos are all of wood, polished, inlaid, some local, some exotic – walnut, yew, Bermuda juniper, though the carvings are as usual made of the softer and lighter lime. The altarpiece seems almost like a frame without a picture, for it is a geometrical abstraction of cross and star-shaped intarsia. This apotheosis of pure meditation is framed by carvings of Baroque garlands, swirling acanthus, winged cherub heads, so exquisitely done that you might think the frame is the centrepiece. Although there is no documentation, the style suggests that this can only be by Grinling Gibbons, the virtuoso woodcarver of his day. These works in Trinity Chapel date from around 1693, between his commissions for Petworth House and Hampton Court.

And now to the garden. Trinity was the first college to have an open quadrangle. Begun in 1688, the Garden Quad has three ranges, with the east side opening out into the green. This was a departure from the monastic enclosure, such as you can still see in the neighbouring Durham Quad, which preserves the spirit of the medieval quadrangle. The original formal garden was replaced at the end of the

18th century by a wide expanse of lawn, and the claim that Trinity is a great place for a picnic is borne out by the number of Trinitarians that lie on the grass reading, sleeping or playing croquet – academic life at its best. I was reminded of their predecessor John Aubrey, who in the 17th century enjoyed what he called 'the greatest felicity of my life' here. The President at the time was the formidable Dr Ralph Kettell, who 'was wont to say that Seneca writes as a Boare does pisse, *scilicet* by jirkes… He was irreconcileable to long haire; called them hairy Scalpes.'

If you visit Oxford in the winter and go into Blackwell's in Broad Street, you'll be greeted by a real fire in a real fireplace. How many other bookshops offer their customers such a warm welcome? (At least they did when I last went there, and I hope they still do.) Somewhere on the wall I once read a sign which proclaimed the customer's 'Right to Browse', which is a pleasure in itself. But you will also buy something, if only to take possession of one of those Oxford-blue Blackwell carrier bags. In this store alone, you have a choice of about 250,000 books, and there are many thousands more in the other three Broad Street branches. If you can't find a book in Blackwell's, then it just doesn't exist.

At the point in the entrance where a different coloured carpet begins, the first Blackwell shop ends. Benjamin Blackwell opened it at 50 Broad Street in 1879, in the house with the Queen Anne façade. It covered an area of 12 square feet, and initially he dealt mainly in second-hand books. In those days you could have bought a first edition of Hobbes' *Leviathan* for 18 shillings (90 pence). In 1889 Benjamin's successor was born on the first floor above the shop. He grew up to be Sir Basil Blackwell, and it was he who in the 1920s founded his own publishing firm which, among others, published the first works of Graham Greene and Aldous Huxley when they were still students. At 8 Broad Street he opened the first children's bookshop in England, and when he began to run out of space upstairs, he expanded in the direction of Middle Earth. Blackwell's is probably the only firm that has spread itself out underneath a college – namely, the south-east quadrangle of Trinity. With its three miles of shelves, the subterranean Norrington Room made its way into the Guinness Book of Records.

When asked if he did any sport, Maurice Bowra, the Warden of Wadham, answered, 'Once a week I walk from Wadham down to Blackwell's – on a Saturday afternoon. And that's my weekly exercise.' Blackwell's is more than just a bookshop – it's an institution and in itself a piece of literary history. Colin Dexter's Inspector Morse was one of its customers, as is the hero of Javier Marías' novel *All Souls*, who on the second floor of Blackwell's comes across a don rapt in reading Pushkin and 'beating time to the perfect cadence of those iambic stanzas'.

B. H. Blackwell Ltd is still a family firm, now in its fifth generation, and it has six branches in Oxford, more than eighty throughout Britain, and its annual turnover is approximately £130 million.

The Old Ashmolean and the Sheldonian Theatre

'I am quite well aware ... that an Oxford decoration is a loftier distinction than is conferrable by any other university on either side of the ocean, and is worth twenty-five of any other, foreign or domestic.'
Mark Twain, on receiving an honorary doctorate at Oxford, 1907

Opposite Blackwell's and next to the Sheldonian Theatre stands a house that is full of astronomical, optical and mathematical instruments and apparatus. The Museum of the History of Science is England's oldest public museum, and was opened some seventy years before the British Museum in 1683. It was probably designed by a local master mason named Thomas Wood, and commissioned by the University of Oxford because twenty-six boxes came down the Thames from London. These contained the Tradescant Collection which Elias Ashmole (see p. 81) had passed on to Oxford, together with his own collection of rarities. The nucleus of this *Wunderkammer* is now housed in the Ashmolean Museum (see p. 156). The so-called Old Ashmolean in Broad Street was where the university originally held its science lectures, and the *Officina Chimica* (chemistry lab) down in the vaulted cellar was one of the first in England.

There they lie in their glass cases: clocks, compasses, globes, armillary spheres, quadrants, sextants, polyhedral sundials, and a thousand other instruments that symbolize the never-ending human desire to pin-point the time and the place, and to measure the earth, the sky and everything else. There are 150 astrolabes alone, some going back as far as the 9th century. These instruments were used to measure the altitude of the sun and stars – engraved discs of gleaming brass, of which this is the biggest collection in the world. Such instruments have a beauty and a magic of their own, designed with the utmost precision and elegance. There are miniature Japanese compasses, barometers, thermometers, aiming devices for gunners, dental and surgical instruments, a collection of early cameras, kaleidoscopes, cinematographic apparatus, Lewis Carroll's photographic equipment, Charles

Babbage's calculator, and George III's silver universal microscope. And there is even the blackboard on which Einstein chalked his ground-breaking formula on 16 May 1931, during his Oxford lecture on the Theory of Relativity. Einstein stayed for two summers in Christ Church. 'He divided his time between his mathematics and playing the violin; as one crossed the quad, one was privileged to hear the strains coming from his rooms,' recalled a Fellow. 'His general conversation was not stimulating. I am afraid I did not have the sense that, so far as human affairs were concerned, I was in the presence of a wise man or a deep thinker.'

In the staircase of the Old Ashmolean is a glass dial – a sundial window with the inscription: *Vesper in ambiguo est / Mora noxia, cras nil*: 'The evening is uncertain, hesitation harmful, tomorrow nothing' (17th century). Along with all the astro-nomical and mathematical instruments, for the manufacture of which Oxford was already famous in the Middle Ages, there are zoological rarities: horns, antlers, the swords of swordfish, and a collection of birds' eggs. It is this mixture of science and the miracles of nature that gives the Old Ashmolean its incomparable charm.

Back outside on Broad Street we come to a strange phalanx of stylites in a semi-circle in front of the Sheldonian Theatre. They are called Emperors' Heads, but these monstrous stone heads look less like Roman Caesars than college Masters. Whoever these bearded gentlemen may be – gods or philosophers – their aura of antiquity succeeds both in capturing and in parodying the *genius loci*. What we see today is the third generation of heads, made in 1972 – copies of the previous two generations that had mercifully succumbed to the weather. Originally in 1669 there were fourteen of them, placed like Roman hermae and commissioned by the architect of the Sheldonian, none other than Christopher Wren.

Wren's model for the D-shaped Sheldonian was the open-air Theatre of Marcel-lus in Rome, although the English climate naturally demanded a roof. At that time, Wren was a young professor of astronomy with no experience of architecture, but the roof is already a spectacular sign of his genius. It is flat, with no supporting columns, and spans 80 feet by 70 feet, hovering overhead like a great gliding bird, and it astonished his contemporaries. There were no iron girders in those days, which makes his structure of supporting beams all the more extraordinary. It is well worth climbing up through the roof trusses, not just to admire Wren's inge-nuity, but also to see the octagonal lantern that was added in 1838, and from which there is a magnificent view.

The Sheldonian was commissioned and paid for by Gilbert Sheldon, Arch-bishop of Canterbury, who was Warden of All Souls and a personal friend of Wren's. From the beginning, after its official opening in 1669, it fulfilled several different functions: degree ceremonies, the conferral of honours which had previously taken place in St Mary's, meetings of the Congregation, the election of the Chancellor, lectures and concerts. Generations of students and scholars, writers, politicians, and public figures from all over the world have made their entrance on this stage beneath the Baroque sky of virtues painted by Robert Streeter, whose ceiling depicts religion, art and science triumphing over envy, ignorance, hatred and malice – an optimistic allegory of the academic world.

Handel held concerts in the Sheldonian, and in 1834 there was a standing ovation for the Duke of Wellington when he was elected Chancellor and, to the great delight of the students, got into a muddle with his Latin. He was impressed, though, by his reception from the students, and announced, 'Let these boys loose in the state in which I saw them, and give them a political object to carry, and they would revolutionize any nation under the sun.' In 1992, the French star of deconstruction Jacques Derrida earned the applause that a more down-to-earth Cambridge had denied him. A year earlier, Giovanni Agnelli, head of Fiat, also found himself among the Oxford lions, for he was the first industrialist to hold the annual Romanes Lecture. This is the most prestigious public lecture, which is held in the Sheldonian during Trinity Term and was inaugurated in 1892 by prime minister Gladstone, followed in later years by such illustrious speakers as Theodore Roosevelt, Karl Popper and Saul Bellow.

One Saturday in May, I attended a Degree Ceremony here. With Ascot hats, cameras and proud expressions, the parents, guests and dignitaries all sat crammed together on the benches – which must be the most uncomfortable seats in England – and up in the galleries, whose wooden columns are painted to look like marble. Leading the way are the Marshal and Bedels (heralds) with their silver maces, followed by the Vice-Chancellor, who is accompanied by two Proctors, the officers in charge of undergraduate discipline. College by college the candidates are called forth, and gather in gown and mortarboard behind their respective Masters, who presents them to the Vice-Chancellor. He then dubs them in traditional academic style by knocking them on the head with a Bible – which is why this ceremony is also known as 'Bible bashing'. Then they leave the room, only to return shortly afterwards in their new gowns, and as bachelor, master or doctor they then bow or curtsey to the Vice-Chancellor. 'Forget it. I love everything but don't expect me to understand what it's all about,' says the American Harvey Metcalfe when the ceremony is explained to him in Jeffrey Archer's *Not a Penny More, Not a Penny Less*.

The Sheldonian is also the setting for the climax of all of Oxford's rituals, the Encaenia, at the end of the academic year. This takes place in June, on the Wednesday of the last week of Trinity Term, when the 'Noblemen, Heads of Houses, Doctors, Proctors and Gentlemen' assemble on the invitation of the Chancellor, wearing the various coloured gowns – scarlet, dark blue, grey – that denote their faculties and titles. After enjoying Lord Crewe's 'Benefaction', the traditional breakfast of fruit and champagne, in one of the nearby colleges, they make their way in procession to the Sheldonian, where honorary doctorates are conferred amid a veritable pantomime of Latin formulae, bowings and scrapings, mortar-boards coming off, mortarboards going on, in a kind of academic *commedia dell'arte*. Afterwards, though, they are all given the chance to unwind with lunch-eon at All Souls, a garden party at Trinity, strawberries and cream, and so much champagne that many of the dons end up with legs as crooked as earlier their faces had been straight.

Joseph Haydn, Isaac Stern, Archbishop Desmond Tutu, Federal President Roman Herzog, UN General Secretary Kofi Annan, EU President Romano Prodi, Nadine Gordimer, Seamus Heaney, Willy Brandt, Anna Achmatova, Judi Dench, Placido Domingo…the list of those who have received an honorary doc-torate is longer even than the face of Margaret Thatcher when in 1985 she did not receive one. That was the first time that Oxford had refused the honour to a prime minister from its own ranks, and it was a protest against her policy on Higher Education. The Iron Lady proceeded to extract her revenge by founding the Mar-garet Thatcher Chair of Enterprise Studies– in Cambridge. A real handbagging to Oxford.

The classical end to Broad Street is provided by the Clarendon Building (1711–15). It has a monumental portico with columns, and on the balustraded roof stand the Muses. This temple-like building was designed by Nicholas Hawksmoor to house the University Press, but it is also a kind of propylon to those other great temples of learning, the Schools and the Bodleian, which can be reached through a barrel-vaulted passage. The Clarendon was named after the 1st Earl of Clarendon, who was a close adviser to King Charles I during the Civil War. His *History of the Rebellion* (1702–4) was a best-seller, and its royalties helped to finance the new building. In 1830, the OUP once again moved to a larger site (see p. 193). The Vice-Chancellor now has an apartment in the Clarendon, but the rest of the rooms are part of the Bodleian. Underground, however, sit the 'bulldogs', the guardians of the university, watching their monitors in case of any trouble. The silver maces are kept there too. Ted East, former Marshal of the university, showed me the mace of the Theological Faculty. Engraved on the head are the words *EGO SUM VIA* [I am the way], and at the bottom is the biblical continuation *VERITAS*

ET VITA [the truth and the life]. When the herald walks in front of the Chancellor, he holds the mace with its head upwards, but when he walks in front of the Vice-Chancellor, he holds it the other way round. Such are the fine details of Oxford's rituals.

Between Wadham and New College

'We drank 8 Bottles of Port, one Bottle of Madeira besides Arrac Punch,
Beer and Cyder. I carried my drinking exceedingly well indeed.'
Rev. James Woodforde, Fellow of New College, 27 July 1774

The Oxford style is epitomized by Lord Peter Wimsey's proposal to Harriet Vane: as casual as possible, carried out at the traffic lights on the corner of Holywell Street, though spiced with the true passion of the Latin lover: '*Placetne, magistra?*' – an allusion to the formula used during the degree ceremony in the Sheldonian when the graduand is presented. The corner of Holywell Street is still a favourite haunt of the students – or to be precise, the pub on the corner is, which is The King's Arms, commonly referred to as KA. It offers live music and ale from the barrel. Its name goes back to 1607, in honour of James I, and like The Mitre it actually belongs to a college – Wadham, which rents out the top rooms and neighbouring houses to its students.

A sweet and heavy scent wafts over the walls of Wadham and into Parks Road. It is the scent of a pendent silver lime. But we're not going to the garden yet. First we shall take a look at Wadham's buildings, for nowhere in Oxford is there a more impressive example of early 17th-century college architecture than this. It was begun in 1610 and completed in 1613. It is a unified whole that has scarcely been altered since, apart from some extensions. The frontispiece of the quadrangle shows the two founders, Dorothy and Nicholas Wadham, landowners from Somerset, and above them a statue of James I. There is a classical symmetry in the ground plan and the façades, which deliberately combine various medieval stylistic features: Gothic windows and crenellations, the hammer-beam roof of the hall, the fan vault of the gatehouse. This stylistic continuation of the past corresponded to a statute obliging students and Fellows to attend chapel twice a day, at five in the morning and eight at night, an early 17th-century imposition of monasticism on academic life.

It was in Wadham that a group of great minds came together and gave birth to an idea that became The Royal Society. They included scientists like Robert Boyle and Robert Hooke, and their contemporary Christopher Wren. Later the 'People's Republic of Wadham' established a reputation for its left-wing politics, and the former Labour leader Michael Foot studied here.

Out in the garden now, and it's time to admire Wadham's trees: the copper beech of 1796, the great tulip tree, the dawn redwood from the province of Szechuan. Below the branches of a Katsura tree sits Oxford's strangest monument to a don: an empty bronze armchair, from the back of which pokes the head of Sir Maurice Bowra, a much respected teacher and Warden of Wadham. From the 1930s, this sharp-tongued classical philologist was regarded as the Falstaff of his field – a virtuoso conversationalist and hedonist. When asked what were his beliefs, Bowra reputedly replied, 'Looking forward to meeting God. Got six questions to put to Him. *Unanswerable.*'

When you turn the corner at the King's Arms, and go into Holywell Street, you will see Georgian plaster façades and half-timbered gables, with a mixture of 17th- and 18th-century houses that make this into one of the most beautiful streets in the city. Stone coats of arms on the façades announce the owners: Wadham, New College, and particularly Merton, which has been the biggest landlord in Holywell Street since the 13th century. Here you will find some of those few houses of the late Middle Ages to have survived the expansion of the college, for most of them were demolished.

From Bath Place a lane full of picturesque nooks and crannies leads off to the Turf Tavern, one of the legendary centres of Oxford's pub culture. In the public rooms, beneath the low wooden beams of the ceilings ('Duck or Grouse'), and outside in the beer gardens, which on winter evenings are warmed by flickering braziers, the students sit drinking their pint of Adnams or Old Speckled Hen – real ale on draught. It is scarcely surprising that the Turf was one of Inspector Morse's favourite pubs, and it was also here that Thomas Hardy's mason Jude suddenly came upon the wife who had left him some years before.

As simple and modest as a Methodist chapel, Holywell Music Room is another of the attractions in Holywell Street. It was opened in 1748 (see p. 80) and has four round-arched windows, an organ, and those typical hard wooden benches on which St Cecilia's devotees drink in their chamber music as if they were sitting on the lawns at Glyndebourne. Two chandeliers give this ascetic room an unexpected glow. Once they were hanging in Westminster Hall, during the coronation of King George IV, but later the king gave them to Wadham, who are the owners of Holywell Music Room. It has been described as Europe's oldest and coldest concert hall. I had the privilege of attending a recital by the Russian virtuoso Alexander Ardakov – a wonderful performance, featuring a piano and two heaters right beside the pianist.

Oxford is full of music. Every evening during term-time a little group of black-clad boys goes from Mansfield Road into Holywell Street, and then disappears into the gatehouse of New College. When William of Wykeham, Bishop of Winchester, founded his Oxford college in 1379, he made provision for sixteen choristers, and together with a dozen older singers they have been practising for over 600 years, are now world-famous, and still meet in the chapel for evensong. I never heard a finer rendering of Mozart's *Agnus Dei* (see p. 77).

The elongated neo-Gothic wing with the present main entrance in Holywell Street dates from the late 19th century. Behind it is the college that William built, right up against the medieval city wall, like a fortified monastery. With seventy scholars and a Warden it was then the biggest of all the colleges. As Lord Chancellor under two kings, the bishop knew that both Crown and Church needed qualified people to run their affairs, and so he founded New College and also, as a preliminary rung on the ladder to greatness, a Latin school, Winchester College. This systematic education from public school through to university was a new concept, and became a pedagogical model that was followed some sixty years later by Henry VI with his double foundation of Eton and King's College, Cambridge. Until the middle of the 19th century, New College only accepted Wykehamists, who had learned their Latin in the exclusive surroundings of Winchester. Students entered New College between the ages of fifteen and twenty, and the rules were strict, in accordance with Wykeham's motto: 'Manners Maketh Man', thus anticipating the Oxonian ideal of the true gentleman. The bishop did not like football or chess, which he considered to be 'dishonourable games', but times have changed and they are no longer banned. Nor, since 1979, are women. Virginia Woolf visited the college in 1933, but was not exactly dazzled by the Fellows: 'Represent culture, politics, worldly wisdom gilt with letters. Nothing to whizz one off one's perch at New College: all in good taste, & very kind. But Lord to live like that!'

The educational vision of the founder was reflected by the architectural design, which was both generous and original. Firstly, all the buildings were conceived as a unit, and after just six years, work was more or less complete – probably carried out under the supervision of the royal master mason William Wynford, with whom Wykeham also worked in Winchester. All around the Great Quad are the permanent elements of college life: on the north side the hall and chapel back to back (as they were later in All Souls and Magdalen, which were both founded by Wykehamists); in the east wing the library, and to the south accommodation for the seventy scholars, with students and Fellows for the first time under the same roof; in the gatehouse, above the entrance – an example also followed by later colleges – the residence of the Warden, who from here could keep an eye on the whole quad, the entrance and New College Lane. Today the old gate is opened by a numerical code. With perfect symmetry, an oval lawn nestles within the rectangular quad – also a prototype for college architecture.

New College Chapel is large and beautiful. From the ante-chapel you go into a long, tall nave. At the eastern end, filling the wall, are rows of stone apostles and saints. This reredos and the hammer-beam roof with its winged angels seem authentically Gothic, but this is only thanks to the restorative work carried out by Sir George Gilbert Scott (1877–81). The late 14th-century stalls, however, still contain much of their original material, with carved misericords that tell fascinating stories: a lecture, a stabbing among students, acrobats, a six-headed monster – a mixture of everyday scenes and nightmares straight from the Middle Ages. With its eight windows (1385–90), New College Chapel has one of the very few virtually complete series of medieval stained glass, designed and executed by Thomas Glazier of Oxford, who was one of the earliest known exponents of the art. It is said that he used his own face as a model for every saint. There are three other exceptional items to note: William of Wykeham's mitre, which is a virtuoso piece of gold work from the late 14th century; Jacob Epstein's dramatic *Lazarus* in the ante-chapel (see p. 68); and the west window of the ante-chapel, with a *Nativity* and the Seven Virtues below, designed by Joshua Reynolds in 1777. This was his only large-scale window, and the shepherd dressed in a saffron-coloured coat and looking at us over his shoulder is a self-portrait. 'Washy colours' was Horace Walpole's verdict, with which Nikolaus Pevsner agreed, but I beg to differ. The transparency of the enamel paint and the subtlety of the grisaille and sepia tones make this a window to remember – but go and see it for yourself.

A mighty holm oak with blue and black foliage arches over the lawn in the cloister, and on the tracery are tangles of honeysuckle and roses. The cloisters west of the chapel, completed around 1400, were used for processions, funerals and academic meditation. They incorporate the monastic tradition of the college, while the gardens are part of its country-house character. The Garden Quad is an inner quadrangle that opens out onto the garden. It was begun in 1682. The Palladian side wings are linked together by filigree wrought-iron railings whose gate is decorated with Wykeham's motto: 'Manners Maketh Man'. There the students lie on the grass and read, though occasionally one will stand up and do a cartwheel to impress his girlfriend…youth and summertime….

The garden has two distinguishing features: the city wall and the Mound. The massive walls are of local, weatherproof coralline limestone, made in the 13th century, with battlements and bastions whose task it is now to protect and defend the flowerbeds of the gardens. The Mound, in the centre of the lawn, was built in 1594, but in the interim has shrunk considerably and is covered with vegetation. This is a relic of what was once an elaborate formal garden. It was a hill with a view, which the Fellows of New College used to call 'Parnassus'; this certainly endowed it with rather more dignity than 'The Mound'.

In 1856 the American author Nathaniel Hawthorne stood beneath the trees of New College. They had, he wrote, 'lived a quiet life here for centuries, and have been nursed and tended with such care, and so sheltered from the rude winds, that certainly they must have been the happiest of all trees.' Had he had the good fortune to study here himself, no doubt he would have been the happiest of all students, for such 'a sweet, quiet, sacred, stately seclusion cannot exist anywhere else.' Let not these words be read in Cambridge.

North-West of Carfax

'There is more going on than meets the eye of a man walking
through the streets. It is a unique centre of thought and religion –
the intellectual and spiritual granary of this country.'
Thomas Hardy, *Jude the Obscure*, 1895

From Carfax Tower, Cornmarket Street runs in a northerly direction. 'The Corn' was Oxford's corn market in the Middle Ages, and the street was full of merchants, craftsmen and taverns. In the middle was a pillory – the stocks for punishing petty criminals, like butchers or bakers who had cheated their customers. That ended in 1810. The street is still a hive of activity with banks, shopping centres, fast-food restaurants, and a house with a Shakespearean connection.

At no. 3, above a betting shop, the Oxford Aunts run an agency for nursing staff. I was amazed when the manageress rolled the wooden panelling to one side and revealed murals from the middle of the 16th century: roses, grapes, passion flowers painted on an ochre-coloured background, above which is a frieze with various religious maxims, like 'feare God above all thynge'. This Painted Room was part of the Crown Tavern, and the landlord was a friend of Shakespeare's, who used to lodge here when he was travelling between Stratford and London. The story also goes that the landlord had a beautiful wife whose son, Sir William Davenant – a popular dramatist himself – boasted that Shakespeare was not only his godfather but also his father. What is certainly true is that Shakespeare's theatre company gave several performances in Oxford between 1604 and 1613.

A few blocks further on is the Golden Cross Shopping Arcade, and here you may actually see the remains of the Golden Cross Inn: an inner courtyard with half-timbered, plastered wings (15th–17th century) and fragments of frescoes. It was the olden-day variation on the modern pizzeria, where for centuries town and gown would come to eat and drink, until it was restored to death in the 1980s. Opposite, in the Clarendon Shopping Centre, the medieval intruder (the Clarendon Hotel) has been completely demolished.

How Do You Become Prime Minister?
The Oxford Union Society

'This House prefers women on top.'
Motion before the Oxford Union, 1998

I n St Michael's Street, off 'The Corn', is the headquarters of the Oxford Union Society. No club in Oxford has better toilets, according to John Betjeman, but these are not the only qualities in this legendary debating society. At least once a week, generally on a Thursday evening, the great debating chamber of almost a thousand seats is filled to bursting point. All that happens here is that people talk. Only in Oxford could a debating society be as popular as a disco. The topics are not always original, and the rules are very strict, but where else could you find yourself engaged in a live discussion with Bill Clinton, Diego Maradona, Gore Vidal and other stars from all walks of life? And what better place to start your own course to stardom?

When the Tory politician Michael Heseltine began his studies at Pembroke College, at his very first evening meal in hall he banged his glass with his spoon. 'Why did you do that?' asked his neighbour. 'Practising to be President of the Oxford Union,' replied 'Hezza'. 'Why do you want to do that?' 'It's the first step to being Prime Minister.' Michael Heseltine did indeed become President of the Union in 1954, but although he had a successful career in Westminster, he never got to the very top. Seven others did, including Gladstone, Asquith, Macmillan and Heath, not to mention innumerable ministers, bishops, judges and diplomats who honed their public-speaking talents here.

The Oxford United Debating Society, as it was originally called, was started in 1823 by a group of aristocratic students and their friends. At first they met in the colleges of the various members so that they would not attract too much attention, for at that time public debate – especially on political and religious themes – was frowned on by the authorities. But after a few years, the club began to gain a reputation and a degree of self-confidence, especially when in 1830 a certain old Etonian took over the presidency. His name was William Gladstone. It was at the Oxford Union that this great debater first revealed his political gifts, and by the age of twenty-three he was already in the House of Commons. Four times in all he became prime minister for the Liberals, and even when he was eighty-three years old, he could still talk for two and a half hours in Parliament. It was he who once said, 'To call a man an Oxford man is to pay him the highest compliment that can be paid to any human being.'

In the middle of the 19th century, the Union moved to a home of its own in St Michael's Street – a collection of Victorian brick houses. The most interesting feature from an art-historical point of view is the Old Library, which was the original Debating Hall of 1857. This high, neo-Gothic room has a gallery all round and wall paintings that no one would take any notice of were it not for the fact that they are early works of the Pre-Raphaelites, heroically disastrous illustrations of the Arthurian legends (see p. 64). A new and bigger debating hall was made to measure in 1878 by Alfred Waterhouse, at a time when the nation was enjoying a peak of political self-confidence. As in the House of Commons, the speakers sit opposite one another on the ubiquitous wooden benches, flanked by the busts of former prime ministers. The President sits on a raised platform, dressed in tails with a white bow tie, and on either side sit the treasurer and the librarian, while the secretary is in front of them. All of these offices have been increasingly occupied by women since the late 1960s. The 'honourable speakers' present their case for or against the motion from dispatch boxes with brass trimmings, there are speeches from the floor, and finally a division when the 'honourable members' vote by leaving the room through the door for the ayes or the door for the noes. It is an exact parallel if not a parody of the procedure in the House of Commons.

The nation's problems and prejudices, moral principles and current political crises have been debated here: Northern Ireland, the abolition of the monarchy, the death penalty, armed intervention by the UN, homosexuality in the army. 'This House believes that in Socialism lies the only solution to the problems facing this Country.' That was a motion debated in 1932. One year later there took place the most famous debate in the history of the Union. Shortly after Hitler had seized power, a student from St John's proposed: 'That this House will in no circumstances fight for its King and country'. The vote in favour of pacifism shocked the nation and was seen by many as a betrayal of the country (see p. 225). Churchill condemned it as 'that abject, squalid, shameless avowal' and never went to the Union again.

Other resolutions have created a major stir beyond the confines of the Union itself: in 1975 the House voted for Europe, but in 1991 it voted against. In 1996, with wonderful foresight, the motion was: 'This House believes that Tony Blair would make a great Conservative Prime Minister'. Some major debates have been televised live by the BBC, as if they were an accurate barometer of the nation. Cambridge and other universities also have their debating societies, but none of them carry the same weight and prestige as the Oxford Union. This is partly due to the calibre of their guest speakers. Ronald Reagan, Douglas Adams, the Dalai Lama, their own former Chancellor Lord Jenkins, Malcolm X, Mother Teresa, Yasser Arafat, Helmut Schmidt, Joseph Beuys, George Soros, Lord Saatchi, and a host of famous authors from W. B. Yeats to Toni Morrison – all of them have spoken at the Union, and they were not paid a penny. Here the American Defence Minister Caspar Weinberger had his first public set-to with a member of the Peace Movement, and here the Sinn Fein leader Gerry Adams was allowed to defend his point of view when he was banned from appearing on British television. 'The Union has become more famous than the University itself,' reckoned Lord Jenkins. In 1992 US President George Bush Sr, in the first televised debate with his challenger Bill Clinton, confessed, 'I'm not a professional debater. I'm not an Oxford man.' It was a vain attempt to present himself as a homespun Yale man in contrast to the ultra-sophisticated Oxonian.

The yearly motion of no confidence in Her Majesty's government is as much a part of the routine as the Farewell Debate – fun and games at the end of term, with motions like 'God is an Englishman'. The union has made very few changes in its rules, but many in its profile. In the 19th century it was Conservative, but in the 1930s became a forum for the left. In 1975, however, the Labour politician Barbara Castle complained that it had become 'the cadet class of the Establishment'. But even this independent institution can scarcely avoid being affected by the *Zeitgeist*, and in addition to the big names from politics and culture, it has turned increasingly to entertainers and fashion and media stars like Jerry Hall and Michael Jackson, not to mention headline-grabbers like O. J. Simpson and Gennifer Flowers.

The Oxford Union has long since shed its image as a gentlemen's club for the upper middle classes, for now it is a massive organization with more than 10,000 members in Oxford itself, and around 100,000 'live members'. For a yearly fee of some £170, it offers its members far more than debates. There are films, cabarets, quizzes, fashion shows, a bar with disco, a restaurant, snooker – all under one roof. There is also a library with about 100,000 volumes, and the most comfortable leather armchairs in the city. Only in its original field does the Union have a modern competitor: L'Chaim Society, founded in 1988 by the American rabbi Shmuel Boteach. This flamboyant 'Moses of Oxford', author of *Dating Secrets of the Ten Commandments* and various other best-selling sex books, has made his debating society into the second largest student union in Oxford, with around 2,000 members of all confessions.

Murder in St Frideswide,
Tea in the Randolph

'But he had not expected to find a corpse up there, had he?'
Colin Dexter, *Service of All the Dead*, 1979

William Morris's marriage lasted somewhat longer than his fresco in the Oxford Union. In 1859 he married Jane Burden just a few steps away from the Union in St Michael's. Built of rubble, the west tower soars skywards at the corner of Cornmarket and Ship Street, a great relic of the early 11th century. The narrow, round-arched twin windows with their thick columns and 'long and short work' are typical of the late Anglo-Saxon style. The church itself, however, is of more recent vintage, and one outstanding feature is the so-called Lily Window in the Lady Chapel: Christ crucified on a lily – part of an Annunciation dating from the 15th century. The tower of St Michael at the North Gate (the full name of the church) was originally precisely that, as it was built at the northern gate of the city; next to and above the gate lay the *bocardo* or prison. This medieval symbiosis ended in 1771, when the city gate was demolished.

Right behind St Michael's stands the next church: St Mary Magdalen. Which of the two is St Frideswide, the scene of those horrific serial killings in Colin Dexter's *Service of All the Dead*? The Gothic font, the sweet smell of incense, the curtain next to the organ behind which is the entrance to the tower – Dexter's collage is so skilful that you will have as much trouble identifying the church as Inspector Morse has identifying the murderer. St Mary Magdalen is also a little confusing architecturally, for it is as broad as it is long. There has been a great deal of rebuilding and extending since Norman times, much of it Victorian – 'painfully so' in the words of the sexton. It is seen as the centre of the High Church, with its traditional Anglo-Catholic liturgy. Candles burn in front of the portrait of Charles I, the martyred king, whose feast day is celebrated every year on 30 January with a High Mass. One might add a candle for 'all the dead', and also for John Aubrey, the great biographer, who was buried in 'St Mary Mags' in 1697.

On the north side of the church is Martyrs' Memorial, in commemoration of Bishops Cranmer, Latimer and Ridley, not far from the place of their terrible execution (see p. 137). The monument to these heroic heretics was installed in 1843, at the height of the theological disputes surrounding the Oxford Movement. For art historians, George Gilbert Scott's construction serves as an example of archaeologically correct neo-Gothic; for students it is another tower to stick a chamber pot on.

An even more popular meeting place than the steps of the memorial is the Morse Bar in the neighbouring Randolph Hotel. Since its opening in 1866, the Randolph has offered the plushest Victorian comfort, and if you want tea in style, or a champagne cocktail called Dreaming Spire or Oxford Blue (vodka with curaçao), this is the place for you. Otherwise, just go and eat there every five years, as the Oxonians do after electing their new Professor of Poetry. Sir Osbert Lancaster's illustrations for *Zuleika Dobson* are here, though their local fame far outweighs their quality. In the Chapters Bar (as it was originally called), Morse sat recovering from the shock of seeing the corpse in Room 310: 'Mrs Laura Stratton lay neatly supine on the nearer side of the double bed. She wore a full-length, peach-coloured dressing robe and (so far as Morse could see) little else. And she was dead.' A tourist dies, a work of art disappears – Colin Dexter's *The Jewel That Was Ours* leads us directly to the Ashmolean Museum.

Ashmolean Museum, Worcester College

'It was not Napoleon
Who founded the Ashmolean
He hardly had a chance
Living mostly in France.'
Edmund Clerihew Bentley (1875–1956)*

There are about 400 university collections in Great Britain, including some of international renown: the Courtauld Institute in London, the Hunterian Art Gallery in Glasgow, the Fitzwilliam in Cambridge – but there is only one with a chamber of wonders. It's on the first floor of the Ashmolean, Room 27. A Chinese hibiscus goblet carved out of rhinoceros horn, cherry pips and plum stones exquisitely carved, Henry VIII's stirrup, an Eskimo paddle, a chain of cat's teeth – a vast array of strange and exotic objects are on display in this little room. There is

---

*A graduate of Merton College, whose four-line nonsense poems became known as 'clerihews'.

also 'the robe of the King of Virginia', a deerskin coat embroidered with shells, believed to have belonged to an American Indian chief, Powhatan, the father of Pocahontas. These 'Rarities and Curiosities' were collected by John Tradescant the Elder and his son John Tradescant the Younger in the early 17th century, and this Cabinet of Curiosities became the basis of the Ashmolean Museum.

The fact that the history of a museum should begin with two gardeners is in itself a rarity. John Tradescant the Elder was 'Keeper of His Majesty's Gardens, Vines and Silkworms' in Stuart times – a botanist and plant-hunter who during his travels collected anything and everything natural, man-made, exotic, eccentric that the world could offer. 'Tradescant's Ark' was the name given to his collection, and his son opened it up for public viewing in their house in Lambeth. Its move to Oxford came about because of Elias Ashmole. A rather pompous gentleman, in a full-bottomed wig, a red velvet coat, and the gold chains of honour awarded to him for his *History of the Order of the Garter* – thus he appears in his portrait (*c.* 1681), the frame of which is a considerably greater work of art, having been carved by Grinling Gibbons. The story goes that John Tradescant the Younger was tricked when drunk into bequeathing his rarities to Ashmole, who then gave them, together with his own collection (notably of coins), to the University of Oxford. The museum was opened on Broad Street in 1683 as a centre for scientific study, with Ashmole's collection as merely a sideshow. The Old Ashmolean had nothing to do with art, and this did not change until the 19th century, when the university built a museum to house all the sculptures, paintings, drawings and archaeological objects that it had acquired over the years. The University Galleries opened in 1845, and in 1908 officially changed their name to the Ashmolean Museum.

The client wanted a building of 'Greek character', and that was what Charles Robert Cockerell (who was also Architect to the Bank of England) delivered. He designed a museum with elements of the Greek revival at a time when this style had long since been dismissed as old-fashioned on the Continent. From the mountains of Arcadia and the Temple of Apollo Epicurus at Bassae, Cockerell copied the Ionic columns and the monumental portico, where Apollo is enthroned above the sculptures on the pediment. He combined this classicism with a marked emphasis on the Baroque, with projecting wings that were taller than the central section: white Portland stone alternating with yellowish Bath stone. In the east wing, on St Giles' Street, this movement culminates in a giant order of Ionic columns crowned with four female figures. This is the entrance to the Taylorian Institution, and the four women personify the countries whose languages have been studied there since 1845: France, Italy, Germany and Spain. The Taylorian was named after Sir Robert Taylor, an 18th-century architect who left his fortune to the university 'for the teaching and improving the European Languages'.

One of the first comparatists of the Taylorian was a polyglot Indologist and mythologist who had emigrated from Germany: Friedrich Max Müller, a Victorian polymath whose chief claim to fame in Oxford was to have initiated the study of comparative religion.

The Ashmolean is sheer delight for visitors, not least because it is smaller than the National Gallery and the British Museum, but is of the same quality. Its collections of drawings by the old masters, archaeology and eastern art are the most important outside London. The gallery of antiquities on the ground floor is a treat in itself, with Roman statues, busts, beautiful stelae, and the heart of the collection – a piece of collecting history – the famous 'Arundel Marbles', which go back to Thomas Howard, Earl of Arundel, England's first classical connoisseur in the 17th century. If we stay on the ground floor, next to the Egyptian section we shall see a display of eastern art which matches that in the Victoria and Albert: early ceramics from the Han and Sun dynasties, blue-and-white Ming porcelain, Indian illuminations, and above them all the reflective calm of a spiritual guide, the fig-wood figure of a Chinese Bodhisattva from the 13th century.

On the first floor the main focus is on archaeology and European art. Cycladic idols, Luristan bronzes, Etruscan statuettes, Assyrian reliefs from the Palace of Nimrud – all finds from legendary archaeological expeditions, many of them by Oxford men, the most famous being Sir Arthur Evans, who excavated the Palace at Knossos. It was thanks to him that the Ashmolean acquired the biggest collection of Minoan art outside Crete. There is a storage jar whose swirling octopus might have been painted by Picasso. The pottery alone is a history lesson: vases with black and red figures, dishes, amphorae and lecythi, showing not only the complete development of Greek ceramic art, but also giving a panorama of Greek life and mythology.

If you asked me to pick just one room, it would be Room 39, Renaissance Department, despite Maurice Bowra's verdict: 'Too many Gaddis and Daddis'. Madonnas by Giotto, Bellini, Giorgione; Titian's *Giacomo Doria* and Bronzino's Mannerist portrait of Giovanni de' Medici; *cassones* and ivory miniatures, and one glowing nocturnal painting that shines out even in this galaxy of star attractions: Uccello's *Hunt in the Forest*, a masterpiece of precision and painterly passion, so evocative that you can almost hear the calls of the hunters. The bronze statuettes from the Renaissance are part of the Ashmolean's substantial collection of sculptures, and I will mention just one more highlight, which you will find in Room 43:

the marble bust of the young Christopher Wren, one of those true-to-life, English Baroque portraits (by Edward Pierce, 1673).

Almost hidden away in the staircase vestibule on the first floor are some of the most priceless items of all. You press a button, and out of the darkness of the display cases come heads and hands, the agonies of a crucifixion, the flowing mane of a stallion, a horseman falling – these are just a few of the drawings by Raphael, Michelangelo, Titian, carefully preserved because they are so sensitive to light. In the Print Room, which can only be seen by appointment, there are no less than sixty-eight drawings by Raphael – the largest collection in any single museum. They were part of the estate of the painter Sir Thomas Lawrence, as were the fifty-four drawings by Michelangelo. But even these are only a small part of the collection. Botticelli, Guercino, Tiepolo, Grünewald, Dürer, Holbein, Rembrandt, Watteau and all the other great names are there in the Print Room. There is also an important collection of 19th-century German drawings, most of which were donated by an emigrant from Berlin, the art historian Grete Ring, a niece of the painter Max Liebermann.

Such donations have constantly added to the Ashmolean's storehouse of treasures, from John Ruskin's gift of Turner drawings (as well as his own) to the Impressionist works of Camille Pissarro, bequeathed by his son Lucien, who was also a painter and who settled in England. Thomas Girtin, John Sell Cotman and J. M. W. Turner, the great English watercolourists, are as well represented here as the satirist Thomas Rowlandson, the visionary Romantic Samuel Palmer, and Edward Burne-Jones, whose painted cupboard – a wedding present for his friend William Morris – is one of the attractions in the Pre-Raphaelite room on the second floor (see p. 65). There you will also find a wonderful collection of Dutch still lifes, botanical cabinet paintings from the 17th century. You may, however, prefer the early Worcester porcelain, the Huguenot silverware, the coins and medals, the watches and engraved glasses, or at the end of the show, the silent world of the Hill Collection. The star turn in this orchestra of musical instruments is a Stradivarius of 1716. One of its owners used to boast about it but would never produce it, until one day someone said that this violin was like the Messiah: always promised, never appeared. Now it rests in its glass case, the famous Messiah Violin.

I must mention one more star. It is the centre-point of Colin Dexter's *The Jewel That Was Ours*: the Anglo-Saxon King Alfred's Jewel. Made of gold, enamel and rock crystal, it bears the inscription '*Aelfred mec heht gewycran*': Alfred had me made. It is probably the endpiece of a pointer used in reading manuscripts, and it dates from 871–899.

The Ashmolean entered the 21st century with another extension, in neoclassical Retro-style – the last twitch of postmodernism. A rotunda following the pattern of a Greek round temple leads from St John Street to the new Sackler Library by Robert Adam (2001). This is part of a larger extension project that includes a gallery devoted to 19th and 20th-century Chinese painting, a centre for antiquities (by Evans & Shalev), and a gallery for modern art. Perhaps then we shall once again see the Ashmolean's one and only Cézanne, which was stolen on the eve of the new millennium.

The Ashmolean can't complain about its neighbours. Beaumont Street is the only fully preserved Georgian street in Oxford, built between 1822 and 1833. The three-storey terraced houses have ashlar façades whose proportions are as harmonious as the individual details – porches with columns, pedimented doorways, cast-iron balconies. Beaumont Street is an address for lawyers, doctors, stockbrokers and architects, and it was a great investment for St John's because all the houses belong to the college, which had them built in the first place.

On the southern side of the street, diagonally opposite the Ashmolean, is the Playhouse, which opened in 1938. It is the best known of Oxford's four theatres, and its stage has been graced by such stars as Dirk Bogarde and Alec Guinness, though none caused such a stir as those who performed in a 1966 production of Christopher Marlowe's *Dr Faustus*. Straight from Hollywood came Richard Burton and Elizabeth Taylor. It was a sort of homecoming for Burton, as he had spent six months studying English at Exeter College – long enough for him to be claimed as an Old Boy of Exeter, and to persuade him to hand over the funds to build the Burton-Taylor Theatre. The Oxford University Dramatic Society has staged many of its productions in The Playhouse, which has been the springboard for countless successful careers in show business: Rowan Atkinson, Maggie Smith, Michael Palin, John Schlesinger, Kenneth Tynan and Lindsay Anderson are just a few of the famous names that once acted for OUDS.

Beaumont Street ends where Worcester College begins, for directly facing you is its neoclassical façade. When you have gone through the gate and seen the tall buildings on your right and the little houses on your left and the lawn in between, you will – if you are a Lewis Carroll fan – go rushing towards the narrow, ogival passageway in the south-west corner. And through this tunnel you will hasten like Alice 'into the loveliest garden you ever saw'. It's a landscape garden with a pond, and the real Alice Liddell often used to come here with Lewis Carroll to feed the ducks in the 'pool of tears'. The land on the Oxford Canal used to be a swamp, but it was laid out in around 1817 with lawns and clusters of trees, winding paths and a serpentine lake. Today it offers the perfect natural setting for open-air theatre, and once a stage version of *Alice's Adventures in Wonderland* was performed here in the presence of Lewis Carroll himself. It was a charity event at which the audience did not have to pay to get in, but did have to pay to get out. In June 1949 Shakespeare's *Tempest* was performed here, and ended magically on the nocturnal lake. It was directed by Nevill Coghill, tutor of W. H. Auden, and according to Peter Zadek 'the only man who knew how to handle me'. The son of Jewish emigrants from Berlin, Zadek looks back on his school and university career (he studied at St John's) as 'a permanent disaster', except that Oxford gave him the spur to launch himself into the theatre.

Worcester College owes its foundation in 1714 to a baronet from Worcestershire. It is in fact the third college to have stood on this site, on the western fringes of the city. Around 1283 it was a monastic college for Benedictines. After the Reformation, all that remained of this Gloucester College was a row of modest cottages, forming the south wing of what is now Main Quad – a relic of the Middle Ages which only survived in the company of its classical neighbours because the money ran out for the new buildings. The central entrance block contains the hall and chapel on the ground floor and the library on the first floor, above the arcades of the cloister.

Worcester's chapel is unique: it has a high Victorian interior by William Burges (1864–66). Burges at the time was still a young architect, and he designed a decorative scheme that was as broad theologically as it was stylistically – a superb pot-pourri of Assyrian, Pompeian and Japanese sources, with biblical symbols and *quattrocento* motifs executed in all kinds of materials and techniques, wall paintings, stained glass (by Henry Holiday), mosaic floors, a lectern made of alabaster, and a menagerie. You will find the latter on the bench-ends, carved in wood: unicorn, owl, rhinoceros, hippopotamus, cockerel, pelican, crocodile, elephant, a tortoise, an anteater, and even a dodo. But perhaps none of these creatures is quite as strange as the thought that when Rupert Murdoch, the Australian media tycoon, was studying at Worcester, the object he kept on the mantelpiece of his room was a bust of Lenin.

Millionaires and Methodists:
Between Lord Nuffield and St Peter

'Rich men don't give nearly enough money away.'
Lord Nuffield (1877–1963)

The skyline on the western edge of the city is dominated by a massive tower with a copper-green spire. This is the tower of Nuffield College, an outsider among the dreaming spires and a comparative newcomer as edgy and individualistic as the man who put it there, Lord Nuffield (see p. 86). He made his fortune as a car-manufacturer, with his various models of Morris, and he gave it away as a philanthropist, which took him into the ranks of the aristocracy. His college was founded in 1937, and was intended to train engineers and businessmen, but it turned into a postgraduate college for the social sciences. 'That bloody Kremlin,' fumed the great man, 'where left-wingers study at my expense.' Architecturally, he got what he wanted: college buildings in the style of a Cotswold country house. There are gables, windows with stone jambs, roofs covered with Collyweston slabs, plus a dash of Manhattan Art Deco, and a high-rise library that could easily stand on the Hudson.

Austen Harrison, former government architect in Palestine, designed Nuffield College in 1939, but it was not built until after the war, and was completed in 1960. Even then the Lutyens-inspired spirit of the 1930s seemed at best nostalgic. Part of the Cotswolds country-house idyll is the pond in the inner quadrangle, though this also reflects a little piece of history, in the form of the canal basin where coals from Staffordshire used to be unloaded before this part of the Oxford Canal was filled in to make way for the college. Today Hythe Bridge marks the end of the canal and the beginning of a towpath that runs all the way along the canal to Jericho and beyond.

Opposite Nuffield College rises the green bulk of Oxford's ruined castle. On top of the grass-covered mound there once stood the keep of 1071, and at its foot was the Chapel of St George. The Norman crypt has survived, as has the mighty west tower, but they have long been closed to the public, because from 1785 until 1996, the old courtyard was the site for Her Majesty's Prison. As always in such 'corrective' institutions, there was a treadmill; the 'hanging cell', which was still used in the 1950s for executions, was in St George's Tower. There is an escape story attached to this, and it took place in December 1142. At that time there was civil war between King Stephen and Henry I's daughter Matilda. After a siege lasting several weeks, Matilda was lowered from the tower on a rope and, clad in white, escaped across the snow-covered fields to Wallingford.

The more romantic the story, the more melancholy the reality: this rule of thumb for tourists certainly applies here. Near the former prison, which is to become a hotel and fitness complex alongside a museum and heritage centre, the County Council has its neo-Norman headquarters; opposite is the Westgate Shopping Centre, and next to this is another mass of concrete in the form of a multi-storey car park. In this urban wilderness there are, or rather were, just two glimmers of light: Simon House for the homeless (in Paradise Street, where the Franciscans once had their garden) and Morrell's Brewery. Here in St Thomas' Street the exquisite beer had been brewed since 1782, with malt from Wallingford, hops from Worcester, and water from the Cotswolds and the Chiltern Hills – the recipe for a beer-drinker's nectar. The lion of the Morrell coat of arms on the cast-iron door held high its branch of hops, but alas not high enough. The last family brewery in Oxford has finally closed, and 'The Lion Brewery', as it is now called, has been turned into an apartment block. St Thomas may not be weeping, but I certainly am.

One member of the Morrell family was the lawyer Philip Morrell, MP and paci-fist. From 1913 onwards, his wife, the eccentric Lady Ottoline, used to hold a salon on their country estate at Garsington, near Oxford, and here High Society and the 'intellectual underworld' (in the words of Leonard Woolf) would mix as felici-tously as hops and malt.

Parallel to Cornmarket Street – for we have now come full circle in our wander-ings – is one of the oldest streets in Oxford: New Inn Hall Street. It was once called the Lane of the Seven Deadly Sins, but then it became a centre for Noncon-formist piety. It was at no. 33 that on 14 July 1783 John Wesley delivered a sermon that shook the Anglican Establishment to the core. This house was the Methodists' first place of worship in Oxford – a rubblework cottage with broad lattice windows – and today its occupants are students from Brasenose. Half the street belongs to the college, including Frewin Hall, which in the Middle Ages was a study convent for the Augustinians. Although Methodism had one of its roots in Oxford, Wesley found very few followers here in spite of his genius for preaching, not to mention that of his pupil George Whitefield. Not until 1878, when Noncon-formists were officially admitted to study, did the Methodist community acquire the self-confidence to build a larger church in the street where it was born – the Wesley Memorial Church.

Nearby, between two church towers, a bishop from Liverpool founded St Peter's College in 1929. If you make such a late start, and you want such a central position, you have to make do with what you can get. A Georgian parsonage became the main entrance, the Victorian parish church of St Peter-le-Bailey became the college chapel, and the Master moved into the former headquarters of the Oxford Canal Company, whose insignia can still be seen over the portico. Since then, St Peter's has filled every available nook and cranny with new buildings, which makes for a bit of an architectural conglomeration, but the students seem to like it. One of them, Edward Akufo-Addo, became President of Ghana, and the former law student Ken Loach is a famous film director.

North-East of the Martyrs' Memorial

'Having once been to the University of Oxford
You can never really again
Believe anything that anyone says.'
Louis MacNeice, *Autumn Journal*, 1938

T he two streets running from the north into the city centre converge like a cone into St Giles' Street, which is the widest street in Oxford. Lined with plane trees, The 'Giler' is a majestic, green avenue with a character all its own, for it rises and falls under its asphalt, its sides refuse to run parallel, and it has scarcely set out on its course (from St Giles' Church) when it comes to an abrupt halt (at the Martyrs' Memorial). It seems to have decided that this, after all, is not the place to be a boulevard.

St Giles' Street and its church are named after St Aegidius, one of the fourteen auxiliary saints, who became very popular in the Middle Ages as the patron saint of beggars and cripples. His feast day is 1 September, and this is the origin of St Giles' Fair, which takes place every year on the Monday and Tuesday after St Giles' Day. It is one of the last great fairs to have survived from medieval England, and town and gown from far and wide come together in this street which, for two glorious days, is closed to traffic and wide open to entertainers, sideshows, merry-go-rounds, and even female wrestlers wearing corsets and black suspenders. For the rest of the year, it's business as usual for the academics and the theologians. Dominicans, Benedictines, Anglicans, Baptists, Quakers – all kinds of religious communities have peopled St Giles' Street. There is also a beautifully symmetrical pattern of colleges and pubs: St John's is directly opposite St Cross, and next to them are the Eagle and Child and the Lamb and Flag. To each his own.

Surviving from the 18th century, when a suburb developed around St Giles' Street eventually to become North Oxford, are some fine Georgian houses now occupied by professors, and law and university offices. On the west side, near the Taylor Institution, the Dominicans built Blackfriars in 1921 – a priory with a seminary. Exactly 700 years before that, in 1221, they had founded their first hall in Oxford. Many influential scholars and preachers were trained there, until the Reformation drove them out of England. Today Blackfriars is regarded as the most liberal Catholic community in the city, and is heavily involved in matters relating to Aids and the environment. Next door is Pusey House, named after the Victorian scholar Edward Pusey, one of the leading lights of the Oxford Movement. Having developed from Pusey's theological library, this Anglo-Catholic institution – a 'house of sacred learning' – has been in existence since 1884, and now shares its premises with the postgraduate college of St Cross. The nearby Classical Revival block on Pusey Street, begun in 1938, is the citadel of the Baptists, Regent's Park College. But before you continue along this, the most pious mile in Oxford – heading for St Benet's Hall, where the Benedictines are – I suggest you stop off at a truly ecumenical establishment: the Eagle and Child.

This pub, dating from 1650, was the local frequented by J. R. R. Tolkien, C. S. Lewis and their friends, known as the 'Inklings'. 'Not another fucking elf,' groaned C. S. Lewis when Tolkien read out his fantasy tales. Between 1939 and 1962 the Inklings used to meet regularly in the wood-panelled Rabbit Room, where amid the swirls of pipe-smoke there would be a manly exchange of hobbits, Beowulf and all the latest college gossip. The Eagle and Child, known locally as the 'Bird and Babe', has a classical pub sign: the eagle carrying off Ganymede, the handsome youth that Zeus had his lustful eye on. From ancient mythology to Christian iconography is not too big a step, as we can see from the pub sign opposite. The Lamb and Flag is named after the attributes of John the Baptist, and here under the chestnut tree you will find the students from St John's, the college which has owned the pub since around 1695. 'Let us eat and drink; for tomorrow we die,' it says in Corinthians, and the Lamb and Flag is as good a place as any to follow the Bible's instructions.

Tony Blair's College:
St John's

'I could never stand the Oxford intellectual establishment.
They seemed to have a poker up their backsides.'
Tony Blair, 1994

Tony Blair, England's twenty-fifth 'made in Oxford' prime minister, was known as a singer in the rock band Ugly Rumours but not as a speaker in the Union. In 1980, five years after getting an upper second degree in Law, he got married in true Oxford style in the chapel at St John's. The college where he studied is so rich that even its gutters are gilded. It is said that you could walk all the way to Cambridge from here and never leave the property of St John's. That may be a slight exaggeration, but it is certainly true that the college owns a great deal of North Oxford and of London's West End, plus estates in Switzerland – enough to offer some 400 students the most comfortable years of their lives. The academic standards expected of them are correspondingly high.

The façade stretches along St Giles' Street with two entrance towers, which makes it seem like two separate colleges. In fact the walls of St John's also encompass the remains of St Bernard's, a Cistercian college that was founded in 1437 and closed two hundred years later. Under the name of 'Collegium Divini Baptistae Johannis', it was founded anew by Sir Thomas White, a wealthy Merchant Taylor and former Lord Mayor of London. He was also president of the Tailors' Guild, and John the Baptist is the patron saint of tailors. The royal patron of the college was the Catholic Mary Tudor, and so this was a Counter-Reformation foundation. When there was renewed persecution of the Catholics under Queen Elizabeth I, one of the victims was a prominent member of St John's, the Jesuit Edmund Campion. He was tortured and hanged in 1581, but later beatified and eventually canonized in 1970.

There are at least two good reasons to spend some time in St John's: the Canterbury Quad and the garden, for both are quite extraordinary. St John's has six quadrangles. The oldest of them is the Front Quad, with its perfectly round lawn set in a stone square, and behind this is another green quad. You are immediately struck by the peacefulness of the place, and its grandeur. From the shadows of the round-arched arcades you look across the lawn at the colonnade of the west wing opposite, and all around you is what seems like perfect symmetry and harmony.

But this quad, begun in 1631, is in fact an architectural hybrid, and if you look more closely you will see that it combines an astonishing range of classical, Gothic, Baroque and other elements. In the Canterbury Quad, for the first time in Oxford, the ground floor was conceived as an open loggia. There are arcades in the style of the French and Italian Renaissance, and above them are narrow, Gothic windows and crenellations. The main arches in the two wings are accentuated by a two-storey frontispiece with twin columns and a pedimented arch that provides a Baroque-style frame for the niches containing two royal figures: Hubert le Sueur's lead statues of Charles I and Henrietta Maria (1633). It was in their presence that William Laud, Archbishop of Canterbury, opened this magnificent quadrangle in 1636, which as Chancellor of the University and former President of the college he had commissioned and paid for. But who was the architect? It may have been Adam Browne, a master carpenter from London whom Laud had used in Lambeth and elsewhere. Or it may have been Nicholas Stone, the royal master mason. The only records are of the names of the latter's assistants, who carried out many of the works to be seen in the Canterbury Quad, for instance the busts of the virtues, and the *artes liberales* in the spandrels between the arches.

Archbishop Laud, St John's greatest benefactor, was – like his king – executed during the Civil War for high treason. Now, it is said, at nightfall they play bowls with their heads in the library on Canterbury Quad. Laud's grave is in the chapel, and in the Old Library is the cap that he wore on 10 January 1645 on his way to the scaffold. His diary, oriental manuscripts and other rarities from his estate are kept in the college library. This houses other treasures too: some of William Caxton's incunabula, letters written by Jane Austen, the archives of the poet and novelist Robert Graves (author of *I, Claudius* and *The White Goddess*), who wrote his doctoral thesis here in 1924 on *Poetic Unreason*, manuscripts by the poet A. E. Housman, who failed his examinations here but went on to become a Latin professor in Cambridge. 'Oxford terrified me. Public schoolboys terrified me. The dons terrified me.' So said another great English poet, Philip Larkin, of his years at St John's; in the summer of 1943, shortly before his Finals (first-class), he reported: 'I am spending my time doing an obscene Lesbian novel, in the form of a school story. Great fun.'

Behind the Tuscan columns at the end of the Canterbury Quad is a little gate. After this architectural feast, it is difficult to imagine anything other than an anticlimax, but as so often happens in Oxford, the smallest entrance can lead to the greatest wonders. A broad expanse of lawn stretches out before you, like a great breath of fresh air after the concentrated enclosures of walls and pillars. This, enthused Henry James, is one of those places where you can 'lie down on the grass forever, in the happy faith that life is all a vast old English garden, and time an endless English afternoon.'

As well as the head gardener of St John's, there is 'The Keeper of the Groves', who is one of the Fellows. Under him, generations of amateur botanists have contributed beautiful, unusual, local and exotic plants – particularly trees: tulip tree, Judas tree, davidia, tree of heaven, eucalyptus, the rare weeping oak, the strangely twisted witch hazel. There are 250 types of ilex growing here, and a total of some 2,500 trees and shrubs. George III said he'd never seen anything like it when he visited St John's garden in 1785. Such places have sometimes been love-nests for the dons as well as the students. A diary of 1825 records that a 'very revd. fellow' was caught at 1 p.m. in flagrante delicto with the Proctor's daughter. 'Oh shame! The old fellow buttoned up his inexpressibles and set off with his *inamorata* to Trinity gardens, where he probably renewed his games.'

A wrought-iron gate leads from the college garden into the Garden Quad of 1993. Richard MacCormac designed this combination of student lodgings and lecture rooms as a series of rectangular towers of yellow brick, cream-coloured concrete, wood and glass. The towers of the Elizabethan Hardwick Hall, and John Soanes's suspended domes which span the space like bat's wings, are among the elements that MacCormac has taken up, using the materials and the spirit of modern times. The domed opening in the basement grants a view over the inner quad right up to the sky, and inside, the ceilings are painted with *trompe-l'oeil* clouds. This new building shows that St John's is still more expert than most colleges when it comes to combining the old and the new.

The Go-Getting Girls of Somerville

'LMH for Ladies,
St Hilda's for games,
St Hugh's for Religion
And Somerville for Brains.'
Anonymous, *c.* 1920

S t Giles' Street splits like a tuning fork, right into Banbury Road, left into Woodstock Road. Follow the bells of St Giles', but this time instead of going to the church, go to the parsonage at 1 Banbury Road. The street could hardly get off to a better start than the Old Parsonage, which is now a small and cosy hotel. It was here that Oscar Wilde lodged in 1877 when he was a student, and the hotel prospectus delights in quoting (not without a degree of irony) his comment on his final, rather shabby accommodation in Paris: 'Either this wallpaper goes or I do!'

Nearby, and branching off Woodstock Road, is Little Clarendon Street, where there are enough cafés, bistros and boutiques to take your mind and eye off the concrete blocks that house the university's administration. This little street was already trendy in the 19th century. In a room above a bakery, the early Somervillians used to gather to listen to lectures on Greek history. These were the modest beginnings of Somerville College, which was founded in 1879 and was the second Oxford college for women only, after Lady Margaret Hall (see p. 174). The first twelve students lived in a rented Victorian villa, Walton House, between the Radcliffe Infirmary and St Aloysius Church, which meant that their neighbours were either ill or Catholic – both qualities making them into outsiders like the 'bluestockings' themselves. At this safe distance from the men's colleges in the centre of the city, the Somervillians developed their own profile and expanded their premises between Walton Street and Woodstock Road. Today they have almost 400 students, half of them men, to whom the doors were opened in 1994.

There are three Old Somervillians who made the college famous: Dorothy L. Sayers, Margaret Thatcher and Indira Gandhi.

Indira Gandhi, daughter of India's first prime minister Jawaharlal Nehru, spent a year at Somerville and a year in prison, through her involvement in the struggle for independence. She became prime minister herself in 1966, survived charges of malpractice and corruption, and returned to power in 1980, only to be assassinated four years later by members of her own Sikh bodyguard. It's a story that scarcely fits the image of the dreaming spires.

Dorothy L. Sayers took a first-class degree in Old French Literature, though she did not receive it until five years later, in 1920, when women were finally admitted to the degree ceremony. As a student, she was in charge of bicycles, sang in the Bach choir, and founded the M.A.S. or Mutual Admiration Society, a literary club for – in case you haven't guessed – mutual admirers. She returned to Somerville's High Table as the Queen of Crime, dressed in billowing black crêpe de Chine.

An unusual number of writers have graduated from this college of high-flying women, ranging from Iris Murdoch to Penelope Fitzgerald, and it is they more than anyone who have given it its liberal, intellectual left-wing image. Apart, that is, from their arch-Conservative fellow Somervillian Margaret Thatcher. When she became prime minister, it was like an industrial accident. 'We'd rather have seen Shirley Williams become the first Labour prime minister,' one of the dons assured me. Margaret Roberts, as she then was, joined the John Wesley Society and every weekend used to go with her Methodist friends into the surrounding villages to preach. It was there that she learned to hone her public-speaking talents, with the fiery, missionary preacher's tone that was vastly more characteristic of her delivery than the usual Oxford love of irony and ambiguity. 'She meant to get into Parliament,' recalled Nina Bawden, her contemporary, 'and there was more chance of being "noticed" in the Conservative Club, just because most of the members were a bit dull and stodgy.' In academic circles, the future Lady Thatcher made herself very unpopular because of her open scorn for all intellectuals, and in particular those who were not millionaires. After she had proceeded drastically to cut the budget for education and research, the university – usually so loyal to the Establishment – refused to grant her an honorary doctorate in 1985. A short time later, when she was visiting All Souls, protesting students pelted her with eggs. And yet when she began her studies in 1944, she did so in the best Somerville tradition as a natural scientist. Her chemistry tutor was Dorothy Hodgkin, who was later awarded the Nobel Prize. The two of them are now reunited, at least institutionally, by way of the Margaret Thatcher Centre in the Dorothy Hodgkin Quad.

These new buildings have one huge advantage: they should knock Somerville right off the tourists' list of sights to see. The same applies, however, to its Victorian and neo-Georgian buildings.

Unlike LMH, an Anglican foundation, Somerville was non-denominational right from the start, but all the same a chapel was built in 1935. With no pictures and no atmosphere, it is more like a container than a chapel.

Keble College:
Holy Zebra and the Parks

'I'm privileged to be very impertinent, being an Oxonian.'
George Farquhar, 1701

Just a few years ago, there was a club in Oxford called the Society for the Destruction of Keble College. Every new member had to bring to the meeting a brick from the college walls. Evidently Keble College has survived this initiation ceremony better than the society, which now exists only as an idea – a peculiar echo of the controversies that have surrounded the college ever since it was founded in 1870.

It stands at the corner of Parks Road and Keble Road, as massive as a Victorian lunatic asylum, with its glowing red bricks and weird patterns. 'Early Bloody' was the style attributed to England's first redbrick college. This neo-Gothic brick building marked a break with the tradition of local stone, and that was not the only break with tradition. The name itself embodies the spirit of the Oxford Movement (see p. 42), for John Keble was one of its leading figures. When he died, his admirers invited subscriptions of public and private money to found a college of religious and social renewal. They wanted to create an establishment that would follow the principles of the High Church, spiritual, plain, and accessible to all and not just the privileged few. Next to Somerville, Keble remains one of the least exclusive and also one of the poorest colleges.

The main buildings were financed by an importer of guano and designed by William Butterfield. His life's purpose was to reform Christian architecture, and his trademark was polychrome ornamentation in brick, with geometrical or striped patterns. Contemporaries dubbed the college chapel the 'Holy Zebra' once he had finished tattooing it. 'All this is not beautiful, in fact it is actively ugly.' Such was Pevsner's verdict, which followed on in the best tradition of Oscar Wilde: 'In spite of Keble College Oxford remains the most beautiful thing in England.' However, I beg to differ, for if you look more closely, you will see Gothic Revival at its finest. The two large quads are not completely enclosed, as Butterfield left gaps to look through, creating a remarkable impression of space, and the different heights of the buildings, the jagged outlines and broken symmetry all create an unusual and unquestionably original effect. He also departed from another Oxford tradition by arranging the students' rooms along corridors instead of following the medieval principle of staircases. Recent restoration work on the hall has shown Butterfield's interior of 1878 in a new light, with its patterned stencilled ceiling panels, decorated trusses and gold bosses.

Keble Chapel, the 'Holy Zebra', dominates all the other buildings. The position of the windows over the blind arcades increases the impression of height and lofty aspirations. It was opened in 1878 but never consecrated – a temple of Anglican piety beyond the control of the Church of England. The stalls are not situated opposite one another, as in other college chapels, but facing the altar – a liturgical emphasis on the sacraments which accords with the principles of the Oxford Movement. In the side chapel, illuminated at the press of a button, is the most admired and most criticized painting of the Victorian Era: Holman Hunt's *The Light of the World* (see p. 65). Carlyle called it 'a mere papistical phantasy', but for Ruskin it was 'one of the very noblest works of sacred art produced in this or any other age'. The painter's models for the head of Christ were Christina Rossetti and Elizabeth Siddal, the archetypal Pre-Raphaelite beauties. He intensified the iridescent lighting effects by painting in moonlight or by gas and candlelight – the epiphany of an obsessive realist. The painting in Keble Chapel is the first version, done entirely by his own hand. In St Paul's Cathedral, where Hunt lies buried, there is a later version which when exhibited overseas in 1905–7 created as much of a sensation as an appearance by the Madonna herself. Keble's second, and even more important art treasure rarely leaves the college library: it is a collection of illuminated manuscripts from the Middle Ages – the finest collection in Oxford outside the Bodleian. Once a week, after Mass, the college chaplain invites his flock to his rooms, which never run dry thanks to the 'Keeper of the Chaplain's sherry'. The last chaplain, Douglas G. Rowell, was made Anglican Bishop of Gibraltar in 2001.

If you want to go for a picnic, just step outside Keble's front door and you'll find yourself in the Parks. The plural is correct and apposite. Where in a single park would you find more than 800 different types of tree, a Victorian cricket pavilion, and a bridge that takes you directly to Mesopotamia? Oxford must indeed lie on the Euphrates and the Tigris since the land between the two arms of the Cherwell is quite definitely Mesopotamia, even though the locals call it 'Mespots'. This is the southern end of the Parks, covering an area of 36 hectares, where during the Civil War the Royalists 'parked' their artillery (hence, perhaps, the name). Later Charles II walked his King Charles spaniels here, to be followed by generation upon generation of dog-lovers, and you will also find philosophers, joggers, idlers, lovers, cricketers, hockey and rugby and tennis and croquet players, and

Parson's Pleasure. I have my suspicions about the parson, for this is where young men used to bathe naked while the ladies had to leave their punts, walk round the fenced-in bathing-place, and get back in their boats on the other side.

If you sit down at the right place, you will be in hobbit territory, for one of the park benches is 'in memory of Tolkien' with a pointer to two nearby trees 'representing Telperion and Laurelin'. The magnificent trees in the Parks don't really need to represent anything but themselves: Atlas cedar, giant redwood, shellbark hickory, tulip tree, trumpet and pagoda tree, Wild Service tree, tree of heaven – a vast arboretum full of rare specimens collected since the middle of the 19th century, when the university acquired the land from Merton College. Oxford is as much a city of trees as it is of books. You can walk down an avenue of different types of maple leading to Rainbow Bridge and a path along the Cherwell, through the water meadows to Marston.

On the northern edge of the Parks, Oxford's first women's college was founded in 1878: Lady Margaret Hall, far away from the city centre, which had already been occupied by the men. One advantage was that they had a stretch of the river all to themselves and 'a garden of their own'. A hundred years later, however, they were sharing it with the men after all. Apart from the trees and flowers, I am told that their garden contains some 250 different types of wild flora, 69 species of bird, 20 species of butterfly, and 183 species of moth. Out of this hallowed habitat emerged such luminaries as the former Pakistan prime minister Benazir Bhutto, the former Chairman of the Joint Intelligence Committee Dame Pauline Neville-Jones, and the writers Antonia Fraser and Caryl Churchill.

LMH was named after Lady Margaret Beaufort, the mother of Henry VII. 'She was a gentlewoman, a scholar, and a saint, and after being married three times she took a vow of celibacy; what more could be expected of any woman?' wrote Elizabeth Wordsworth (great-niece of the poet), who founded the college. Lady Margaret also founded Christ's and St John's in Cambridge as well as professorships of Divinity at both universities. From 1896 onwards, LMH spread out in its own buildings, with hipped roofs and neo-Georgian brick – a little schoolmarmish for my taste, but the chapel is certainly outstanding: a cruciform, domed church in Byzantine style, designed in 1931 by Sir Giles Gilbert Scott. As far as the future is concerned, we learn all about it in P. D. James's sci-fi novel *The Children of Men*: in the year 2021, 'Lady Margaret Hall has become the massage centre for Oxford.'

Home of the Dodo and the Dinosaurs:
University Museum and Pitt Rivers

'Yes
You have come upon the fabled lands where myths
Go when they die.'
James Fenton, 'The Pitt Rivers Museum, Oxford', 1995

E rect and ready to pounce, the iguanodon stands waiting for the visitor to the University Museum of Natural History. He is surrounded by the skeletal casts of other prehistoric creatures: a 14-metre-long *Tyrannosaurus rex*, and a local *Cetiosaurus oxoniensis*, which the experts assure us is a vegetarian. Over the spectacular hall curves a roof of iron and glass, making it seem a little like a dinosaur railway station. The first exhibit in this museum is really the entrance hall: cast-iron compound piers divide up the five aisles of the rectangular space, which is encompassed by arcades and galleries, like a cloister. Pointed arches bear the weight of the glass-covered saddle roof. This neo-Gothic cathedral of knowledge, built with the technology of the Railway Age, was designed in 1855 by a little-known architect named Benjamin Woodward, with the assistance of ironwork specialists from Coventry. The elegance of the spandrels with their floral and filigree decorations anticipate Art Nouveau, and together with the wrought-iron capitals they illustrate themes from natural history: the leaves, blossoms, flowers and fruits of chestnut, lime, palm and other trees. The arcades are also a lesson in botany and geology. Every shaft is made from a different British stone, and every capital depicts different plants. The models came live from the Botanic garden, and the masons were nearly all Irish, with the brothers O'Shea very much to the fore.

The emphasis on the Gothic, on craftsmanship, and on nature as the source of all the ornamentation was particularly dear to John Ruskin, who was one of the driving forces behind the project and identified himself so closely with it that it was almost a continuation of his *Stones of Venice*, the book in which he had recently expounded his aesthetic credo. In order to illustrate his own gospel, he even got involved in the building work himself. Together with some of his students, he erected one of the brick columns in the interior – but did it so badly that it had to be taken down and then rebuilt.

It was Ruskin's idea to build the chemistry laboratory next to the Museum as a copy of the Abbot's Kitchen in Glastonbury, with an octagonal pyramid roof and lantern. The fact that glass and iron were materials used for the railways and were not exactly in the Gothic spirit was less of a problem for Ruskin than for some of his contemporaries. 'Perfectly indecent,' was Alfred, Lord Tennyson's verdict, but there were far more serious conflicts going on at the time.

In the year of its opening, 1860, a legendary debate took place in the University Museum. Samuel Wilberforce, Bishop of Oxford and a pillar of the Anglican establishment, and the zoologist Thomas Henry Huxley held a debate in front of more than 700 people on the evolutionary theory of Charles Darwin, whose epoch-making work *On the Origin of Species* had been published just a few months before. The bishop, nicknamed 'Soapy Sam' because of his slippery rhetoric, asked, 'Is it on his grandfather's or his grandmother's side that the ape ancestry comes in?' Huxley, who according to an eyewitness was white with anger, replied, 'For myself I would rather be descended from an ape than from a divine who employs authority to stifle truth.'

During the years in which the Darwin debate continued to rage, Oxford's museum offered a rich variety of material to the researchers and to the general public. A good 500,000 fossils, tens of thousands of minerals, three million insects – the museum can display only a fraction of its vast hoard of treasures. And so, you ask, where is the dodo? What remains of this strange and long-extinct bird of the *Raphidae* family – a claw, a skull and its mythological aura – is still just where Lewis Carroll and Alice first saw it, in Oxford's University Museum. You will find it in a glass case on the ground floor, a relic from Wonderland or, to be more precise, from Mauritius in the Indian Ocean. That is where *Raphus cucullatus*, that giant flightless fowl, fell victim in the 17th century to its own bulk and the appetite of sailors. Only twelve dodos were brought alive to Europe, and soon they existed only as a figure of speech: 'as dead as a dodo'. It was as part of Tradescant's collection of rarities that this particular specimen came to Oxford in 1683. When the last dodo's remains were thrown away in 1775, a curator managed to rescue the skull and claw.

Lewis Carroll, whose real name was Dodgson and who is known to have had a stammer which turned his name to 'Do-do-Dodgson', clearly had a soft spot for the long lost bird, and gave it a leading role in the third chapter of *Wonderland*, thereby making it immortal. When all the animals get soaking wet in the pool of tears, it is the Dodo that suggests a 'Caucus-race' to make them dry again, and after they have run around for half an hour, he declares that they have all won. 'But who is to give the prizes?' quite a chorus of voices asks. 'Why, *she*, of course,' says the Dodo. Somehow it always comes back to Alice.

Just like a Russian doll, the University Museum has another museum tucked away inside it. The second one is the most unusual in Oxford, was built in 1885, and is called the Pitt Rivers Museum. The display cabinets are packed tight, and each one is full of instruments and weapons, cloths and masks, knives, amulets, fans, lighters, opium pipes, belts, fetishes, shrunken heads, an Eskimo sealskin coat, and towering over them all is a 12-metre-high totem pole from the Queen Charlotte Islands. It's like entering a global attic in which is stored everything that people from distant, earlier cultures once used and then discarded.

The collection that formed the basis of the Pitt Rivers Museum of Anthropology and World Archaeology, to give it its full name, was donated to the university by General Augustus Henry Lane Fox Pitt Rivers. He had fought in the Crimean War and had been commissioned by the army to research the development of firearms. Like Darwin, he was obsessed by the concept of evolution, but in his case it was the evolution of objects. The simple developed into the complex, the musket into the rifle, and so in 1852 he began to collect and compare firearms of all sorts, flint arrowheads, locks and keys, various instruments and pieces of apparatus, until his house in London was positively bursting. In 1883, he gave some 20,000 ethnographic and archaeological items to the University of Oxford on condition that they established a Chair of Anthropology – the first at any British university.

Pitt Rivers' idea was to display comparable material typologically, and not geographically or chronologically. This very useful system has been abandoned elsewhere but retained here. It is, therefore, an authentic Victorian collection, encyclopedic, perhaps a little pedagogical, but never boring. It still has most of the original, handwritten labels in sepia ink, and by comparison to your modern designer museum, in which objects disappear into virtual space, the old-time charm of the Pitt Rivers seems almost revolutionary.

When he was a Slade student in Oxford in 1944, the sculptor Eduardo Paolozzi spent a good deal of his time in the Pitt Rivers, fascinated by the African masks and fetishes and by this whole treasure chamber of fading imperial memories. 'It's a bit eerie, this place, even in broad daylight,' says Inspector Morse, when investigating the case of the *Daughters of Cain*. A knife has disappeared from Cabinet 52 in the Pitt Rivers. It turns up in the back of a drug dealer. But now it's in Cabinet 52 again as if nothing had ever happened – a Rhodesian hunting-knife with a wooden handle, and in the museum shop it's being sold as a postcard, signed by Colin Dexter.

The Pitt Rivers now has more than a million objects – and a chronic shortage of cash, like all university museums. In the annexe at 60 Banbury Road, you will find a wonderful collection of musical instruments from all over the world: nose flutes from Assam, oboes of willow bark, whistling arrows from China that were fired as signals when the Emperor was travelling through the land, so that the people would have time to disappear from view. Don't miss the Baines Music Garden behind the house. Plants are grown there from which musical instruments are made, and flowers with such mellifluous names as trumpet lilies, angel's trumpets, horned violets, bellflowers, Berlioz tulips and Handel roses.

Labland:
The World of the Laboratory

'It is almost impossible to win a Nobel Prize at twenty-two, but it is perfectly possible at that age, after studying at Oxford, to know precisely what one needs and has to do in order to win a Nobel Prize.'
Alan Ryan, Warden of New College, 2000

B ehind the University Museum, along South Parks Road, is the Science Area. The laboratories of Labland are a conglomerate of brick, concrete and glass, spiritually and architecturally a complete contrast to the colleges in the city centre. Until well into the 20th century, Oxford was essentially a university for the arts, even though it had also boasted many eminent scientists from Roger Bacon through to the Fellows of Wadham who had founded the Royal Society. But it was not until the middle of the 19th century that the natural sciences began to emerge from the shadows of ecclesiastical and literary orthodoxy. The building of the University Museum signalled the beginning of this renaissance, because here for the first time the science subjects, which had hitherto been scattered among different houses, were united (albeit briefly) under one roof. In 1872, the physicists moved out again, and into the neighbouring Clarendon Laboratory, which was one of many new institutes that sprang up around the museum.

With the Clarendon, which was founded in 1870 before the more famous Cavendish Laboratory in Cambridge, Oxford took the lead in atomic and laser research. The driving force was Frederick Lindemann, physicist, cosmopolitan, eccentric director of the Clarendon from 1922, and an influential adviser to Winston Churchill during the Second World War. It was he who developed the concept of blanket bombing of German cities. Nicknamed 'The Prof', Lindemann was the only professor ever to have played at Wimbledon. He had studied in Berlin, which was then the leading centre of theoretical physics, and it was thanks to his initiative that scientists such as Franz Simon and Kurt Mendelssohn came to the Clarendon from Nazi Germany. In 1933 they succeeded in liquefying helium, and in the newly opened Lindemann Building (1939) a team under Simon worked on the Tube Alloys Programme, which was the code name for the atom bomb. Today, scientists in the Clarendon are, among other things, working on instruments for NASA expeditions to Mars and Titan, the moon of Saturn which will take seven years to reach.

In Labland, behind the Clarendon, are the laboratories for the chemists, anatomists, pharmacologists, botanists and biogeneticists, together with the eight-storey Department of Microbiology. There were violent protests by the anti-vivisectionists when the Sir William Dunn School of Pathology was opened in 1927 at the east end of South Parks Road. It was there that in 1939 the pathologist Howard Florey together with the biochemists Norman Heatley and Ernst Boris Chain, another emigrant from Berlin, achieved the decisive breakthrough in isolating and purifying penicillin, which the bacteriologist Alexander Fleming had accidentally discovered in Oxford in 1928. Today, just like their Cambridge counterparts, Oxford's scientists have their own hi-tech firms and research laboratories on the outskirts of the city. There has been a very successful partnership between the university and industry in the field of biotechnology – commerce-orientated research based on the American model. The university spends some £200 million a year on biomedical research, which is even more than Cambridge. 'The *idée fixe* that Cambridge is the refuge of the natural sciences and Oxford that of the arts is no longer valid,' says Alan Ryan, Warden of New College.

The importance of Labland is in reverse proportion to the mediocrity of its architecture. Even the corner building opposite the Pathology Department is no exception. It was designed by Sir Leslie Martin to accommodate both the zoologists and the psychologists (1966–70). The blocks are divided up in steps like the decks of an ocean liner, with walls of prefabricated concrete slabs, the whole thing being reminiscent of the most brutal Le Corbusier-style functionalism. So is there nothing of interest in Labland's architecture? Well, just one building, right opposite, though you might not think so at first sight.

Linacre College was named after the doctor and humanist Thomas Linacre, and was founded as recently as 1962 – a postgraduate college with the emphasis on science. In 1994, on the edge of the Cherwell meadows, they opened a new student hall of residence in Queen Anne style, with Dutch gables and various Georgian features. Nothing is more frowned upon in Oxford than the impression of newness, but behind this old-fashioned façade is some forward-thinking architectural technology: the materials used are natural wood and slate, the paints are organic, and there are no synthetic products at all. The Abraham Building uses considerably less gas and electricity than conventional buildings, rainwater is stored and filtered, bathwater is re-used to flush the toilets, and throughout, recycling is an integral part of this exemplary eco-architecture.

How to Make a Cowboy into a Gentleman: The Rhodes Scholarships

'The Rhodes Scholars had not – how could they have? – the undergraduate's virtue of taking Oxford as a matter of course. The Germans loved it too little, the Colonials too much. The Americans were, to a sensitive observer, the most troublesome – as being the most troubled – of the whole lot.'
Max Beerbohm, *Zuleika Dobson*, 1911

What is the link between Bill Clinton, Howard Florey and Adam von Trott? Well, you've seen the chapter heading, so you know that the American President, the Australian Nobel laureate and the German resistance fighter were all Rhodes Scholars at Oxford University. These international awards were founded by Cecil Rhodes who had a mighty dream: to change the course of history for the better through a worldwide Oxford elite. He himself studied at Oriel (see p. 185), and the house from which his legacy is administered stands in South Parks Road. Rhodes House was opened in 1929, designed by Sir Herbert Baker, who was Rhodes's favourite architect. Only the circular foyer and the temple-like portico echo the imperial style of Baker's houses in Pretoria and New Delhi, and the rest is simpler, with a mixture of colonial and Cotswold country house. At the top of the rotunda, which is a monument to the Rhodes Scholars who died in both world wars (including the Germans), sits a mythical bronze bird from Zimbabwe, formerly Rhodesia. Set in the floor below the dome with the Aristotle quote is a slab of granite from the Matopo Mountains, where Rhodes lies buried. 'Non Omnis Moriar' [I shall not wholly die] is the inscription above the door to the vestibule – a proud line from the Horace *Ode* that begins 'A monument, more durable than brass'.

The classics figure prominently in the house of the classical imperialist, who demanded 'Equal rights for every white man south of the Zambezi'. Cecil Rhodes was a vicar's son who rose to be prime minister of Cape Colony having made a fortune from the Kimberley diamond mines in South Africa. When he died in Rhodesia in 1902, the moon was not yet British – 'I would annex the planets if I could,' he once said – but about a quarter of the world's landmass was coloured pink in the atlas, and that meant it was part of the British Empire. 'And as He is manifestly fashioning the English-speaking race as the chosen instrument by which He will bring in a state of society based upon Justice, Liberty and Peace, He must obviously. wish me to do what I can to give as much scope and power to that race as possible,' he wrote in 1877. This was the background to his foundation – the philanthropic legitimization of his policy of expansion. He saw Oxford as the energizing source of Empire, where his scholars should learn how to govern the world. That is to say, the English-speaking world. And of course, the world should speak English.

The first Rhodes Scholars came to Oxford in 1903, from the British colonies, America and also from Germany, which he added to the conditions laid down in his will because he hoped that 'an understanding between the three strongest Powers will render war impossible and educational relations make the strongest tie.' Germany broke away from Cecil Rhodes's world order for the first time in 1914. After the war, they had to be punished, and German scholars were not readmitted until 1929 – and then only two instead of the original five. One of the last was Adam von Trott (see p. 139) before Germany once again fell from grace in 1939. Then it took until 1969 before they were allowed back into the fold (with four scholars), and they remain the only European beneficiaries.

The racist, chauvinist principles that drove Cecil Rhodes have long since been revised by the trustees of his Foundation. Many black students, even African revolutionaries from the ANC, have now come to Oxford on Rhodes Scholarships, though women were not included until 1976. Today there are up to 90 scholars from 18 different countries – an elite within the elite, and the best possible ambassadors for Oxford. Past beneficiaries have included prime ministers of Australia, Malta and Jamaica, the German economist E. F. Schumacher (*Small is Beautiful*), the Texan country-and-western singer and actor Kris Kristofferson (*Billy the Kid*), US Secretary of State Dean Rusk, Senator J. William Fulbright, and various NATO generals and directors of the CIA. Though we may think of Americans first and foremost as cowboys, there can be little doubt that most Rhodes Scholars go back to the States as Oxford gentlemen, and they have made a major contribution to the lasting reputation of Oxford on the other side of the Atlantic.

At the beginning of the new millennium, the Rhodes trust stood at more than £200 million. It is not only the scholars who meet at Rhodes House, for with over 400,000 books it is a study centre in itself (and forms part of the Bodleian Library). The main emphasis here is on material from the Commonwealth and from colonial history, with important archives like those of the Anti-Slavery Society and the Anti-Apartheid Movement. Cecil Rhodes could never have imagined the direction his foundation would take.

In the entrance hall – and this certainly has nothing to do with Rhodes's principles – is a Pre-Raphaelite tapestry, woven in 1901 by Morris & Co after a lost painting by Edward Burne-Jones: *The Pilgrim in the Garden* – love's dream in a garden of roses.

Between Manchester and St Catz

'If you really want to see me married, try St Cross Church, Oxford, tomorrow at two.'
Dorothy L. Sayers, *Busman's Honeymoon*, 1937

If you would like to follow the Pre-Raphaelites through Oxford, do not miss Harris Manchester College. All the windows in their Victorian chapel are by Edward Burne-Jones and executed by the firm of his friend William Morris. This was the last work they did together at their old university (see p. 64). Where did the college's strange double name come from? It was founded in Manchester in 1786, went to London, and finally came to rest in Oxford in 1889. It was renamed 100 years later in honour of Sir Philip Harris, a carpet manufacturer who gave the college £3.6 million – always the most direct way to get your name up on high. The American cornflakes king Will Keith Kellogg followed the same route to establish Kellogg College, which the students have dubbed 'Korpus Krispie'.

Nearby, Mansfield College lies happily off the beaten tourist track between Mansfield Road and Love Lane. It was founded in 1886 as a theological college of what is now the United Reformed Church, and from the very beginning was as open ecumenically as it is architecturally, thanks to the design of the Victorian architect Basil Champneys. Mansfield has the highest state school intake in Oxford, an interdisciplinary department for environmental, ethical and social research, and the world's first Professor of Animal Theology. Reverend Andrew Linzey is concerned with the 'higher rights' of animals, for instance suitable ceremonies for the baptism or burial of our beloved pets. His book *Animal Rites* – again the world's first liturgically correct prayer book for all animal occasions – is dedicated to his late, great friend Barney, 'still wagging his tail, in heaven'.

Not far away, in Holywell Cemetery, lie some of the higher mammals that lived, learned and taught here: the beauty-loving Walter Pater, the theatre-loving Kenneth Tynan, the battle-loving Wadham Warden Maurice Bowra. There is ivy growing over the graves, and the wind whistles through the Cherwell willows across to the remains of Kenneth Grahame, whose classic Edwardian children's book is still a best-seller. He left both the manuscript of *Wind in the Willows* and all the royalties to the Bodleian Library. Grahame went to school in Oxford, became a bank clerk in London, but wanted to spend the rest of eternity among the moles and toads of his Oxford childhood. Here he lies in this Victorian cemetery, by the little church of St Cross, and here too is his son Alistair, who killed himself in Oxford.

In the meadows on the other side of the Cherwell is St Catherine's College, founded in 1963. Parallel to the river there is a moat-like canal with water lilies, and beyond is a stretch of lawn leading to the extended entrance of glass and clinker. In front of the porter's lodge sits the college cat Plops, with serious expression and arthritis. 'Catz' is the only college that has been completely built in the second half of the 20th century. It was designed by the Danish architect Arne Jacobsen, together with the furniture and all the lighting, and it is a great success, continuing the old traditions in an unmistakably contemporary manner, even if the sand-coloured bricks seem as alien to Oxford as the red bricks of Keble used to do.

Arne Jacobsen's buildings are flat, reflecting the horizontal forms of the river landscape. His design incorporates the traditional Oxford ground plan of the quadrangle, but the wings are open at all four corners, and the quads no longer lead directly into one another. Between the two residential blocks, each of them 180 metres long, are the lecture rooms, library and dining hall, and there is a circular lawn between the rectangular buildings. Even the bicycle stand at the entrance is a perfect circle, while the Music House is hexagonal. There is geometry everywhere, including the square 'garden rooms' and the rectangular grey slabs. This architecture combines purism, functionalism and self-discipline with an impression of generosity, openness and liberality. The fact that today Oxford University is a secular institution, and a modern place of learning, is nowhere more evident than in this college. It does admittedly have a bell tower, but it is the only college without a chapel. The dining hall is the largest in Cambridge and Oxford, with 400 seats but no portraits. It was given to the college by Esso, and was officially opened by the then Chancellor Sir Harold Macmillan, who in his speech remarked: 'Surely this must be Esso's largest filling station.'

St Catherine is the patron saint of learning and libraries, and her blessing certainly lies on her college which, in 1993 – just thirty years after its foundation – received the finest possible accolade for its architecture: along with England's medieval cathedrals and country estates, it was declared 'Grade I Listed'. All the same, there are clear deficiencies: the rooms are too small, the sound insulation is poor, the glass fronts afford too little privacy, and in summer it's like living in a greenhouse. But I have never heard any of the students complain.

The first and founding Master was the historian Alan Bullock, whose biography of Hitler (1952) was a worldwide best-seller. Lord Bullock's portrait for the Fellows' Dining Room was painted by Tom Phillips, himself a graduate of Catz. Oxford's youngest college can already claim one prime minister (of Trinidad and Tobago) and one major – if highly controversial – figure both in and out of the Blair cabinet (Peter Mandelson). The West End impresario Cameron Mackintosh endowed a Chair for Contemporary Theatre, and some of the greatest playwrights have held workshops and master classes here, including Arthur Miller, Peter Shaffer and Alan Ayckbourn, and actresses like Diana Rigg have done the same. At the southern end of the campus is a small, open-air amphitheatre with a backcloth of cedars, cypresses and a Judas tree. The picture is completed by the green expanse of the college sportsfields on the River Cherwell.

In 1991, St Catherine's opened a branch in the Japanese port of Kobe, financed by a local steel company. The Kobe Institute is a college in miniature, and is the very first branch of Oxford University to be built outside Oxford.

From North Oxford to Jericho

'Shall we ever, my staunch Myfanwy,
Bicycle down to North Parade?
Kant on the handle-bars, Mars in the saddlebag,
Light my touch on your shoulder-blade.'
John Betjeman, 'Myfanwy at Oxford', 1940

In the evening, Colin Dexter tells me, Inspector Morse generally leaves his bachelor flat in North Oxford and goes 'under the giant horse chestnut trees, along roads with such splendidly memorable names as Middle Way and Squitchey Lane, to one of the local hostelries.' Dexter also lives in North Oxford, at the top end of Banbury Road.

In this district, Summertown, when you stand at the checkout queue in the supermarket, you usually expect to be next to a Nobel laureate or at least a former government minister. In North Oxford live writers like James Fenton, Craig Raine and John Bailey, and celebrity scholars like Richard Dawkins, Roger Bannister and Desmond Morris, behind whose house ('Sunnyside') there was once a little Victorian summer house – the 'scriptorium' in which Sir James Murray compiled the *Oxford English Dictionary*.

In the memoirs of countless academics you will read about the legendary 'Donland'. You will find its literary transfiguration in the nostalgic irony of John Betjeman's poems, and in Barbara Pym's novel *Crampton Hodnet*, which offers an amusing insight into the secret life of this quarter and its upper middle-class inhabitants in the pre-war years. 'Belbroughton Road is bonny, and pinkly bursts the spray / Of prunus and forsythia across the public way / ...And open-necked and freckled, where once there grazed the cows, / Emancipated children swing on old apple boughs,' writes John Betjeman in his 'May-Day Song for North Oxford'. This is where T. E. Lawrence, Kenneth Grahame, Antonia Fraser and Lord Olivier went to school, along with the children of ambitious dons. And this is where hobbit fans may have glimpsed the father of all hobbits, J. R. R. Tolkien, who lived here for a while at 20 Northmoor Road. If every house in North Oxford had plaques commemorating the famous people who had lived or died there, you would see more plaques than walls. That would be a pity, because architecturally this most Victorian of all England's Victorian suburbs is a delight to see. North Oxford stretches for some three kilometres along Banbury Road and Woodstock Road, between St Giles and Summertown. Most of it belongs to St John's College, which began to turn its fields into building land in the middle of the 19th century, and thereby created a goldmine for itself.

The oldest settlement here is Park Town, designed between 1853 and 1855 by Samuel Lipscomb Seckham: two crescents in the middle of which is an oval park, and another crescent at the eastern end, Park Terrace, with individual detached houses and large gardens in between. This alternation between terraced and detached houses in the green created a combination of community and privacy – a mixture of town and country life that anticipated the garden city movement of the early 20th century. In the decades that followed, more houses went up in the surrounding areas: the Victorian High Gothic of Norham Road and Norham Gardens, Crick Road, Canterbury Road, Bardwell and St Margaret's Road. The southern section of Banbury Road is the real, inner North Oxford, but it was never a purely academic quarter.

A wine merchant, a lawyer, two chemists and a photographer built the first villas in Park Town. The dons didn't come until later, because at the time they tended to live in the colleges, most of them being bachelors. It was only in 1877 that the ban on marriage was lifted for the Fellows, and then there was a demand for homes near the colleges and for large family houses with room for the servants – gardener, cook, nanny, maid. These houses reminded Betjeman of parsonages, 'for indeed they were built to house monks set free'. Professors, clerics, retired dons, widows of dons – they all lived in this enclave of academic domesticity, on the fringes of which there arose theological seminaries and the first women's colleges. 'The New Jerusalem' is what they used to call North Oxford, not without a certain degree of Oxford irony.

Well into the 20th century, this remained the favourite hunting ground of those who liked 'plain living and high thinking'. The fashionable dress then was corduroy trousers, grey flannels, navy blue jerseys and shoes with thick soles (bought from Ducker's in The Turl). Their rooms would have been lined with Morris wallpaper, which Walter Pater introduced to Oxford. On Sundays they would go to 'Phil and Jim', the Anglican service in St Philip and St James in Woodstock Road, where George Edmund Street had built the new parish church in 1860–66 for the rapidly expanding community – as aspirational as the people themselves, with lancet windows and round shafted pillars of polished, rose-coloured granite. When the children were barely three years old, off they went to the famous

Dragon School, and then to the High School for Girls in Belbroughton Road, or St Edward's, the public school for boys in Summertown. That was how things were done in North Oxford. And of course there were dinner parties, and there were holidays too: Cornwall in the spring, the Dordogne in the summer. It was not by chance that in 1977 the star French chef Raymond Blanc opened his first gourmet restaurant 'Quat' Saisons' in Summertown, even if it was squashed in between the Oxfam office and a shop selling ladies' underwear. 'I do remember some dons who really appreciated good food,' he recalls, 'but obviously they were mean people, because of course in college they had everything for nothing, so to have to pay for it was a different matter.'

Walking round North Oxford is like visiting an open-air exhibition of Victorian housing. Almost every style is to be seen here, from neo-Renaissance to Edwardian neo-Georgian. After the early Italianate villas in Park Town, with their stucco façades, came the neo-Gothic of the 1860s in yellowish brick. From the 1880s the fashion was for Queen Anne style and red brick, in stark contrast to the pallid Cotswold stone of the medieval city. The decorative fantasy of the Victorians and their delight in historical disguises can be seen wherever you go. And the front gardens – at least, those that haven't been made into parking spaces – are full of pansies, laburnum and the scent of lilies.

For a long time people turned their noses up at Victorian architecture, and North Oxford was a target for developers and speculators. The fact that this area has remained largely intact is due in no small measure to John Betjeman, the prophet of the Victorian Revival. He played a vital role in getting North Oxford officially designated a conservation area in 1968. The large family houses have long since been turned into offices, institutes and an increasing number of language schools, mostly in and around Banbury Road. Many London commuters live here now – businessmen, consultants, media and advertising people – because this is the address to have, if you can afford the price. Seckham's villas in Park Street now cost around £1.3 million, which leaves most of the dons looking elsewhere. The Right Reverend Richard Harries is there, though, in Linton Road, but as the Bishop of Oxford he has friends in high places.

Between the Pasternak Museum
and the Radcliffe Observatory

'Yesterday my wife drove my father to the Spiritualist Chapel in Oxford's
Summertown. They passed Aristotle Lane. "Aristotle," said my father.
"Wasn't he a Greek millionaire?"'
Craig Raine, 1994

In 1999, a new museum opened in Oxford, and its admission times are as exclusive as its address: the Pasternak Museum in Park Town, on the first Sunday of the month for two hours *by appointment only*. It is the house of the painter Leonid Pasternak, who came from Odessa and whose son, the novelist Boris Pasternak, became even more famous than his father. Leonid, a Russian Jew, left his home after the Russian Revolution, went to Berlin in 1921 (as did Nabokov), stayed there until it was impossible to go on living in Germany, and emigrated to England in 1938, where seven years later he died in his Park Town house, in the first room on the left of the entrance. On the walls hang the pictures that accompanied him on his long journey from Moscow to Oxford: portraits, interiors, still lifes – mostly chalk and pencil drawings, but also pastels and oil paintings. Some of his best portraits were of friends like Tolstoy, Rachmaninov, Einstein and Rilke. These are pictures by a Russian Impressionist from the generation before Malevich, somewhat academic but filled with moments of colour and flashes of family life, rescued from the shadow of Lenin whose unfinished portrait was found on the easel of the 83-year-old artist. Living in this private museum today is Leonid's granddaughter Ann Pasternak Slater, Fellow of St Anne's and wife of the English poet and don Craig Raine. He had his doubts about admitting the public: 'What you want is a visit of mute admiration by a bladderless millionaire who doesn't need the lavatory, pays for the postcards with an ingot and instructs you to keep the change.'

Opposite Park Town, on the other side of Banbury Road, is St Hugh's College, one of the original four ladies' colleges that were established in North Oxford at the end of the 19th century. Elizabeth Wordsworth founded St Hugh's in 1886, and named it after a medieval Bishop of Lincoln. For the first thirty years, the students were lodged in rented accommodation, until a new building was constructed for them in 1916 in St Margaret's Road – the first college in Oxford to be specifically designed for women. Of more interest than the neo-Georgian architecture, however, is the story of one of their graduates: Aung San Suu Kyi, Burmese winner of the Nobel Prize for peace and an indefatigable campaigner for civil rights in her country. She spent over a decade under house arrest, and when her husband – Michael Aris, a Tibetologist in the neighbouring St Antony's College – died in Oxford in 1999, the Burmese military authorities would not even let her leave to go to the funeral.

St Antony's College, situated closer to the city centre on Woodstock Road, is one of the intellectual powerhouses of the university. It's a postgraduate college, relatively new, correspondingly poor, and individualistic enough to spell its name without an 'h'. It really ought to be called St Antonin's, after its founder Antonin Besse, a wealthy French merchant who left school with no qualifications at all and thought that 'Antony' was the English equivalent of his French name. In 1950 work began on his college in the dim Victorian buildings of a former convent, whose chapel was turned into a library. Since then, there have been several new buildings, including the Nissan Institute for Japanese Studies.

An unusual feature of St Antony's is that it specializes in the politics, economics and history of particular regions: Eastern and Western Europe, Russia, the Middle East, Japan, China, Africa and Latin America. 'We're more like an international studies centre than your normal college,' I was told by Ralf Dahrendorf, who was Warden of St Antony's until 1997. Lord Dahrendorf is the archetypal liberal who likes to call himself a 'mondialist', a citizen of the world who refuses to recognize any intellectual borders, and it is he more than anyone who has contributed to the international reputation of this college, whose eminent members include the expert on Eastern Europe, Timothy Garton Ash (see p. 84). There is a visiting professorship for German historians, which is regarded as an interface for Anglo-German relations, though there is still much work to be done in order to improve the negative image of the Krauts and Huns in Britain.

The neighbouring St Anne's College, a pioneer in the education of women, has also been taking male students since 1979. They call it 'Stan's'. It has an impressive list of alumni: politicians like Edwina Currie and Baroness Young, the first woman to become Leader of the House of Lords; Sister Wendy Beckett, nun and art critic; the poet Elizabeth Jennings; the magazine editor Tina Brown; and the chemist Mary Archer, an expert on solar energy and how to deal with Jeffrey. The building-block architecture, however, is not worth a detour. Much more attractive, on the other side of Woodstock Road, is the Tower of the Winds.

This classical tower is Radcliffe Observatory, though it doesn't look like an observatory. Instead of having a dome, it is crowned by two lead figures, Hercules and Atlas, holding up a copper-green globe. At ground level there are two long wings flanking the octagonal tower, the first floor of which is divided up by Ionic pilasters, while above the windows are the signs of the zodiac in relief. This observatory was the first Greek Revival building in Oxford, begun in 1772 and completed by James Wyatt in 1794. As on his model, the Hellenistic Tower of the Winds in Athens, Boreas, Zephyr & Co. – the winged personifications of the winds – are flying round the cornices in the form of eight stone reliefs by John Bacon, who also created the Atlas/Hercules group. Until 1935, the astronomers' telescopes stood in Wyatt's noble octagon. Today the Radcliffe Observatory belongs to Green College, a postgraduate college specializing in medicine, which was founded in 1979 by Ida and Cecil Green of Texas Instruments, manufacturers of chips for mobile phones.

Between Green College and Somerville is the Radcliffe Infirmary, also named after the royal physician John Radcliffe (see p. 133). A local policeman named Albert Alexander was the first patient to be treated with penicillin, on 12 February 1941 in this, Oxford's oldest hospital (1759–70). It is a strictly neoclassical building that is considerably more interesting than its various extensions. These were strewn higgledy-piggledy over the area during the last two hundred years, culminating in a modern clinic in the suburb of Headington, the JR2, built in 1979. A mere trumpet call away from these too, too solid walls is Jericho.

A Lively Place of the Dead: Jericho

'There was the High Anglican smell of incense, prayer books and
furniture polish. I had a sudden feeling that this was where the bodies
would be discovered with their throats cut. I uprooted the church (St Barnabas)
from Oxford to Paddington.'
P. D. James on her novel *A Taste for Death*, 1986

Jericho is a no-man's-land as far as tourists are concerned. No colleges, no
museums, and not even a shopping mall. Two-storey houses hide away in the
chessboard streets of north-west Oxford – terraced houses of brick, two up and
two down. Many of them have a tiny front garden, there are milk bottles standing
outside the pastel-shaded front doors, a cat wanders round the corner.... Idyllic
suburbia, just fifteen minutes' walk from the city centre.

Jericho lies between Walton Street and the Oxford Canal, bounded in the south
by Worcester College and in the north by the cemetery of St Sepulchre's. It was
once the working-class counterpart of the Park Town villas and was built in the
19th century, when dock and railway workers came to live near the canal. They
were joined by the factory workers from Lucy's Ironworks and the printers from
Oxford University Press. The popular explanation for the biblical name is that the
houses were built so quickly and cheaply that when a conductor from the nearby
railway blew his whistle too loudly one day, the walls came tumbling down. In
fact, though, the name was taken from fields called Jericho Gardens where, around
1680, a tavern called Jericho House was built, in Walton Street. Until recently it
was The Philanderer & Firkin, but it is now The Jericho once more, and is next to
the Phoenix Cinema. A little further on is the pub named Jude The Obscure after
Thomas Hardy's hero, the stonemason who found cheap accommodation and a
sad end in this area, fictionalized as Beersheba.

A literary 'Taste for Death' in Jericho runs from P. D. James – born at 164 Walton
Street – to Colin Dexter, but real life as usual has far transcended fiction. In the
19th century, poverty, prostitution and cholera were rife, and after the Second
World War it seemed that nothing could halt the downward slide of the whole district. But then came an exemplary clean-up campaign. Property was still cheap,
and so in moved the artists, musicians, students, yoga instructors, acupuncturists
and spiritualists, and the crumbling backyard workshops were transformed into
studios and hi-tech centres, while the workers' houses became 'des res' for academics. Then designer shops, delicatessens, cafés and bistros like Le Petit Blanc

opened on Walton Street. You can even find Oxford's best jazz club here, in the dim light that filters through the stained windows of St Paul's, a Greek Revival church of 1836, closed in 1969 and then re-opened under the name of Freud's Café.

Jericho is now a completely different place, bustling, fashionable, but without the gloss of Chelsea chic. If you are as thirsty as Inspector Morse, you may start looking for The Printer's Devil, but its actual name is The Bookbinders and it stands 'beneath the looming, ominous bulk of St Barnabas' great tower' – one of the locations in which Colin Dexter's *The Dead of Jericho* takes place. The 'Bookies' was the local for the printers who worked at OUP, and St Barnabas ('Barneys') was the workers' church of the Oxford Movement – the Anglican Reform movement that attracted many of the poor souls who lived in Jericho. The church must have seemed to them like the promise of Jerusalem when they left their little homes on a Sunday and entered into this expanse of opulence: the Byzantine glow of gold in the apse, the baldachin over the High Altar, the mosaics above the arcades. Sir Arthur Blomfield, son of the Bishop of London, designed this, the most original Victorian church in Oxford (1869), with neo-Romanesque arches, red bands of brick, and a bell-tower that soars high above the rows of terraced houses. This campanile on the canal is Jericho's contribution to the skyline of dreaming spires.

If you regard the iron cross on the tower as a signpost, it will point you in the direction of where it was made: Lucy's Eagle Ironworks. From the early 19th century, this foundry in northern Jericho produced drain covers, streetlamps, railings, bollards, and all the other ornamental necessities of the Cast-Iron Age. But today it is as still and silent as the cemetery which its red brick walls enclose on three sides – a monument to unemployment. St Sepulchre's Cemetery, which goes back to the middle of the 19th century, is Jericho's Victorian garden of the dead. Ground elder and bellflowers grow between the graves along with holly, ash and dark yew. Somewhere beneath the copper beeches lies the body of Thomas Combe, superintendent of the OUP, who financed the building of St Barnabas. The high-flying Benjamin Jowett, Master of Balliol, was also laid to lowly rest in St Sepulchre's in 1893.

Words, Books and Dictionaries:
The Oxford University Press

'Mechanically wonderful – but morally even more so.'
William Gladstone on the OUP, 1831

If you interrupt your tour of Jericho for a cappuccino in Freud's Café and look over to the other side of the street, you will see a neoclassical building of Bath stone that is as monumental as the Bank of England. The Oxford University Press has been there since 1830, and it is a national institution. What it publishes can lead to upheavals as drastic as a stock market crash. When the Press put an end to its poetry list in 1998, public controversy was such that questions were asked in Parliament and the House of Lords held a debate. What other publishers could create such a stir?

The first book printed in Oxford appeared in 1478, a *Commentary on the Apostles' Creed Attributed to St Jerome*, printed on the hand press of Theodoric Rood, who came from Cologne. Oxford's publishing history began with a misprint, because Rood accidentally left out the Roman numeral X, so that the year of publication was wrongly given as 1468 (which would have put him nine years ahead of Caxton). His printing press only lasted ten years in Oxford, and in any case the link with the university was tenuous. It was not until 1585 that the OUP was well and truly founded by Robert Dudley, Earl of Leicester.

After various locations, it finally moved from the Clarendon Building to its present headquarters on Walton Street: the Bible Press is in the southern wing, the Learned Press in the northern, though the old division between religion and learning has long since disappeared. The best-sellers are no longer Bibles and prayer books but dictionaries like *The Oxford Advanced Learner's Dictionary*, which sell all over the world. The English Language department is one of the biggest and fastest-growing areas of the OUP. An earlier ground-breaking success was *The Oxford Book of English Verse*, edited by Arthur Quiller-Couch in 1900, which gave rise to a new formula: the Oxford anthology. All that is missing now is *The Oxford Book of Cambridge*.

The OUP opened its first branch in New York in 1896, which was followed by others in India, Africa and Australia. Wherever it went, it played a key role in education, from Calcutta to Kuala Lumpur, and today with branches in more than fifty countries, it is by far the biggest university publishing house in the world. It produces some 4,000 titles a year, and its yearly turnover is in the region of £390 million. Responsibility for this global industry is still in the hands of a committee – a system set up in 1633 by Archbishop Laud, who was then Chancellor of the University. The 'Delegates of the Press' consist of 21 academics from different faculties. They in turn are nominated by another committee of 13 dons who change virtually every year – also specialists in their fields but amateurs in publishing. It is a perfect recipe for discontinuity and chaos, so the critics say, and the fact that this bizarre system actually works is yet another of Oxford's wonders. An important factor is the London branch, which operates autonomously, for its commercial success helps to offset the losses sustained by the Clarendon Press – the purely academic department of the company. This is where items even more obscure than volumes of poetry have always been published. In 1878, on Darwin's recommendation, they accepted a book on *Certain Variations in the Vocal Organs of the Passerers that have Hitherto Escaped Notice*. In twenty-five years it sold twenty-one copies. But even such worst-sellers have helped to establish the OUP's unique reputation, as have the talents of editors like Leofranc Holford-Strevens, copy-editor for Learned Editions and Fellow of Christ Church, who can understand no less than forty languages. When this polyglot took his exams in 1967, he was given a text in Ancient Greek with the bare instruction: 'Translate!' He proceeded to translate it into a language that no one could identify at first. Eventually, the examiners discovered that it was a dialect spoken by Frisian farmers in the 19th century.

Architecturally, there is not a great deal to see, but the OUP is famous for its books not its buildings, and there are two that are an absolute must. Firstly, a work of reference containing the biographies of every important person in the history of Britain and its colonies: 63 volumes of *The Dictionary of National Biography*, published between 1885 and 1901. The DNB, a National Portrait Gallery in words, was one of those monumental Victorian concepts designed to promote the national identity. Its first editor was Virginia Woolf's father, Sir Leslie Stephen, who was not exactly a forerunner of the feminist movement since he chose 35,000 men and just 1,000 women. Later supplements attempted to rectify the balance. Despite the lexicographers' scrupulous care, at least two biographies sneaked in of people who never existed: Adam Anglicus and Thomas Cutwode – fictional pieces of Oxford nonsense. In 2004 a completely new edition was published, containing 55,000 biographies and the collective memory of a nation (available online at www.oup.co.uk/newdnb).

The second mighty project of the 19th century, which has continued uninterrupted through to the 21st century and has cost about £35 million to produce is *The*

Oxford English Dictionary, one of the true wonders of linguistic scholarship. The first volume (A–Ant) was dedicated to Queen Victoria and was published in 1884, exactly thirty years after the Brothers Grimm had published Volume I of their German dictionary – which was the model for the Oxford lexicographers. Their equivalent of Grimm was James Murray (see p. 87), a Scottish philologist who originally intended to complete his work in four volumes and ten years. He died in 1915, still working on Ta, and it was to take another thirteen years before the twelfth and final volume was ready, with the last of the 414,825 key words (Zyxt). This gigantic inventory of the English language, 'the longest epic ever written' (Anthony Burgess), was compiled in his 'scriptorium', a corrugated iron shed behind Murray's house in North Oxford – a 'horrid, corrugated den', as his editors described it. There he sorted, classified and stored everything that his freelance colleagues sent him from all over the Empire – more than one thousand notes every day, together with literary references for every word, right through to the longest word in the OED: floccinaucinihilipilification (the action or habit of estimating something as worthless). The novelist Julian Barnes also worked for a while as an OED lexicographer, his specialist subjects being sport and obscenity.

The second edition of the dictionary, OED2, was published in 1989 and comprised twenty volumes. A new version (also online at www.oed.com) appeared in 1998 in preparation for a third edition, and although it was much praised, it was also criticized for pandering too much to the zeitgeist. But Murray's disciples are only recording the changes in the language, and if Americanisms and neologisms like Prozac, Blairism and sex tourism are omitted from the OED, where is the bewildered reader to find help? There is a long and winding road from Oxford English to the international language of the Internet, but whatever new words you find there and elsewhere, be sure to send them to the editors of OED3 in Oxford. For this complete revision, which is scheduled to be ready by 2016, every one of the 750,000 key words will be re-examined, along with their 2.4 million references.

Murray lived at 78 Banbury Road, which is where the zoologist Desmond Morris now lives, and in front of the house you will still see the red pillar box which the Post Office kindly placed there for the great word-collector's correspondence.

The Green Edge of the City:
The Oxford Canal and Port Meadow

'I will take you walking with me to a place you have not seen –
Half town and half country – the land of the Canal.
It is dearer to me than the antique town: I love it more than the rounded hills:
Straightest, sublimest of rivers is the long Canal.'
James Elroy Flecker (1884–1915), 'Oxford Canal'

Behind the houses of Jericho shine the waters of the Oxford Canal. There are willows on the banks, and alders and hazel-bushes. Wild ducks go soaring upwards, and a moorhen minces across the towpath. Tied to the bank are Shakespeare and Petrarch, two brightly coloured narrow boats. They all seem to rejoice in weird names: Bill the Lizard, Rosamund the Fair, Tinworm, Poohsticks, Serendipity. Some of them, further down towards Hythe Bridge, have been there for years – houseboats with letterboxes, washing lines and even a little front garden with irises, clematis, strawberries, jasmine, rosemary growing in the narrow strip between boat and path. England's tiniest gardens lie on the Oxford Canal, on the green and grey fringes of the city where the boat people live: drop-outs, the unemployed, the early retired, students, odd-job men.

The canal is 133 kilometres long and runs between Oxford and Coventry. It was begun in 1769, when there was canal fever all over England, and it was finished in 1790. There is a fine cast-iron bridge over the Isis Lock, where the canal cuts through to the Thames, but occasionally its beauty is somewhat marred by the fishing out of suicides. The canal joins the Thames and the Mersey, and it was the route along which coal was transported from the mines in the Midlands – far cheaper than by sea.

It is only one and a half metres deep and never wider than 4.8 metres, which is just broad enough for two barges to pass each other. The narrow boats had a standard width of seven feet, which is the same as the towpath. Everything was calculated very precisely. But no one's calculations included the railways. In 1844 the Great Western reached Oxford, and it was so much quicker and cheaper that commercial traffic on the canal gradually dwindled to virtually nothing. Where once the coal used to be unloaded on the docks of Jericho, canal boats are now rented out to holidaymakers. The Oxford Canal marks a clear border between town and country; it's an industrial watercourse that cuts through the idyllic countryside, but first, as it makes its way between the railway line to Birmingham and Lucy's Ironworks, it reveals its old and grimmer face, grey with the labour and poverty of yesteryear. It was this darker side of Oxford that fascinated poets like W. H. Auden and Stephen Spender when they were students – the disturbing, working-class, humdrum reverse of the cerebral college world tucked away in its quiet corners and quadrangles.

'It's a watery, raffish, amiable, trickster-like world of boat dwellers and horse dealers and alchemists. The character of this part of Oxford is very ancient, quite unmistakeable, entirely unique and now, alas, in some peril,' Philip Pullman wrote recently, in a plea for the preservation of the Alchemy Boatyard in Jericho, which is under threat from developers. This part of the canal was the model for some scenes in *His Dark Materials*. It is where his boat-dwelling 'Gyptians' live and work, and where his heroine Lyra is rescued.

Horses graze on Port Meadow, between the Isis and the embankment. The sky arches over the green and treeless plain on the north-west edge of the town. Port Meadow has never been built on or cultivated, and it is one of the few landscapes in England that has served the same purpose for over a thousand years: pasture-land for grazing. When an American visitor asked to be shown Oxford's oldest sight, he was taken not to a church, and not to a college, but to Port Meadow.

Even the Domesday Book of 1086 mentions the great stretch of common land outside the city walls, for which the burgesses of Oxford paid the king the yearly sum of six shillings and eightpence. The 'freemen', the merchants and craftsmen, fiercely defended their grazing rights down through the centuries, particularly against any attempt to exploit the 160 hectares for profit. The last legal battle began in 1732 and ended in 1970, with confirmation that Port Meadow was and is common land, and that some 200 of Oxford's citizens still have grazing rights. Of course, it is not only the freemen and their cattle that benefit. Walkers, joggers, dog-owners and birdwatchers can all enjoy this vast open stretch of land. Once there were even horse races here, and students played cricket in the summer, while in the winter when the meadow is partly flooded and freezes over, out they all come with their ice-skates. It has never been treated with any kind of chemical, is probably the best-documented piece of land in the country, and has been given the official status of 'Site of Special Scientific Interest'. Burnet and small scabious grow here in abundance, and you can see most of the 207 kinds of bird that have been recorded around the city, including snow geese, bar-tailed godwit and, as spotted on 18 May 1981, a hoopoe.

To Binsey and Godstow:
Alice Doesn't Dream Here Any More

'I have been at Oxford; how could you possibly leave it? After seeing that
charming place, I can hardly ask you to come to Cambridge.'
Horace Walpole, 1736

I t was a late summer's day in September when I walked from Aristotle Lane
across the fields to the Isis. There were a few children flying their kites over
Port Meadow. I crossed the bridge to Binsey and went past The Perch, the old pub
on the river where you can drink your beer in the garden under the willow trees,
and along the Isis to The Trout and to Godstow. Generations of students have sat
here by the river, with their pint and the image of Oxford's towers and the dreams
of a long summer's evening. There is no lovelier path away from the city of books,
and there is no better way to go back to its beginnings.

A path leads across the fields to the village church of Binsey. It is small and simple, lit only by paraffin lamps. Behind it is St Margaret's Well, the spring that is
magically linked both to the legend of St Frideswide, the patron saint of Oxford,
and to Lewis Carroll's tale of the treacle-well. The healing powers of the water,
particularly for eyes, stomach and fertility made Binsey a goal for medieval pilgrims, and its lasting popularity has been ensured by The Perch, with its thatched
roof and its draught beer. Down below by the river, the leaves of the Binsey
Poplars* begin to rustle in the wind, perhaps weeping for the fallen aspens so
movingly lamented by Gerard Manley Hopkins when he saw them lying 'all
felled' before him (see p. 53).

Godstow means 'the place of God'. This is not because of The Trout Inn, and the
Trout Inn is no longer the place of trout, as they have long since disappeared from
the Isis, but there are still photos of anglers on the walls, and there is good ale and a
room with relics of Inspector Morse. Opposite the inn, on the other side of the
river, lie the ruins of Godstow Abbey, the scene of a tragic medieval love story. In
this Benedictine convent Fair Rosamund Clifford, the legendary mistress of
Henry II, found refuge. She died there in 1176, but whether it was from a broken
heart, or from poison forced upon her by the jealous Queen Eleanor, not even
Inspector Morse can tell us.

---

* Hopkins' aspens (*Populus tremula*) have since been replanted, but with a different type (*Populus nigra*).

The path to Binsey and Godstow is a reminder of the creative bond between fiction and reality that is so typical of Oxford. It was here on the Isis that Lewis Carroll first told his stories of Wonderland to little Alice and her sisters. They rowed from Folly Bridge upriver for about five kilometres to Godstow, and picnicked near the ruins of the abbey. It was 4 July 1863, 'on that blazing summer afternoon with the heat haze shimmering over the meadows', as Alice Liddell later recalled in her memoirs. The meteorological records, however, say that that 'blazing afternoon' was actually 'cool and rather wet'. But then most memories of Oxford tend to become gilded with the passage of time.

Cambridge
History and Culture

Microsoft Meets the Middle Ages:
A Short History of Cambridge

'It seems so strange to be in a place of colleges that is not Oxford.'
Matthew Arnold, 1853

O f all the towns in Europe, Bill Gates chose Cambridge as the place for his first Microsoft branch outside the USA. When I read this headline in May 1997 ('Techno goldrush boost for Cambridge), I was sitting in the Garden House Hotel on the River Cam. There were cows grazing beneath the willows in Coe Fen. 'Cows in the middle of Cambridge!' said a businessman at the table next to mine. Why on earth was the American computer giant coming to this little market town in the fens of East Anglia?

With an investment of millions, followed by the biggest programme of scholarships in England, Bill Gates put himself right up in the superleague of benefactors that have financed the University of Cambridge since the Middle Ages. Isaac Newton taught here, Charles Darwin began here as a theologian and finished as a naturalist, and Stephen Hawking sits in Newton's professorial chair and tells us all about the black holes in the universe. Atoms, computers and genes – these three great scientific emblems of the 20th century are as bound up with Cambridge as the Tudor coat of arms is with King's College Chapel. The discoverers of the structure of DNA, Francis Crick and James Watson, the pioneers of calculators and artificial intelligence, Charles Babbage and Alan Turing, nuclear physicists like Ernest Rutherford and James Chadwick – all of them played their part in the Cambridge phenomenon that has blossomed in the shadows of the old colleges. Now there are hundreds of hi-tech firms in Silicon Fen, England's answer to California's Silicon Valley. Oxford had Bill Clinton, but Cambridge has Bill Gates.

The history of a place is often the history of a word. In the Anglo-Saxon Chronicles of 875, there is mention of Grantabrycge – the first recorded use of the word 'bridge' in English. From the Norman Grentebrige or Cantabriegge eventually came the name Cambridge. It was after this and not the other way round that the river received its present name of Cam, but in its upper reaches between Silver Street Bridge and Grantchester it is still called the Granta. Derived from this name, and far more famous than the river, is the literary magazine *Granta*, now based in London though it began life as a student magazine. Cambridgeshire is the only county in England to have taken its name from a bridge. The one in question used to be near what is now Magdalene Bridge. Beyond this crossing, on the chalky scree slopes at the southern end of the Fens – a huge area of swampy marshland that was reclaimed in the 18th century – the first Bronze Age settlers built their huts. Sooner or later, everybody came here: Romans, Anglo-Saxons, Vikings, Normans. One lot drove out the other lot, as usually happens in such places where the bridgehead creates a strategic stronghold. Cambridge thus developed into an intersecting point for routes running from the Thames Valley, the Norfolk coast and the Midlands; it became a little trading station between the rival kingdoms of Mercia and East Anglia.

When the monks of Ely packed their bags in 695 to seek a shrine for St Etheldreda, they came to Cambridge and found only a 'civitatula quondam desolata' – the ruins of the Roman *Duroliponte* at the foot of Castle Hill. The centre of the new Anglo-Saxon settlement gradually shifted to the other side of the river, to what is now Bridge Street, the old Roman road to Colchester, and then southwards along Trumpington Street to Swinecroft Marsh, where Downing College is today. The Domesday Book (1086) lists some 375 houses in the little Norman fortress town of Grentebrige. It also mentions the mills at the end of Mill Lane, where you can still see the mill pond. Here the corn was ground for the settlement, which then developed into the main centre for the whole county. Long before Milton's river god 'Camus, reverend Sire' could deck himself out with the pearls of his colleges, there were docks and warehouses on the Backs. The Cam and the Great Ouse linked Cambridge to the North Sea, to King's Lynn and the Baltic ports.

The round Church of the Holy Sepulchre marks the centre of Norman Cambridge. Where the High Street branches off from the old Roman road, there once stood the Hospital of St John, founded by the citizens and the Bishop of Ely in around 1200 to care for the sick and poor. Another of the charitable religious institutions founded by the medieval community was the lepers' hospital, at a safe distance east of the town beyond the Augustinian Priory of Barnwell. The Jews also had their place in the town and in the medieval world picture. The Jewry was opposite Trinity College. But around 1275, the people of Cambridge – with the King's blessing – drove them out of the town even before their general expulsion from England.

'The oldest of all inter-university sports was a lying match,' said the historian F. W. Maitland, referring to the battle over which of the two universities is the older. One of the myths concerning the foundation of Cambridge runs as follows: Athenian philosophers who were followers of Prince Cantaber, the Spanish son-in-law of the King of the Britons, Gurguntius Brabtruc, founded the *Alma Mater Cantabrigiensis* in the 4,321st year after the creation of the world, i.e. 4004 BC. The following story, however, is a little more plausible: two Oxford scholars accused of murdering a prostitute were condemned and hanged in 1209. In protest, Oxford's *Magistri* downed their teaching tools and departed – some of them to Cambridge, and some elsewhere. A new foundation caused by an exodus from an old one is not in itself so unusual – Leipzig University was the result of a secession from Prague. But in that case, why did the university grow up in Cambridge, and not in Northampton, or Stamford, which were equally prosperous market towns where other Oxford scholars had already gone to live? And indeed, why not in London, or in a cathedral city like Lincoln, where there was already a cathedral school?

However obscure the origins of the university might be, what is beyond dispute is that a community of teachers and students were able to obtain the protection of both Crown and Church, a basic precondition for survival in the face of a hostile township. By 1225 Cambridge's *Magistri* had elected a Chancellor from among their members, and his authority – and by extension the autonomy of the university itself – was confirmed by Henry III. Shortly afterwards, in 1233, came recognition by Pope Gregory IX, a canonical privilege that Oxford was not granted until 1254, as the Cambridge archivist Elisabeth Leedham-Green notes with some satisfaction ('As so often Cambridge had started after Oxford and finished first.') An even more important step, however, was the guarantee given by Henry III and his successors that both universities would enjoy monopoly status, and indeed until the 19th century – a period of 600 years – Oxford and Cambridge remained the only universities in England. Nowhere else in Europe was there such a monopoly.

Like Oxford, Cambridge University had no buildings of its own at first. People taught and lived wherever they could in rented rooms. From early on, the students lived in hostels under the supervision of a Principal. By 1280 there were thirty-four such hostels in the town before these private establishments were replaced by the colleges, which had their own rules and regulations and were established with endowments that ensured their permanence and their independence.

In 1284 the Bishop of Ely, Hugh de Balsham, founded Cambridge's first college, Peterhouse. Right down to its statutes, it followed precisely in the footsteps of Merton, the episcopal college which had been founded twenty years earlier in

Oxford. Peterhouse was to have a Master and fourteen Fellows, with two deans for the daily services, two bursars for financial administration, an almoner and, if enough money could be found to pay him, a porter. Apart from two or three places for needy students, it was a postgraduate college, forming a community of advanced scholars along the lines of the Sorbonne in Paris. It was not until the early 14th century, with the foundation of King's Hall by Edward II, that there came into being the pioneering concept of the college as a community of students to live and be taught together. 'The King's Children', as they were called, were indeed children, for they entered college at the age of about fourteen.

Who were the students at that time? Initially they were mainly the children of small landowners and town dignitaries, rather than the aristocracy and the landed gentry. Students during the early Middle Ages lived in strict and monastically Spartan conditions, and often the only ones granted a room of their own were the qualified Doctors of Divinity. All the other Fellows shared their rooms with a group of students – 'not more than two to a bed, unless they be under fourteen', according to the statutes at St John's. Chapel was compulsory in the early morning and evening, and lectures and disputations were held in cold, bare rooms whose floors were covered with straw. There was no such thing as sport or organized leisure. The only diversion was the taverns in the town, and the ladies to be found therein. Even in 1342 there were already complaints about eccentric fashions among dons and students: 'Disdaining the tonsure, the distinctive mark of their order, they wore their hair either hanging down on their shoulders in an effeminate manner, or curled and powdered…; they were attired in cloaks with furred edges, long hanging sleeves not covering their elbows, shoes chequered with red and green, and tippets of an unusual length; their fingers were decorated with rings, and at their waists they wore large and costly girdles, enamelled with figures and gilt: to their girdles hung knives like swords.'

The academic year was divided into three, as it is now. Cambridge, like other European universities in the Middle Ages, offered courses in the *artes liberales* (also dubbed the arts of unemployment): grammar, logic and rhetoric, the so-called *trivium*, followed by the *quadrivium* of arithmetic, music, astronomy and geometry, and then the three philosophies of metaphysics, and moral and natural philosophy. If you passed your examinations after seven years of study, you became a Master of Arts, and were entitled to teach. But if you wanted to make a career for yourself at the court or in the Church as a Doctor of Jurisprudence, Medicine or Divinity, you had to go through another ten years of study – a total of seventeen years, and not even a Gates Scholarship to sustain you.

From the earliest days, Oxbridge graduates had the best chance of success in their chosen fields. Particularly after the Great Plague of 1348–49, which accounted for about a third of the population in England, the need for fully trained clerics, administrators, lawyers and doctors became acute. By 1370 there were eight colleges in Cambridge, and about two dozen hostels. The whole university had some 700 members, which is fewer than a single college like Queens' today. Not until the 15th century did Oxford's poor cousin finally catch up in size, even if not in importance. There are notebooks from this period which tell us what was studied at the time: along with Aristotle, the main focus was on the works of Oxford scholars. Both universities, however, in contrast to Paris for instance, were already establishing a tradition of experimental science in the Middle Ages, together with mathematical and symbolic logic, as apparent in the subtleties of Duns Scotus as in the scepticism of Ockham.

Before the first universities were founded in Europe, monasteries and cathedral schools were the centres of higher education. That was where manuscripts and sacred texts were collected, and that was where the few literate people in a largely illiterate society would gravitate to. In Cambridge too there were monasteries long before there were colleges, and these attracted different branches from the different orders. As the university grew, so did the number of monks, and they exercised a stabilizing influence on the academic community. Many of the early scholars – even those who were not studying divinity – were clerics or became clerics. The language of the Church, Latin, was also the lingua franca of scholars from Bologna, Salamanca, Cambridge and elsewhere. As at many other universities, the Franciscans and the Dominicans were the main rivals for the most important professorships, but inevitably there was a rising trend towards freedom of discussion, as opposed to adhering to the traditional doctrines of the Church. Cambridge soon became a hotbed of heresy. With their teaching, the clerics themselves forged an instrument of what German historian Kurt Flasch has called the 'declericalization of knowledge'. In the late 14th century, around three-quarters of Cambridge's theologians belonged to one of the religious orders, and among the laymen there were four times as many jurists as theologians. The smallest faculty was that of medicine.

Colleges in the Middle Ages were also geared to the salvation of the soul, and so they had chantries with a permanent obligation to hold masses for their founders. Indeed the foundation of a college was regarded as a religious act on a par with that of a monastery or an altarpiece. The founders of the first colleges were by no means confined to the Church. Kings and their wives were among them, as were noblewomen like Elizabeth de Clare and the Countess of Pembroke. There were state officials, merchants, and a few bishops. The most unusual patrons were those of Corpus Christi, which is the only college in Cambridge or Oxford to have been founded (in 1352) by two of the town's guilds. Thirty years later, the good people of Cambridge very nearly destroyed it.

Conflict here, as in Oxford, between town and gown was far from unusual in the Middle Ages. In 1231 Henry III complained to the Mayor on behalf of the scholars about exorbitant rents. The burgesses in turn complained about the many rights enjoyed by the university, ranging from licensing taverns to having their own jurisdiction – privileges which all the English monarchs from the 13th century onwards granted to both universities and some of which continued *pro forma* right through to the reign of Elizabeth II. It caused a lot of bad blood, which reached a climax in 1381 when the Peasants' Revolt hit Cambridge. Led by the Mayor himself, the mob proceeded to plunder the students' quarters, the colleges, and even the university chest in Great St Mary's. Documents were destroyed, and books and papers burned in the market place: 'Away with the learning of the clerks, away with it!'

The town had to pay dearly for its excesses of 1381. Once more the king entrenched the position of the university by giving it control over weights, measures and the price of food in Cambridge. It was even put in charge of the leisure pursuits of the townspeople, including football, theatre, cockfighting and bearbaiting. Not until Parliament passed a law in 1856 did the university lose its right to supervise the markets and fairs in the town, to grant licences and to hold its own courts of justice. But its ancient right to protect its students from the most dangerous of worldly temptations remained in force until 1894: they could arrest prostitutes and license theatre performances. Until 1974 the university still sent four representatives to the City Council. And finally, it took until the beginning of the 21st century for Blair's government to take away the last of all the privileges, going back to a Charter signed by Richard II in 1382: the right to grant pubs a licence for wine.

Even more so than with Oxford, the history of Cambridge is the history of its university. Nothing changed the medieval townscape as much as the colleges, and nothing annoyed the townsfolk as much as the university's increasing appropriation of the land. It's easy to imagine all this if you sit on the little wall in front of King's College. The lawn behind you was once covered with rows of houses, lanes led down to the river, and where there are now courtyards and lawns and the famous chapel, once there was a complete district – razed to the ground in order to make way for Henry VI's grandiose foundation in 1441. Hundreds of workers' houses and shops were demolished along what used to be Milne Street, one of the main streets running parallel to the river; all that is left of it now is Trinity Lane to the north, and the present Queens' Lane to the south. It was a typical piece of what we nowadays like to call 'redevelopment', not to mention property speculation, and it marked the beginning of a radical change in the town's structure. The business district on the river turned into a campus with one of the most beautiful college parks in Europe: the Backs.

In the meantime, the university had constructed its very first building: the Old Schools (c. 1350–1475) with lecture and assembly rooms, library and administration. Around this academic centre the colleges began to take up their positions: Clare, Trinity Hall, Gonville Hall. Gradually the warehouses disappeared along with the docks and the quays on the Cam. By around 1500 there were a dozen colleges in Cambridge, most of them between High Street and the river, stretching from Peterhouse in the south – already outside the town walls at Trumpington Gate – to Trinity College and St John's in the north, though both of these came later. The division soon became apparent: the university expanded to the west, and the east remained predominantly town not gown.

The invention of the printing press was a great aid in spreading the ideas of the humanists. No one embodied the classical spirit of this great European Renaissance more brilliantly than Erasmus of Rotterdam (see p. 259). And Erasmus came to Cambridge. He came, moaned about the weather, the flat beer, the useless copyists and virtually everything else in Cambridge, but he stayed on and off for nearly three years. Between 1511 and 1514 he had lodgings in Queens' College, taught theology and Greek, wrote, translated, edited, corresponded, and did all of these things with matchless energy, style and grace. He was more than a prestige catch for Cambridge. Instead of medieval scholarship, he turned attention back to its sources, switching the focus from theology to rhetoric, from training people for the priesthood to making them into educated public servants. For a long time afterwards, it was classical languages and literature that dominated the curriculum in English universities. The Cambridge humanists' preoccupation with Greek and Hebrew led to critical editions of the Bible and the works of the Church Fathers. All of this prepared the way for the Reformation.

A key role in this development was played by the man who had brought Erasmus to Cambridge: his friend John Fisher. He was Master of Queens', Bishop of Rochester, and for thirty years Chancellor of the University – a scholar and organizer of immense influence, not least through his position as father confessor to

Lady Margaret Beaufort, mother of Henry VII. Instead of giving her fortune to Westminster Abbey, she was advised by the pious don to save her soul by supporting Cambridge. And what support she gave! First a chair of divinity (1502), the oldest in Cambridge; then a college, Christ's (1505); and posthumously a second college, St John's (1511). The completion of King's College Chapel by Henry VII was also thanks to John Fisher. Spectacular gifts, rising numbers of students, a humanist curriculum – all of this helped Cambridge rise to become a university of European rank, and for the first time to draw level with Oxford. John Fisher was a reformer, but he remained orthodox at heart, for while he brought the temperate Erasmus to Cambridge, he had the writings of Martin Luther burnt in public. Finally, he himself stood on the scaffold. Among his opponents was a former Fellow of Jesus College, Thomas Cranmer, Archbishop of Canterbury (see p. 258). It was from him that Henry VIII received the information that the Cambridge theologians would interpret the canonically tricky question of divorce in his favour. Fearing the threat of sanctions, the university said yes, but its Chancellor said no. He was beheaded in 1535 for high treason. Four hundred years later, however, he was canonized.

Unlike conservative Oxford, Cambridge and its dons soon embraced Luther's teachings. Around 1521, the dons met in the White Horse near King's, and they discussed the new ideas that had come from Germany. 'Little Germany' was the name given to this group of sympathizers, and if their tavern had not been long since demolished, there would surely be a sign there now saying, 'Here drank the pioneers of English Protestantism'. Hugh Latimer, Thomas Cranmer, Miles Coverdale, Matthew Parker, William Tyndale – as Bible translators, bishops and archbishops, these allies of 'Little Germany' all played a major part in disseminating the ideas of the Reformation throughout England. Two books played a particularly important role: Tyndale's Bible and Cranmer's liturgy, *The Book of Common Prayer*.

William Tyndale had left Oxford because of the threat of persecution, had continued his studies in Cambridge, and had actually met Luther in Wittenberg. He was the first man to translate the New Testament into English, and his version was published in 1525–26 in Worms; it was written in plain and simple prose which helped to spread the spirit of the new movement all over the country. For his pains, he was burned at the stake. The same linguistic qualities applied to *The Book of Common Prayer* (1549), which was initiated by Archbishop Cranmer and had an even greater influence. Through the Act of Uniformity, which was passed in the same year, it was made compulsory for every church and every house to read this handbook of the Protestant Revolution – a book that left an indelible mark on the English language and is even today seen as a worldwide symbol of English culture. Cranmer's liturgy, Tyndale's Bible and the works of Shakespeare all represent the triumph of this small island's language, and it should be added that twelve of the thirteen men who worked on the prayer book were from Cambridge.

In the light of Henry VIII's power politics, however, one should not overestimate the influence of the universities. In both Oxford and Cambridge the monasteries were dissolved, but the king's advisers were still not satisfied. They wanted the college silver, the endowments and the estates. In 1545 Henry VIII signed a law ordering the dissolution of all the larger chantries and all the colleges. How Oxbridge, amazingly, escaped this death penalty is a mystery, but somehow the bursars must have succeeded in proving that their colleges were a total write-off, for on reading their accounts the king remarked, not without a degree of irony, that 'he had not in his realm so many persons so honestly maintained in living, by so little land and rent.' He then left the colleges in peace to go on racking up more debts, and while he carried on sacking the chantries, the richest and most majestic of all, King's Chapel, was given its magnificent interior with his blessing.

It is one of the paradoxes of his reign that this flamboyant king, who never showed much interest in Cambridge, actually endowed it with five Regius professorships. But in a time of such upheavals, the Crown needed Oxford and Cambridge to provide it with a reservoir of reliable administrators, jurists and preachers to give academic backing to his regime. It was not, therefore, just out of royal generosity that in 1546 Henry VIII himself founded a college. This he did by combining two older colleges into a massive new one that left all its predecessors in the shade: Trinity College. It is still the only one in Cambridge whose Master is not elected by the Fellows but is nominated by the Crown, on the recommendation of the prime minister.

In 1553, Henry's Catholic daughter Mary Tudor succeeded to the throne of England. Heretics were put on trial, college Masters were deposed, and three of the leading figures in the Reformation, Cranmer, Latimer and Ridley were burned at the stake in Oxford (see p. 137). Many Protestants fled to the Continent, while others failed to find peace even in the grave. On 6 February 1556, the corpses of the Protestant theologians Martin Bucer and Paul Fagius were exhumed, their coffins chained to stakes, taken to the market place in Cambridge and set on fire, as if they had now become heretical ghosts.

When the Protestant Elizabeth I came to the throne, the university gradually settled down again, though even this change of regime had its problems. There were fierce debates about the authority of the Bible and the Church, and having to swear an oath of allegiance to the Anglican faith caused many a crisis of conscience among both Recusants and Puritans who were totally loyal to Elizabeth. The 'Virgin Queen' introduced the rule of celibacy for all the Fellows except the Master, and from 1570 onwards this ban on marriage became part of the university statutes, and remained so officially until 1861. New colleges were founded for the advancement of the true faith – Emmanuel (1584) on land confiscated from the Dominicans, and Sidney Sussex (1596) on former Franciscan territory – and in order to demonstrate their break with the Catholic past, both chapels were built facing north instead of east.

Only once, in summer 1564, did Elizabeth I visit Cambridge, for her sympathies (and her generous gifts) were directed towards her 'dear Oxford'. However, during her long reign, the University of Cambridge enjoyed closer relations with the throne and with the powers-that-be than ever before and indeed ever since. For forty years, its Chancellor William Cecil, Lord Burghley, used his ministerial influence to protect and promote his Alma Mater. Cambridge graduates followed one another as Archbishops of Canterbury and into all the other high offices of Church and State.

As the religious climate settled down, the numbers of students increased from 1,630 in 1570 to around 3,000 in the 1620s. A growing proportion came from the gentry, and there were three distinct categories of student: the noblemen, who paid higher fees, gained their academic titles without taking exams, and as 'fellow commoners' were privileged to take their meals ('commons') at the same table as the Fellows; then came the 'pensioners', who were from the middle classes and paid less for their tuition and accommodation; and finally the 'sizars', who came from a poorer background, did not pay any fees, but were obliged to work for the college. The basic mode of tuition in this three-class system was the 'supervision', which developed through the 16th and 17th centuries and also formed part of the college economy, as the young Fellows earned their living by means of these supervisions.

For centuries the town of Cambridge was merely the setting for the university, providing a reservoir of cheap labour. As recently as 1954, the Irish dramatist Sean O'Casey on a visit to Cambridge wrote: 'It sidles and lurches round the colleges, looking like a shabby fellow waiting for a job from a rich relative.' The more the colleges expanded, the greater was the need for porters, janitors, cleaners and craftsmen. Cambridge itself remained relatively small – in 1801, the year of the first census, there were no more than 9,000 inhabitants. It was just a little market town in the centre of a prosperous agricultural region. Farmers lived here, and stonemasons, brewers, tailors, shoemakers, merchants. There were no large town houses, for the rich burgesses lived on their country estates outside the town. Just once a year, though, they would come into the town together with visitors from all over the country, including coaches from London, and merchants from the Continent. This was in September, and the event they came for was the Stourbridge Fair.

By about 1211 King John had bestowed on the burgesses the privilege of holding a market on the common land east of the town. Stourbridge Fair became the biggest of its kind in England. Clothiers and wine merchants, tanners, chandlers, book-sellers, horse dealers – all of them had their stalls here, and there were entertainers too, conjurors, puppet-masters, clowns, dwarfs, giants, 'wild beasts and wild men'. It was a gigantic fiesta complete with bars and brothels, catering for all tastes and needs. The colleges stocked up with candles, the scholars with books, and Isaac Newton is said to have bought his prism there. John Bunyan is believed to have used Stourbridge as his model for Vanity Fair in *Pilgrim's Progress*. But in the 19th century it began to lose its appeal, and in 1934 it came to an end. All that remains is one street-name: Garlic Row, where the garlic- and spice-sellers once had their stands.

The Stuart kings preferred Oxford. They regarded Cambridge as a stopping-off place on the way to the horse races at Newmarket. When James I stayed at Trinity in 1614, the college had to ban smoking because it was well known that the king hated tobacco. For his entertainment the dons offered him a 'philosophy act' – a mock debate on the subject of whether dogs can make syllogisms. The conclusion was that dogs cannot think, whereupon the monarch declared that his dogs were an exception, which the dons confirmed with loud cheers. There is no doubt that at the time Cambridge was intellectually buzzing with theological and political discussions that everyone enjoyed, including the youthful John Milton. At Sidney Sussex, a student named Oliver Cromwell got to know the ideas of the Calvinists, and in 1640 he was elected Member of Parliament for Cambridge with a majority of just one vote. 'That single vote had ruined both Church and Kingdom,' observed the poet John Cleveland, Fellow of St John's.

When the Civil War began, the university – unlike the town – was generally Royalist. In 1643 Cromwell returned, made the colleges into barracks, and Cambridge into the headquarters of the parliamentary movement in East Anglia. Most Masters were deposed, half of all the Fellows – more than two hundred – were sacked, and some fled to Oxford, where Charles I held court. William Dowsing, on behalf of Parliament, now set out to destroy everything in the colleges that had survived the Reformation: angels, icons, and anything that might be condemned as papist. For all the barbarism of this iconoclast, it is clear that he represented the concept of piety that inspired many of Cromwell's contemporaries.

'Beware of sleeping at prayers and sermons for that is the sleep of death,' warn the rules for Trinity students from around 1660. 'Play not at Chesse or very seldome, for though it be an ingenious play, yet too tedious and time-devouring. Refraine foot-ball, it being as it is commonly used a rude, boisterous exercise, & fitter for Clownes than for Schollers.'

After the restoration of the monarchy, the Act of Uniformity re-established the old Anglican order, and court favourites were imposed on the university as Chancellors. For many years, professorial chairs also reflected the Protestant–Catholic fluctuations of the monarchy. The Cambridge Platonists, however, a group of liberal religious philosophers, continued to do their teaching and their research with Cartesian incorruptibility, and they were not alone: 'Reason is the candle of the Lord,' was the watchword, and as faith searched for rational justification, reason found a new religion of its own: the natural sciences. After the foundation of the Royal Society in London (1660), chairs were established for mathematics, chemistry and astronomy. The star of Isaac Newton shone brightly over Cambridge. The most heated debates among the scholars took place in the coffee houses, where Puritans and Rationalists enjoyed the new 'in' drink amid orgies of sobriety. The coffee houses were now the centres for new theories, the latest gossip, students' poetry, and in due course the first newspapers. These precursors of our Internet cafés proved so popular that in 1750 the Vice-Chancellor and the Heads of Houses issued a decree banning any morning visits to such establishments.

Unlike Oxford, Cambridge was relatively isolated from London, which may have been a factor in its comparative independence. Not until 1792 was there a regular, direct stagecoach, and the journey then took seven and a quarter hours. For most of the 18th century, the Crown and Parliament left the university to its own devices. Dons and students did what they liked best – a bit of study and a lot of entertainment. They went fishing and hunting, frequented their beloved coffee houses, and went to the theatre and the brothels. With this concentration of celibate Fellows and academic stallions, the prostitutes were on to a good thing.

In the Combination Room at St John's, with its fine Georgian setting, one can sense something of the elegance and the opulence of 'the exceedingly comfortable and respectable century', as Virginia Woolf's father Leslie Stephen called it. The image of dozing dons and hunting-shooting-fishing-drinking students is one of the Oxbridge clichés of the time, and indeed the escapades of the eccentric young aristocrats certainly attracted more attention than the bent backs and lowered heads of the bookworms. The majority of students, however, came from less moneyed backgrounds, worked hard, and hoped at least to finish up with a parish living to keep body and soul together. Nevertheless, many of the professors in Georgian Cambridge gave no lectures at all and indeed were often conspicuous by their absence.

By around 1800, the reputation of both Cambridge and Oxford had gone rapidly downhill. Two other universities had taken over top spot, particularly in the sciences: Edinburgh in Scotland, and Göttingen in Germany, the latter having been founded by George II and having soon become the most renowned university of the Hanoverians. Also, for the first time, Oxbridge had lost its monopoly and now faced competition within England itself from Durham (1832) and London (1836). At the same time, more and more people wanted to study. The prosperous middle classes needed new institutions of higher education, and in the increasingly industrialized and commercial society of the Victorian Age, even Cambridge began to realize that perhaps it should try to make itself useful. Reform was long overdue, and the man who gave it a kick start was a prince from Coburg: Victoria's husband Prince Albert.

In 1847, by a narrow majority, the University of Cambridge elected this none-too-popular German to be its Chancellor. To the Queen's relief, Prince Albert at last had something to do in his own right, and as it happened, he knew more about education in Germany and in England than did most British academics. He had rather too much respect for Cambridge's traditions, and was by nature perhaps a little too ready to compromise for his reforms to be truly radical, but the University Act of 1858 brought about a revision of the statutes and of the curriculum; furthermore, the cosy autonomy of the colleges was restricted, and the time of academic privilege came to an end. By now the Catholics were demanding full academic rights, and women also wanted the chance to study.

When Miss Emily Davies began to teach her five students in 1869, it was the most modest and yet the most decisive of beginnings. Girton was Britain's first college for women, followed two years later by Newnham. Intellectual and social freedom for young ladies? 'No good will come of this,' growled the die-hards. Indeed, Victorian society had very different ideas of what constituted progress. But gradually the professors got used to seeing girls at their lectures, even if Sir Arthur Quiller-Couch still insisted on addressing his mixed audiences as 'Gentlemen'. In 1890, the best examination result of that generation of students was achieved by a girl. All the same, women were not allowed to earn a degree. The gentlemen saw to that with their veto in the Senate. Cambridge was the last British university to grant women full academic rights, ranging from having a vote to attending the degree ceremony. This had to wait until 1948, twenty-eight years after Oxford – another record. King's and Churchill were the first men's colleges to accept women (in 1972), and Magdalene was the last (in 1987). In those heroic days, when 'we went mixed,' according to the Head Porter at St John's, 'my predecessor Bob Fuller wore a black armband, and our college flag was flown at half mast.' Today more than a third of all Cambridge students are female, though only six per cent of the Fellows are women.

A law that ended discrimination against Nonconformists came into force in 1871, but before then anyone who wanted to take a degree or to become a teacher had to take an oath to abide by the Thirty-Nine Articles, a practice introduced in 1563, which entailed swearing allegiance to the Anglican Church. Catholics, Jews and other Dissenters were generally barred from Oxbridge. Despite this long delayed move towards religious tolerance, it was still compulsory for all students to attend prayers in chapel every day, and this rule was only lifted at the end of the First World War (though it lasted even longer in some colleges).

The fact that Cambridge was gradually emerging from the Middle Ages became apparent in 1861, when it took on its first married don. One year before, the university had officially lifted its ban on married Fellows, but as the individual colleges were allowed to take their own decisions on the subject, it was only after 1880 that the fashion really caught on. It started off a baby and building boom in Cambridge, as the new academic families required suitable new housing. It also brought an end to the college way of life, in which Fellows and students were symbiotically housed under one roof.

There are, however, some dons who still yearn for those good old days. 'I believed in the colleges as a family, really as single-sex institutions,' said David Watkin, Fellow of Peterhouse. 'My ideal was a place where the dons lived in college and the undergraduates were *in statu pupillari*. It was an extraordinary society which existed very satisfactorily and was changed really with very little thought just following an idle egalitarian fashion. And I don't welcome any egalitarian elements in a place of higher education.' From a genetic point of view, the lifting of the ban led to a wondrous intensification of the Oxbridge factor. Intermarriage between academics led to children who in turn became dons, headmasters at places like Eton and Rugby, and leading figures in political, literary and public life. Such Oxbridge dynasties included the Arnolds, the Adrians, the Butlers, the Huxleys and the Stephens, Quaker families like the Gurneys, the Frys, the Gaskells and the

Hodgkins, and illustrious names like Macaulay, Trevelyan and Darwin, the latter joining forces with Keynes. These few families produced a disproportionate number of eminent and influential personalities between the turn of the century and the 1930s – a very conservative 'intellectual aristocracy' whose physical and mental interrelationships have been documented by the Cambridge historian Noel Annan, one of the last great heirs to the tradition who, incidentally, married a member of the Berlin House of Ullstein.

This Oxbridge inbreeding also had its reverse side, for even after the various reforms, working-class people still had very little chance of gaining entry. 'The real reason for our exclusion,' wrote Charles Kingsley, 'is because we are poor.' The eponymous hero of his novel *Alton Locke* is a tailor and poet for whom Cambridge in 1850 is as inaccessible as Oxford was to be for Thomas Hardy's stonemason Jude. Kingsley himself, whose historical novels have virtually disappeared apart from the place name of 'Westward Ho!', became Regius Professor of Modern History at Cambridge. Prince Albert engaged him as tutor to his eldest son (Edward VII), who was a student at Trinity and who was impressed by Kingsley's 'muscular Christianity'. As champion of the working classes, royal tutor, Christian socialist, Catholic-hater, and pure embodiment of all the contradictions of his time, Kingsley was immensely popular among the Victorians.

In 1870 the Chancellor of the University, William Cavendish, 7th Duke of Devonshire, founded a chair for experimental physics along with a laboratory, both named after one of his ancestors, the physicist Henry Cavendish. It was the beginning of a great leap forward in the study of the sciences in Cambridge, and the catalyst was the Cavendish Institute. On the other hand, the Industrial Revolution passed Cambridge by. At least the railway managed to get there in 1845, after a fierce tug-of-war between the town and the university, the latter (just like Oxford) being opposed to it. The Vice-Chancellor protested vehemently against the introduction of cheap Sunday returns to London, for such sinful things were 'as distasteful to the University authorities as they must be offensive to Almighty God and to all right-minded Christians.'

At least the university succeeded in getting the station built on vacant land far away from the centre. There, in the eastern part of the town, arose the estates of terraced houses for the railway workers – 'Little Russia' as the district of Romsey was then dubbed – while in the west, beyond the Backs, the dons settled down in their magnificent villas. In the 19th century the population of Cambridge quadrupled to almost 50,000. Many lived in the medieval centre, squashed together in the narrow lanes and courtyards around Petty Cury. Undernourishment, typhus and prostitution were all part of everyday life. The sewage flowed directly into the Cam. When Queen Victoria visited the town in 1868, she looked down from a bridge and was surprised to see hundreds of scraps of paper floating by. 'Those, ma'am, are notices that bathing is forbidden,' explained William Whewell, Master of Trinity.

During the First World War, Cambridge became a garrison. Nurses moved into the colleges, and field hospitals stood on the cricket squares. In the chapels there was soon an endless, tragic succession of memorial services, for this university alone lost more than 2,000 students before the bells of Great St Mary's finally announced Armistice Day on 11 November 1918. Then magically the 1920s seemed to take Cambridge back into Edwardian times, and the spirit of the dead but eternally young Rupert Brooke became the epitome of the beautiful and clever young things of Cambridge, swirling through a world of punting parties, May Balls and crème brulée.

Between the wars, Cambridge was a place of social elegance and intellectual controversy, dominated by towering figures such as Bertrand Russell, Maynard Keynes and Ludwig Wittgenstein. Philosophy, economics and the sciences flourished, but so too did student theatre groups and debating societies like The Heretics, the Moral Science Club and, most exclusive of all, the Apostles (see p. 223). Then Hitler's rise to power brought a deadly serious tone to the discussions. Virginia Woolf's nephew Julian Bell and his friend John Cornford were among the young Cambridge volunteers who died in the Spanish Civil War, carrying *Das Kapital* in their knapsacks. After 1933, Marxism seemed to many students and dons the only respectable alternative. The historian Eric Hobsbawm, Fellow of King's, remained a member of the Communist Party right through to the 1990s. In this simmering intellectual cauldron, the KGB was able to recruit spies like Kim Philby and Anthony Blunt, but the British Secret Service also recruited some of the top brains for its decoding team in Bletchley Park – above all, the brilliant mathematician Alan Turing, who played the main role in cracking the Enigma Code that was so crucial to the German military machine.

In 1938–39 alone, some 40,000 Jews sought asylum in England. One of them was the eighteen-year-old Gottfried Ehrenberg from Tübingen, who under the name of Geoffrey Elton became one of the most important Cambridge historians of the Tudor period. But as a result of Britain's strict immigration policy, only one in ten asylum-seekers was accepted during Hitler's reign of terror. The Academic Assistance Council, an aid organization which began work in 1933, helped some refugees – particularly scientists – to find refuge in Cambridge, and one of these was the Viennese chemist Max Perutz, who in 1947 founded the world-famous laboratory for molecular biology. For his lifelong research on haemoglobin, Perutz together with his colleague John Kendrew received the Nobel Prize in 1962.

If you wander round the Cambridge colleges today, you will find that nearly all of them have memorials to those who died in the Second World War; there were sixty alone in a small college like Peterhouse, and 389 in Trinity.

The number of students has steadily increased. In 1938 there were 6,000, by 1984 more than 12,000, and today the thirty-one colleges cater for around 17,000. The new foundations include some purely graduate colleges – Darwin, Wolfson and Clare Hall – and the university now spreads far beyond the narrow confines of the city centre. This development actually began in 1934 with the building of the University Library, and by the end of the 20th century there was a huge new campus in the west of the city, with science again predominant.

In summer 1959 a lecture took place in Cambridge that caused an uproar and is still quoted even today, although its subject was not even new at the time: 'The Two Cultures and the Scientific Revolution'. The argument was that scientists were lacking in literary culture, while those trained in the arts didn't know the first thing about thermodynamics, and the complaint came from the Cavendish physicist and novelist C. P. Snow. His thesis concerned the growing economically and socially disastrous gulf between the sciences and the arts, and it caused a stir even beyond Cambridge. Surely Bertrand Russell, mathematician and winner of the Nobel Prize for literature, was living proof of the counter-argument. A don from Downing, F. R. Leavis, who was the literary guru of his time, became Snow's most vociferous critic, but his argument has long since been discredited. The most radical changes in society of recent years have been brought about by genetic and information technology, and the cultural mandarins have had little part to play.

The thinking elite of Cambridge had latched onto this trend before most of their colleagues elsewhere in England, and not only through the foundation of Churchill College. In 1970, Trinity initiated the establishment of the Science Park, which proved to be a springboard for cooperation between hi-tech research and industry, and between town and gown. The university concentrated on the sciences, though not at the expense of its traditional strengths in the arts. A new faculty, the School of Technology, grew out of the Engineering Department, and yet all these developments took place against the background of a higher education policy that viewed both Cambridge and Oxford as a relic of the old elitism. It was Shaw who said that Oxbridge aimed to produce gentlemen and not businessmen, and it was Margaret Thatcher and her government that decided they should pay the penalty. The university now had to adhere to the new commercial priorities, and so in came controls on efficiency, productivity and measurable statistics, and of course subsidies were drastically cut. The personal tutor system was badly hit, as was anything that couldn't prove itself to be economically profitable. Out went the Tories, and in came Tony Blair's New Labour, but to the dismay of many, nothing changed. Oxbridge continued to be punished. Margaret Thatcher and Tony Blair, two Oxford graduates, waged an unbroken patricidal campaign against the academic principles that had produced them both. Instead of improving the state school system, the Labour ideologists could only denounce the dominance of the independent schools.

'Want a place at Cambridge? Go to a state school'. Under this headline, *The Independent* reported in January 2000 on a pioneering attempt by Clare College to give priority to candidates from state schools and underprivileged families over those from private schools. Critics understandably called it 'social engineering' and discrimination against the independent schools, but nevertheless by 2004, the number of new entrants to Cambridge from state schools had risen to 55 per cent, as opposed to the still disproportionate 45 per cent from the private sector. The difficulty is to achieve the right balance without lowering standards and without abandoning the principle of entry on merit.

Mass production and mediocrity in higher education both in England and on the Continent only serve to reinforce the arguments of those who defend Oxbridge, such as Noel Annan, who pleads the case for the elite university on the grounds that 'Excellence breeds excellence'. Excellence does not have to be heavy-handed, though. The more playful side was illustrated by a poetry competition which has been held since the 18th century for Sir William Browne's Medals, named after a Fellow from Peterhouse. In 2004 the challenge was to write either an epigram in ancient Greek on the subject of junk food, or an epigram in Latin on junk mail. Thus do the old and new go hand in hand in modern Cambridge. In this context of excellence, it is perhaps worth noting that the university has the lowest rate of drop-outs in England at 1 per cent (in Germany the rate is 50 per cent).

While the university found itself facing crises of finance and identity, the city and the region enjoyed an unprecedented boom. A symbol of this 'Cambridge phenomenon' is the above-mentioned Science Park, built in 1970 on the north-eastern outskirts of the city. It was the brainchild of John Bradfield, the bursar of Trinity College, which has owned the land since 1443. He planned it along the lines of similar parks in America, where innovative companies do their development work, combining basic research with economic exploitation to the mutual benefit of university and industry. With about seventy companies now based there, the Cambridge Science Park is now the biggest concentration of IT and biotechnology in Britain, and yet this 50-hectare space with its pavilions and its green setting looks more like a holiday camp than a hive of industry. If you are not interested in the experiments being conducted by Abcam, Xaar and NAPP, then just go and view it as an arboretum. Dr Bradfield is a zoologist, and as a true nature-lover, he had a second vision to go with the laboratories – namely, to plant as many types of tree between them as the alphabet has letters, from the alder to the zelkova.

The success of this park, which was the first in England (Scotland already had one in Strathclyde) had been preceded by other less spectacular initiatives. About ten years after the hi-tech boom in California's Silicon Valley, a number of small, highly specialized firms were set up in and around Cambridge. They were generally started by young scientists – spiritual descendants of Newton – who preferred to work independently rather than take badly paid teaching jobs. This was the entrepreneurial spirit of Thatcherism. The inventor of the World Wide Web, the physicist Tim Berners-Lee, was a Cambridge graduate, as was England's first Internet millionaire Mike Lynch, who started the software company Autonomy. In the middle of the 1980s there were more than 400 such firms in the area, and 'Silicon Fen' was trumpeted as a shining example of Thatcherism at work, and indeed it gave a massive economic boost to the whole region.

In 1987, St John's College set up its own Innovation Centre opposite the Science Park. The link between future technology and a centuries-old academic tradition in the creative environment of Cambridge University worked like a magnet. Sony, Olivetti, Microsoft and many other global players in this new, post-industrial revolution have also sunk their research roots in the Fens. And what better place could there be to foster Europe's centre for the key technologies of the 21st century? There are now nearly 1,500 firms with about 33,000 employees in the area, and for several years Cambridgeshire has been the fastest-growing county in England. 'The gown-town has become a boom-town,' wrote *The Independent* in 1999. The down side, inevitably, is a vast excess of road traffic and an acute shortage of accommodation.

Every day about 40,000 commuters drive into Cambridge from the surrounding villages. Traffic jams during the rush hour are worse than on Blackfriars Bridge in London. Even the 'Park & Ride' bus schemes on the edges of the city have done little to relieve the claustrophobic conditions. Cars are no longer allowed in the narrow streets of the city centre, but there it's bicycles that are the problem. Campaigns by the Pedestrians Only lobby to have them banned from the centre have not only mobilized town against gown, but have also set the Labour City Council (pro-cyclist) at loggerheads with the Conservative County Council (pro-pedestrian) – not that they need much encouragement to oppose each other. Tourists are another major contribution to the congestion, since about 3.5 million of them descend on Cambridge every year. The City Council has even considered mounting campaigns like the 'Great Cambridge stay-away day', with the slogan 'Cambridge is full...we don't want you!'

The city is indeed full, with more than 120,000 inhabitants. Every year house prices go up by about 20 per cent thanks to the massive demand and the boom in Silicon Fen. Even tiny Victorian terraced houses in the old working-class suburb of Romsey are fetching more than £150,000, while in the west of the city they might cost almost triple that amount. As for a villa in Storey's Way, you will be looking at £1 million plus. The result is that many people prefer to live in Ely or Huntingdon and commute. Tens of thousands of new houses need to be built in the next few years – but where? The planners have a real problem on their hands (see p. 256). A rural university has suddenly become an economic centre, though it still has the infrastructure of a small, medieval market town. That too is part of the Cambridge phenomenon.

'It seems our destiny is to turn into a show place.' Such were the prophetic words of Henry Sidgwick, a Trinity don, in 1869. 'Learning will go elsewhere and we shall subside into cicerones. The typical Cambridge man will be the antiquarian personage who knows about the history of colleges, and is devoted to the *culture des ruines*'. More than most other places, Cambridge is a socially divided city, but the division is no longer between town and gown. The academic middle classes are distinct from the software millionaires from Silicon Fen, while the intellectual and technological elite are distinct from the crowded ranks of the less well-paid workers. Unemployment is low, but some of the employed live right on the poverty line, for example in problem areas such as Arbury in the north of the city. All the same, the groups do mix and social tensions are not a major problem. You will not find equality in any town or indeed in any western society, but Cambridge appears to have achieved as fine a balance as one could hope for.

Apostles and Spies:
'The Cambridge Homintern'

'I hate the idea of causes, and if I had to choose between betraying my country
and betraying my friend I hope I should have the guts to betray my country.'
E. M. Forster, 1951

In 1820, a student got together with his friends at St John's to start a debating
society called The Cambridge Conversazione Society. As originally there were
twelve of them, they became known later as the Apostles. Their founder, George
Tomlinson, ended his days as Anglican Bishop of Gibraltar. One of the most
famous members of this society died in Moscow in 1988, a highly decorated spy for
the KGB, by the name of Kim Philby. These were the two extremes of the Cambridge elite, brilliant and mysterious, like so much else that has emerged from the
history of this university.

The Apostles, whose early members included the poet Alfred Tennyson, met
once a week, at first in St John's and then later in Trinity. There they discussed anything and everything that took their fancy, and they had only two rules: absolute
openness among themselves, and absolute silence outside. They were rationalists
and agnostics, whose only faith was doubt. They questioned everything that was
orthodox in church and state, in science and in morality. Such nonconformism was
dangerous in Cambridge. They therefore cultivated their subversive thinking in
typical English fashion by forming a strictly private club. They were subtle masters of the art of undermining the Establishment without breaking away from it or
from its comforts.

The fact that this secret society became world-famous was due to the celebrity
of its members and to their predilection for writing memoirs. Leonard Woolf,
Lytton Strachey, John Maynard Keynes, Rupert Brooke, Bertrand Russell, Ludwig
Wittgenstein, E. M. Forster, G. M. Trevelyan – all of these in their time were members of the Apostles. At the beginning of the 20th century they were a dazzling
constellation. Most of them were at Trinity, the richest and most aristocratic college of them all, and many were also part of the Bloomsbury circle. 'Love, the
creation and enjoyment of aesthetic experience and the pursuit of knowledge' was
how the philosopher G. E. Moore summed up the ideals of the society whose
president he became. With his *Principia Ethica* (1903), a theory of relativity concerning goodness, Moore influenced a whole generation of students.

'The most important event of my Cambridge life was being elected to the Apostles,' wrote Virginia Woolf's nephew Julian Bell in 1930. 'I really felt I had reached the pinnacle of Cambridge intellectualism.' They called one another 'brother', and anything connected with the Apostles was designated 'reality' while the rest was 'phenomena' – mere appearance. In schoolboy manner they loved making up code words of their own: old members were 'angels', candidates were 'embryos', and sardines on toast were 'whales' (that was the traditional meal at their Saturday evening meetings). They would discuss topics like 'Is I me?', 'Are crocodiles the best of animals?', and 'Can we mean anything when we don't know what we mean?' 'When we divided last term on "Can we love those we copulate with?" the presence of women in the discussion would have been invaluable,' observed Bertrand Russell in 1893. Women were not admitted to this masculine circle until 1971. The first 'sister' was Juliet Annan, a student at King's and daughter of the 'angel' Lord Annan. Some of the Apostles considered homosexual relations to be a loftier form of love, and in the framework of what Lytton Strachey called 'higher sodomy', everything was permissible provided it fitted in with their own code of ethics. In this climate of intellectual games and adventurous morality, people also began to dally with Marxism.

At the beginning of the 1920s, a young Russian immigrant named Vladimir Nabokov was surprised at some of his fellow students who, 'for all their decency and refinement, would lapse into the most astonishing drivel when Russia was being discussed.' One of these inanities – or was it perhaps a subtle joke? – came from the art historian and Trinity Apostle Anthony Blunt, who after a trip to the Soviet Union in 1935 declared that Communism could be just as interesting as Cubism. Not all the Apostles were blind in the left eye. Maynard Keynes warned his colleagues that Marxist economics were 'an insult to our intelligence'.

There were two main reasons why, during the 'pink decade' between the wars, so many left-wingers in England sympathized with Marxism: one was a class system with three million unemployed, and the other was the growing threat of Germany's National Socialism. Communism seemed to be a more acceptable alternative than the Labour Party, a policy of appeasement, and the 'hypocrisy' that John Le Carré described as 'an essential component of our social equipment'. 'Little wonder that the young men of Oxford and Cambridge, longing to escape from the tight rules of conduct in bourgeois England, grasped at the blue flower of Communism during the 1930s.' But the majority of the 'bright young things' in Oxbridge were either Liberal or Conservative in those days, and certainly not Marxist. The strength of pacifist feeling, however, was demonstrated by the

Oxford Union with the famous debate on 9 February 1933, shortly after Hitler had seized power. By a majority of 275 to 153, they voted that 'this House will in no circumstances fight for its King and Country'. The Cambridge Apostles interpreted this burning question of morality and political loyalty in their own way.

While Julian Bell died fighting for the left in the Spanish Civil War, his fellow Apostle and lover from Trinity days, Anthony Blunt, became an agent for the Soviet Secret Service. He had been recruited by his friend Guy Burgess, a gambler with a power complex. In 1933 Kim Philby, another Apostle and Trinity dandy, had already entered the service of the KGB. The other man in the group was Donald MacLean, a graduate of Trinity Hall, whom Guy Burgess met up with again at the Foreign Ministry and recruited for the cause. Both of them were working at the British Embassy in Washington in 1950, and there MacLean had access to the American nuclear weapons programme. In 1951 they both fled to Moscow, after receiving a tip-off from the 'third man', Philby.

Philby was the super-spy in this group – the KGB's most successful double agent. After taking his degree in history, he entered the British Secret Service and became head of MI6, responsible for counter-espionage in the eastern bloc. For hundreds of agents and opposition groups in Eastern Europe, Philby's double game had the direst consequences. He was not exposed until 1963, when the American Michael Straight, yet another former Trinity man and Apostle, confessed to the FBI. Philby fled to Moscow, where he lived for another twenty-five years with the state pension of a KGB general, a supply of Cooper's Oxford marmalade, and the books that he went on getting from Sherratt & Hughes in Cambridge right to the very end.

A year after his flight, in 1964, the 'fourth man' was also exposed. He was none other than the Queen's adviser on art, whom she had knighted for his services as curator of the royal collection. He was given immunity from prosecution in exchange for a full confession, and it was not until fifteen years later, when he had long since retired from all his public offices, that in November 1979 Prime Minister Margaret Thatcher finally revealed to Parliament the name of the fourth traitor: Sir Anthony Blunt, Surveyor of the Queen's Pictures and secret agent in the service of Joseph Stalin. This scandal shook the Establishment even more than had the abdication of Edward VIII. Blunt, after all, was 'one of us', cut from the same cloth, sharing the same clubs, the same institutions, even the same beds. The Cambridge spies had betrayed their class, and that was even worse than betraying their country. 'I chose conscience,' declared Blunt. This Apostle had not turned traitor, then, simply for a few pieces of silver. Philby and Burgess also saw themselves as traitors by conviction. The protagonists of what the Oxford don Maurice Bowra dubbed the 'Homintern' were masters of the double life and the double standard – intellectual adventurers whose shadows fell darkly over their background and over the club of the Apostles.

Had it not always been a secret society, right from the start? Many former members were now subjected to painful interrogation. What came to light no longer had anything to do with KGB moles but everything to do with the entanglements of a mixed-up generation. The fact that not even the Hitler–Stalin pact of 1939 could sow a seed of doubt in the minds of Cambridge's Marxist elite showed the extent of the self-deception – it was one of the 'Masks of Treachery' described in detail by the historian John Costello. Since then, the aura of conspiracy has if anything added to the myth of the Apostles. Its members are elected for life, and they include such influential public figures as Lord Rothschild, Neal Ascherson and the Marxist historian Eric Hobsbawm.

Kim Philby and his friends were not the only spies to have come out of Cambridge. The Apostles were mainly literary men, but there was also a mole in the Cavendish: Pjotr Kapitsa, protégé and colleague of Ernest Rutherford. Kapitsa passed on all the results of their nuclear research to Moscow, providing key information for the Soviet nuclear weapons programme. And then there was George Blake: not an Apostle, not a social lion, not a sex symbol – just an ordinary graduate from Downing College who betrayed a large number of Western agents during the Cold War. He also gave away the secrets of 'Operation Gold', the Anglo-American plan to dig a tunnel into the Soviet sector of Berlin in order to tap the telephone network of the Soviet Army. The building of this tunnel is the subject of Ian McEwan's novel *The Innocent* (1990).

Through books, plays and films, and as endlessly fascinating characters from Cambridge folklore, the Kremlin moles have dug their way deep into the national psyche. When Anthony Blunt died in 1983, *The Times* gave him a full, three-column obituary – the sort normally reserved for a statesman. It was the same with Kim Philby, whose belongings were auctioned by Sotheby's in 1994 like the memorabilia of a pop star.

Cambridge produced Stalin's finest spies, but the finest spy novels came from Oxford men: Graham Greene, who dedicated the first editions of his books to Kim Philby (and himself spent three years working for MI6); John Le Carré, who as a student spied on his left-wing colleagues for the Secret Service. Smiley, his melancholy hero, is the very embodiment of the conflict of loyalties so dramatically resolved by the Cambridge spies.

In Corpus Christi hangs a portrait (probably not authentic) of one of its most illustrious alumni, the dramatist Christopher Marlowe. A rival to Shakespeare, he was a master of the arts of theatre and deception. While still a student, he was alleged to be an atheist, a homosexual, and a member of the Secret Service. He was also said to have been recruited by Elizabeth I's Privy Council to spy on Catholics in the college, who were sent to the English Jesuit College in Reims to be trained as priests and potential enemies of the State. But was he a double agent? He met a violent, premature end in a tavern brawl – or did he? Was it murder, or a cover-up?

Marlowe was not the only precursor of the Cambridge spy network. His contemporary John Dee, graduate of St John's College, mathematician, geographer, alchemist and cabbalist, was one of the most enigmatic scholars of the time. Dr Dee was not only Elizabeth I's astrologer, but also went on diplomatic missions to the Continent. His coded letters were signed '007'. Strangely enough, the movie incarnation of Ian Fleming's master spy James Bond also studied at Cambridge.

Byron and Bear, Nabokov in Goal:
Literary Cambridge

'I do not know if anyone will ever go to Cambridge in search of the imprints which the teat-cleats on my soccer boots have left in the black mud before a gaping goal or follow the shadow of my cap across the quadrangle to my tutor's stairs; but I know that I thought of Milton, and Marvell, and Marlowe, with more than a tourist's thrill as I passed beside the revered walls.'
Vladimir Nabokov, *Speak, Memory: An Autobiography Revisited*, 1966

Downing College had a cat called Pickwick. Sidney Sussex had a cat called Stella – named after Sir Philip Sidney's love poems to a young lady of that name (1591). And in Pembroke College I met a cat called Thomasina – the purring monument to Thomas Gray, who lived here in the 18th century and wrote a heart-rending ode to a cat that drowned in a goldfish bowl. Thomasina's successor also bears a literary name: Kit, which is the four-legged abbreviation for Christopher Smart, Gray's great rival at the college who sadly went insane, but not before writing a hymn to his cat Jeoffry, so touchingly poetic that the present Master of Pembroke has given his chocolate-coloured Burmese cat the same name.

This feline digression leads us with catlike smoothness to the subject of literature. Cambridge is full of it. From Milton's mulberry tree to Byron's Pool, and from the manuscripts displayed in Trinity Library to tea with honey in Rupert Brooke's Grantchester. An advertising slogan used by the bookshop Deighton Bell in 1951 provides a classic summary: 'The Cambridge Poet of today is generally the Oxford Standard Author of tomorrow'.

Elizabethan poets such as Edmund Spenser and Christopher Marlowe, the big three of English Romanticism, Wordsworth, Coleridge and Byron, Victorian favourites like Edward Bulwer-Lytton and Alfred, Lord Tennyson, winners of the Nobel Prize for literature Bertrand Russell and Patrick White, and best-selling authors of our times like Douglas Adams, Robert Harris, Nick Hornby, Salman Rushdie, Zadie Smith – all of them studied at Cambridge. It was in Cambridge and not in London that the Bloomsbury Group first took root. And it was here that the most tragic of 20th-century love stories began, when Ted Hughes and Sylvia Plath met at a party one night in 1956.

Cambridge has the best writers, and Oxford the best novels according to the Oxonian Evelyn Waugh, whose *Brideshead* was more popular than any novel about Cambridge. In the literary Boat Race, Cambridge is several shelf-lengths ahead of its rival. It is part of the great intellectual competition that in all things, including style, they should emphasize the differences rather than the similarities. The harsh climate of the Fens and the centuries of isolation encouraged the 'sterner virtues', a greater moral intensity than in the more sociable, metropolitan Oxford, writes Peter Ackroyd, and this atmosphere may have helped to encourage the subtleties of poetry rather more than the frivolities of the novel. Ackroyd, himself a Cambridge man and a novelist, might have added that in Oxford there was also a more favourable climate for the art of nonsense, for witty absurdities ranging from Lewis Carroll to *Charley's Aunt*. Oxford is also dominant in the spheres of fantasy and detective fiction. Could it be that there is some truth in what they say about the *genius loci*?

'Cambridge, the mother of poets' was the description given by Virginia Woolf's father, the Cambridge literary historian Sir Leslie Stephen. The university is right to be proud of its poets, but what, he asked, did Cambridge ever do to help its geniuses? Nothing, replied Tennyson in a sonnet of 1830: '...you that do profess to teach / And teach us nothing, feeding not the heart.' The biographies and works of Cambridge authors are full of complaints about their Alma Mater. They complain about the dons: '...abundance of leisure and small variety of reading' (Bacon); 'The country is so disgustingly level; ...the studies of the University so uninteresting, so much matter of fact' (Tennyson); 'the quiet ugliness of Cambridge' (Coleridge); 'Quam male Phoebicolis convenit ille locus!' [How badly that place agrees with Phoebus's sons!] wrote John Milton in a pentameter as perfect as any that he had studied. The criticisms were as much about the weather as about the fossilized dons. Cambridge was 'the very palace of winds', wrote Coleridge, whose rooms in Jesus College were so damp that in his very first term (1791) he took to his bed (and also to his opium) with rheumatics. His predecessors George Herbert and Laurence Sterne died of consumption, which may well have been the consequence of their time at Cambridge. A more modern Oxonian complaint came from Kingsley Amis in 1964, after a two-year stint as a fellow of Peterhouse: 'Inhospitable despite the ceaseless ceremonial parade of hospitality.' The fact that this magic mountain in the Fens, this university of Newton, this Mecca for all scientists, has produced any poets at all, let alone such vast numbers of them, is little short of a miracle.

Although Cambridge has more literary associations than any other place outside London, very few authors seem to form a lasting attachment. Most have been 'youthful birds of passage, acquiring influences, knowledge and friendships, wrinkling their noses at systems and dogmas, passing on,' writes Graham Chainey in his *Literary History of Cambridge*. The university has always been a stopping-off place – an intellectual power station for many, and a bridge to fame for some: 'Cambridge Fame-bridge' was Frederic Raphael's way of putting it, and his career as a novelist and screenwriter (*Glittering Prizes*, and Stanley Kubrick's film *Eyes Wide Shut*) confirms the concept. Those writers that did stay in Cambridge tended to be introvert and not very productive – eccentric college recluses like Thomas Gray, A. E. Housman and, in the end, even E. M. Forster, who failed to heed his own warning that Cambridge was 'not a place in which a writer ought to remain'.

The first literary pilgrims to visit the haunts of the great were themselves writers – the tourists only came later. When he was a student, Tennyson went to see the places where Wordsworth, Byron and others had been before him. Wordsworth himself describes in his autobiographical poem *The Prelude* how he and a friend went to Milton's rooms in Christ's and drank 'to thy memory' – until for the first and only time in his life he was completely drunk. In Book III he also describes a trip to Trumpington, the setting for one of Chaucer's *Canterbury Tales*.

It is in this village south of Cambridge, we are told in Chaucer's *Reeve's Tale*, that the vain and 'deynous' (arrogant) Simkin has his mill on the River Cam. He is a thief, but when he tries to cheat two clever law students named Aleyn and John, it is they who outwit him. They have come from their college, 'the Soler-halle at

Cantebregge' to ask him to grind some corn for them, and by the end of the tale, the miller's 'wife is swyved [bedded], and his doghter als', which only goes to prove that 'a gylour [cheat] shall him-self bigyled be'. With *The Reeve's Tale* as a counterpart to *The Miller's Tale*, which is set in Oxford, Chaucer even-handedly gave students from both universities their glorious debuts in world literature.

Today only specialists read Roger Ascham's *Toxophilus* (1545), a dialogue between two Cambridge scholars on the art of archery. The author's name became synonymous with a cupboard for storing bows and arrows. Roger Ascham was a humanist, and private tutor and Latin secretary to Elizabeth I, having studied at St John's, which was also the college of Sir Thomas Wyatt, who translated Petrarch and thereby introduced the sonnet into English Literature. Wyatt was Anne Boleyn's lover, and since at the time he was in the diplomatic service of Henry VIII, he was risking a great deal more than the future of the sonnet. Another towering figure of the time was Edmund Spenser, who in the fourth book of *The Faerie Queen* (1590–96) described his Alma Mater as 'My mother, Cambridge'. In this verse epic on the Faerie Queen Gloriana and her ideal kingdom, Elizabeth I graciously recognized her own reflection, and granted Spenser a lifelong pension – a truly fairytale success for a poet who had begun his career as a poor scholar in what was then Pembroke Hall.

All of this has more or less faded into literary history, but still read and still produced are the plays of Christopher Marlowe, whose end was as bloody as that of his tragic heroes – stabbed in the eye on 30 May 1593. He was twenty-nine years old, and Shakespeare's greatest rival. At Corpus Christi College he was supposed to study divinity, but became a radical free-thinker as well as a renowned university wit who overstepped all the marks of Renaissance moderation. Like all scholarship students at the time, the cobbler's son from Canterbury was forced to wear drab colours and cloth caps, while the young noblemen strutted around in velvet. This may well have sharpened his class consciousness and the sense of social injustice that permeates his work, but college drills also taught him something else: to write in the classical metre of Ovid and Virgil. He wrote his first play while he was still at Cambridge, the tragedy of *Dido, Queen of Carthage*, and he began *Tamburlaine the Great*, with a superman hero and blank verse that teems with rhetorical devices and impressive learning – dramatic, emotional, excessive, and his first triumph on the London stage. Bad boy Marlowe led a hectic double life as a poet and a spy, popular with the public, protected by the Crown, and ever present in Cambridge, for if you want to experience the very best of student theatre, you should go to a production by the Marlowe Society in the Arts Theatre.

Their very first production was directed by Rupert Brooke in 1907, and the play was Marlowe's *Doctor Faustus*.

When Stalin ordered the blockade of Berlin in 1948 and had a 400-strong Cossack choir singing on the Alexanderplatz, the British Council sent the Marlowe Society to the cultural frontline. Under the direction of George Rylands, they performed Shakespeare's *Measure for Measure* and Webster's *The White Devil*.

How remote from us are the 17th-century poets? Not at all, if Robert Herrick is anything to go by. In just six lines *Upon Julia's Clothes*, he encapsulates the whole art of lyrical seduction: 'When as in silks my Julia goes, / Then, then (me thinks) how sweetly flowes / That liquefaction of her clothes. / Next, when I cast mine eyes and see / That brave Vibration each way free; / O how that glittering taketh me!' Herrick graduated from Trinity Hall and became a country parson in Devon; he kept a trained pig that could drink out of a beer mug, and delighted his congregation with songs about the countryside and the girls therein – a pastoral poet of joy who while, leading a godly life, also knew how to 'Live Merrily, and to Trust to Good Verses', as one of his poems puts it. Robert Herrick was one of an astonishing collection of 17th-century poets that came from Cambridge, the greatest of them all being John Milton. But it is well worth getting to know the others – for instance, George Herbert: he was a Fellow of Trinity, Member of Parliament, public orator, and 'the jewel of the university' according to James I, but then he turned his back on a glittering career in London and became a parish priest in Wiltshire, where he died at the age of forty. Soon after his death in 1633, the only collection of his poetry was published under the title *The Temple*, and it became a cult book for the Puritans during the Civil War and the Restoration. Many of George Herbert's hymns are still sung today. The fact that they were published at all was due to Nicholas Ferrar, a friend from his student days in Cambridge.

Ferrar also turned his back on his career and went to a remote corner in the north-west of the county to found a religious enclave: the commune of Little Gidding. In its combination of practical work and meditation, of common sense and common prayer, this lay community (which has since been revived) represents a very English kind of spirituality, rooted in practicalities and mystic experience. The last of T. S. Eliot's *Four Quartets* is about this unlikeliest place of pilgrimage, for he went from Cambridge just to see Little Gidding in 1936. It was a modern mind's journey back into the 17th century, just as it had been in 1926 when he had delivered his lectures on the metaphysical poets in the hall at Trinity. He analysed and elucidated their complex imagery as a synthesis of spiritual and sensual experience, and through these Clark Lectures he was largely responsible for a reassessment and a revival of interest in the lesser-known Cambridge metaphysicals like Richard Crashaw and Andrew Marvell.

The first thing I read of Richard Crashaw's was some lines carved into the glass door of the Lady Chapel in Little St Mary's; it was not just the calligraphy that was striking. Crashaw was an Anglican priest here in this church, before the Puritans deprived him of his fellowship in nearby Peterhouse. As a Royalist, he fled to the Continent, converted to Catholicism, and died in 1649 in Loreto while still in his mid-thirties. His best-known work is *Steps to the Temple*, a book of religious poems influenced by the imagery of the Counter-Reformation and by Spanish mysticism – ecstatic, Baroque and, in the eyes of the Calvinist Puritans, the work of the Devil.

On the opposite, Protestant side of the fence was Crashaw's Cambridge contemporary Andrew Marvell: admirer of Cromwell, Latin secretary to Lord Carlisle, and MP for his home town of Hull until his death in 1678. Marvell was a graduate of Trinity, and John Aubrey said of him that he had no equal in the composition of Latin verse. During his life he was famous as a patriot, a Republican and a satirist, but as a poet he was virtually unknown. Not until modern times were his ironic and sometimes enigmatic poetry, his urbane wit and his *concetti* recognized and taken to the nation's heart. 'The Grave's a fine and private place. / But none, I think, do there embrace.' The poem *To His Coy Mistress* is alone enough to guarantee his immortality. His love of paradox and word play masked the hopes and doubts of the Puritan soul that characterized that deeply divided period. These were epitomized by the work of Marvell's great friend and patron, John Milton.

For modern readers, the faith and culture underlying Milton's work are of mountainous proportions, but the climb is well worth the effort. You need not tackle the epic *Paradise Lost* straight away. The most personal if not necessarily the easiest approach is through the early poems and sonnets. The Latinized syntax of his verse, and the richness of the biblical, mythological and literary allusions are a reflection of the seven years he spent studying at Cambridge, the end of which is marked by his Ode *Il Penseroso* (1632), in which the poet wishes always to walk 'the studious cloisters' of his college in a 'dim religious light' while the choir sings 'full voiced' bringing all heaven before his eyes. Although the university itself was a disappointment to him ('These studies neither delight nor instruct nor promote any common good'), Cambridge was the turning point of his life. He wanted to be a poet, not a priest, and with great, sonorous organ peals of his verses, Milton became the mouthpiece of the Puritans, with a matchless moral and poetic authority. In 1637, after the death of a student friend who was drowned in a shipwreck, he wrote *Lycidas*, a meditation on the uncertainty of life, the meaning of death, and his own poetic destiny. It contains some of the best-known lines in English poetry – 'Fame is the spur that the clear spirit doth raise / (That last infirmity of noble minds)' – and is one of the most beautiful of all English elegies. 'Tomorrow to fresh woods and pastures new.'

So long as there have been courts and there have been poets, there have been court poets. Twelve of the twenty-one men who have held the title of Poet Laureate have come from Oxbridge. Oxford may have produced the majority (seven to five), but the quality surely came from Cambridge. The first one was appointed in 1668 by Charles II, and he was John Dryden – a Cambridge man. He wrote successful plays, satires, didactic poems, literary criticism and brilliant translations. He was a Cromwell supporter, but then a Royalist, converted to Catholicism, moved this way and that, and even preferred Oxford to Cambridge. But you don't have to like a man in order to admire him.

Personally I am a fan of Samuel Pepys, not because he liked Cambridge, or because he kept going back there and eventually left his private library – that treasure chamber of a lost culture – to his old college, Magdalene, but because today we can read him with as much pleasure as earlier generations did. The diaries of this son of a London tailor, who rose to become Secretary to the Admiralty and President of the Royal Society, give such a vivid and fascinating account of his daily life that we can picture him even now as he visited Magdalene on 25 May 1668, 'and there drank my bellyful of their beer, which pleased me as the best I ever drank.'

In the 18th century, we meet the first great Cambridge novelist, who described his four years there as 'a piteous delay'. Laurence Sterne was given a scholarship to Jesus College, was constantly short of money, notoriously lazy in an environment that was thoroughly conducive to laziness and whose pseudo-learning he parodied in *Tristram Shandy*, a novel that is one long and fantastic digression. Sterne used his time there to read just about everything that was not on the curriculum but that he found stimulating: Cervantes, Swift, Rabelais – the latter, we are told, under a walnut tree in First Court, which Sterne's friend John Hall-Stevenson described as follows: 'It overshadow'd every room / And consequently more or less, / Forc'd every brain in such a gloom / To grope its way, and go by guess.'

Let us follow Sterne's principle of digression and talk about the trees of the Cambridge poets – a dendrological history of literature, for why should we merely stop at Milton's mulberry? 'Ye fields of *Cambridge*, our dear *Cambridge*, say, / Have ye nor seen us walking every day? / Was there a *Tree* about which did not know / The *Love* betwixt us two?' Thus did the poet and Trinity Fellow Abraham Cowley mourn the death of his friend William Hervey in 1656. The cypresses in the garden of Christ's have equally elegiac roots, for they were bred from the seeds of the cypresses growing around Shelley's grave in Rome. The ash – 'this lovely tree' – that William Wordsworth sought out on moonlit winter nights, 'alone, beneath this fairy work of earth' (described in *The Prelude*, VI, 66–94), is no longer standing in the garden of St John's, but as a consolation you can see ash trees growing from barrels in the college chapel. More of this anon. You can, however, follow in the footsteps of Henry James and admire the old horse-chestnuts, whose mighty branches have bowed to the ground, sunk their own roots, and now grow upwards even mightier than the trunk – 'one of the most heart-shaking features of the garden of Trinity Hall,' observed the tree-loving American author. But Cambridge's most beautiful monument to a poet is to be found in the Backs, where an avenue of cherry trees was planted by the Fellows of Trinity College in memory of their colleague A. E. Housman: 'Loveliest of trees, the cherry now / Is hung with bloom along the bough, / And stands about the woodland ride / Wearing white for Eastertide.'

To end our dendropoetical excursion, we shall get a yew-tree to take us into the 18th century. It is the yew of Thomas Gray and his *Elegy Written in a Country Churchyard* (1751), and in its evergreen shade is 'Each in his narrow cell for ever laid'. Like the people of the hamlet in his elegy, Gray lived 'far from the madding crowd's ignoble strife', tucked away snugly in Pembroke, where he was a Fellow. 'Cambridge is a delight of a place, now there is nobody in it,' he wrote in August 1760 to a friend. 'I do believe you would like it, if you knew what it was like without inhabitants. It is they, I assure you, that get it an ill name and spoil all.' Apart from a few journeys, he spent his entire life in Cambridge, the strangest and most enigmatic college hermit of his time (see p. 260). Few English poets have written as little as Gray, but his lines are quoted more often than those of any other 18th-century poet. The elegy, so perfect in form and sound, combines classic elements of style with a new vision of nature and of human emotion that typifies the Romantics for whom most certainly he paved the way.

In Georgian Cambridge, and in the hard-drinking, vain and envious clique of the scholars that were his Pembroke colleagues, Gray was an outsider whose inhibitions concerning his own writing were – according to Leslie Stephen – made worse by the barbs that were constantly being fired at him, 'as though a singing bird should build over a wasps' nest'. Among his few friends was Horace Walpole, and among his rivals at Pembroke was the eccentric Christopher Smart, who once remarked: 'Gray *walks* as if he had fouled his small-clothes, and *looks* as if he smelt it.' Nevertheless, Smart deserves to be more than a footnote in the story of Gray. He wrote poetry of a strangely sporadic, jerky intensity, influenced by Horace and by the Psalms, with rhythms and a religious ecstasy that were highly unconventional by comparison with Gray, who stuck to the conventions both in life and in his writing. Kit Smart, poet and religious maniac, spent a good deal of time in an insane asylum, and ended his days in a debtors' prison.

On a gloomy day in October 1787, a first-year student proudly entered his new lodgings at St John's. He was 'a northern villager', and had come from the hills of the Lake District to the flattest of flatlands; he now found himself in 'a nook obscure' above the kitchen in First Court. His 'unlovely cell' has been extended and converted into a conference room, and it is called The Wordsworth Room. In 1791, when William Wordsworth had just left Cambridge, Samuel Taylor Coleridge was beginning his studies at Jesus College. Not until four years later did they meet, become friends, and change the course of English literature. These heavenly twins of Romanticism, long canonized as the authors of the *Lyrical Ballads*, were both academic failures. Coleridge dropped out without even taking his exams, and Wordsworth scraped through 'without distinction' (whereas his younger brother Christopher went on to become Master of Trinity). They both felt hemmed in by college rules and regulations. It was compulsory to attend chapel twice a day, and as every absence cost a fine of twopence, Coleridge was forced to conform: 'I am remarkably religious upon an economical plan.'

Cambridge did not do the Romantics any harm. King's College Chapel and his own portrait inspired Wordsworth to write sonnets, though they were hardly his best, and the only official poem that he wrote as Poet Laureate was a not very good ode on the installation of Prince Albert as Chancellor of the University in 1847. Three years later, Wordsworth was dead. *The Prelude*, however, unfolds a splendid panorama of Cambridge – a collage of impressions that would have been shared by generations of students: the hopes and fears, the expectations and disappointments. 'I was the Dreamer, they the Dream.' This section of his autobiographical poem, Book Sixth, bears the beautiful title 'Cambridge and the Alps'. Indeed it is mountains and not books that first open the poet's eyes to the sublimeness of nature and the human imagination. *The Prelude* is a key work of English Romanticism, and it was dedicated to Coleridge, who created more of a stir in Cambridge than his more reserved friend.

Fired with enthusiasm for the French Revolution, Coleridge joined in the student demonstrations of spring 1793, when they burned the slogan 'Liberty and

Equality' into the sacred college lawn. He and his friends shocked the Tory Establishment just by their Jacobin appearance: long hair and striped pantaloons, instead of the normal powdered hair and silk knee breeches. In his first year, Coleridge won a gold medal for a Greek ode on the slave trade, and after that he and his Oxford friend Robert Southey published a verse drama about Robespierre. These events, however, had considerably less impact on the university authorities than his desertion of academia to join a regiment of dragoons, registering himself under the pseudonym of Silas Tomkyn Comberbache, in order to escape from his debts in Cambridge. When he returned, the university put him under college arrest and made him do a ninety-page translation from the Greek. In the circumstances, it is not altogether surprising that Coleridge and Southey planned to emigrate to America and set up a 'pantisocracy'. The plan never came to anything, which was fortunate for the history of English Literature.

One of the heroes of college folklore was Lord Byron, the youngest of the Cambridge trio of Romantics. Unlike Wordsworth and Coleridge, who were scholars from a relatively poor background, Byron enjoyed all the privileges of the aristocrats. He dined in gold-embroidered gown at the table of the Trinity dons, and had a four-in-hand carriage, liveried servants and, since dogs were banned from college, a tame bear named Bruin. The young lord used to take his chained pet for walks, and when asked what he intended to do with it, would reply, 'He should sit for a Fellowship.' He informed his tutor that he had no liking for mathematics and that 'To *bewilder* myself in the mazes of Metaphysics, is not my object.' Lord Byron certainly set the standards for future generations of eccentric students.

Cambridge, Byron wrote to Elizabeth Bridget Pigot on 5 July 1807, was 'a *Monotony* of *endless variety*.' And on 26 October 1807: 'Oh! The misery of doing nothing but make *love, enemies,* and *verses*.' His letters suggest that his studies consisted mainly of boxing and fencing, gambling, hunting and swimming, and those pleasures which brought him a dose of gonorrhoea. Byron was not, however, quite the wastrel that is implied by his volume of poems *Hours of Idleness*. Behind the mask of aristocratic languor was an ambitious student who translated Virgil and Anacreon, started writing a novel, and published his first volume of poetry at the age of eighteen, *Fugitive Pieces* (1806). These early works were heavily influenced by Pope and Anacreon – light-hearted, conventional verses, but already tinged with that melodious world-weariness which was to become his trademark. When he visited Cambridge a few years later, in 1814, he was greeted in the Senate House with wild applause. By now he was famous throughout Europe as the author of *Childe Harold's Pilgrimage*, a verse epic about a romantic hero and his passions. This is the book that is clutched in Byron's marble hand, as part of the monument in Trinity Library.

Byron himself said that in Cambridge he spent 'the happiest, perhaps, days of my life'. This was due in no small measure to a fifteen-year-old choirboy at the college, John Edleston, with whom he enjoyed 'a violent, though pure *love* and passion'. Having a boyfriend in the choir was part of Trinity tradition, and indeed all homoerotic relationships in this masculine world were a natural social undercurrent, as they were later in the women's colleges. After the premature death of this friend, Byron dedicated the elegy 'To Thyrza' to him. But it was another friendship that really touched Victorian England – a friendship that began at the same college and ended in lamentation.

In 1828 Alfred Tennyson, a short-sighted, long-haired, rather timid student at Trinity, got to know a younger student whom he soon loved even more than the pet snake which he kept in his room. Arthur Henry Hallam was a gifted linguist and orator, and like Tennyson he adored the Romantics; they were both Apostles, went travelling together, and were happy in Cambridge. Hallam's sudden death in 1833 at the age of twenty-two came as a terrible shock to Tennyson, and in the same year he began the threnody *In Memoriam A.H.H.* which by the end comprised no less than 132 poems – one of the greatest of English elegies and described by T. S. Eliot as 'a poem of despair, but of despair of a religious kind'. Soldiers and widows found consolation in these verses, as did Queen Victoria after the death of Prince Albert. In the year of their publication, 1850, Tennyson followed Wordsworth into the post of Poet Laureate, and in 1884 he became a lord.

Can one read Tennyson today? One can and one should. He was a fascinating master of form and sound, and was the disturbing yet representative voice of his time. Just read *Tithonus*, one of his finest poems, begun when he was still a student before he left Cambridge in 1831 (without a degree). *Tithonus* is the dramatic monologue of a man who grows ever older but cannot die – 'cruel immortality', which has become strikingly topical in this age of biogenetics.

Edward Bulwer-Lytton was another exemplary Victorian. He found Cambridge 'excessively academic', and became the highest paid author of the 19th century with historical novels such as *The Last Days of Pompeii* and *Rienzi* (which Wagner made into an opera). Today he is remembered chiefly by way of a prize named after him – for the worst beginning to a novel. In his first best-seller, *Pelham* (1828), which made the so-called 'silver-fork school' of High Society novels fashionable, he tells the story of the dandy Henry Pelham, one of whose prestigious stopping-off places was Cambridge: 'I had a pianoforte in my room, and a private billiard-room at a village two miles off; and, between these resources, I managed to improve my mind more than could reasonably have been expected. To say the truth, the whole place reeked with vulgarity.'

Unlike Bulwer-Lytton, his fellow student William Makepeace Thackeray is one of the enduring novelists of the time, with his social satires including, above all, *Vanity Fair* and the *Book of Snobs*. Thackeray's student life in Cambridge was much like that of the hero of *Pendennis* (1850) – drinking, gambling, fencing every day, and after just five terms leaving the place with massive debts and no degree.

After leaving Trinity, he remained friends with 'Old Fitz', Edward Fitzgerald, another fellow student who achieved lasting fame through a book which he had not even written himself, but had translated so brilliantly from the 12th-century Persian that his English version was regarded as entirely his own work: *The Rubáiyat of Omar Khayyám* (1859). 'Fitz' continued his student life on the coast of East Anglia, a clever idler who raved about muscular sailors that looked like 'one of the Phidias Marbles dressed in blue Trowsers and Guernsey Jacket'. His first published work, *Euphranor* (1851), was a Platonic dialogue between Cambridge students who, over a beer and a game of billiards in The Three Tuns, discuss the joys of youth and the narrow-mindedness of English university education.

Of the many writers who studied at Cambridge, none were more radical than John Cowper Powys in their claim that it had made no impact on them: 'The university *as* a university had not the least influence upon my taste, my intelligence, my philosophy or my character!' He owed nothing to Cambridge, but everything to Cambridgeshire. The road to Ely, village graveyards, fields of turnips, the meadows on the way to Grantchester with their poplars and willows – 'these are my masters, my fellows, my libraries, my lecture-halls; these are my Gothic shrines!' It was on his long, lonely walks with his oak cane 'Sacred' that Powys, who studied history at Corpus Christi but was originally destined for the priesthood, experienced his literary awakening, 'a sort of Vision on the Road to Damascus'. Forty years later, in his autobiography of 1934, he vividly conjures up 'the indescribable happiness of my calm, dazed, lulled, wind-drugged, air-drunk spirit'. This ecstatic experience of nature and objects was the beginning of Powys' journey into the myths and strange histories that inform the finest of his novels.

The most beautiful and most penetrating descriptions of Cambridge were written by a woman who never studied at the university. Her father, however, taught there, her brothers were students there, and she met her husband there too. Had it not been for Cambridge, Sir Leslie Stephen's daughter would not have been called Virginia Woolf, and there would never have been a Bloomsbury Group.

In spring 1900, Thoby Stephen invited his sisters Virginia and Vanessa to the May Ball. They arrived like characters in a Chekhov play, 'in white dresses and large hats, with parasols in their hands, their beauty literally took one's breath away'. That was how Leonard Woolf described his first meeting with Virginia and her sister in the room of his Trinity friend. There too Vanessa first met her future husband, Clive Bell. It was in his rooms, in Trinity's New Court, that the members of the Reading Club would meet at midnight every Saturday to declaim poetry by Milton, Shelley and themselves. Clive Bell, Leonard Woolf, Thoby Stephen and Lytton Strachey were all members of the Midnight Society, which eventually formed the nucleus of the Bloomsbury Group. There were also some friends from King's College, including Edward Morgan Forster and John Maynard Keynes, who were members of the Apostles – that much-discussed secret society to which Leonard Woolf and Lytton Strachey were admitted in 1902. What linked them all was their unshakeable belief in reason, intellectual honesty and complete openness in all things, including personal and sexual relationships. When their student days were over, this circle of Cambridge friends found a new meeting place in the London house of the two Stephen sisters, in the district of Bloomsbury. From then on, Cambridge was given the ironic honorary title of 'Bloomsbury-by-the-Cam'.

'No place in the world can be lovelier,' said Virginia Woolf in 1904. She loved Cambridge, but she also hated it as the embodiment of a man's world. She was born in London, but regarded Cambridge as her home town. Sir Leslie Stephen, first a student and then a Fellow of Trinity Hall, was the prototype of the Victorian scholar. Virginia saw him as 'an admirable model of the Cambridge analy[tical spirit]', but also as a patriarch of atrophied emotions. The ambivalence of the place and of her own background haunted her for the rest of her life. She had been 'born within the Polar region of Cambridge', she wrote to Ethel Smyth (11 October 1930), and even without a university education 'I am naturally of that narrow, ascetic, puritanical breed'. She visited it and wrote about it again and again. At first she lodged with her Aunt Caroline, nicknamed 'The Quaker', at 33 Grantchester Street, and then later at Newnham College, where yet another member of the Stephen clan was Principal. In October 1928, Virginia gave a talk to the students of Newnham on the subject of 'Shakespeare's Sister: Women & Fiction', and a week later she gave the same talk at Girton, after being invited by the ODTAA Society (One Damned Thing After Another). 'I blandly told them to drink wine & have a room of their own,' she noted in her diary. 'I felt elderly & mature. And nobody respected me.' It was on these lectures that she based *A Room of One's Own* (1929), which with its digressions on androgyny became a classic, not only for feminists.

'Perhaps Cambridge is too much of a cave.' However much Virginia Woolf may have criticized this hotbed of envy and vanity, she was still drawn to it, and never ceased to write about its charms – most strikingly in Chapter 3 of her novel *Jacob's Room* (1922). It is almost as if she was trying to give a second, fictional life to her brother Thoby, who had died of typhus in 1906, for her hero, Jacob Flanders, begins his studies in 1906, lives in a room in Trinity, but dies in the First World War. Her description of the light of Cambridge is a *pièce de résistance* of impressionistic irony: the college lit up at night, the dons as comical beacons of scholarship, like Erasmus Cowan who slurps his port wine and intones his Latin with incomparable melodiousness 'as if language were wine upon his lips... Nowhere else would Virgil hear the like.' And Sopwith, the tutor with the silver tongue: 'Talking, talking, talking – as if everything could be talked – the soul itself slipped through the lips in thin silver disks which dissolve in young men's minds like silver, like moonlight. Oh, far away they'd remember it, and deep in dullness gaze back on it, and come to refresh themselves again.'

Lytton Strachey would also have liked to become an eminent don, and even as a student he cultivated the appearance of one even to the point of caricature. 'The Strache' was pale, myopic, thin, always slightly hysterical, infinitely tall, 'and could be even twice his height if he were not bent as a sloppy asparagus,' observed Cecil Beaton. With a falsetto voice and flaming red beard, Lytton Strachey haunted Cambridge years after he had taken his degree, because for him this was the perfect place for intellectual and homosexual adventures. 'Cambridge whose cloisters have ever been consecrated to poetry and common sense.' After he had applied in vain for a professorship at Trinity, he wrote the book that was to make him famous: *Eminent Victorians* (1918), a masterly critique of national heroes. This mandarin without a chair spent the rest of his life commuting between Cambridge, Bloomsbury and the reading-room at the British Museum, and he lived in a *ménage à trois* with the painter Dora Carrington and her husband.

'It is perhaps as difficult to write a good life as to live one.' These words of his friend Lytton Strachey were reaffirmed by the novelist E. M. Forster (see p. 240). Lytton nicknamed him 'The Taupe' in the circle of the Apostles on account of his timidity and inconspicuous appearance. The opulent film adaptations of his novels – *A Passage to India, Howards End, A Room with a View* – cannot disguise the fact that as a man he suffered all his life from the issue of his homosexuality, although this disposition may well have helped him in his portrayal of love transcending the rigid barriers of morality and class. Only after his death in 1970 was a novel called *Maurice*, begun in 1913, found in his rooms at King's. 'Shocked to the bottom of his suburban soul', Maurice – a student at Cambridge – falls in love with an aristocratic fellow student. The novel ends with a passionate indictment of the persecution of homosexuals. Forster himself, however, regarded *The Longest Journey* (1907) as his most personal novel, a homage to Cambridge and to his own values of friendship and aesthetic experience – the Bloomsbury values.

The great champion of these values was the moral philosopher and Apostle George Edward Moore, whose *Principia Ethica* appeared in 1903. He was a don at Trinity who 'pursued truth with the tenacity of a bulldog and the integrity of a saint' (Leonard Woolf). He made an important contribution to a more open-minded attitude towards homosexuality, and for students like Keynes and Forster he was an almost Messianic figure who represented the liberating voice of reason. 'As Cambridge filled up with friends it acquired a magic quality,' wrote Forster: 'People and books reinforced one another, intelligence joined hands with affection, speculation became a passion, and discussion was made profound by love.' After giving several guest lectures at Cambridge, Forster finally returned there in 1946 and spent the rest of his life in his old college, 'a blue butterfly' as Virginia Woolf called him, who found his cocoon on A Staircase at King's.

Also on A Staircase, when his studies began in 1906, were the rooms of Rupert Brooke before he moved to Grantchester (see p. 366). His name is legendary and as hugely overrated as his poetry. He may have been the second national hero to have emerged from Cambridge, but another Byron he was not. He died young and beautiful, like James Dean and Marilyn Monroe, and what's more he died in the First World War. 'He was all that one would wish England's noblest sons to be': Churchill's obituary of him in *The Times* sealed the myth of the poet soldier and made him the symbol of his generation. W. B. Yeats called him 'the handsomest man in England'. Rupert Brooke was irresistible – especially to men. 'A young Apollo, golden-haired, / Stands dreaming on the verge of Strife, / Magnificently unprepared / For the long littleness of life' (Frances Cornford, 1908). While the Apollo of Grantchester perfectly matched the androgynous ideal of the Bloomsbury Group, he was no pacifist like the rest of the Apostles. Until the 1980s the manuscript of his idealized, patriotic war sonnets was on display in front of the war memorial in King's College Chapel. But today the voice of this lost generation is much more recognizable in the anti-war poetry of his contemporaries Siegfried Sassoon and Wilfred Owen. The latter experienced the full horror of trench warfare before he fell in Flanders at the age of twenty-five. Brooke's fame ultimately rests on a single poem, *The Old Vicarage, Grantchester*, a sentimental hymn to England, dismissed by his mentor Lytton Strachey as 'a bloody affected concoction'.

If one reads Rupert Brooke's correspondence with James Strachey, Lytton's younger brother, one gets the impression that students at Cambridge in those days only thought about three things: mountaineering, socialism and sex. One of the handsome young men, the 'Queens of King's' was the history student George Mallory, who died climbing Everest in 1924. The historian Oscar Browning, a legendary King's don whose interest in young men was not merely pedagogical, wrote an Alcaic ode to the penis: 'Partner of our days, / King potent over men / Troublesome author of anxieties you are....' Even so open-minded an author as D. H. Lawrence, when he visited Trinity College in 1915, felt ill at ease in the homo-erotic ambiance of the Apostles. 'I went to Cambridge and hated it beyond expression.' He was bitterly disappointed with Maynard Keynes and the other dons whose way of thinking and living seemed to him to be intolerably self-indulgent and aesthetic against the background of a savagely cruel war. He could not stand 'the smell of rottenness, marsh-stagnancy,' he wrote to his host, Bertrand Russell; 'How can so sick people rise up? They must die first.' T. S. Eliot, who also lectured in Cambridge in 1915, found the academic world 'serious, industrious, narrow and plebeian'. Ultimately, it all depends on the eye of the beholder.

During the First World War, many volunteers had one particular volume of poetry in their knapsacks. It was first published in 1896, but only became popular in the war, and has remained so ever since: *A Shropshire Lad*, elegiac verses about rural England, unrequited love and lost youth – 'the land of lost content'. The author of these variations on *le temps perdu* was Alfred Edward Housman, an eminent Latinist who began to teach at Cambridge in 1911 (see p. 262). With his pastoral, ballad-like, bittersweet verses, he became the model for the Georgian poets gathered round Rupert Brooke. For T. S. Eliot and the modern poets, however, he was a living anachronism. He lived for 25 years in Trinity College, published a five-volume edition of Manilius, but only one more thin book of poetry. He was a *poeta doctus*, a bachelor and an outsider, like Thomas Gray, did not like appearing in public, and kept his passions buried inside him – for poetry and also for his own sex. 'Deliberately he chose the dry-as-dust, / Kept tears like dirty postcards in a drawer; / Food was his public love, his private lust / Something to do with violence and the poor,' wrote W. H. Auden in his sonnet to Housman. Not until sixty years after his death, in 1996, was he honoured by a memorial window in Westminster Abbey's Poets' Corner. It was unveiled by his best-known student at Cambridge, translator of Thucydides and Tory politician Enoch Powell.

One of the writers who had a lifelong love of Housman's poetry was Vladimir Nabokov. As a student, he used regularly to see the melancholy don with the drooping moustache sitting at High Table in Trinity, like a man from another world. The young Nabokov, an emigrant from Tsarist St Petersburg, began his studies there in 1919, reading zoology at first but then switching to French and Russian. In his autobiography, with Proustian intensity he describes these first years in exile as 'the story of my trying to become a Russian writer'. On the other hand, one might also get the impression that his main preoccupations then were football, punting and 'several love affairs simultaneously', as if he were trying to confirm his fictitious Uncle Henry's views 'that these three years of aquatics in Cambridge had gone to waste'.

In actual fact, Nabokov worked extremely hard. In addition to a serious entomological essay on lepidopterology in the Crimea, he was the first to translate *Alice's Adventures in Wonderland* into Russian (and later defamed Lewis Carroll as the first Humbert Humbert), reviewed and translated poems by Rupert Brooke, and also wrote 'rather sterile Russian poems' of his own. In 1921, along with his tennis racket, boxing gloves and a first-class degree, he returned to his family in Berlin, which was then the centre for Russian emigrants. The emigrant milieu of the 1920s, between Cambridge and Switzerland, is the setting for his novel *Glory* (1930), whose hero, Martin Edelweiss, experiences his happiest moments – as Nabokov did – playing in goal for Trinity.

Literary history is often a story of meetings that never happened. After Nabokov had left Cambridge, Christopher Isherwood arrived; he then went to live and teach in Berlin. Their paths crossed, but never at the same moment. Isherwood's Berlin novels and stories, on which were based the Broadway and London hits *I am a Camera* and the musical *Cabaret*, were as different from Nabokov's Berlin as Nabokov's Cambridge was different from Isherwood's. In his fictionalized autobiography *Lions and Shadows* (1938), Isherwood conjures up an anarchic counter-world to the academic city of the dead which is Cambridge; he calls the latter Mortmere, and it is populated with necrophiliacs, pornographers, the *nouveaux riches* and dung-eaters – a surreal revenge for his own, not very happy time there. 'When the time came for him to take his tripos,' reports his friend Stephen Spender, 'Isherwood answered all the questions in limericks and blank verse. In this way, he achieved his aim of getting himself sent down.'

Malcolm Lowry was still a student at St Catharine's when he wrote his first novel, *Ultramarine* (1933), whose hero Hilliot is told by his tutor, 'You are not nearly so unusual a type as you think you are!' Nevertheless, Lowry's tutor accepted the novel in lieu of a dissertation. According to a friend, even at this time Lowry was sober for at most one or two hours a month, but even from under the pub tables he could play the ukulele splendidly. Throughout his short, hectic, nomadic life – he lived in Mexico (*Under the Volcano*) and then British Columbia for some years – 'deceitful memories' of his college years would keep returning: 'Ah, the harbour bells of Cambridge!'

Post-war literature in Cambridge began with a love story that could hardly have ended more tragically. Ted Hughes and Sylvia Plath met at a party in February 1956, 'and then he kissed me bang smash on the mouth... And when he kissed my neck I bit him long and hard on the cheek, and when we came out of the room, blood was running down his face.' More than thirty years later, in his *Birthday Letters* to his dead wife, Ted Hughes recalls the bite of that first kiss 'that was to brand my face for the next month. / The me beneath it for good' ('St Botolph's'). Sylvia Plath was a Fulbright Scholar from Massachusetts, and had found the 'big, blasting, dangerous love' that she had been looking for. He was an 'incredible' man, she wrote to her mother, 'always the same black sweater and corduroy jacket with pockets full of poems, fresh trout, and horoscopes.' The incredible man was a graduate of Pembroke College and university archery champion who wanted to emigrate to Australia, but instead took on the role of 'the male lead in your drama'.

They were married in June 1956 and moved into an apartment on the edge of Grantchester Meadows (55 Eltisley Avenue). Ted Hughes worked as a teacher at the Coleridge Secondary Modern School while Sylvia Plath studied for her literature examinations at Newnham, but meanwhile they were both writing – mainly poetry: 'We romp through words.' Sylvia Plath's notes in her Cambridge diaries show the joy of these shared beginnings, but also the burning, fanatical desire to achieve everything at once – academic, literary and familial. Five years later she perished beneath the weight of her obsessions – not because of but in spite of Ted Hughes. Her suicide made her into a martyr and him into a monster, but this was a feminist distortion of an infinitely complex story.

In the mid-1960s, even Cambridge was affected by the universal student unrest. At best, however, this privileged environment only produces reformers and not revolutionaries, as Australian writer Clive James has pointed out, even though he then regarded himself as a radical Socialist: 'The lovely façades, the sweeping lawns... were meant not just to lull but to disarm: nobody who had once lived in these emollient surroundings would ever again feel sufficiently alienated from society to be anything more troublesome than a reformist.' Someone like his fellow student Salman Rushdie, from Bombay's upper classes and studying history at King's, would not rush to the barricades but instead would go to the cinema, watch Godard and Antonioni, listen to Bob Dylan and Mick Jagger and – as

Rushdie says himself – read Herbert Marcuse and 'the two-headed fellow known to Grass readers as Marxengels'.

The conflicts of those years are reflected in David Hare's play *Teeth 'n' Smiles* (1975), which is set at a stormy May Ball in Jesus College. David Hare is not the only giant of modern theatre to have studied at Cambridge. His fellow dramatists Howard Brenton and Peter Shaffer, the directors Peter Hall and Trevor Nunn, and actors Derek Jacobi, Ian McKellen and Emma Thompson all cut their dramatic teeth on the stages of Cambridge.

Far jollier than revolutionaries are comedians, and in this field Cambridge has truly excelled. The satire boom of the 1960s began with a revue called *Beyond the Fringe*, written and performed by two men from Cambridge and two from Oxford. First performed in Edinburgh, it then took London by storm and began a trend that led from *Private Eye* through to *Monty Python*. Of the four participants, Jonathan Miller (Cambridge) qualified as a doctor and is one of the finest stage and opera directors of our time; Alan Bennett (Oxford) is one of England's leading dramatists; Peter Cook (Cambridge) was regarded by many as the funniest man of his day, and Dudley Moore (Oxford), as well as being a fully-fledged concert and jazz pianist, carved out a successful career as a film actor. The Pete & Dud double act was a classic of its kind, but both men sadly failed to reach old age.

The Cambridge Footlights were at the very heart of the satire boom. This annual treat, which is still one of the highlights of May Week, has marked the debut of some of England's finest writers, including – apart from those mentioned above – Michael Frayn, an extraordinarily versatile novelist and playwright whose work ranges from the sublime farce of *Noises Off* to the intellectual and scientific complexities of *Copenhagen*. Frederic Raphael and the author and actor Stephen Fry ('born to be Wilde') were also involved with the Footlights, but the most dazzling comedy to have been spawned by this institution in recent times was undoubtedly Monty Python, with John Cleese, Graham Chapman and Eric Idle leading the way. The absurd, anarchic wit of their sketches, which from their BBC debut in 1969 made *Monty Python's Flying Circus* into a worldwide cult, was in fact part of a tradition stretching way back beyond even the fringe of the 20th century. The Footlights began with a performance for the inmates of a lunatic asylum in Cambridge. The success was so great that in 1883 the students started a theatre group which was called the Cambridge Footlights Dramatic Club. They put on musical comedies in the style of Gilbert & Sullivan, pantomimes and revues. Men played all the parts, for women were not admitted until 1957, but unlike their counterparts in Oxford, where the actors were not even allowed to wear women's costumes, the 'girls' dressed up so attractively that this drag tradition actually became a speciality of the Footlights.

More comedy came from Tom Sharpe's campus satire *Porterhouse Blue* (1974). The vegetating dons, the unpopular reformist Master, and the surly head porter Skullion made people laugh more than some university people would have liked. 'The spirit had gone out of them since the war. They got grants now. They worked. Who had ever heard of a Porterhouse man working in the old days? They were too busy drinking and racing.' It is pointless to ask what was the model for this nostalgic caricature of the old college glory. Tom Sharpe studied at Pembroke, but it was Peterhouse that got tarred with the Porterhouse brush.

What I find really strange is that the majority of campus novels are set in Oxford and not Cambridge, even though many more authors have come from Cambridge. The campus detective story in particular seems to be an Oxford speciality – because the place is more criminal, or more picturesque, or more varied? Here's another brain-teaser: did Sherlock Holmes study at Oxford or Cambridge? And here is one true fact: P. D. James was born in Oxford, the eldest child of a Cambridge tax official, and named her famous detective Adam Dalgliesh after a Miss Dalgliesh who taught English at the Cambridgeshire High School for Girls.

It is impossible to cover the whole list of prominent Cambridge authors, but here are a few of the outstanding ones that have studied here and made their mark in recent years: The Booker Prizewinner Penelope Fitzgerald, A. S. Byatt and her sister Margaret Drabble, the poets Thom Gunn, Geoffrey Hill, John Holloway and Michael Hofmann, the novelists Sebastian Faulks, Robert Harris, Nick Hornby, Graham Swift, Howard Jacobson and Alain de Botton (whose book *How Cambridge Can Change Your Life* is eagerly awaited). In her final year at King's, 1999, the twenty-four-year-old Anglo-Jamaican Zadie Smith shot to literary stardom with her first novel, *White Teeth*.

One can scarcely depart from the literary scene without also mentioning some of Cambridge's illustrious critics. Ever since Sir Arthur Quiller-Couch occupied the then comparatively new chair for English Literature in 1912, Cambridge has been blessed with a succession of outstanding literary historians, ranging from the Shakespeare gurus George Rylands and Sir Frank Kermode to the flamboyant feminist Germaine Greer. They and charismatic teachers like F. R. Leavis and George Steiner have left an indelible mark on many generations of students. The finest Goethe biography of our times was written not by a German but by Nicholas Boyle, a Fellow of Magdalene. The first writer whom the University of Cambridge made an honorary Doctor of Literature was an Oxonian: John

Ruskin. Two Germans have received the same honour: Thomas Mann in 1953 and Stefan Heym in 1991. 'Rarity of a double doctorate in Oxford and Cambridge,' Thomas Mann noted in his diary, and added: 'Dinner lousy, accommodation fair.'

Cambridge graduates are also increasingly prominent in the media: columnists, reporters and correspondents like Neal Ascherson, John Simpson, Roger Scruton, Martin Bell, Simon Hoggart, the Pepys biographer Claire Tomalin, and the founder and editor of *The London Review of Books* Karl Miller, as well as TV celebrities like David Frost and Jeremy Paxman. Between 1874 and 1932 every single editor of the legendary satirical magazine *Punch* came from Cambridge, many of them having earned their first journalistic laurels with *Granta*. Ronald Searle, born in Cambridge in 1920, drew cartoons (left-handed) for *Granta*, and with the money he earned, he financed his studies at the Cambridge School of Art – where he was taught by Darwin's granddaughter Gwen Raverat. In 1979, the magazine was taken over by Bill Buford, a twenty-four-year-old Californian scholar at King's College. With a number of literary discoveries, he made *The Granta* (as the first issue of 18 January 1889 was called) into an internationally renowned literary magazine with the widest circulation in England. In 1990, Bill Buford and *Granta* moved to London, and in 1995 he was fiction editor of the *New Yorker*. Even in a small city there is still room for the occasional meteor.

The Philosophers' Stones:
Architecture and Town Planning

'How indeed, she thought, could the heart be indifferent to such a city where stone and stained glass, water and green lawns, trees and flowers were arranged in such ordered beauty for the service of learning.'
P. D. James, *An Unsuitable Job For A Woman*, 1972

The charm of Cambridge cannot be attributed solely to its architecture, any more than it can be explained by the aura of scholarship. Whatever it is that makes this place so fascinating must be more than the sum of its colleges. Cambridge is an aesthetic combination of disparate parts, much like a Shakespeare play in which the King and the Fool, the tragedy and the comedy, the emotional verse and the calculating prose all combine into a perfect whole. The magic lies in the alternation of dimensions and materials, where the cosiness gives way to the majestic, limestone is a neighbour to brick, half-timbering to reinforced concrete. It lies in the classical colonnades and the willows on the banks of the Cam, in stylistic contrasts and harmonies, never more pleasing than in the Backs behind the colleges: Renaissance Clare, Late Gothic King's Chapel, Classical Gibbs Wing, Wilkins' Romantic neo-Gothic – like a catwalk of architectural fashions parading through the great riverside park.

Architecture in Cambridge is predominantly college architecture. The city has no cathedral, but it does have a college chapel that is more regal than Oxford's cathedral. At about the same time as King's College Chapel was completed, on the other side of the street the university and the town joined forces to renovate St Mary the Great. This modest parish church, which served the whole university, was completely overshadowed by a chapel serving just one college – a contrast that demonstrates clearly who held the purse strings at the time. Many of the colleges had rich founders who were keen to build; the university itself was poor and, as an institution, too impersonal to attract former students as sponsors. Not until 1730 did it have a building of its own in which to perform its official ceremonies – the Senate House. Only when the scientists needed laboratories in the 19th century did the university begin to build substantially.

For all their individuality, the colleges follow a basic ground plan that reflects the academic way of life. Around a rectangular court (and not 'quadrangle', as in Oxford), are grouped the dining hall, chapel and library, the Master's lodge, and the residential wings for the Fellows and the students. A passage called the 'screens', which also contains the notice boards, leads between hall and kitchen into the second court, and if two courts have proved to be insufficient, there will then be a third. These courts are like a succession of thoroughfares leading through to the gardens at the rear, where once you would find fruit and vegetables grown for the college kitchen, and later bowls and croquet for the Fellows. That is the basic pattern, though there are of course many variations on the theme. Typologically, it was the continuation of a feudal form of construction.

The college ground plan developed in Oxford only reached Cambridge in 1448, with the building of Queens'. Its Old Court (and that of Corpus Christi) is the best example of a perfectly preserved medieval inner court. Here you can sense something of the intimacy of such places, the peacefulness and the secure privacy that they gave to the occupants. As they are on a much more domestic scale, they are like miniature versions of the great quadrangle at New College, Oxford.

Queens' took over the cloister, which was a central element of monasteries and cathedrals, but other Cambridge colleges decided that this was unnecessary. As in the manor houses of the 14th and 15th centuries, the hall would be opposite the entrance gate, with the Master's Lodge next to it. A feature that is different from Oxford, however, is the fact that the hall and chapel are not always next to each other. As for the rooms in the early colleges, the Oxford staircase principle was adopted here too. Several Fellows and students would share a room, but each would have a study niche to himself; in the middle stood the 'truckle beds', which were of different heights so that they could be pushed into one another to save space, like a nest of tables. Each staircase was (and still is) a unit in itself, with a group of rooms for which one or two Fellows were responsible, thus paving the way for the tutorial system.

'This is the city of perspiring dreams,' according to Frederic Raphael's parody of Arnold. But Cambridge has its dreaming spires as well. Oxford's oldest colleges may be more splendid, but Cambridge has magnificent Tudor gatehouses, triumphal arches of academic splendour, from Queens', Christ's and Trinity to the apotheosis of gatehouse glory at St John's. With their towers and battlements, mighty portals and heraldic emblems, these gatehouses resemble medieval castles – proclaiming the message: Beware, this is a Fortress of Learning. Quite apart from their symbolic function, the gates used to protect students from the dangers of the outside world: prostitutes, heretics, hostile townies. Some of the gatehouses, such as over the entrance to Queens', would also house the treasure chamber, where the college silver and important documents were kept. Today's gatekeepers are just as effective as the old portcullis, for you only have to step in front of the Porter's Lodge to hear the dreaded message: 'Sorry, we're closed.'

Cambridgeshire is brick country, and Cambridge shows it. In the gatehouses, this working-class material has a nobility of its own. Bricks are always popular when there are no good stone quarries in the vicinity. Before 1500, almost all of Cambridge's buildings were made from clunch, a soft limestone from the hills in the south-east of the county. Clunch was easy to quarry, in Cherry Hinton or nearby Reach in the Fens, and it was easy to work, as one can see for instance in Bishop Alcock's superb memorial chapel in Ely Cathedral. But it was not durable and it was not weatherproof. In the 17th and 18th centuries many colleges had to restore their old limestone walls, and they gave them new façades, preferably of cream-coloured Ketton limestone, which was also used for King's College Chapel, Clare, Trinity and elsewhere. The best Ketton stone, a Jurassic oolite, came from quarries in Northamptonshire and Rutland, but it was expensive and so it was used only sparingly. The veneer of Ketton stone on the medieval walls of Peterhouse, Christ's and Trinity Hall is only a couple of inches thick. The alternative was brick, and Queens' was the first college to use large quantities of red brick over a core of clunch. The triumph of brick art extends from the Tudor gatehouses to the ornamentalism of the Victorians, for example in Newnham – a Cambridge tradition which was continued by Robinson College in 1977, with multicoloured bricks from Swansea and a monumental quotation of a gatehouse.

Anyone who has wandered through Oxford and Cambridge will have noticed that the building materials are not the only major difference. In Cambridge, many of the colleges open out onto the river, whereas most Oxford colleges are tucked away between High Street and Broad Street, with their backs to the street. Cambridge, writes Nikolaus Pevsner, is 'buildings in a landscape', whereas 'the Oxford image is a landscape made of stone'. Oxford is urban, and Cambridge is countrified, and although Cambridge has a marketplace, it has no piazza comparable to Radcliffe Square. 'Cambridge is certainly a cosy, sympathetic spot after the grim grandeurs of Oxford – quite middle-class, which is always such a relief – at any rate for a day or two,' said Lytton Strachey. In 1951, the town was granted a city charter, and no one was more surprised than the people of Cambridge. It is said that this was George VI's way of thanking them for the wonderful time he had as a student at Trinity.

Such a place offers a fine opportunity to wander through the history of architecture, from the Anglo-Saxon church tower of St Bene't to the ultramodern hi-tech laboratories. The turbulence of the Reformation helped to delay the arrival of the Italian Renaissance in England, but eventually it came, first in the form of ornamentation, and then at its most magnificent in the choir screen and stalls of King's Chapel (c. 1535). Most colleges initially held to their Gothic traditions, but then colleges like Gonville and Caius began to incorporate new styles into their medieval environment. The pilasters and pediment of the Gate of Virtue (1567), the round-arched gateway with victories in the spandrels just like a Romanesque triumphal arch, are pure Renaissance and not in the least characteristic of Elizabethan architecture. One of its companion pieces, the Gate of Honour, harks back to obelisks and other details from the repertoire of the Bolognese architect Sebastiano Serlio. In his immensely influential work *L'Architettura* (1537–51) English architects found the five classical orders of columns and everything else that belonged to the post-antique style.

Inigo Jones never built anything in Cambridge, but there is part of a choir screen that he designed in 1638 for Winchester Cathedral. As it did not fit in with its

Gothic surroundings, it was taken down in 1820, and the central section was re-erected in 1912 on the top floor of the Archaeological Museum in Cambridge. While Inigo Jones was in London winning support for the great classical revolution, the taste in Cambridge even after 1638 was still for ogival windows and a Gothic fan vault, as in the gatehouse at Clare. At the same time, this college began to renovate its Old Court as if it were a Renaissance palace. The dons of Christ's also wanted to live in the spirit of the new age, and so their symmetrical Fellows' Building (1640–43) stands in bold and splendid isolation, demonstrating what John Evelyn praised as 'exact architecture'. And then along came an Oxford man and showed the people of Cambridge the meaning of the word 'classical'. He was a professor of astronomy who had never built anything before, and his name was Christopher Wren.

In spring 1663, even before he had begun work on the Sheldonian Theatre in Oxford, Wren showed his uncle Matthew, a Fellow of Pembroke, his design for a college chapel. It is extremely plain, with pilasters, pediment, and not much decoration, and it is Cambridge's first purely classical building. Wren took his inspiration not only from the pattern books of Serlio, but also from contemporary French and Italian architects, including Bernini, whom he subsequently met in Paris in 1665. A year later he designed a second chapel, for Emmanuel, this time with Baroque elements. But his masterpiece in Cambridge is the Trinity Library, begun in 1676 when he had already been appointed surveyor general. With this library, conceived on a grand scale and perfectly executed down to the last detail, he gave to Palladian classicism an unmistakeable character of its own.

Wren's assistant Nicholas Hawksmoor was also in Cambridge, but in contrast to Oxford, none of his monumental designs (from 1713 on) became reality – neither for King's College (a court almost 90 by 90 metres with cloister and bell tower), nor even more ambitiously for the town centre. If Hawksmoor had got the go-ahead, today we would walk down a majestic avenue all the way along Petty Cury from Christ's to King's Chapel, where a *forum academicum* with colonnades would have stood. He also wanted to broaden and straighten Trinity Street, and decorate it with obelisks like the Piazza Navona – a Baroque 'Cantabrigia Romana'.

Viewing the world from castles in the air has its own charms. Imagine how the little town in the Fens might have looked if Capability Brown had had his way. The king of landscape gardening suggested in 1779 that the Backs should be transformed into one continuous park. Instead of the zigzag route across separate colleges, there would now be serpentine paths along the Cam, which would end in a narrow lake – and there would be no Queen's Road and no traffic. In 1784 Robert

Adam, then at the height of his fame, also submitted designs, and they were also rejected: a new university library and a circular dining-hall for King's. However, what was actually built in the 18th century certainly stood up to the competition.

Once again, as in Oxford, it was James Gibbs who modified and executed Hawksmoor's design for King's. His Fellows' Building (1724–32) is best seen from the Backs, and shows how contrasting styles can stand together and enhance one another: the classicism of Gibbs beside the Gothic of King's Chapel, the dramatic Perpendicular vertical next to the gentle, elongated horizontal, the white Portland stone of the wing beside the warm, yellowish Ketton and York stone of the Chapel – a triumph of architectural counterpoint and an object lesson in bold planning. The Georgian dignity of the Senate House (1722–30) was also the work of Gibbs, and was the first new university building for more than two hundred years.

I was told by a porter that one night a group of students parked their Austin 7 on the roof of the Senate House. A touch of Alice in Cambridge, I thought, until I read *The Night-Climbers of Cambridge*. This classic of 1937 describes some of the hair-raising exploits that have taken place on the roofs and towers of the colleges, complete with names like the routes up Mount Everest: the Chetwynd Crack at King's, the Trinity Kitchen Plateau, the Drain-Pipe Chimney in the New Court of St John's. Night-climbing is a somewhat elaborate way of getting to grips with the peaks of college architecture; it is an extreme sport for the academic flatlands of the Fens. The scale of these expeditions ranges from the practical joke – like replacing Henry VIII's sceptre over the Trinity gate with a chair leg – to acts of protest like tying a 'Ban the Bomb' banner between the pinnacles of King's College Chapel. True roof-climbing, though, is *l'art pour l'art*: jumping, for instance, from a narrow window in the Victorian corner tower of Caius onto the cornice of the Senate House, and then jumping back, which is even more difficult. The Senate House Leap of more than two and a half metres was once a famous test of courage for Caius students, though one doubts if it was part of James Gibbs' master plan.

Apart from the dominant figure of Gibbs, it was mainly two amateur architects who gave form to the new Georgian taste in Cambridge. Sir James Burrough, later Master of Caius, designed the Palladian wing for Peterhouse (1738–42) and the pilastered chapel for Clare (1763–69). With a thin façade of ashlar, sash windows and gables, he Italianized the first court of Trinity Hall as if it were an entirely new classical construction, giving it an 18th-century facelift. Burrough had set the example, and from now on the Middle Ages were out, and since conservation was not in, many colleges proceeded to modernize, especially if they could not afford completely new buildings. For instance, Christ's and Emmanuel were given their new faces by Burrough's younger colleague James Essex. Behind the smooth Georgian façades and the tall, light windows from the Age of Reason, you will often find the small, dark panelled rooms of the Middle Ages.

In the early 18th century the appearance of the town altered considerably. The medieval architecture virtually disappeared, and the half-timbered houses with their overhanging upper storeys were replaced by brick buildings of classical proportions. One of the best examples, still in the Queen Anne style of 1701, is the Master's Lodge at Peterhouse, opposite the college itself on the other side of Trumpington Street. Cambridge does not have the elegant squares and crescents of Georgian Bath or London, but it does have their 19th-century reflections in the fine terraced houses along Malcolm Street and Park Terrace.

After the Napoleonic Wars, the rising number of students led to a college building boom. Downing, begun in 1807, was the first new foundation since the 16th century, and it was Cambridge's first college in pure Greek Revival style. But by the 1820s, the medieval look was back in fashion, particularly in the older colleges, which now wished to emphasize their venerable age through ogival windows, pinnacles and crenellations. William Wilkins, who built Downing in Greek style, produced successful neo-Gothic designs for Corpus Christi, Trinity and King's. Along with Wilkins, the leading architects of the day all joined the triumphant Gothic Revival, especially Sir George Gilbert Scott, with the New Buildings at St John's, and Alfred Waterhouse (Pembroke, Caius, Girton). Why this huge swing to the Gothic? The medieval fashion was part of European Romanticism, but was also an 'extraordinary English phenomenon', according to architectural historian David Watkin. In the intellectual triangle between Oxford, Cambridge and London he discerns the real powerhouse of the Gothic Revival, to which two Catholic movements made a decisive contribution: the Oxford Movement and the Cambridge Camden Society, which was founded in 1839. This Ecclesiological Society, as they were named after their journal, wanted to reform both the liturgy and the architecture of the churches. Their ideal was 14th-century English Gothic, and their prophet A. W. N. Pugin. He converted to Catholicism in 1835, and in the chapel at Jesus College he left shining examples of historically correct designs. The 'decay of faith' had led, he wrote, to the adoption of 'the luxurious styles of ancient Paganism'. Away, then, with the classical, and back to Gothic!

'As to Cambridge, it is rather a hole of a place, and can't compare for a moment with Oxford.' Nevertheless, the Oxonian William Morris and his firm did also reach Cambridge. Works by his Pre-Raphaelite friends Edward Burne-Jones and Ford Madox Brown, especially stained glass and tiles, can be seen in Peterhouse,

Queens' and the chapel at Jesus. All Saints Church is a Victorian masterpiece in the spirit of Pugin, with painted walls, ceilings and windows, designed in 1863 by G. F. Bodley, an architect from the second generation of Gothic Revivalists.

In an environment like Cambridge, every new building is a risk. With one stylistic rehash after another, the 19th century preferred to abide by the conventions rather than be suspected of trying to break with tradition. The results are often mediocre. Yet the Victorian Age got off to a promising start, with Charles Robert Cockerell's Old University Library and George Basevi's Fitzwilliam Museum, both begun in 1837, the year Queen Victoria came to the throne. By the end of her reign, Cambridge was marked by the most extraordinary upsurge in the natural sciences and the most depressing agglomeration of laboratories and institutes. To this architectural horror story, set mainly between Pembroke, Emmanuel and Free School Lane, Oxford's master of styles T. G. Jackson made a major contribution.

One of the English architects most admired by Hermann Muthesius, co-founder of the German *Werkbund*, at the turn of the century was Mackay Hugh Baillie Scott, whose name is all but forgotten today. He designed virtually nothing except family houses, a dozen in and around Cambridge, of which five are in Storey's Way. The best known of these is no. 48, built for a Fellow at Caius and typical of Baillie Scott's style: interior and exterior, house and garden conceived as a single unit, with all the fittings in the best Arts & Crafts tradition. Baillie Scott has been totally overshadowed by his more famous contemporary Sir Edwin Lutyens, though the latter left only a second-rate piece of work in Cambridge, the over-extended wing in Magdalene's Benson Court (1930–32).

In the early 1930s, a twelve-storey book-tower grew up over the trees beyond the Backs. No tower block can have been more controversial than the new University Library by Sir Giles Gilbert Scott. Like his Battersea Power Station, built in the same year (1934), this building is a piece of abstract monumentalism, a compromise between tradition and modernity. The truly avant-garde architect of that period, however, was rejected by Cambridge. Walter Gropius, founder of the Bauhaus, fled from the Nazis and lived in exile in London from 1934. In 1936, he and Maxwell Fry designed an extension to Christ's College, but the Fellows turned it down, choosing in its place a neo-Georgian anachronism in Third Court. Thus it was not Cambridge but Harvard that offered Gropius the Chair of Architecture in 1937.

Cambridge only entered the 20th century in 1959. That was the year in which Sir Basil Spence designed the Erasmus Building for Queens', Cambridge's first building in the International Style. Until then, the contribution of the colleges to modern architecture could be summed up in the words of Nikolaus Pevsner, who for a while was Slade Professor of Fine Arts in Cambridge: 'It seems as though in this century of ours intellectual leadership has moved a long way from aesthetic leadership.' But very soon, the 'Herr Doktor Professor' (John Betjeman) was to be proved gloriously wrong. Between 1954 and 1974, seven new colleges were founded, and many extensions were built – a boom that did not always lead to masterpieces, but did produce a surprising amount of contemporary architecture. It is worth keeping an eye open, even in the old colleges, for the modern buildings which are often hidden away in the second or third court. My favourite is the Cripps Building at St John's, a meandering structure of white Portland stone, uncompromisingly modern and yet sensitively incorporated into its surroundings (Powell & Moya, 1966–67). Cambridge's most radical and most controversial post-war building, however, was commissioned by the university itself: the Faculty of History by Sir James Stirling – a monumental block of industrial glass and red brick (1964–68). 'Anti-architecture,' cried Pevsner, 'aesthetically as neutral as the glazing of a tomato-frame...actively ugly' – a verdict as historical as the History Faculty itself, which now stands under a preservation order.

In the last third of the 20th century, Cambridge became a parade ground for all the big names of British architecture – far more so than Oxford. Sir Norman Foster, Sir Michael Hopkins, Richard MacCormac, Ralph Erskine, Eldred Evans and David Shalev, John Outram, Quinlan Terry, Edward Cullinan – all of them built in Cambridge, as did two Danish architects, Henning Larsen and Erik Sørensen. Here you will find new concepts for old commissions like chapels and libraries, research laboratories and factories. The range extends from John Outram's spectacular Management Institute in Pharaoh style to the Schlumberger Research Centre, the hi-tech tent by Michael Hopkins which became an emblem of the new Cambridge.

On the western outskirts of the city, in the green area between the M11 and the A1303, the university is developing one of its two most ambitious 21st-century projects: the West Cambridge campus for science and computer technology. On this site south of Madingley Road, the new Cavendish Laboratories and the Vet School are already established. Other research institutes are to follow, with joint ventures between science and industry including Microsoft's European Research Centre, right next to the William Gates Building, the university's computer lab.

The second major new project is growing in the south, around New Adden-brooke's Hospital – the campus for biomedicine. Sir Alec Broers, an Australian nanotechnologist and former Vice-Chancellor of the University, had a vision for the new millennium: 'a whole corridor for biomedical research' stretching from Addenbrooke's to Hinxton Hall. On this estate south of Cambridge, the double winner of the Nobel Prize for chemistry Frederick Sanger developed the Human Genome Campus, Europe's foremost genetic archive for 21st-century medicine. The present head of the Sanger Centre, Sir John Sulston, was awarded the Nobel Prize for medicine in 2002, together with the molecular biologists Sydney Brenner and Robert Horvitz, former colleagues of Crick and Watson.

What do the structures of life have to do with architecture? Even for its boldest visions, the university needs planning permission. This is where Brian Human comes in, as assistant director of the town-planning department, where the old town versus gown conflict finds its modern continuation. The university and the colleges own almost 30 per cent of all the land, and 70 per cent in West Cambridge. Often the city can only build if the colleges give their consent; the colleges, however, like any landowner, are subject to the authority of the town-planners. The new West Cambridge site, whose master plan was drawn up by the architect (and Trinity graduate) Richard MacCormac, had to go through the usual planning procedures. 'The University very much took the view that it was in a sense its own backyard, its own land, that they were the planning authority there rather than us,' says Brian Human. 'There is perhaps a feeling sometimes that because they've been here a long while, for them the imposition of the planning system is relatively new.' It is always the same, although there is 'a sort of creative tension, encouraging flexibility on both sides. But nevertheless there are certain limits.' One of these limits is set by what is known as the Green Belt.

Parker's Piece, Christ's Pieces, Jesus Green, Midsummer Common – Cambridge is blessed with green spaces whose survival is as wonderful as their names, for this is common land in the middle of the city, never built on thanks to a vision shared by town and gown. In addition, there is a green belt all round the city and its neighbouring villages which goes back to the Holford Plan of 1950. This plan, named after the architect Sir William Holford, places historic Cambridge like a crown jewel on a cushion of green silk. There was to be no outward expansion into the fringes, and new firms must go further afield into the Fens. In the 1960s, only a relatively prosperous town like Cambridge could afford to refuse planning permission to a company like IBM. With the hi-tech boom following on from the Science Park, however, this restrictive policy found itself going more and more on the defensive. Problems of accommodation and traffic became increasingly urgent. Cambridge had become a victim of its own success.

'Grow or die' – how was it possible to promote economic growth without destroying the character of the city and the quality of its lifestyle? At the end of the 1990s, it became the task of 'Cambridge Futures' to find a way out of this dilemma.

After an exemplary debate, the think-tank of academics, townspeople and business people came up with the following options: intensify building within the city; recycle derelict areas; develop sites within the Green Belt – which the less environmentally conscious considered to be flat and boring anyway.

In the Fens west of Cambridge, there is now a new village of some 3,300 houses. Cambourne was built according to a master plan designed by the architect Terry Farrell. 'Such small settlements dispersed over a large rural area are not the solution,' says Brian Human. 'If you're talking about what meets the housing needs of the Cambridge area, you're talking almost about another settlement the size of Cambridge.' And if one is talking about the requirements of the ever-growing number of students, one is talking about the need for new colleges. On a 57-hectare university site on the north-west outskirts of the city, one or more new colleges are to be built by 2025, together with research institutes and accommodation – the largest expansion project in the long history of the university.

Brief Lives:
A Galaxy of Cambridge Stars

Jeremy: Sir I have the seeds of rhetoric and oratory in my head. I have been at Cambridge.
Tattle: Ay, 'tis well enough for a servant to be bred at a University, but the education is a little too pedantic for a gentleman.
William Congreve, *Love for Love*, 1695

LORD BYRON (1788–1824)

Poet and rebel, sexual adventurer, archetype of the Romantic artist whose life was identified with his greatest work, the verse epic *Don Juan* (1819–24). Of Cambridge he wrote in 1805: 'This place is the *Devil*, or at least his principal residence, they call it the University, but any other appellation would have suited it much better, for Study is the last pursuit of the Society.' He was already creating the basis of his own myth in Cambridge. At Trinity he developed from a shy, rather tubby youth into a dandy with pale complexion and brown curls, 'mad, bad and dangerous to know' (Lady Caroline Lamb). From then on he fostered the Romantic image of the outsider with a mixture of world-weary poetry and scandalous affairs, until he died of marsh fever while fighting for the Greek insurgents against the Turks. His statue in Trinity Library was rejected by Westminster Abbey, and it was not until 1968 that the *poète maudit* was finally honoured with a memorial plaque.

THOMAS CRANMER (1489–1556)

Cambridge moulded him, Rome condemned him, and Oxford burned him. Cranmer was a student and then Fellow at Jesus College, intellectual father of the English Reformation, and its most prominent martyr. He sanctioned the marriage of Henry VIII to Anne Boleyn and established the Church of England. In 1533 he became the first Protestant Archbishop of Canterbury. His *Book of Common Prayer* (1549–52), which is still used by the Church of England today, is not only an educational work but is also a masterpiece of the English language. Instead of Latinisms and humanistic pomp, its prose is sublimely simple, powerful and memorable. As an author in his own right, he contributed the eighty-four short prayers known as the Collects – miniature prose poems of extraordinary beauty.

FRANCIS H. CRICK (1916–2004) AND JAMES D. WATSON (BORN 1928)

What Mad Pursuit is the title of Crick's autobiography, and it is also his description of what he and Watson achieved in Cambridge in 1953: the discovery of the double helix as the molecular structure of DNA. For this epoch-making deciphering of the genetic code, they and Maurice Wilkin were awarded the Nobel Prize for medicine in 1962. Crick, the son of a Northampton shoemaker, worked till 1976 in the Cambridge Laboratory for Molecular Biology before taking up a post as a neurobiologist at the Salk Institute in La Jolla, California. A self-confessed atheist, he hoped to discover through his research on the brain 'what the soul really is' (the title of his book of 1994). James Watson comes from Chicago, and returned to America in 1956. Until 1976 he taught at Harvard, and from 1989 to 1992 he was director of the National Center for Human Genome Research. He is a pioneer in the study of heredity, and believes that evolution can be improved upon through genetic technology. His book *The Double Helix* (1967), which will remain compulsory reading for future biology students, was so candid that it almost destroyed his friendship with Crick, who tried in vain to prevent it from being published.

CHARLES DARWIN (1809–82)

He broke off his study of medicine at Edinburgh and studied theology at Cambridge, which he later described as the 'most enjoyable' years of his life, but he did not want to become a country parson. In 1831, as an unpaid naturalist on *HMS Beagle*, he set off on a five-year expedition to South America, where he collected the material for a study that was to revolutionize the world. His ground-breaking work *On the Origin of Species by Means of Natural Selection* (1859) destroyed the biblical myth of Creation. His contemporaries had difficulty accepting the idea that apes were their common ancestors, and when Darwin sent a copy of his book to his old professor, the geologist Adam Sedgwick, the latter's response was: 'I have read your book with more pain than pleasure.' Unlike the theories of Karl Marx, Darwin's evolutionary model has remained valid even for the sociobiologists and biogeneticists of our day. Darwin withdrew to his family home, Down House in Kent, and went on researching and writing, his last work being on *The Formation of Vegetable Mould Through the Action of Worms*. He died in 1882, an agnostic, and was buried in Westminster Abbey, not far from Newton's tomb. His sons and grandsons were also scientists, and there is now a Cambridge college named after him. The university herbarium has more than 950 dried plants from the *Beagle* expedition that Darwin sent to his friend John Henslow in Cambridge.

ERASMUS OF ROTTERDAM (C. 1469–1536)

'Vulgus Cantabrigiense inhospitales Britannos antecedit' – The Cantabrigians are even more inhospitable than the English, wrote Erasmus, who was fond of rhetorical hyperbole. Nevertheless, the great Dutch humanist was also fond of England, 'where the walls have more culture and eloquence than our people have at home'. It was England that first recognized Erasmus, in the circle of humanists around Thomas Morus. After a period at Oxford (1499–1500), this controversial pacifist and media star of his day taught at Cambridge for three years (1511–14). His critical editions of ancient authors and of the New Testament set the standard for undogmatic scholarship. His aim was to synthesize faith and knowledge, antiquity and Christianity. He also wanted religious reforms, but stopped short of the split that marked the Reformation. Table talk at Queens' may have been the model for his *Colloquia familiaria* (1518), a best-seller of its day and still an amusing guide to the art of living and to *civilitas*, the cheerful and friendly way to deal with people.

EDWARD MORGAN FORSTER (1879–1970)

As it was for Rickie, the hero of his novel *The Longest Journey*, Cambridge was E. M. Foster's 'only true home', first as a student in the Bloomsbury group of friends, and later as an Honorary Fellow at King's. In between came restless years in Florence, Alexandria and India. At thirty-five, Forster had already written five of his six novels, among the most vivid portraits of the Edwardian middle classes, their rituals and their inhibitions, and then after *A Passage to India* (1924) he wrote only critical works and essays. At King's he spent the last and longest period of his life 'tea-tabling', as Christopher Isherwood called it. He was a shy, friendly, owlish man, fully conscious of the idleness of his existence, the transient traces of which he noted in his Commonplace Book: 'Farts. With and without smell'.

THOMAS GRAY (1716–71)

His father, a scrivener, was so violent that his mother, who was a milliner, eventually separated from him. Of their twelve children, only Thomas survived. He was a poet and a hypochondriac, an English Bartleby, who shied away from all the demands of the academic and literary world. He became famous through his *Elegy Written in a Country Churchyard*, a hymn to melancholy. With his Eton and Cambridge friend Horace Walpole, he went on the Grand Tour, but then returned to Pembroke College, where he remained for the rest of his life as a Fellow. The urbane Dr Johnson found him boring: 'dull in company, dull in his closet, dull everywhere.' Gray's reputation as a lone wolf is as incontrovertible as his niche in the history of English literature. He was a poet of resignation, whose emotions and conflicts were caught up in classical conventions of form. He was also a brilliant letter-writer.

GERMAINE GREER (BORN 1939)

In the 1960s she was the feminist whom men actually liked: flamboyant, notorious for her sexual exploits and her well publicized tirades. She was born in Australia, went to a Catholic convent school and then university in Sydney, but has lived in England since 1964. She did her doctorate in Cambridge on the subject of Shakespeare's women characters, went through marriage and divorce in just three weeks, and became the heroine of the feminist movement with her best-seller *The Female Eunuch* (1970). Newspaper columnist, media celebrity, academic femme fatale, but always independent enough to change her mind, she taught at Newnham College, but since 1998 has been Professor of English and Comparative Literature at Warwick University. She has written several books on the role of women in art and literature (*The Obstacle Race, Slip-Shod Sibyls*), age and the menopause (*The Change*), a monograph on the Earl of Rochester, a disillusioned look back over the feminist movement (*The Whole Woman*, 1999), and a provocative look at boys in art (*The Boy*, 2003).

STEPHEN HAWKING (BORN 1942)

Theoretical physicist from Oxford, who at the age of twenty-one contracted amyotrophic lateral sclerosis, a form of motor neurone disease which normally leads to death within a few years. Hawking nevertheless married, is the father of three children, and in 1979 was appointed Lucasian Professor of Mathematics (Newton's chair) at Cambridge. *A Brief History of Time* (1988) – his account of modern cosmology and the search for a universal theory – became the most successful science book of all time and made its wheelchair-bound author into a media star. After divorcing his wife, Hawking married his nurse, made an appearance on *The Simpsons*, and although his cosmology has become increasingly speculative (*The Universe in a Nutshell*, 2001), he is certainly the outstanding Cambridge don of the moment. One of his former assistants, Nathan Myhrvold, became the main strategic adviser to Microsoft and a multi-millionaire.

THOMAS HOBSON (1544–1631)

Cambridge coachman who transported the academics and their luggage. He became rich by renting out horses, and his name became a household expression as 'Hobson's choice' (see p. 339). He was popular with town and gown, was several times mayor, insisted on driving his eight-in-hand coach himself even in old age, and was as tough as teak. But death finally caught up with him: 'Showed him his room where he must lodge that night, / Pulled off his boots, and took away the light. / If any ask for him, it shall be said, / Hobson has supped, and's newly gone to bed.' So ends John Milton's epitaph for Hobson, who is buried in St Bene't's.

ALFRED EDWARD HOUSMAN (1859–1936)

He failed as a student at Oxford, but in 1911 he became a Latin professor at Cambridge. He spent the years between as an employee at the Patent Office in London, but published a book of poetry that became a best-seller: *A Shropshire Lad* (1896). A. E. Housman was the poet of pessimism, a late Romantic who is still popular as the epitome of pastoral, patriotic and nostalgic emotion, though this makes him correspondingly suspect in the eyes of the modernists ('Shropshire lead'). He spent the last twenty-five years of his life at Trinity College, Latinist, gourmet, member of the bachelors' club The Family, but otherwise as tightly closed as a secret drawer. Tom Stoppard's play *The Invention of Love* (1997) is all about this hidden life and the obsessions that went with it.

TED HUGHES (1930–98) AND SYLVIA PLATH (1932–63)

No modern book of poems has been as big a best-seller as *Birthday Letters* (1998) by the then Poet Laureate Ted Hughes: eighty-eight poems about a fatal love which began in Cambridge in 1956: 'Fame will come. Fame especially for you. / Fame cannot be avoided. And when it comes / You will have paid for it with your happiness, / Your husband and your life.' ('Ouija'). The Cambridge graduate from Yorkshire met the Fulbright Scholar from Boston at a party, they got married in 1956, and the marriage ended in 1963 when she committed suicide after Ted Hughes had left her and their two children to live with Assia Wevill, who also killed herself and her child five years later. From the burial chambers of this biographical constellation, it is becoming ever clearer which are the texts that are truly outstanding: Sylvia Plath's *Ariel* especially, and her letters and diaries; Ted Hughes' children's books, translations of the classics, essays on poetry, but above all his many animal poems, whose poetic passion was often criticized for its violence.

SIR JOHN MAYNARD KEYNES (1883–1946)

The most famous economist of the 20th century, born in the year that Karl Marx died. At the age of five, he was already busying himself with cricket statistics, timetables and numbers of all kinds, and his great-grandmother wrote to him: 'You will be expected to be very clever, having lived always in Cambridge.' Keynes shone in many roles, as a professor, diplomat, speculator, art collector, *homme de lettres* and patron of the arts. He was equally at home in the Bloomsbury circle and in the world of finance, and he was just as adaptable in his sexual life. His friend James Strachey called him 'an iron copulating machine', before Keynes married Nijinsky's ballet partner Lydia Lopokova in 1925. After taking his degree at King's, he made a career at the Treasury, which he represented at the Versailles Peace Conference in 1919, and then again in 1944 as a key adviser in negotiations on the post-war economic order. His *General Theory of Employment, Interest and Money* (1936) turned Keynesianism into a key economic concept. The basis of his theory is that the market does not regulate itself, but if necessary the State must intervene in the economy. As we have seen repeatedly, this is no panacea either. King's College, where he was bursar, also benefited from his financial genius. One of his basic tenets was: 'When I see that I'm wrong, I change my mind. What do you do?'

FRANK RAYMOND LEAVIS (1895–1978)

Gaunt, thin-lipped, with open-neck collar and sandals, bolt upright on his old bicycle, heading for Downing College – that was how people saw F. R. Leavis until he was well into his sixties. He was the dominant literary historian and critic of his time, on the opposite side of the fence from C. P. Snow in the battle of the 'two cultures'. He was born and raised in Cambridge, and he died there – the personification of traditional Puritan rigour, a literary missionary who moulded generations of English scholars (known as 'Leavisites'). 'To live properly is to live in and for great literature.' His method of close reading focused on text analysis, social context and the moral responsibility of literature. In books like *Revaluation* (1936) and *The Great Tradition* (1948), he set out his canon, from John Donne to Jane Austen, bastions of (English) culture against the barbarism of the mass media. The fact that Wittgenstein went to the cinema was 'shocking'. He was an early champion of Gerard Manley Hopkins, D. H. Lawrence and T. S. Eliot, but misjudged James Joyce and Virginia Woolf. He and his wife Queenie edited the magazine *Scrutiny* (1932–53), which became an influential forum for literary criticism in Cambridge and, of course, a mouthpiece for its greatest polemicist. His limitations and insular provincialism became all too evident when George Steiner arrived on the scene (see p. 266).

JOHN MILTON (1608–74)

The Lady of Christ's was his nickname, because he had a gentle face and a sharp tongue. As a Puritan he supported the Parliamentary side in the Civil War. In 1649 the Council of State appointed him Secretary for Foreign Tongues. He was Cromwell's Latin secretary, and set out the Republican's policies in letters and pamphlets, including a justification for the execution of the King. However, he defended freedom of conscience, freedom of the press, reason and religious tolerance against every State and Church authority. This impressed his contemporaries more than his poetry, which only achieved a growing reputation from the Romantic period onwards. Milton was the most argumentative of all English poets, his style was as remote from the vernacular as Cambridge is from Blackpool, and his attempt to justify the ways of God to man was probably the most difficult of all his tasks. He had to dictate his great verse epic *Paradise Lost*, because from 1653 he was completely blind. 'They also serve who only stand and wait.'

SIR ISAAC NEWTON (1643–1727)

Farmer's son from Lincolnshire, went to Trinity College at seventeen, became professor of mathematics at twenty-seven. His great treatises on *Philosophiae Naturalis Principia Mathematica* (1687) were the result of his years at Cambridge, and soon became an integral part of the teaching there as well as adding enormously to the prestige of the university. With Newton began the dominance of the sciences. His laws of dynamics and gravity for the first time proved the physical unity of the universe, and this rationally explained synthesis of earthly and heavenly appearances presented a totally new picture of the world. Newton was reputed to be a lone wolf, unsociable and with no interest in women or in men. In 1705, by which time he had become Master of the Mint and President of the Royal Society, he was the first scientist to be knighted. On the day of his state funeral in London in 1727, Voltaire said of him that he was the precursor of the Enlightenment. In the chests that he left to the university, however, there were various writings on alchemy and theology. At the end of his life, 'the last of the magicians' (J. M. Keynes) was seeking a divine plan for salvation and for a natural law of Creation. William Blake depicted him as an ambiguous genius (*The Ancient of Days*, 1795), providing a model for Paolozzi's monument to Newton in front of the British Library – the rationalist measuring eternity with his dividers. His own view of himself was more modest: 'to myself I seem to have been only like a boy playing on the sea-shore, and diverting myself in now and then finding a smoother pebble or a prettier shell than ordinary, whilst the great ocean of truth lay all undiscovered before me.'

SAMUEL PEPYS (1633–1703)

To his college, Magdalene, he left not only his private library but also more than 3,000 pages of encoded shorthand which made him famous – his diary. After his studies, Pepys went back to his hometown, London, rose rapidly in the naval service, and became Secretary to the Admiralty, organizing England's mighty fleet. He was an expert on shipping, President of the Royal Society, an MP, an art-lover and a 'man of pleasure', hedonistic, cosmopolitan, curious, vain – the ideal qualities to produce a diary that became a classic. In minute detail, Pepys recorded domestic and state affairs with matchless honesty and wit, creating a unique chronicle of everyday life. The refrain that runs through his many visits to Cambridge is one that could apply throughout his life: 'We were very merry.'

KIM PHILBY (1912–88)

His real name was Harold Adrian Russell Philby, but he was called Kim after the hero of Rudyard Kipling's novel, who had a similar gift for espionage, or 'the great game'. Philby was born in India, and finished his studies at Cambridge in 1933 as a convinced communist. The perfect gentleman-spy, a double agent working ostensibly for the British Secret Service but in reality for the KGB, he fled in 1963 to Moscow, where he was the only one of the Cambridge spies to be honoured posthumously with a postage stamp. One of his friends to the end was Graham Greene, whose spy novel *The Human Factor* (1978) can be read as Philby's story.

SIR BERTRAND RUSSELL (1872–1970)

Married four times, the last at the age of eighty, lost three parliamentary elections, imprisoned twice for his pacifist principles, awarded the Nobel Prize for literature in 1950 for his sensational book *Marriage and Morals* (1929). Studied and taught at

Trinity College, where he developed a mathematically based logic which his pupil Wittgenstein immediately deconstructed. He wrote almost continuously: some 60,000 letters, hundreds of essays, 71 books. His *History of Western Philosophy* (1945) became a best-seller. 'The Voltaire of our century' (Golo Mann) stated late in his life that he had only gone over to philosophy when he became too stupid to do maths, and to politics when he became too stupid to do philosophy. With his pipe and his silver hair, Russell became one of the great symbols of the protest movements against the Vietnam war and in favour of nuclear disarmament; he was also a pioneer in matters of sexual freedom, and his excessive bed-hopping earned him the reputation of being 'a man all brain and balls, with nothing much in between' (Jane Dunn). A London taxi-driver recalled the famous Lord Russell getting into his cab. 'So I asked: "Well, guv, what's it all about, then? I mean, why are we here?" And you know what? He couldn't tell me!'

GEORGE STEINER (BORN 1929)

Son of a Jewish Viennese banker, born in Paris, emigrated to America in 1940, brought up trilingual, an international commuter in literature and ideas. His dissertation on a theme of comparative literature was turned down by Oxford and became his first major success: *The Death of Tragedy* (1961). In the 1960s, Steiner shone in Cambridge, then in Geneva, before returning to Oxford in 1994 as the first Professor of Comparative Literature. For many insular academics, the cosmopolitan, nomadic intellect of this literary mandarin was suspect, and he has remained an outsider, the typical Oxbridge hybrid. His main preoccupations are the relationship between art and barbarism, between language and silence. His autobiographical *Errata: An Examined Life* (1997) is an apotheosis of the eternally restless Jewish mind fighting against the metastases of mediocrity.

ALAN TURING (1912–54)

Studied mathematics at Cambridge, 'the most gifted of all the many Queens of King's' (Clive James). One of his teachers was Wittgenstein. Starting out from the *Entscheidungsproblem*, then a much discussed problem in mathematical logic, he devised the Turing machine in 1936, a model for modern computer systems. He began his *Computing Machinery and Intelligence* (1950) with the famous line: 'I

propose to consider the question, "Can machines think?"' As part of the deciphering team at Bletchley Park, he played a major role in cracking the Enigma Code of
the German *Wehrmacht*. However, he could not cope with the codes of the world
around him. In 1952 he was charged with homosexuality, and was compelled to
take female hormones ('I'm growing breasts!'). He committed suicide by eating an
apple containing potassium cyanide.

LUDWIG WITTGENSTEIN (1889–1951)

The youngest of eight children, his father was a Viennese steel magnate, and he
grew up in a Jewish-Protestant household. He began by studying aeronautics in
Manchester before he met Bertrand Russell in 1911 in Cambridge. Russell wrote:
'At the end of his first term at Cambridge he came to me and said, "Will you please
tell me whether I am a complete idiot or not?" I replied, "My dear fellow, I don't
know. Why are you asking me?" He said, "Because if I am a complete idiot, I shall
become an aeronaut; but, if not, I shall become a philosopher."' In 1914 he volun-
teered to join the Austrian army, and after the war finished his *Tractatus
logico-philosophicus*, gave away the fortune he had inherited, and worked as a
monastery gardener, village schoolteacher, and architect. In 1929 he returned to
Cambridge, declared that first time round he had got everything wrong, and spent
the next eighteen years trying to get 'a whole cloud of philosophy condensed into
a drop of grammar'. 'Only let's cut out the transcendental twaddle when the whole
thing is as plain as a sock on the jaw.' During his lifetime he published no more
than a hundred pages, but for his disciples he was the Sun King of philosophers, an
absolutist in thought as in life, monomaniacal, self-tormenting, a pain to the academic Establishment, 'unclubbable'. He was a Trinity don who read American
pulp thrillers in preference to the philosophical magazine *Mind*. To escape from
the black holes of philosophy he would take himself off to the cinema, to Ireland,
to Norway, to anywhere away from the world of signifiers. In 1947 he gave up his
professorship just a few years before he died of cancer in Cambridge. The ethical
rigour and the analytical elegance of this great linguistic thinker continue to fasci-
nate even today. The definitive, bilingual *Wiener Ausgabe* [Vienna Edition] of his
work is being prepared at the Cambridge Wittgenstein Archive, and began publication in 1993.

North of Market Hill

'I feel frightfully important coming to Cambridge.... I don't
want to be horribly impressed and intimidated, but am afraid I may be.'
D. H. Lawrence to Bertrand Russell, 2 March 1915

It gets off to a great start: a completely flat square named Market Hill. Ever since the Middle Ages, the farmers from the surrounding villages have set up their stalls here in the centre of Cambridge. There's cheese, fish, fresh fruit and vegetables, books, antiques – but of a hill there is no sign, and there never was. This open space – and that, strangely enough, is what the word 'hill' means in Cambridge – once extended further east as far as the churches of Holy Trinity and St Andrew's. As usual in such small towns, you can find everything you need grouped around the market place: the Guildhall, churches, cafés, banks and shops. In this somewhat amorphous collection of buildings, the Art Nouveau shop window at 21 Market Street looks a little like a lost soul.

On the north side of Market Hill, where Rose Crescent swings gently round the corner, a bronze plaque commemorates the tobacconist's shop Bacon's. Among the regular customers of this family business, which had flourished in Cambridge since 1810, were such Victorian smokers as the young Alfred Tennyson and Edward Fitzgerald. Professors like Charles Kingsley also used to go to Bacon's to stock up on tobacco, clay pipes and stormproof Vesuvius matches. Of this temple of blue vapours, which closed in 1983, all that remains is a few lines cast in bronze: 'Ode to Tobacco' by Charles Stuart Calverley. He wrote it in 1862, when he was a Fellow at Christ's. Calverley was a brilliant parodist, who translated English classics into Latin or Greek and with equal facility could leap over a coach horse. He was as addicted to athletics as he was to smoking: 'Smith, take a fresh cigar! / Jones, the tobacco-jar! / Here's to thee, Bacon!'

Petty Cury branches off Market Hill, *le petite Curye* branches off Petty Cury, and *parva cokeria* branches off *le petite Curye*. Petty Cury was the first street in Cambridge to be cobbled in the 18th century. It was surrounded by lanes and backyards – very much old town, which 'progress' passed by until recently. Instead of the area being restored, however, it was demolished and replaced in 1975 by a shopping mall – a bad mistake, as the planning department now admits. In the middle of Lion Yard, a red lion stands on a socle, denoting what used to be the Red Lion Hotel. Behind the shopping centre, a car park and a county court complete the inner-city disaster. By the side of the road, Michael Ayrton's bronze statue of Talos delivers its ironic message: Talos, the mythical watchman, was supposed to protect Crete from harm.

At the rear of the Guildhall, opposite the Tourist Information Centre, stands a long brick building of 1874, the Corn Exchange. This Victorian centre for the Fen farmers is now a multi-purpose hall, good for pop concerts, but acoustically unsuitable for a symphony orchestra. Just round the corner is Peas Hill, where there were never any peas but there was fish. Peas is a corruption of *pisces*. Here you will find the Arts Theatre, which has welcomed many of the established stars as well as the stars of the future, performing in the productions of the Marlowe Society. It was the economist John Maynard Keynes who both initiated and financed the Arts Theatre, and at its opening in 1936 his wife, the Russian ballerina Lydia Lopokova, played Nora in Ibsen's *A Doll's House*. In the foyer hangs a copy of a double portrait of this art-loving couple; it is by William Roberts, a member of the Vorticist movement. As a collector and a sponsor, Keynes knew what to spend his money on. Even when he was still a student, in 1904, he bought rare items such as a first edition of Newton's *Principia* from the antiquarian Gustave David. If you want to follow in his footsteps you can, for just a few yards away from the Arts Theatre is David's, the bibliophile's delight, in the idyllic lane next to St Edward's churchyard.

Print and Prayer:
Cambridge University Press and Great St Mary

'For Cambridge people rarely smile,
Being urban, squat, and packed with guile.'
Rupert Brooke, 'The Old Vicarage, Grantchester', 1915

David's treasure house is as discreetly hidden as the University Press and Bookshop is majestically prominent – right opposite the Senate House. The CUP's shop window has only been situated in the stately brick building on the corner of St Mary's Street since 1992, but books have been sold there since at least 1581. That is why 1 Trinity Street proudly proclaims itself to be 'the oldest bookshop site in England'.

As in Oxford, the first printer in Cambridge was a German: Johann Lair from Siegburg. John Siberch, as he was known, came to Cambridge with his hand-press in 1521, printed ten books, and then went straight back to Germany in 1522. Censorship made the printing business an extremely risky one. Siberch's initiative, however, was a purely private affair and had nothing to do with the university. It was not until sixty years later that the next books were printed in Cambridge, for although Henry VIII had granted the university the licence to print and sell 'omnes et omnimodos libres', this was initially prevented by the Stationers' Company. Until 1584 this London-based company preserved its monopoly, but then at last the university printer Thomas Thomas was able to publish his first books, one year before his rivals in Oxford.

In the beginning was the Word – the Geneva Bible of 1591 – and the Word in Cambridge developed into a multi-million pound business. It was this edition of the Bible that Shakespeare used and the first English settlers took to America. The CUP shared with its Oxford colleagues the privilege of being allowed to publish the Bible and prayer books. The enormous demand for religious literature in the early 19th century brought correspondingly enormous profits to the press, which enabled it to finance its academic programme. But of course, it was not able to accept everything that it was offered. Ludwig Wittgenstein's *Tractatus logico-philosophicus*, for instance, was turned down. When Bertrand Russell and Alfred North Whitehead submitted the 2,500-page manuscript of their *Principia Mathematica* – a Herculean attempt to deduce all mathematical theorems from logic – the CUP syndicate hummed and hawed so long that in the end the authors agreed to pay a proportion of the expected losses themselves. Later Russell admitted that no one to his knowledge had ever read the three volumes through to the end: 'I used to know of only six people who had read the later parts of the book; three of these were Poles, subsequently (I believe) liquidated by Hitler. The other three were Texans, subsequently successfully assimilated.'

Of the long succession of Cambridge University printers, one in particular stands out: John Baskerville, one of the most innovative of all the great European printers of the 18th century. His name entered the language through the serif type-face that he invented. He was a trained calligrapher and type founder, and was constantly in search of pure typographical lettering. During the few years when he was active in Cambridge, he produced many classic editions, including the New Testament in Greek lettering and the famous Folio Bible of 1763. The finest examples of his craft are to be seen in the college library at Newnham.

The CUP published works by Erasmus, Milton, Newton and John Donne, as well as popular anthologies and encyclopedias, and it also prints timetables, examination papers, specialist journals, prayer books, textbooks, and dictionaries that go all over the English-speaking world. It has long since grown into an international concern, with branches and offices in some sixty different countries. In 1981 most of the press left its Victorian headquarters, the Pitt Building in Trumpington Street, and moved into new buildings on the other side of the Botanic Garden. More than 24,000 authors from about 100 countries have now seen their work published under the CUP banner, and every year there are around 2,400 new publications – enough for a good forty launch parties a week at 1 Trinity Street.

Part of Cambridge's publishing history and indeed forerunners of the CUP in this corner building were two Scottish brothers, Daniel and Alexander Macmillan. They were booksellers from 1845, and soon became publishers as well. At 1 Trinity Street students, professors and bookworms from every walk of life came together, Thackeray and Tennyson gave readings, and in 1857 the Macmillans published Thomas Hughes' *Tom Brown's Schooldays*, the Victorian best-seller about life at a public school. And so the famous London publishing house of Macmillan began its career in Cambridge.

As you leave the bookshop and wander along Market Street, you will hear the chimes of Big Ben. This may surprise you, since London is a fair distance away, but your ears do not deceive you. The catchy phrase adapted from Handel's *Messiah* ('I know that my Redeemer liveth') to mark each quarter of an hour first rang out from the tower of the Cambridge University Church of St Mary the Great. A professor of law from Trinity Hall, Reverend Joseph Jowett, installed the chimes in 1793, and the melody became so popular that in 1859 it was used for the clock tower of the new Houses of Parliament. Under the name of Westminster Chimes, the erstwhile Cambridge Chimes proceeded to ring all round the world, from the clock towers of several American universities to the City Hall in Sydney.

Great St Mary's was a completely new building constructed after 1478 on the site of an older church. It has crenellations, high slender arcades and Perpendicular windows, with ornamental tracery carved in the soft limestone of the spandrels. The hammer-beam roof, donated by Henry VII in 1505, is made from a hundred oak trunks and is decorated with Tudor bosses. From a very early stage this town church was also the university church. Masters and Fellows held meetings here in the 15th century, until the completion of the Old Schools, and the university kept its documents here too – it was virtually the seat of government. Until 1730, when the Senate House was built, disputations, degree and other ceremonies were held in Great St Mary's, and in the galleries along the side aisles students and townsfolk would throng together to listen to famous visiting preachers. The gallery reserved for Masters and doctors, now demolished, was nicknamed Golgotha – the place of the skull. This is one of the few churches in England still to have a movable pulpit, which rolls on rails into the nave.

For centuries the university church has stood in the shadow of another sacred building – the famous King's College Chapel. 'Poor St Mary,' people might say, except that nothing can compare to its glorious and incomparable chimes. The twelve bells are a good deal more impressive than the architecture, and if you do not already know anything about the fine English art of change ringing, this is the place to go. If you are really lucky, you might hear the Cambridge Guild of Change Ringers performing a movement of Stedman Triples, though you will need a few spare hours if you want to hear it from start to finish. The mysterious records of change ringing are listed on the panels of the bell-ringers' chamber, which you will pass on your way up the spiral staircase to the top of the tower, and from there you will look down on the brightly coloured market stalls, the church towers and the college courts of Cambridge.

As always, things are a little more sober when you see them again at ground level. In front of Great St Mary, on Senate House Hill, are marble benches and bollards with pretentious gold lettering – small town adornments in big city style. To recover from this sight, I recommend that you go straight to Auntie's Teashop, after which you might wish to pop into the internet café next door.

The Heart of the University:
Senate House and Old Schools

'People will actually have to work when they get to Cambridge. *If* they get to Cambridge.'
'What, everybody?'
'Yes, everybody.'
Nicholas Monsarrat, *Life is a Four Letter Word*, 1967

Once a year, to the accompaniment of Great St Mary's chimes, a picturesque procession wends its way along King's Parade to the Senate House, led by the bedels holding their staffs of office, with the University Chancellor (or Vice-Chancellor) following in his gold-braided robes, and then the dignitaries, Masters and Fellows in the shining gowns of various colours according to their faculties – a cross between solemn funeral and colourful carnival. The conferral of honorary degrees is the highlight of the academic year. Field Marshal Blücher, Archbishop Desmond Tutu, the entomologist Miriam Rothschild, Piotr Tchaikovsky, Thomas Mann, Jürgen Habermas and countless other representatives of the great and the good have trodden this path to academic honour.

While you and I might look at the classical façade with a greater or lesser degree of interest, in June there are hordes of students who can't take their eyes off it. Their reactions will range from delight to despair, for next to the entrance hang the lists of their exam results. Not long after, on Degree Day, they, their tutors and their relations will troop into the Senate House for the degree ceremony, though not as you might expect according to the alphabetical order of their colleges. Even this ritual reflects the hierarchy of the elite within the elite. It begins on Friday morning with King's, Trinity and St John's – the great and old and rich – and it ends late Saturday afternoon (by which time the lawn in front of the Senate House has been trampled to mulch) with the poor cousins from Robinson, Homerton and Darwin.

The Senate House is the stone heart of the university. Here the senate sits, and here all the big and little decisions are taken that determine the present and future life of the university, from the great debate on women's academic rights to the affair of Jacques Derrida's honorary doctorate. It has also been the showplace for memorable events such as A. E. Housman's one and only public lecture, in May 1933, on *The Name and Nature of Poetry*, and C. P. Snow's unveiling of his thesis of the *Two Cultures*, given as the Rede Lecture in 1959. By comparison with this, the

most prestigious of all Cambridge lectures, which began in 1524, the Senate House
is relatively young. It was built in 1722–30, and was designed by the Scottish architect James Gibbs, at the same time as his London masterpiece St Martin-
in-the-Fields. The façade (made of the same light Portland stone that Wren used in
London) is divided up by massive columns and pilasters, with a pediment over the
slightly projecting central section, and there is an alternation of round and pointed
arches above the ground-floor windows, while the roof has a balustrade crowned
with majestic urns. This classical elegance is a mixture of Palladian motifs, the
Wren tradition, and Roman Baroque. The interior is a long, light hall with galleries, with a coffered plaster ceiling in Rococo style and statues by Michael
Rysbrack and Joseph Nollekens. On the lawn outside is a bronze copy of the
Roman Warwick Vase. Unauthorized visitors, which includes most of us, are kept
at bay by thick black railings, erected in 1730 and, incidentally, among the first cast-
iron railings to be used in England. It is worth noting how the corners of
Cambridge lawns are marked off: with cast-iron spirals outside the Senate House,
with elaborate stone scrolls in the front court of Emmanuel College, and with
black lanterns in the Old Court at Peterhouse – a theme with many variations in
this paradise for lawn-worshippers.

The Senate House was the only project to be realized out of a number of new
buildings planned for the centre of Cambridge in the 18th century. Not only
Hawksmoor had Baroque visions for the centre; Gibbs himself wanted a good
deal more: a Senate Court with wings and with Great St Mary marking its eastern-
most point. A shortage of funds and an abundance of criticism meant that the view
of King's Chapel remained undisturbed. It was not until more than thirty years
later that a new library was built next to the Senate House (1754–58). Stephen
Wright's design is rather more masculine than Gibbs' Senate House, but it creates
an admirable ensemble, built of the same Portland stone and very much in the
spirit of Palladio, whose Venetian windows were particularly popular among his
English successors. Wright's Palladian wing replaced the original east wing of the
Old Schools. Behind the Georgian façade of the latter beat the heart of the
medieval university. This Cobble Court had everything that was required by such
an institution: rooms for meetings and for administration, a library, and lecture
halls for the different schools or faculties. It all began with the theologians, whose
Divinity School (c. 1350–1400) was the first individual faculty building to be constructed – though it was in no way comparable in grandeur to its Late Gothic
Oxford counterpart. The west wing for canon law (c. 1430–60) was built of rubble
stone, while the south wing for philosophy and civil law (1457–70) was of brick.

Above the lecture halls was the university's first library. Scarcely any of this is now to be seen, let alone visited, for the Old Schools, which have undergone countless renovations and conversions, are now the university's administrative backrooms. Part of the administrative centre is the adjacent West Court, which was originally King's Old Court and which the university bought from the college in 1829. Sir George Gilbert Scott virtually rebuilt this court in 1867, as he did the entrance in Trinity Lane.

We should not leave this architectural rectangle without casting a glance at the Cockerell Library (1837–42), directly west of the Senate House. This second extension of the university's library was designed by the Victorian architect C. R. Cockerell, with a masterly feeling for space and surface; the interior is magnificent, stretching over the entire length of the building and roofed with a barrel vault which is beautifully furnished with a diagonally ribbed coffered ceiling – certainly the finest 19th-century library in Cambridge. In 1992 the university, whose vast quantity of books had long been transferred to new and much larger premises, leased its Old Library to Gonville and Caius College opposite for 350 years. This is the sort of time scale on which people think in Cambridge.

Gonville and Caius:
The Gate of Honour

'Ah! my old friend Dr Harvey... I remember he kept a pretty young wench to wayte on him, which I guesse he made use of for warmeth-sake as King David did.'
John Aubrey (1626–97) on William Harvey, who discovered the circulation of the blood

Gonville and Caius not only has a double name, but it was also founded twice: first in 1348 by Edmund Gonville, a parson from Norfolk, and then in 1557 by John Keys, a doctor from Norwich who latinized his name in the humanistic style to Caius (which is also pronounced *Keys*). The majority of people abbreviate the name to Caius.

Dr Caius was physician to Edward VI and to Mary Tudor, and he was one of the richest doctors of his time. He had studied medicine in Gonville Hall and in Padua, had lived for some years in Italy, and taught philosophy before pursuing a medical career in London. Dr Caius refounded and revitalized his old college, and became its Master, though as a Catholic he was not particularly liked by the Fellows. The new court that he built in 1565–69 next to Gonville Court was the first in Cambridge to have just three wings and a wall with a gate on the south side. Caius Court was designed to be bright, open and airy – a sanitary measure with symbolic overtones: away with the mustiness of the Middle Ages! Through the enclosed inner courtyards of the past came the new and open spirit of the Renaissance.

With three equally symbolic gates, Dr Caius leads us along the educational path of the Elizabethan humanist: 'Humilitatis' is the first through which the student must pass, followed by 'Virtutis', whose reverse side spells out 'Sapientiae', and finally comes the Gate of Honour, which leads directly from the college to the Old Schools, examinations, degree, career. The academic rite of passage is still practised ceremonially in Caius today. Normally there are only two occasions when the Gate of Honour is opened: on Degree Day, when the students go to collect their degrees from the Senate House, and when a Fellow dies. In order to pay final respects to the deceased, there is a Requiem Mass in the chapel, after which his coffin is borne through the Gate of Honour to the hearse waiting in the Senate House Passage.

Nowhere else in Cambridge is there an iconographic academic programme like the gates of Caius. The Gate of Humility has in the meantime been transplanted to the Master's Garden, where perhaps it was more urgently required, but the key word *Humilitas* still greets us in its old position, for it is above the entrance in Trinity Street. A charming avenue of whitebeam trees leads across the Victorian Tree Court to the three-storey Gate of Virtue (1567). Historians of architecture assure us that this is one of the earliest relics of the English Renaissance, but as is so often the case in life, its noble purity proves to be less attractive than the exotic hermaphrodite that awaits us in the next court. The Gate of Honour, which was built posthumously according to Caius's own design (1575), is a fantastic collage of arches, columns, pediments, obelisks and finials, crowned by a hexagonal tower with dome and sundials – a mass of different motifs within the most confined of spaces. The Elizabethans loved such *concetti*, and the greater the ornamentation, the greater the honour.

The fact that Dr Caius was more concerned with fame than with humility is clear from his monument in the college chapel: a columned baldachin of marble and alabaster. His Gate of Honour bears two inscriptions: one, with Virgilian pathos, 'Vivit post funera virtus' [Virtue outlives death], and the other a strikingly brief autobiography, 'Fui Caius' [I was Caius]. He was not, incidentally, the only famous doctor to come from this college. William Harvey, who discovered the circulation of the blood, was one great 'Caian', and Edward Wilson, who died with Scott in the Antarctic in 1912, was another. The college flag that he hoisted at the South Pole now hangs trophy-like at the head of the hall. There, beneath the Victorian hammerbeam roof, in the biggest gold frame of the portrait gallery, is a portrait of an astrophysicist for whom the doctors gave up hope long ago: Stephen Hawking, the most famous Fellow of Caius (see p. 261). To give his lectures, programmed into a computer, he used his last two movable fingers to operate his voice synthesizer – a superbrain in a wheelchair making his way to the very frontiers of space. 'My goal is simple. It is complete understanding of the universe, why it is as it is and why it exists at all.'

Gonville and Caius was the first college to lift the ban on marriage for its Fellows in 1860, and it was one of the last to admit women students in 1979. The chapel and hall are part of the medieval Gonville Court, the historical heart of the college, which was 'modernized' in 1753 with a neoclassical façade by Sir James Burrough, Master and amateur architect. It is simple and well proportioned, in contrast to the overwhelmingly pompous First Court built in 1870 by Alfred Waterhouse in the style of Early Renaissance French chateaux. The self-satisfied splendours of this towering Victorian block are best seen from King's Parade, where they compete disastrously with their neighbours, the Senate House and Great St Mary.

Clare's Tears, the Backs and Trinity Hall

'If I were called upon to mention the prettiest corner of the world, I should have a tender sigh and point the way to the garden of Trinity Hall.'
Henry James, *Portraits of Places*, 1883

The entrance to Clare College is a little remote, behind the Old Schools at the end of Trinity Lane. The simple elegance of the architecture, and indeed all the beauty of this college, is only to be seen from the river side, against the great setting of the Backs. Clare rises up like a country house out of the meadows, next to its glorious neighbour, King's Chapel.

Twelve silver tears on a black background frame the Clare coat of arms. These are the tears that Lady Elizabeth de Clare wept for her husbands, for she was wid-

owed three times. All of them were rich men, however, and that was the good fortune of the college, which had been founded by the University Chancellor
Richard Badew in 1326 without sufficient funds. In 1338 the college found a second
and more powerful patron in the Countess of Clare. Nothing is left of the original
buildings, and what we now see is the result of a rebuilding programme begun in
1638, interrupted by the Civil War, and only finished in 1715. Despite this construction time of seventy-seven years, Clare College appears completely harmonious,
as if it had been built in a single phase. It has an urbane aura, with the grandeur of a
Renaissance palace.

The Old Court is the first totally classical court in Cambridge. And yet the elaborate, almost Mannerist gatehouse of 1638 still has a Late Gothic fan vault – one of
the last examples of this retrogressive fashion. The court itself, however, has all the
elegant proportions and disciplined dignity of the new style. Monumental Ionic
pilasters punctuate the river side of the west wing, and the upper storey has a
rhythmic succession of alternating segmental and triangular pediments. Local
masons, Thomas Grumbold and his son Robert, were responsible for the building
and also in part for the design, which clearly shows the influence of Christopher
Wren. A portal with a Baroque shell-shaped porch leads into the chapel, which
was designed by James Burrough in 1763 along similar lines to Wren's chapel for
Pembroke College. The entrance, an octagonal antechamber, is original, though,
with its high, light lantern. The altarpiece, an Annunciation, is by Giovanni Bat-
tista Cipriani, one of the founder members of the Royal Academy. What Clare's
students like most about the chapel, however, is the crypt, where they hold their
discos (or 'bops', in student parlance).

Stepping out of college courts into the open arms of nature is always a pleasure,
especially at Clare. A bridge with three arches spans the river, and there are balls of
stone balanced on its parapet – a playful piece of architectural water music
designed by Thomas Grumbold in 1639. No guide ever forgets to ask the crucial
question about Clare Bridge: 'How many stone balls are there on the parapet?'
Everybody confidently says 'Fourteen!' But the correct answer is 13 ⅞, because
one of the balls has a segment missing. This is the oldest surviving bridge over the
Cam, and if you approach it by boat, you will see the mythical singer Arion on his
dolphin carved in relief on the outside of the parapet.

Since 1688, even before the filigree wrought-iron gate was erected (1714), the
Fellows of Clare used to walk along the avenue of lime trees to go into their garden. At the entrance is a Judas tree, which bears purple blossoms in May; there
are herbaceous borders with yellow mulleins, light blue poppies and dark blue

delphiniums, and a sunken water garden surrounded by hedges of yew; at the end
of Dean's Walk is a dove tree or davidia, which waves hundreds of white handker-
chiefs at you in June, because it is also known as the handkerchief tree. And in May
Week every fan of glorious gardens and shimmering Shakespeare goes to the out-
door production in the Fellows' Garden at Clare.

If you leave the Cam-side colleges through the back door, you will enter one of
the most beautiful landscapes to be found in any European city: the Backs. They
stretch from Darwin and Queens' in the south to St John's and Magdalene in the
north, a unique combination of water meadows, colleges, leisure park, fields, gardens, bridges and avenues. Picnics on the river bank, punting on the river, cows
grazing against the backcloth of King's College Chapel – all the picture postcard
clichés come to life here in scenes that symbolize the unique nature of Cambridge.

It seems scarcely possible that this idyll has not been here since time immemo-
rial. And yet in the early Middle Ages, the Backs were an industrial zone. From the
High Street, narrow lanes ran past warehouses and colleges all the way to the
docks, where river trade went on between Cambridge and King's Lynn. The other,
western bank was constantly susceptible to flooding, and so it was left largely
untouched. When Henry VI bought the land for King's College in 1447, he also
acquired land on the other side of the river. 'Kynges college backe sides' is the
name given to it on old maps, and in time this became shortened to the Backs.

So long as the Cam was a commercial waterway and formed part of the munici-
pal sewage system, the colleges turned their own backs on the evil smelling river.
The Backs were their backside, so to speak, and nothing changed until the 16th
century. The *vedute* of the British engraver David Loggan that appeared in 1690 in
Cantabrigia Illustrata already depict avenues running through the Backs, and college gardens along the banks of the river: kitchen gardens, orchards, hops, and also
bowling greens and pastureland for the Fellows' horses. By the end of the 18th century, the Backs looked more or less as they do today – a park rather than a food
store – while the colleges had taken on their dual character, with forbidding gatehouses at the front, defending them against street and town, and idyllic gardens
and river scenes at the rear. 'I visited the little town of Cambridge,' wrote Joseph
Haydn in 1791, 'and saw all the universities [sic], which are built very cosily in a
row, one after the other, though each one for itself; each university has a very spacious and beautiful garden at the rear as well as a fine stone bridge in order to pass
over the river which runs all around.' Ever since, visitors have wandered with
delight through these academic havens of green. Even without any contribution
from Capability Brown, this is the English Garden par excellence, a piece of *rus in*

urbe which offers the additional attraction that one can breathe in the pure air of the spirit. Nowhere in the world will you find a riverside park with a higher concentration of top IQs.

For all the impressiveness of the Backs, Henry James considered that the little river itself was only there for decoration and as an excuse to build pretty bridges. Between Clare and Trinity Bridges there is now a slender modern one of pre-stressed concrete, built in 1960 and offering a view of another enchanted garden which is the preserve of ancient horse-chestnut trees and the rather less ancient Fellows of Trinity Hall.

With the ever-popular Georgian cosmetic front of smooth ashlar and large sash windows, this college cleverly hides its true age, at least in its front court. The passage next to B Staircase, however, will take you straight from the 18th to the 14th century, to the rear of the north wing, where you can still see the medieval masonry of rough-cut clunch and narrow Gothic windows. Trinity Hall was founded in 1350, and its founder, Bishop William Bateman, gave it the name of his own cathedral: 'The Holy Trinity of Norwich'. A few years earlier, England had been ravaged by the plague, and with this foundation Bishop Bateman hoped to train a new generation of urgently needed clerics and lawyers. Here men of Church and State learned the basics of their trade, from Bishop Stephen Gardiner, Mary Tudor's Lord Chancellor, right through to Sir Geoffrey Howe, Foreign Secretary under Margaret Thatcher. Trinity Hall is still *the* college for law (as well as for oarsmen), and Vyvyan Holland, Oscar Wilde's son, was one of its law students.

The elegant lantern above the West Wing marks the dining hall, which has a fine Georgian interior with lime-green panelling and, at the head, twin Corinthian columns with gilded capitals. Opposite the entrance is the Sir Leslie Stephen Room, in commemoration of Virginia Woolf's father, who was a Fellow here, as was Robert Runcie, the former Archbishop of Canterbury, whose passion for cricket illuminates one of the windows in the ante-chapel. Trinity Hall's library is the only one in Cambridge to have basically preserved its medieval character, although the building itself actually stems from the late 16th century. Behind these Tudor brick walls with their stepped gable, there are still books that are chained to the shelves as they used to be in the early chained libraries.

Many of the colleges were originally called halls. The word 'college', derived from *collegium*, actually referred to the scholars who lived in the halls, but later the meaning changed. Of all the old Cambridge colleges, Trinity Hall is the only one to have retained this name, which of course distinguishes it from its neighbour, Trinity College.

Three for Trinity:
Newton, Byron and Prince Charles

'In the whole of the world and throughout infinity,
There is nothing so great as the Master of Trinity.'
Anonymous

The only people in Cambridge who wear bowler hats are the porters at Trinity College. They stand there chatting on the grey cobblestones in front of the Great Gate, while above them at the entrance the King holds on to an elaborate chair leg in place of a sceptre. Not even the apple tree on the lawn beside the gate is a normal apple tree. 'It's Newton's apple tree,' the porter informs me. There is no doubt about it, the tree of knowledge grows here.

Let's get the superlatives out of the way: Trinity is the biggest, richest, most important college in Cambridge. It was the birthplace of Bloomsbury, the home of the Apostles, and the cradle of high treason. It produced spies like Kim Philby and Anthony Blunt, prime ministers like Arthur Balfour, Jawaharlal Nehru and Rajiv Gandhi, future kings like Edward VII, George VI and his grandson Prince Charles. It boasts 29 Nobel laureates, more than any other college in Cambridge or Oxford, and in the 20th century it spawned Fellows of the Royal Society in virtually every branch of the natural sciences. It is largely due to this college, and a range of scientists from Ernest Rutherford to Alan Hodgkin, that Cambridge has earned its reputation as the foremost seat of scientific learning in Britain.

Trinity is also, however, a college of writers, from Lord Byron to Vladimir Nabokov, and an intellectual powerhouse where Bertrand Russell, Ludwig Wittgenstein and the American cyberneticist Norbert Wiener used to meet every Thursday in Russell's rooms to split the philosophical atom at their 'mad tea party' in Nevile's Court. 'Maurice's set had laughed at Trinity, but they could not ignore its disdainful radiance or deny the superiority it scarcely troubles to affirm,' wrote E. M. Forster in his novel *Maurice*.

Trinity College is as large and as flamboyant as its founder, Henry VIII. It came into the world when the King dissolved two older colleges and combined them into one. In 1546 Michaelhouse and King's Hall turned into the College of the Holy and Undivided Trinity, with a view to accommodating a Master and sixty Fellows – bigger than any existing college, and bigger even than Cardinal Wolsey's Christ Church in Oxford. With plunder from the monasteries, Henry was able to endow his college with massive wealth, and one of its land acquisitions was turned into a goldmine during the 20th century with the establishment of the Science Park (see p. 219).

With four crenellated corner turrets of Tudor brick, the Great Gate of Trinity (1518–35) was once the entrance to King's Hall, which Edward III had founded in 1337. It is a gatehouse that resembles an heraldic database of English history. Above it flies the college flag of Trinity, Edward III's standard, which also unfurled itself over the battlefields of Crécy and Poitiers, for in order to symbolize his claim to France, the King was the first to cross a French fleur-de-lys with an English lion. Edward III's coat of arms, placed right in the centre above the entrance, is flanked by those of his six sons – one of whom (with ostrich feathers) was the Black Prince, while another died in infancy and left behind a coat of arms that was white and blank.

Trinity's links with royalty are not confined to the figures that adorn the gate-house – Henry VIII himself and James I, facing the inner court along with his wife and son, the future King Charles I. This is the only college whose Master is not elected by the Fellows but is appointed by the Crown. 'We have our little per-formance when the Master is installed,' I was told by Paul Simm, the Junior Bursar. 'He has to wait outside and knock on the door. The Head Porter then opens the Main Gate, and he is asked if he has his Letters Patent from the Crown, the Letter of Appointment from the Queen which he has to put on the silver tablet. It's then taken to the Chapel and given to the Vice-Master, and he reads that out to the Fellows, and all the Fellows then come out to the Gate. And then the new Master is admitted back in the Chapel, where he is installed.'

Even without the ceremony, it's a triumphal entrance. Ahead of us lies the Great Court – a broad expanse with buildings all round, like a grandiose mixture of piazza and village green, with a fountain in the middle whose gentle, endless bab-ble echoes on all sides and keeps out the noise of the traffic beyond. The Great Court is, of course, bigger than any other court in Cambridge or Oxford, but what makes this court so special is not just its size, or the quality of buildings around it – the chapel and hall, the Master's Lodge, the residential wings and the gatehouses – for these you will find in any college court. What makes this one so impressive and so different is that it is neither square nor rectangular, and its lawns and paths are not symmetrical, and none of its three gates stand in the centre of their wings. As in medieval squares, the heights, ages, materials and even quality of the buildings vary from one to the next. Some have stone façades, others are plastered, many are covered with plants like wisteria, roses, clematis and Virginia creepers. It has the charm of irregularity, the variety that blends into unity with the living confidence which can only reside in something that has developed down through the centuries. The whole spectacle centres (though in fact it is off-centre) on the splashing arabesque that is the fountain, which once supplied the college with its drinking water. It is a late Elizabethan, columned baldachin with a filigree ogival cover (1601–15, renovated in 1715). This eye-catching centrepiece balances out the proportions of the huge court, providing a focal point in the vast and uneven spaces that surround it.

The Great Court in its present form is mainly the work of Thomas Nevile, who became Master of Trinity in 1593. It was he who brought together the disparate elements of Henry VIII's foundation, financed the new dining hall out of his own pocket, and even replaced an entire gatehouse. In order to unify the court, Nevile did not demolish King Edward's Tower (1427–37) but had it dismantled stone by stone and then rebuilt some twenty metres away on the west side of the chapel. King Edward's Tower was the original entrance to King's Hall, and the first gatehouse of its kind in Cambridge, but Nevile's early example of conservation was less concerned with architecture and history than with continuity and with economics: building materials were expensive, but labour was not. The lantern on the tower was added by the Master, as was the statue of Edward III in Elizabethan armour. After all, this King had not only beaten the French and founded the Order of the Garter, but he had also brought Flemish weavers into the country – an enlightened forerunner of European ideals.

King Edward's great clock has just struck – two beats for every hour, the first one heavy, the second light. Wordsworth, sitting in nearby St John's, called it 'loquacious'. But for more sporting natures, this was the greatest challenge of their Cambridge career. Once a year, at midday in October, the students race against the clock in the Great Court Run. Before the clock has finished striking its twenty-four hammer blows (which it accomplishes in 45 seconds), you have to complete the full circuit of the court – 370 metres, to be precise. The first winner of this eccentric race was Lord Burghley in 1927, and he went on to become an Olympic champion. Not until 1988 did two more record-breakers, Sebastian Coe and Steve Cram, beat the clock, but it was said that they cheated, because instead of taking the paved path, they ran on the cobbles, which saved them a good 15 metres. No one has managed the feat since then.

The Great Court Run, which made film history in Hugh Hudson's *Chariots of Fire*, ended in front of the chapel. Mary Tudor, daughter of Henry VIII, financed this Late Gothic building (1555–67), which was one of the few ecclesiastical edifices constructed during the reign of the Catholic queen. The Georgian interior – screen with columns, stalls, reredos – was provided by a none-too-polite classical philologist, Richard Bentley, Master of the College, who used to call his Fellows asses, fools and dogs. He has been resting here – possibly in peace – since 1742. The antechapel is more interesting than the chapel itself, for here we can find a whole gallery of Trinity celebrities, commemorated by brass plaques, marble busts and statues. In this Valhalla sits Lord Tennyson, his pipe half-hidden beneath a laurel wreath, and opposite him the great Elizabethan polymath Sir Francis Bacon, who at the age of twelve declared that the Trinity curriculum was out of date. And towering over everybody, with his genius proclaimed on the socle ('Qui genus humanum ingenio superavit'), the figure of Sir Isaac Newton, complete with prism, portrayed as a young man without a wig – a masterpiece by the Huguenot sculptor Louis François Roubiliac (1755). It was this marble statue that inspired Wordsworth's immortal lines in *The Prelude*: '...Newton with his prism and silent face, / The marble index of a mind for ever / Voyaging through strange seas of thought, alone.'

Newton spent thirty-five years of his life at Trinity. In his own shorthand he recorded his student sins, from skipping chapel to 'using Wilford's towel to spare my owne'. In 1669, there occurred the rare event of a teacher giving up his post to his student, because the latter simply knew more than he did. The rooms of the twenty-seven-year-old maths professor, decorated in his favourite crimson, were in the Great Court, on E Staircase. It was here that he wrote the scientific treatises which formed the basis of a new view of space and time so revolutionary that, in the words of Alexander Pope, 'Nature, and Nature's Laws lay hid in night: / God said, *Let Newton be!* and all was light.' When he wanted to relax, Newton went walking in the garden which in those days lay in front of his rooms, right next to the Great Gate. The apple tree that stands there now was in fact planted in 1954, but it's not a complete fraud. It descends from a cutting taken out of the garden of his parents' home in Lincolnshire, where in summer 1665, as everybody knows, an apple fell on his head bearing all the weight of the law of gravity. The variety of this historic fruit is Flower of Kent, 'absolutely inedible' according to one brave soul who'd tasted it.

Almost every week, someone asks permission to film in Newton's rooms, but the bursar has to refuse because one of the Fellows lives there. 'We don't keep rooms as monuments. We're not a museum – this is a workplace.' If you just take E Staircase alone, the names resonate: William Makepeace Thackeray, novelist; Thomas Babington Macaulay, historian; James Frazer, anthropologist. And just like biblical genealogies, one name begets another: Macaulay leads to his great nephew George Macaulay Trevelyan and his teacher Lord Acton, on to Trevelyan's pupil Steven Runciman, chronicler of the Crusades, and from there to E. H. Carr, Orlando Figes and Richard Evans, creating a phalanx of Trinity Fellows who carried on the great tradition of Anglo-Saxon narrative history. Trevelyan's *English Social History* was a best-seller, and he himself became Master of Trinity. In admiration of the Glorious Revolution of 1688, he had the phone number 1688. The Master until 2004 was Amartya Sen, who is married to a Rothschild, is an expert on world poverty, and has won the Nobel Prize for economics.

In the southern wing of the Great Court, whose gatehouse is embellished with a statue of Elizabeth I, a new student took up residence in 1967. He stemmed from the House of Windsor, had rooms on K Staircase, and for three years studied anthropology and history. Prince Charles was the first royal student ever to sit the exams and actually earn his B.A. (Cantab). He was never one of the true Cambridge wits, but on at least one occasion he certainly made his fellow students laugh. They were sitting together discussing what they would do after their exams, and what careers they wanted to pursue. Charles simply announced: 'I want to be King of Europe.'

It is one of Trinity's rituals that the eight crescent-shaped steps up to the hall should be mounted with a single leap. A pagoda-style lantern crowns the steep roof, which offers another sporting challenge plus 'the finest view-point in the College Alps', according to *The Roof-Climber's Guide to Trinity* (1899). More than 30 metres long, this is the biggest hall in Cambridge, and it was built in 1604–5 and modelled on the Middle Temple Hall in London. It is a grandiose celebration of the traditional medieval hall, though its interior was already old-fashioned at the time – from its minstrels' gallery (i.e. singers' gallery), with elaborately carved balustrade, to the Jacobean hammer-beam roof, which is structurally too thin for its size. The plastic duck that shifts around among the beams bears eloquent testimony to the activities of the Climbing Society.

Two high bay windows with heraldic motifs illuminate the top end of the hall, where there are two high tables reserved for the Master, Fellows and guests of honour. Above them, on the panelled wall, stands Henry VIII, legs astride like a colossus, as he was in Holbein's 1537 wall painting (destroyed) in Whitehall Palace. On the right of the portrait of the Royal Founder, a copy of 1667, hangs one of his daughters, Mary Tudor, as severe as ever, while on his left is a handsome, long-legged youth of fifteen, who in 1791, wearing the gold-braided gown of a Trinity graduate, posed for the artist George Romney: this was Prince William Frederic,

Second Duke of Gloucester, known as 'Silly Billy', who later became Chancellor of the University. He was the first member of the Royal Family to study at Cambridge. This portrait is sometimes switched with one of him as a boy, painted by Joshua Reynolds. You will find no portraits more charming than these two in Trinity's gallery of famous alumni. The students themselves, however, are not to be distracted from life's deeper values by all this splendour, as is clear from their *Alternative Prospectus*: 'The surroundings in Hall are still more impressive than the meals served within them.'

Ludwig Wittgenstein, who was a Fellow at Trinity, rarely dined in hall. On one occasion when he did, he cautiously dipped his spoon into a creamy dessert. 'Sir,' one of the college waiters said encouragingly, 'if you dig a little deeper, you'll find a peach.' It was, according to Wittgenstein, the kindest thing anyone ever said to him in Cambridge.

From the screens, the passageway outside the hall, you enter Nevile's Court or, rather, the balustraded terrace known as Wren's Tribune. From this classical rostrum you can look over Trinity's second court, which was built by the Master Thomas Nevile in 1612. After the medieval exuberance of the Great Court come the harmonious proportions of the Renaissance, with wings and colonnades of Mediterranean elegance where once Newton, with pendulum in hand, tested the speed of an echo. In the middle is an immaculate lawn. 'Students have covered it with furniture,' recalls one of the porters, 'or let white rabbits loose in the court.' Pretty tame stuff when one remembers that Byron used to wander around here with his pet bear. The young lord had furnished his rooms in the north wing of Nevile's Court with Greek style lamps, ottomans and a four-poster bed. He had a servant and a horse, and during his first term, in 1805, he wrote to his half-sister Augusta that he felt 'as independent as a German Prince who coins his own cash'. From his rooms on the first floor, Byron could look across at the Wren Library, where now he is forever commemorated in marble.

Nevile's Court was originally open to the river and was quite homely and domesticated. It only received its monumental west wing when Newton's teacher, the Master Isaac Barrow ('God always acts Geometrically') asked his friend Christopher Wren to design a new college library. Wren did this free of charge, and it is his greatest masterpiece in Cambridge (1676–85). Trinity Library outshone the old University Library just as King's Chapel put the University Church of St Mary in the shade. Wren designed a long building with an open-columned hall on the ground floor, rather like the great halls one sees in old schools. High windows above the arcades take up the rhythm of the round arches in a peaceful, wave-like movement of Ketton stone, which changes colour from cream to peach according to the light, and was beautifully worked by Wren's mason Robert Grumbold. From the balustrades on the roof, four statues gaze down on the court, allegorical figures of Divinity, Law, Physics and Maths, sculpted by Caius Gabriel Cibber, sculptor to William III. While the court side of the building is richly decorated, the river side is simple to the point of severity, divided up only by three portals with columns – quite enough for the Backs, which at that time were not yet the park that they are today.

A single Baroque masterstroke reveals Wren's mathematical and architectural genius. The upper storey which houses the library does not begin over the triglyphic frieze, as it seems to do from the outside, but actually starts below the tops of the arches. By filling these in with lunettes, he was able to conceal the real height of the floor, and by sinking the level of the floor, he gained extra space for the bookshelves and for the large windows, all of which makes for a wonderfully light and spacious interior. With this library, which is on a scale far more massive than appears from the outside, Wren was following examples set by his great Renaissance predecessors, Michelangelo's Laurenziana in Florence and Sansovino's library in Venice.

And what an interior this is! It is a reader's paradise, 46 metres long, 12 metres wide and 12 metres high, with bays in between the bookcases, which range along the walls and at right angles to them – a combination of the English box system and the continental hall library. Wren also designed the stools and tables, with adjustable lecterns in the areas for study, and the oak bookcases stained reddish to look like cedarwood. The carvings are in limewood, and their virtuosity is such that only one man could have done them: Grinling Gibbons – 'a citizen of nature,' as Horace Walpole once called him, 'who gave to wood the loose and airy lightness of flowers.' Between 1691 and 1695 Gibbons covered Wren's bookcases with garlands, fruits, emblems and coats of arms, all of them exquisite, and on top of one of the twenty-four founder's panels sits a carved grasshopper poised to make a great leap. The statue of the Sixth Duke of Somerset, who was then Chancellor of the University, was also done by Gibbons, but it is in marble and rather stiff, for marble was not his material.

In this college it goes without saying that every room of any size is a Valhalla. Trinity's stars fill not only the chapel and hall, but also the library. Forming a double guard of honour before and on top of the bookcases are rows of marble busts – Bacon, Bentley, Newton, and a host of familiar and unfamiliar names – the best being the work of Roubiliac (1751 onwards), along with Greek, Roman and English philosophers and poets, as if on this Olympus of learning even Socrates, Cicero and Shakespeare had once studied at Trinity College. And so we walk over the black-and-white marble tiles to the very end of this magnificent hall, and there, in front of the great south window, Lord Byron sits upon his socle, 'concentrating very hard on looking unhappy', as Bertel Thorvaldsen said of his subject, who had sat for him in Rome. The chapter at Westminster Abbey had refused to allow the scandal-ridden poet to be buried there, and they also rejected Thorvaldsen's over-lifesize marble statue of 1829, and so finally his old college took it in, and set it up in the library. Behind it, a Baroque window illustrates the apotheosis of Trinity's glory: Cantabrigia, the Alma Mater personified, presents her superstars Newton and Bacon to King George III, with Britannia, the allegorical figure of Fame and scantily dressed nymphs all round them.

One might almost forget that the principal purpose of a library is books. Out of a collection of 200,000 volumes, the Wren (as his library is known) stores the 55,000 or so that were printed before 1820. From this sea of words, a few items stand out like coral reefs: a collection of early Shakespeare editions, the Rothschild collection of 18th-century English literature, Newton's personal library together with his cane, and the collection of Piero Scraffa, the Turin economist whom Maynard Keynes brought over in 1927 to Cambridge, where he spent the rest of his life as a Fellow of Trinity. Another of The Wren's treasures is the botanist's Bible, the *Historia Plantarum* (1686–1704) by John Ray, another Fellow of Trinity. Carolus Linnaeus based his system of binomial nomenclature on this encyclopedic description of more than 20,000 different types of plant. But this book-lover's feast is not only for scientists. The cabinets of the Wren Library also contain wondrous literary treasures: the manuscript of *Winnie-the-Pooh*, who was to become even more famous than Byron's bear and whose author, A. A. Milne, also studied at Trinity (pilgrims should head for Whewell's Court, P Staircase); manuscripts of poems by John Milton and A. E. Housman; an edition of *Piers Plowman* from the 14th century, when the first texts to be written in the vernacular were published, and when English replaced French as the official language at Court. There are incunabula, illuminations, over 1,200 medieval manuscripts, including an edition of St Jerome with a decorative capital A that looks like a parody of a tutorial: a man is teaching the alphabet to a dancing bear (12th century). The oldest manuscript in Trinity's library is a Latin copy of a letter from St Paul (8th century), probably written by an Irish monk.

A college safe holds the literary estate of Ludwig Wittgenstein: his diaries, notes, thousands of typescripts. Wittgenstein returned to Cambridge in 1929. 'Yesterday

I sat for a while in the garden of Trinity,' he wrote in his diary, '& there I thought, strange how the well-developed physique of all these people goes together with complete unspiritedness.' Ten years later, he took over as successor to G. E. Moore what he considered to be 'the absurd position of a professor of philosophy'. In a small circle of disciples ('My lectures are not for tourists') he explored the frontiers of language and thought, stammering, pausing, talking in meandering, aphoristic sentences, a gaunt, grey figure of enigmatic lucidity, who could be understood only by the man from Mars with whom he holds discussions in Derek Jarman's film *Wittgenstein*. After every seminar or lecture he would be totally exhausted, and to unwind would take himself straight off to watch something at the 'flicks' – preferably a western.

Wittgenstein lived in a Spartan room in Whewell's Court, on the other side of Trinity Street. One floor below him lived the poet and Latin professor A. E. Housman. Two Fellows of Trinity, both homosexual and both as difficult and melancholy as the other – a situation loaded with potential. However, Housman disliked the philosopher so much that on one occasion of some urgency, he even refused to let him use his toilet.

In the middle of the 19th century, Trinity expanded beyond its Great Gate and out into the old town. Whewell's Court (1859–68) was designed by Anthony Salvin in Tudor-Gothic style. It was named after the then Master, William Whewell, who was tutor to Thackeray and Tennyson – a Victorian polymath of 'unbounded energy and boundless arrogance' (Noel Annan). Next to Whewell's Court is the towering Wolfson Building, a five-storey student hall of residence with two pyramidal inverted lanterns (1968–72). Like a Babylonian ziggurat, this massive block has been stuck right in the heart of the old town. Close by is another residential block for the students of Trinity, Blue Boar Court, an aesthetically rather more pleasing design by Richard MacCormac (1996). The whole area between Trinity and Sidney Street, Green Street and All Saints Passage belongs to Trinity College, the largest landowner in Cambridge. The students living in the former Blue Boar Hotel opposite the college are expected to have a good laugh every time they go into the bar downstairs. It rejoices in the name of 'Ha! Ha!'

Across the Bridge of Sighs to the Wedding Cake:
St John's College

'Theft, murder, incest, notorious adultery or fornication, scaling the walls
or opening the gate at night... to be punished with expulsion!'
From the statutes of St John's, 16th century

It's advisable to take a break between visiting colleges, and the most literary break you can take is at Heffers, the bookshop in Trinity Street. A rank outsider founded this counterpart to Oxford's Blackwell's in 1876: William Heffer, son of a farm worker from the Fens. Heffers too became an institution, until the founder's grandchildren sold the family business in 1999 – to Blackwell's. This takeover, it was said, was like a dead heat in the Boat Race, for the firm keeps rowing under its old name, but Blackwell is now the cox. One of the six branches, the Children's Bookshop in Trinity Street, still has shop windows from the Regency period. If you walk past the 18th- and 19th-century brick houses of this street, with shops below and flats above, and round a gentle bend, you'll come to a little square with benches and birch trees. All Saints Garden was once the graveyard of a church that has long since disappeared. At weekends, artists and craftspeople sell their wares here. In the next lane, gourmets will find Cambridge's finest cheese shop, and hot-heads can be turned into eggheads – 'Get ahead with Ray's Barber Shop'.

The Tudor bricks of St John's College have a pink glow. With its lozenge patterns of blue clinker and its four slender, octagonal corner turrets, the gatehouse is one of the most classic in Cambridge. Like its neighbour Trinity, St John's introduces us at once to its Founder, and it does so in spectacular fashion right at the entrance. Two yales – mythical beasts with antelopes' bodies, goats' heads and elephants' tails – hold up the crowned coat of arms of Lady Margaret Beaufort, mother of Henry VII. The Tudor emblems are displayed here with even more splendour than at Christ's, her earlier foundation: the portcullis and the red rose of Lancaster. Marguerites and forget-me-nots blossom on the heraldic field, alluding punningly to Lady Margaret, whose witty but syntactically obscure motto is 'Souvent me souvient' (which presumably means 'remember me often'). The golden-haired figure in the niche below the Gothic baldachin (1662) is not, however, the royal Foundress but the spiritual patron of the college, St John the Evangelist with his attributes: the eagle and the snake chalice. The monastery hospital of the Augustinians was dedicated to him (c. 1200), and it was on this large site that St John's was founded in 1511, two years after Lady Margaret's death. The driving force behind the foundation was her executor, Bishop John Fisher.

When we have passed through the linenfold panelling of the fine oak portal beneath the fan vault of 1516, we find a succession of courts and buildings that reach from the early 13th through to the late 20th century, extending more than half a kilometre across the river and into the park as far as Queen's Road. 'It's like a little town,' says Don, one of the porters. In terms of area, St John's is the biggest of all the colleges, and only Trinity has more students and more money.

Anything is possible here, as can be seen from the entrance to G Staircase in First Court, where we read: 'Stag Nov 15 1777'. It seems that a stag got halfway up the stairs before being killed by the hunters. First Court is the oldest part of the college, and the young Wordsworth had his rooms on F Staircase (see p. 235). He would not recognize the wing opposite, for the original hospital chapel that he attended was demolished, and only its foundations can still be seen in the lawn; behind this is a neo-Gothic chapel that looms over the whole court. Wordsworth would, however, recognize at least one portrait in the hall, since it is of himself.

With its massive, gold-decorated hammerbeam roof, this is one of the finest halls in Cambridge – pure Tudor, with an additional Victorian bay window. Such bays were also to be found in medieval manor houses, on the level of the high table, so that their Lordships could sit in the light. Above the Master's chair, as in most colleges, hangs the portrait of the Foundress, Lady Margaret Beaufort, kneeling before her book of hours, wearing the white hood of an abbess. Rowland Lockey, a pupil of Nicholas Hilliard's, painted this portrait in around 1598, almost ninety years after her death, and based it on Lady Margaret's sarcophagus sculpture in Westminster Abbey. The 'Johnians' venerate their benefactress, and Cambridge's oldest boat club, founded in 1825, is named after her. The scarlet jackets worn by its members gave rise to the word 'blazer'.

The portrait gallery in the hall offers only a small selection of St John's celebrities, from Lord Burghley, the most influential minister and university politician at the court of Queen Elizabeth I, to Queen Victoria's prime minister Lord Palmerston. The humanist Roger Ascham, tutor to Elizabeth I, her astrologer John Dee – an English Nostradamus – and the saintly Philip Howard, whom she left to die in the Tower, also came from St John's. The scientific reputation of the college is in the hands of such Nobel laureates as Paul Dirac, Sir Edward Appleton and the nuclear physicist Sir John Cockcroft. Other notable pioneers include the first man to cross Antarctica overland (Sir Vivian Fuchs in 1957) and the first man to hitchhike his way through the galaxy (Douglas Adams, 1979).

St John's Chapel is more like a parish church than a chapel. It was designed by Sir George Gilbert Scott (1863–69) in the style of the late 13th century, and it represents a colossal misunderstanding. The proportions are as grotesquely out of tune with the court it stands in as the Ancaster limestone (instead of brick) that was used to build it. Scott based the polygonal apse on the Sainte-Chapelle in Paris, and the T-shaped ground plan with transept and crossing tower on the college chapels in Oxford. What infuriated his contemporaries can now be looked at with a little more detachment, for in itself this is an impressive example of neo-Gothic church architecture with High Victorian decoration. Red granite, green serpentine and various coloured marbles all make an impact, but at the time the costs rose as high above the college as the tower itself. The latter, incidentally, has louvres for the sound of the bells, but no bells to make the sound.

The English love of word play is a constant source of joy, even in death. In the ante-chapel stands the tomb-chest of Hugh Ashton, one of the first Fellows of St John's, who died in 1522. The railings and the tomb itself are decorated with a rebus that makes up his name: an ash tree growing out of a barrel (= ash-tun). The double meaning, sense in nonsense, is accentuated by the double figure of Ashton himself, dressed in academic robes above, and as a skeleton below.

The Fellows still meet in the chapel to elect their Master, but anyone can attend evensong. The choirboys and the 'gentlemen of St John's' have a very individual sound, which connoisseurs can recognize instantly. If you hear Allegri's *Miserere* here on an Ash Wednesday, as I did, you will never forget it. Nor will you forget the chorale which the boys sing from the top of the tower at noon on Ascension Day. There are only two Cambridge colleges with a choir school of their own: King's and St John's. For forty years, until 1991, the St John's choir was conducted by a Welshman named George Guest, who made them famous, taking them on world tours as far as the Opera House in Sydney.

No other college conveys the same feeling of axial symmetry and architectural unity that you find in St John's first three courts as they succeed one another on their way from street to river. Like an echo of the front gatehouse, a second gatehouse stands at the end of the second court, erected in 1598–1602 through the generosity of Mary, Countess of Shrewsbury, whom we can see above the portal. 'She died on the scaffold,' says Don, with a jerk of the neck – 'quite quick for those days.' Then he shows me a room that the Fellows use on festive occasions, the Combination Room on the first floor of the north wing (1599–1601). It is the Master's former long gallery, almost 30 metres in length, with a richly decorated plaster ceiling, panelled walls, silver candelabra – an Elizabethan interior that matches any other that you will find in Cambridge. A mahogany table was specially made in 1963 to go with this room and its Chippendale chairs; it was a copy of the great table at Hardwick Hall. 'Almost 24 metres long,' says Don, 'and room for 180 guests.'

In the 17th century, along with its third court, St John's acquired a new library. This north wing ends with an oriel looking out on the river, and it bears the date 1624. Through the tracery windows with their pointed arches, an almost archaic light falls on this long, Late Gothic room on the first floor, with a box system that makes it seem positively medieval. The oak bookcases have Renaissance decorations, and on the end of each is a little wooden door behind which is a list of the books. Equally user-friendly is the flat stool that originally went with each standing position and enabled even smaller readers to reach the two-sided lecterns, as well as to avoid getting cold feet. In the Upper Library, the college keeps the books printed before 1800, which constituted the academic canon of their time – classical, theological and scientific works, including the first ever book on midwifery to be published in England: *De arte natandi*, 1587. One floor below, in a fireproof, air-conditioned chamber, are 260 illuminated manuscripts from the Middle Ages. There is also an enchanting book of hours, bound in calfskin, which Lady Margaret Beaufort gave to one of her ladies-in-waiting, with the dedication: 'For my good Lady Shirley, pray for me.'

St John's Library also contains first editions of works by its famous alumni, William Wordsworth's teacup and paperweight, and photographs taken by Cecil Beaton, who began his studies in 1922 with the intention to become 'a whole-hearted aesthete'. At the time he was far too shy, but when he left after three years without a degree, his costume designs and stage sets for student productions in Cambridge had already attracted a lot of attention. So too had his first photographic credit in *Vogue* in 1924: a portrait of George Rylands in the role of the Duchess of Malfi.

The majority of St John's 80,000 books are in the new library next door (1993). The architect, Edward Cullinan, extended the Victorian west wing of Chapel Court with a transverse building of red brick and light limestone, crowned with a lantern of steel and glass which serves as a sensor-operated ventilator and looks like a pile of Chinese hats.

Two bridges cross the Cam from the old courts of St John's. The Old Bridge, edged with balustrades, was designed by Wren's master stonemason Robert Grumbold (1709–12). The other is a neo-Gothic extravaganza by Henry Hutchinson, the Bridge of Sighs (1831), covered like its Venetian counterpart, and when in summer the gondoliers of Cambridge stand at the rear of their punts, and with leisurely swings of their poles send the boats gliding gracefully between the arches, the picture postcard cliché is complete. The bridge was covered because of college statutes, which used to impose a nightly curfew on the students. For this reason, the tracery windows contain no glass but only iron bars – reason enough for all those sighs.

To contemporaries, New Court, with which St John's first extended across the river (1826–31), must have seemed like a mirage. A cloister with Gothic windows and crenellations links the two outer wings, and in the middle is a gatehouse flanked by towers and with a lantern on top whose flying buttresses, pinnacles and finials rise to a neo-Gothic crescendo. It was immediately christened 'The Wedding Cake'. Perfectly integrated in glowing Ketton limestone, New Court stands in the green setting of the Backs, Gothic Revival mixed with classical features, designed by Thomas Rickman and his pupil Henry Hutchinson. Rickman was also responsible for the terms 'Early English', 'Decorated' and 'Perpendicular' with which we now classify English Gothic. The stone eagle above the ogee arch of the gate has survived many a student prank. At various times, this attribute of the college's patron saint has been painted red, dressed in a bow-tie, and crowned with a hat. The St John's porters can tell you many other hair-raising stories: 'We had a piano pushed off the roof once into the river – yeah, bits of fun like that.'

The end of New Court is not the end of St John's, for there are still a few pleasant surprises in store. On the river bank you will find a superb example of 20th-century college architecture – a building that curves its way across the park, forming open courts and blending trees with walls in a dialogue with nature that recalls the tradition of the picturesque using the vocabulary of the present. The Cripps Building by Powell & Moya (1966–67) is a residence for 200 students, which is over four times the number that studied at St John's in the 16th century. There are also penthouse flats for Fellows and roof parties for everyone.

When the Lady Margaret Players put on a new production, the theatergoers meet in the School of Pythagoras. This massive stone house, dating from around 1200, is one of the oldest in the country. It was bought in 1270 by Walter de Merton as a possible refuge for his Oxford scholars, and it was not until 1959 that Merton College finally sold its Cambridge exclave to St John's, together with an adjacent group of half-timbered houses known as Merton Hall (16th–17th century).

With its park in the Backs, St John's offers its students plenty of scope to enjoy the freedom of nature. Capability Brown had his own idea of what was natural, and the Fellows' Garden which he designed in 1778 is known as the wilderness. Old oak trees grow there, and chestnuts and a tulip tree, and in spring you will see beneath these trees the golden daffodils immortalized by Wordsworth.

2,903 Books and a Diary:
Samuel Pepys at Magdalene

'Walked to Magdalene College... and there drank my bellyfull
of their beer, which pleased me as the best I ever drank.'
Samuel Pepys, 25 May 1668

A pike is a fish, a pickerel is a young pike, and the Pickerel Inn, diagonally opposite the college, is the local for all the young pikes of Magdalene. There used to be five inns on the short stretch between the river and the crossroads at the end of Castle Street, and just as many brothels. What Magdalene House, a corrective institution for prostitutes, and Magdalene College have in common is Mary Magdalene, patron saint of repentant prostitutes.

Many generations of Magdalene students have celebrated their triumphs or drowned their sorrows in the Pickerel, whose walls are covered with photographs of rugby and hockey players, footballers and the Wyvern Society. New members of this exclusive sports club, it is said, were made to drink three pints in three minutes, the last half pint being mixed with vodka. However, the macho image of Magdalene has suffered greatly since in 1988 it became the last college in Cambridge (as well as Oxford) to admit female students. This bastion of Old Etonians had long had the reputation of being more interested in dog-breeding than in studying, though all that remains of this legend is a little Victorian dog cemetery in the Fellows' Garden. There they lie in the earth of academia, Bumble and Nettle, Ti-Ti and Tim, 'a great pet'. Magdalene (pronounced 'maudlin', and don't forget the all-important 'e' that distinguishes it from the other place) was the only one of the old colleges to be built on the west bank of the Cam. There the Benedictines had established a college of their own in 1428, but after the dissolution of the monasteries, Buckingham College – as it was then called – fell into the hands of Thomas Lord Audley, Henry VIII's Lord Chancellor, who re-founded it in 1542 under the name of St Mary Magdalene. His successors, the Neviles of Audley End, still have the right to appoint the Master of the college.

The first court (c. 1430–1580) is small and intimate, as indeed is the whole college. The monastic emblems over some of the portals are a reminder of its Benedictine origins. In the east wing, distinguished by its seemingly telescopic lantern, is the hall, above the entrance of which is the Founder's motto: 'Garde ta Foye' [keep your faith], which the students like to translate as 'Mind your liver'. One attraction in this hall is its beautifully carved gallery, from where one can look down as in a little theatre on the tables with their flickering candles. Candlelight dinners are the norm, because there is still no electric light here (although of course there is an Internet connection). If I could choose to spend the rest of the day with just one of the Magdalene men whose portraits hang in the hall, I can imagine no more congenial companion than Samuel Pepys (see p. 265). In the 1673 portrait by Sir Peter Lely (or possibly an assistant), painted after his appointment to the Admiralty, you get a clear picture of this *bon vivant* of the Restoration Period. But what he left to his college was an infinitely more fascinating self-portrait in words – the Bibliotheca Pepysiana in the second court.

Most 17th-century collections of books have long since been split up and scattered around. Pepys's collection, however, has remained intact, even in its appearance and arrangement, just as he had it in his London home when he was alive. It was an extraordinarily modern library, with free-standing, glass-fronted bookcases – the first of their kind in England, made in 1666 by Thomas Simpson, master carpenter of the Admiralty. That is why these bookcases are made from the favourite wood of the ship-builders, good old English oak, and not the mahogany or walnut that was in vogue at the time. Pepys organized his library as systematically and economically as his fleet: twelve cases with about 250 books in each, sometimes in double rows, with big books behind smaller ones in order to save space, though they were also divided up according to author and subject matter. The whole of Pepys's wonderfully compact library is stored in a single, relatively small room on the first floor above the arcades. Pepys believed that the library of a properly educated man should only contain what he himself could cope with intellectually and what reflected his own interests and pursuits. These went far beyond what most of us would dream of today.

The details of everyday life were just as important for Pepys as Plato's ideas, and he found it just as normal to read the classics as to read Newton's *Principia Mathematica*, to the first edition of which, as President of the Royal Society, he gave his official approval. Lying in glass cases to protect them against the light are some very rare editions: incunabula printed by Caxton, early handwritten polyphonic music, medieval manuscripts, and a sketchbook with striking watercolours of animals (*Monk's Drawing Book*, c. 1400). In large leather folios Pepys kept etchings by Dürer and Rembrandt, with thousands of drawings, portraits, biblical pieces, topographical scenes, and a collection of calligraphic scripts from the 7th century through to his own time. He also collected ballads and popular books, the so-called 'Penny Merriments', which give a unique insight into the popular culture of the 17th century. Added to this are all the specialized items from his job with the Admiralty: letters, memoranda, statistics, an illustrated inventory of all the weapons used by Henry VIII's fleet, the list of provisions for the Spanish Armada, ship by ship – a treasure chest of extraordinary documents. Pepys had his books bound 'in Decency and Uniformity'. Every one bears his name, his *ex libris* with portrait and emblem (rope and anchor), a double number for filing, and his motto, which is reproduced over the entrance to his library – a quote from Cicero's 'Somnium Scipionis': 'Mens cuiusque is est quisque' [the mind of each man is his true self] (*De re publica* VI, 26). Here, unfolded in all its richness, is the culture of books as it used to be, with the aesthetic pleasure of the bound and printed word, and the spirit and beauty that spreads from each letter to the binding to the bookcase to the whole library.

Pepys had no children, and when he died in 1703, he left this priceless treasure to his old college 'for the benefit of posterity'. In minute detail he stipulated that his library, which he regarded as a work of art in itself, should remain intact 'and no other book mixt therewith'. Richard Luckett, the Pepys librarian, told me, 'Not one of the 2,903 books can leave this room, and they are even restored in here.' If a single book were to be lost, stolen, sold or added, the whole library should pass to Trinity College but, according to Dr Luckett, Trinity has already forfeited this claim anyway, because it failed to fulfil its supervisory duties regularly. No one but the Master of Magdalene is allowed to borrow a Pepys book, and even that is restricted to once a year. 'Since 1819, none of the Masters has made use of the privilege.' And finally, Dr Luckett shows me the book of books: Samuel Pepys's Diary.

The original manuscript comprises 3,100 pages in six volumes, bound in brown calfskin, written in ink on unlined paper in clear, neat shorthand, perfectly reflecting the clear-thinking, orderly man who would often sit down late at night by candlelight, straining his eyes, in order to keep his diary up-to-date. For fear of going blind, Pepys finally abandoned his diary in 1669, after nearly ten years during which scarcely a day passed without him making an entry. He described not only the great events of his time – the Restoration of the Monarchy, the Plague, the Great Fire of London – but also with complete openness and meticulous attention to detail his own daily life, his dreams, eccentricities and adulterous affairs. He used a shorthand that he may well have learned when he was a student, but it was not a secret code, as had long been assumed. Not until 1819–22 did a student from St John's decipher and transcribe Pepys's stenographs, and yet the key to these diaries lay all along in the library itself: Thomas Shelton's *Tachygraphy*, the system of stenography of 1626 that Pepys actually used.

We should cast a glance at the building that now bears his name. The inscription above the central arch in the colonnade reads 'Bibliotheca Pepysiana 1724', but this represents neither the original purpose of the building nor its original date. 1724 was when the library was installed, but there are very few documentary records of the building's history. There is a main block with two wings and double gables, a classically symmetrical façade in light limestone, and a red-brick garden front dating from Elizabethan times (begun c. 1585). The building was completed about a hundred years later. The decorations on the spandrels and windows are 18th-century additions. The Pepys Library is a unique experience, and at the end of it, I could only echo his own words: 'And so away, mightily pleased.'

The best-preserved ensemble of medieval houses in Cambridge is to be found opposite the college in Magdalene Street. Behind these half-timbered houses – and this would have surprised Pepys – Magdalene has constructed three more courts. The entrance to the former Cross Keys Inn (nos. 25 and 25a) leads to Benson Court. This is the place for you to sing *Land of Hope and Glory*, for the words of Edward Elgar's patriotic anthem, still an annual hit at the Last Night of the Proms, were written by the Master of Magdalene, A. C. Benson, who was said to have earned enough with the royalties to finance Benson Court. Only a third of the plans, however, were realized. The court is a massive, over-extended block of brick, designed by Sir Edwin Lutyens (1930–32), and A. C. Benson along with the rest of us can be grateful that the great man did not do any more damage here. If he had had his way, all the other 16th-century houses would have been demolished. Happily, in the 1950s his colleague David Roberts carefully integrated these and adapted them for more student accommodation.

Simple modern buildings have extended 'the village', the domestic area of Magdalene College of which Mallory Court is a part, named after a former student, the mountaineer George Mallory. He died in 1924 on the ridge below the summit of Mount Everest, where his body was not found until 1999. When asked why he wanted to climb Everest, he gave the classic answer: 'Because it's there.'

Round Churches, Crooked Clubs
and a College Full of Cocks

'Debating is public speaking with a kick, conversation with a goal, orgasm without the mess.'
Cambridge Union Society

Of all the bridges over the Cam, Magdalene Bridge is the one where it all began. On this spot was the first and for a long time the only crossing, the Great Bridge, to which Cambridge owes its name. This was where the Roman Via Devana from Colchester crossed the Cam, which formed the border between East Anglia and the Midlands. Countless bridges of wood and one of stone were finally replaced in 1823 by the cast-iron one which today still slightly shakily bears the weight of modern traffic.

Down below, where the punts lie waiting for customers, there was a Viking trading port in the late 9th century. The period of occupation still has a faint echo in the name of a church in Bridge Street: St Clement, who was patron saint of Christian sailors but was also entrusted with the safety of the Viking marauders. A more interesting church from an architectural point of view lies a little further on into the city, where St John's Street branches off from the old Roman road: Holy Sepulchre, generally known as the Round Church.

This is the oldest of the five round churches in England. Its models were Roman and early Christian rotundas over tombs, and especially that above the chapel of the Holy Sepulchre in Jerusalem. Cambridge's Round Church was built in around 1130 by members of the local 'Fraternity of the Holy Sepulchre'. The only original part that remains is the central domed room with its ambulatory. Eight squat, round-shafted piers support a gallery that has even shorter, though equally thick piers and twin arches, and the space is both confined yet monumental, with an intense concentration of power, rather like a weightlifter just before the decisive snatch. Everything else seems superfluous. The north chapel, south aisle and chancel are all 15th-century additions. A radical restoration was carried out in 1841 by the Victorian architect Anthony Salvin, who restored the heart of the church to its ideal Norman form, with new round-arched windows, a columned portal and a conical broach roof. The Round Church would still be a noble place if only someone would drive the money-changers out of the temple: their modern equivalent is the Brass Rubbing Centre and the exhibition with which the so-called Christian Heritage Centre is destroying the visual beauty of its finest showpiece.

During the term, students stream into a Victorian brick building behind the Round Church to attend the debates and parties held by the Cambridge Union Society. It is a few years older than its counterpart in Oxford, indulges in the same rhetorical rituals, and invites equally prominent guest speakers, ranging from Colonel Gaddafi to the prostitutes' champion Lindi St Clair, but it has never achieved the status of the Oxford Union. Why this is so might make for an interesting motion. On 20 February 1815, the Cambridge Union held its first debate in a backroom of The Red Lion in Petty Cury. Two years later, the university authorities forbade it to hold any more meetings because it had dared to debate the government's policy in Ireland. It was a promising beginning. In 1821 it was given permission to start up again on condition that it steered clear of politics (a ban that has, of course, long since been lifted). Motions are now as wide-ranging as they are topical: 'This house believes that a ban on hunting will not help the fox' (1997). Among the early stars was the Trinity student Macaulay, who was as dazzling an orator as his contemporary Bulwer-Lytton, whereas Thackeray only spoke – or rather stammered – there once, on the subject of Napoleon. In 1866 the Union moved into its present neo-Gothic quarters, designed by Alfred Waterhouse – his first commission in Cambridge. In the Debating Chamber, behind the wine-red leather chair of the President, hang the photos of his predecessors, which included Maynard Keynes and no less than five of Margaret Thatcher's ministers: Kenneth Clarke, Norman Lamont, John Selwyn Gummer, Michael Howard and Douglas Hurd. This, however, is not the only reason why every year there is a motion of no confidence in Her Majesty's Government, gleefully debated prior to the inevitable majority verdict in favour of the motion. As in Oxford, the votes are registered by walking through the appropriate door.

If we turn off from Bridge Street into Jesus Lane, we shall pass the only British pizzeria to be dedicated to prime minister William Pitt. His medallion portrait adorns the tympanum above the portico of a small, whitewashed house, in which temple of good taste resides the Pitt Club, founded in 1819 to commemorate William Pitt the Younger, whose career began in Cambridge. Only a very exclusive club like this, traditionally a meeting place for the seriously rich, can afford its own clubhouse (let alone pizzeria). 'The Pitt' has one hundred members, men only, as I was informed by its president, David Watkin, aesthete and Fellow of Peterhouse. What is its programme? 'Just conviviality.' It extended its conviviality to Guy Burgess, super-spy and pederast from the finest stock. While still a student, according to his biographer Tom Driberg, he would drink a whole bottle of German wine with his lunch. He was a 'Liebfraumilch communist'.

Just round the corner in Park Street is the ADC, England's oldest university theatre. The Amateur Dramatic Club was founded in 1851, and received substantial support from Edward VII during his student days in Cambridge. The youngest brother of the current Prince Charles, Edward Windsor, present patron of the theatre, also made his name here as a prince of slapstick. He studied history at Jesus College in the mid-1980s. It is said that since he had been brought up with so many servants, he felt most at home with the college porters, and so you were more likely to find him in the Porter's Lodge than on the rugby pitch. When I visited Jesus myself, however, there was a different regular customer in the Porter's Lodge: the college cat Benson, 'enjoying honorary dining rights'. His successor, I gather, is equally spoilt. I can well understand the advice given by Nick Firman, head gardener at Pembroke: 'If you've got to come back, come back as a college cat.'

At the time of its foundation, 1496, Jesus lay beyond the walls of the town, so sheltered by the water meadows from the din of the outside world that James I said that he would like most to pray at King's, dine at Trinity, but study and sleep at Jesus. The monastic origins of the college are evident from its official name: 'The College of the Blessed Virgin Mary, St John the Evangelist and the Glorious Virgin St Radegund'. Benedictine nuns founded a convent here around 1150 in honour of St Radegund. The virtuous nature of this Thuringian princess was alas not emulated by her nuns at the end of the 15th century, for when John Alcock, Bishop of Ely, visited the nunnery, he found only two nuns there, and one of them was 'infamis' – i.e. of doubtful reputation. Without waiting for the Reformation, Bishop Alcock closed the place down and on its site, in the hope of making it more useful (not to mention more pious), founded a college.

'The Nuns' Run' was the name given to the long, walled-in route from Jesus Lane to the college. More common now is 'The Chimney', an anglicized form of the French *chemin* (path). There are plane trees behind the walls, where the gardens of the Master and the Fellows are situated. At the end of this stone passage rises the gatehouse, the majestic entry to another world. The Jesus College gatehouse was built around 1500 of red brick with a lozenge pattern of cream-coloured bricks on the upper, crenellated storey. Above the baldachin protecting the figure in the niche is a cock on a globe – Bishop Alcock's emblem, punning on the two syllables of his name, with the globe representing 'all'. The cock crowed three times in the Bible, as it does on the bishop's coat of arms, on the college coat of arms, and everywhere you look in the college, for there are cocks of stone and cocks of wood on doorways, railings, windows, ceilings, bench-ends. Jesus even has an historic collection of bronze and silver cocks, and a club named Roosters.

The moment you leave the first court and enter the Cloister Court, you are struck by the peace and quiet of this monastic enclave. There is a small square of lawn surrounded by cloisters, and it was around this former nunnery that Bishop Alcock built his college. He had the aisles of the oversized convent church demolished, turned the chancel and transept into the college chapel, and made the nave into the Master's residence. At mealtimes, the students still eat in the former refectory of the nuns, on the first floor of the north wing. On the walls of the hall, below a roof of walnut beams (c. 1500), are the inevitable portraits of eminent Jesuians: Archbishop Thomas Cranmer, Robert Malthus, who developed a theory of constantly expanding populations, Laurence Sterne and Samuel Taylor Coleridge; Nick Hornby is not there yet, for you have to be more or less dead to take your place on these walls. When Lord Snowdon was still Tony Armstrong-Jones, he studied architecture at Jesus, but failed the exam; all the same, he triumphed as cox in Cambridge's victorious Boat Race crew of 1950, which made him a true blue even before he became a royal.

Jesus Chapel has a special place among the college chapels of Cambridge. Music lovers applaud its chancel, fans of the Pre-Raphaelites adore its decor, and architectural historians are fascinated by the puzzle of its elements, from the Norman round arches of the north transept, the oldest part of the convent church (c. 1150), to the lancet windows of the choir, which look Early English but in fact are 'medieval' Victorian in the spirit of the Cambridge Camden Society. The architect A. W. N. Pugin, who was commissioned to carry out the restoration of the chapel in 1845, replaced Bishop Alcock's Perpendicular east window with these high lancet windows. In order to make his Gothic style authentic, Pugin travelled to Chartres cathedral, where he studied the windows, then adopted the roundels and the principle of galvanized iron frames, and even incorporated fragments of Chartres glass in the eastern windows of Jesus Chapel. But still he wasn't finished. He designed the brass lectern that rests on lions, a copy of the one in St Mark's in Venice, and the painted organ case, the wings of which can be closed like a medieval triptych (1847).

The second phase of restoration was an unqualified success. The nave, crossing tower and chancel were given new wooden ceilings that were painted with angels, coats of arms and floral patterns that all added up to a Pre-Raphaelite vision of the Middle Ages, put together by William Morris (1864–67). Most of the windows received new paintings in the form of glowing allegories of the Christian virtues, saints and church fathers, designed mainly by Edward Burne-Jones, but also by Ford Madox Brown and William Morris, and executed by Morris & Co (1873–77).

In the ante-chapel, as a rare bonus, we can see some of the cartoons for the windows, including a large charcoal drawing of Bishop Alcock himself by Burne-Jones.

Works of art are as ubiquitous in this college as Alcock's cocks. On the lawn of First Court stands Barry Flanagan's bronze *Venetian Horse*; in Chapel Court is Eduardo Paolozzi's *Daedalus*; and on the cricket ground is the strangest of all cricketing monuments, Flanagan's *Cricketing Hare*. The Jesus collection also includes works by Antony Gormley, John Bellany, William Turnbull and Richard Long, who in 1996 adorned the Upper Hall with one of his monumental wall paintings, *River Avon Mud*. Such commitment to modern art and artists is comparatively rare among Cambridge academics, with the notable exception of the ladies of New Hall (see p. 362). The Fellows of Jesus have an art committee which regularly organizes exhibitions of contemporary sculpture at the college and also buys modern works. As the garden committee goes along with this policy, everybody benefits.

In 1996, for the 500th anniversary of its foundation, Jesus College opened a new library, designed by Eldred Evans and David Shalev, architects of the Tate Gallery St Ives. There are green columns rising against the ochre brick façade, with climbing plants wending their way from the bases to the capitals. The windows echo Palladio, and the lattice work echoes Mackintosh, and with all these historical echoes, the architecture bears the patina of somewhat half-hearted modernism. Its over-emphasis on harmony makes it seem to defer to the old buildings instead of establishing itself as a self-confident complement. The interior, however, is more convincing: brightly lit, with bookcases and tables of light American ash, and at the top of the stairs a figure cast in steel by Antony Gormley (ex-Trinity), *Learning to See* (1995). Among the treasures to be found in this library is a manuscript copy of the first Bible to be printed in America, translated into Mohican by a missionary named John Eliot, an emigrant graduate from Jesus, and published in 1663 in Cambridge, Massachusetts. Evans and Shalev also designed the new hall of residence next to the library (2000). Together with the south wing of Chapel Court, it creates a new court which is open on one side, like all the courts in Jesus. The impression of broad spaciousness that you get at this college extends to the many sports grounds that surround it like a green gloriole.

Jesus Green, Midsummer Common – the very names of these riverside meadows are balm for feet that are tired of the concrete. An avenue of plane trees and a network of paths lead across these wide fields, which in the Middle Ages were convent land, then passed into the possession of the college, and have remained in their natural state ever since. On the north bank of the Cam, opposite Midsummer

King's College: Front Court and gatehouse

King's College choirboys on their way to chapel

View of Clare College and King's Chapel from the Backs

Trinity College: Great Court

Mr Hales, Head Porter of Trinity College in the hall

View of Trinity Library from the Backs

Trinity Library by Sir Christopher Wren

Jesus College: Venetian Horse by Barry Flanagan

Jesus College: Rebus of the Founder, Bishop Alcock

Benson, the Jesus College cat, sunning himself in The Chimney

Schlumberger Building by Sir Michael Hopkins

Faculty of History by Sir James Stirling

Alfred Lord Tennyson

Christopher Marlowe

E. M. Forster

Thomas Gray

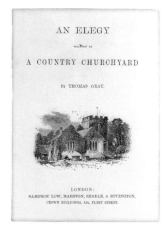

Title page of Gray's Elegy

William Wordsworth

Bertrand Russell

Ludwig Wittgenstein

Sylvia Plath and Ted Hughes

Faculty of Law by Sir Norman Foster

Bicycle shop sign, Laundress Lane

Pembroke College: Ivy Court

Emmanuel College: chapel by Sir Christopher Wren

Queens' College: The President's Gallery

Magdalene College: Pepys Library

Senate House

Newnham College: library extension by Joanna van Heyningen

St Peter's

St John's College: the Bridge of Sighs over the Cam

Common, is a line of boathouses, some dating from Victorian times, with timbered gables, and balconies – bastions of sporting conviviality. The oarsmen set out from here to do their training, rowing upriver to Chesterton and Bait's Bite Lock, in the hope of becoming Head of the River during the Bumps of May Week. At this time – which, you will remember, is in the middle of June – the fields near Fen Ditton are crowded with spectators, picnickers, straw hats (which are known as boaters because of this very association), champagne and buttercups. A feast in the country, like an academic Henley-on-Cam.

Bring me the Head of Oliver Cromwell: Sidney Sussex and Christ's College

'Good professors are not more essential to a college
than a spacious garden sweetly ornamented.'
Lord Kames, 1762

All Saints is the name of the church in Jesus Lane with the tall, pointed spire, and as it lies directly opposite the entrance to Jesus, and was part of its living, it is also known as St Opps. Of all the Victorian churches in Cambridge, this is the most important. It was designed in 1863 by G. F. Bodley in neo-Gothic style, and he and William Morris were also responsible for the painted walls and ceilings, with stylized flowers and foliage, inscribed psalms and the repeated motif of the pomegranate, a symbol of resurrection. To execute the great east window (1865–66) above the high altar, with its assembly of saints, prophets, apostles and kings, Bodley called upon his Pre-Raphaelite friends Edward Burne-Jones, Ford Madox Brown and William Morris – the same artists who afterwards designed the windows of Jesus Chapel. The mysterious dim light that falls on the nave, the dark and solemn colours of the wall paintings, the glow of the east window – all of these create an aura of Tractarian piety that has no match elsewhere. And this is in spite of the fact that All Saints has been left in a truly desolate state.

When I entered this Victorian masterpiece, I was greeted by an icy stench of decay. All Saints has been empty since 1972, saved from total ruin by the Churches Conservation Trust, but still rotting away here in the heart of the rich university city of Cambridge. A Pakistani shop-owner in King Street gave me the key so that I could go and see it for myself. 'You call it the House of God,' he said, 'but I call it grotesque – an empty building, where there are so many homeless people.'

King Street was once beautiful, before the cottages on one side were torn down and replaced by dreary terraced houses. Of equal ugliness is that section of New Court with which Christ's College literally turns its back on the city. All that remains are a few pubs to which the street owes the epithet 'The King Street Run'. 'This House is dedicated to those splendid Fellows who make Drinking a pleasure, who reach Contentment before Capacity and who, whatever the Drink, can take it, hold it, enjoy it and still remain Gentlemen.' These are the words above the entrance to one of the pubs, and I recommend that you recharge your batteries here with the appropriate liquid, for our next college is a spine-chiller.

It happened one dark night in November, in the south wing of the Chapel Court at Sidney Sussex. John Emslie was sitting in his room when suddenly everything went cold, and there was a smell of rotting flesh. The student turned round, and saw a hovering head, pale as wax and without any ears. The next day, a girl student reported that she had seen a pale blue eye in her room – a single, large, pale blue eye. If you want to study at Sidney Sussex, make sure your nerves are in good order. For such extra-curricular phenomena, the experts have an illuminating explanation: it was the ghost of Oliver Cromwell, who returns occasionally to his old college, where he began his studies in 1616. Only twenty years earlier, Sidney Sussex had received its statutes, a posthumous gift from Lady Frances Sidney, Countess of Sussex. The college was strictly Puritan, in the spirit of the Calvinism that so influenced Cromwell. His unshakeable faith in Providence and in himself being one of the chosen, his sense of mission and his self-righteousness all had their roots here, even if he only studied for fourteen months. But let us return to the known facts behind this gruesome tale.

After the Restoration of the Monarchy, fanatical Royalists took their revenge for the execution of Charles I by executing the already dead regicide. They disinterred his body from its tomb in Westminster Abbey, hanged the corpse on the gallows at Tyburn, beheaded it and stuck the head on a pole over Westminster Hall. At some time the skull disappeared, but it resurfaced many years later, having been hidden away in a box, and on 25 March 1960 was secretly buried in the ante-chapel of his old college. Only the Master and the bursar know the exact spot, for who knows, the Royalists might come again to take their revenge.

If you really want to see Cromwell's head, the best Sidney Sussex can offer you is his portrait in the hall, 'warts and all', just as he wanted it, painted by Samuel

Cooper a year before Cromwell's death in 1657. It's a rather coarse face, with averted gaze, the face of an East Anglian farmer who rose to be the uncrowned king, feared, hated, not even loved by his admirers – a national figure, but never a national hero like Nelson. Of all the portraits in all the halls of Cambridge, only Cromwell's has a curtain. Even today, one of the college servants closes this blue damask curtain before the loyal toast is proposed. However, when Queen Elizabeth II visited the college in 1999, the curtain remained open, for in the words of the butler, 'she's got a sense of humour.' Perhaps, though, she should stay clear of John Emslie's room.

Cromwell would not recognize the Georgian interior of the hall, nor would he recognize Hall Court, where he lodged as a student. In those days Sidney Sussex had red-brick façades, and not the Puritanical grey coating of Roman cement with which Sir Jeffry Wyatville plastered the college in 1821. Wyatville, a champion of Elizabethan neo-Gothic, gave the gatehouse its present look, with stepped gables and crenellations. Later additions have also failed to make Sidney Sussex into an architectural silk purse. By contrast, however, there is undiluted pleasure to be had from Arcadia, the college theatre group, with their open-air productions during May Week in the Master's garden. In 1999, more than 400 years after its foundation, a woman became head of the college – Professor Dame Sandra Dawson, sociologist and the first director of the Judge Institute of Management Studies.

It's not every day that you can change your money in a Victorian bank designed by Alfred Waterhouse. It has stood since 1891 at the corner between Sidney Street and Hobson Street, and I mention it only because of the banking hall: an octagon with columns all around and a mosaic floor, terracotta tiling with floral decorations, lime green – an aesthetic bonus even when the exchange rate is falling.

In the middle of this shopping precinct you will find Christ's College. To get in, you will normally go through a narrow door set in the large oak portal of the gatehouse. At once, you are a world away from the hustle and bustle, in a court that leads to another court that leads to a garden that could be in the heart of the countryside. When it was founded in 1505, Christ's College lay on the edge of the town. If the Tudor bricks hadn't disappeared in the early 18th century behind a limestone façade, we would probably have had difficulty distinguishing between the gatehouse of Christ's and that of St John's. Both of them have the same mythical horned beasts (known as 'yales') bearing the royal coat of arms over the ogee arch, and the same Tudor emblems of the portcullis and the red rose of Lancaster, which reappear above the windows, signalling the rank of the same Foundress, Lady Margaret Beaufort. Not only did she found these two colleges, but she also set up professorships at Oxford as well as Cambridge, and was clearly a Tudor super-woman. She was pregnant at twelve, widowed at thirteen, married two more husbands, played a clever tactical game during the Wars of the Roses, and saw her only son, Henry VII, come out victorious. 'Bounteous she was and liberal...of marvellous gentleness to all folk.... All England for her death have cause for weeping, including the students of both universities to whom she was a mother.' Such was the tribute paid to her by Bishop John Fisher at her funeral in 1509.

'Souvent me souvient' [remember me often], Lady Margaret's motto, which we have already seen at St John's, also decorates the colourful coat of arms on the oriel window of the Master's Lodge, opposite the entrance. The upper floor of the Lodge was reserved for the royal Foundress, and from a window in her wood-panelled oratory, she was able to look directly into the chapel next door – a similar link to those found in the chapels of royal palaces. When the Master's Lodge was restored in the early 20th century, four mummified rats were found, and they had died in a remarkably academic nest. It consisted of shreds of manuscripts, four pages of Horace, fragments of a Caxton edition, and four playing cards dating from 1510.

The lawn in the rectangular court is circular, and in the corner by the chapel is a *Magnolia grandiflora*, while an old wisteria spreads its branches over the wall of the Master's Lodge. In the middle of the 18th century, the first court was modernized, with sash windows, classical pediments over the doors, and façades of Ketton stone. This is the college of John Milton and Charles Darwin. Young Darwin came to Cambridge with the aim of becoming a country parson, but somehow this ambition got lost on the way. He enjoyed botanical field trips far more than the study of maths and theology. He was a passionate collector of beetles, and once when he had both his hands full, he even stuffed one in his mouth. John Milton's student career was not quite as untroubled as Darwin's. 'The Lady of Christ's' was the nickname bestowed on him by his fellow students when he entered the college in 1625 at the age of sixteen. He was a gentle, sensitive boy with long hair. 'Why do I seem to those fellows insufficiently masculine?' he wondered. 'Doubtless it was because I was never able to gulp down huge bumpers in pancreatic fashion.' Nevertheless, he stuck it out for seven years, took his degree, wrote odes in Latin, sonnets in Italian, and practised to become one of the greatest of all England's poets. Where did he live? Was it M Staircase or N? Or the now demolished Rat's Hall? We do not know. The college's only authentic relic of Milton is the noble bust by Edward Pierce (*c.* 1656), but this is not normally accessible to visitors, who must therefore make do with the legendary poet's tree in the Fellows' Garden.

A small passageway to the right of the dining hall leads to Second Court and the Fellows' Building (1640–43). This was an epoch-making construction, at least in Cambridge. Detached and all alone in the garden, it was as innovative in the field of college architecture as the stone mullions and transoms of the windows. Ionic corner pilasters reach all the way up the walls, and the dormer windows have alternating triangular and curved pediments, while the windows on the ground floor are surrounded by rustication – it is an almost Mannerist treatment of classical motifs. The symmetry and rhythm of the façade are of a quality that one would like to ascribe to Inigo Jones, but in fact no one knows who designed the Fellows' Building.

Equally innovative, though built some three hundred years later, is Sir Denys Lasdun's New Court (1966–70): this is a residential cascade of prefabricated concrete and glass, constructed in terraces and nicknamed 'The Typewriter'. Such megastructures – though this one has a good deal of variety – made Lasdun into a precursor of the concrete brutalism of late modern architecture.

The Fellows' Garden is full of catalpas, cypresses, crown imperials and all kinds of flowers. Under the trees the dons have placed beehives, and they have given their famous colleague C. P. Snow a splendid resting-place, in an urn beside the swimming pool. Not far from there is Milton's mulberry tree, with its ancient, spreading branches propped up on crutches like a venerable Chelsea Pensioner. Cambridge's most celebrated tree was actually planted in 1608, the year of Milton's birth, and was one of 300 that the college bought with the aid of King James I. His great plan was to establish a silk industry in England, but unfortunately they were the wrong mulberry trees, and so the poor silkworms that should have fed on them instead starved to death. All the same, for a few years at least, this garden may have been a paradise gained for Milton.

South of Market Hill

'Now for the beauty of Cambridge – the beauty of beauties – King's College Chapel!'
Maria Edgeworth, 1 May 1813

Cambridge's old High Street has four names: St John's Street, Trinity Street, King's Parade and Trumpington Street – a *via triumphalis* of great neighbours, from the Tudor gatehouses in the north as far as the Fitzwilliam Museum, with the glorious King's College Chapel in the middle. King's Parade is the very heart of this truly royal promenade, though you should avoid the high season if you can. There is good reason for the crowds to come flocking here. This is the breathtaking centre of the little city, with the Senate House, Great St Mary and King's Chapel creating an ensemble of the classical and the medieval that is unsurpassed. And yet all this architectural splendour might well seem coldly impersonal were it not for the one solitary and enormous tree: the horse chestnut that stands guard before the great chapel.

Houses of brick and timber, from the 18th and 19th centuries, shops, cafés, residences – there is no single house that stands out on King's Parade, but they all form a teeming background to the college opposite. In King's Parade you can buy newspapers, teddy bears and gowns, the correct colour college tie from Ryder & Amies, the finest crafts from Primavera, and if you have a sweet tooth then head straight for Jim Garrahy's Fudge Kitchen, whose entrance is directly opposite King's. In earlier times, people used to meet at least once a day on King's Parade, for this was the college news agency and the centre of university policy-making. 'Remember this,' wrote Francis M. Cornford in his *Microcosmographia academica* of 1908: 'The men who get things done are the men who walk up and down King's Parade, from 2 to 4, every day of their lives.'

Sweet Singing in the Choir:
King's College

'Knock down a couple of pinnacles at either end in King's College
Chapel, and you will have a kind of proportion instantly.'
John Ruskin, *Seven Lamps of Architecture*, 1849

Along King's Parade stretches a stone screen, fantastically adorned with tur-rets, and you can imagine that behind it lie all the splendours of Xanadu. The Front Court shimmers green from behind the bars of the tracery windows, and even the Victorian postbox in front of the gatehouse has a little cupola. 'No bicy-cles' says the notice on the wall where all the bicycles are leaning. There are house martins nesting in the gatehouse vault, oblivious to the daily toing and froing. This is the classical entrance to King's College. Tourists, however, are directed to the north portal of the chapel, but even this back entrance is impressive. John Betje-man once called King's 'the most Oxfordlike' of all Cambridge colleges, which is undoubtedly the highest compliment an Oxonian could ever pay.

'The King's College of the Blessed Mary and St Nicholas' is the full name of the college that Henry VI founded in 1441, just a few months after Eton College. With this doubling of institutions, the nineteen-year-old king was following the exam-ple of William of Wykeham, who some sixty years earlier had founded Winchester School to prepare students for New College in Oxford, which he had established in 1379. King's College was open only to Etonians until 1861, and this elitist band of brothers was not only spared the trouble of taking the usual exam, but they did not even have to subject themselves to the authority of the proctors. 'Kingsmen', in accordance with the wishes of the King himself, enjoyed special status, and it was not until the middle of the 19th century that they lost it. Such privileges did not exactly endear them to their fellow students, but it gave them a very special snob appeal.

Today King's prefers to lay stress on its nonconformist, liberal traditions. In 1973, it was one of the first Cambridge colleges to accept women, and now this for-mer Eton enclave can boast the highest proportion of students from state schools (about 80 per cent). Ethnic minorities found their way into King's earlier and in greater numbers than elsewhere, and another feature of the King's ethos is the egalitarianism of dons and students. The spirit of liberalism and friendship which characterized the Apostles and the Bloomsbury Group has never been more intensely (or idealistically) described than by the novelist E. M. Forster, a Fellow of King's, who said that he would rather betray his country than his friends. At the time when the college was founded, such a statement would have cost him his head.

The statutes of King's laid down that there should be seventy Fellows and scholars, ten chaplains, six clerks, sixteen choristers and a Master who should not be called a Master but a Provost. For a college of this size, then unprecedented in Cambridge, the King needed space. A whole district of the town was pulled down, together with its parish church – demolition on a massive scale, though it was not until centuries later that the new buildings were finally erected. The first phase gave rise only to Old Court, north of the chapel and later to become the Schools. With the downfall of the King in the Wars of the Roses, the funds for the completion of his college were no longer available. It was a miracle that the chapel itself was completed in 1515, but after that it took more than two hundred years for King's to start planning again on a large scale. Once more, though, only one of the plans came to fruition: the Gibbs' Building, opposite the entrance. James Gibbs, architect of the Senate House, designed this long, detached wing of light Portland stone in the rational spirit of classical architecture (1724–32). Over the rusticated ground floor is the piano nobile, and above that another storey, surmounted by balustrades that create a smooth and peaceful finish to the building – in deliberate and striking contrast to the animated, elaborated Gothic of the chapel next door. Only the entrance, like a triumphal arch with a triangular pediment and a crescent-shaped window, brings a degree of excitement to the symmetry of this elegant building, whose simplicity was not altogether uninfluenced by the limitations of its budget.

It was in this building, in room H3 on the first floor, that the first and only meeting took place on 25 October 1946 between two of the great minds of the 20th century. 'Are There Philosophical Problems?' was the subject addressed by Karl Popper, guest speaker at the Moral Science Club. Ludwig Wittgenstein fiddled with a poker, and challenged Popper to give an example of an ethical rule. 'Not to threaten visiting lecturers with a poker,' replied Popper, and Wittgenstein left the room. Did it really happen? Whether it did or not, the legendary quarrel developed into one of the longest and most curious footnotes in the history of philosophy. Today, two Fellows have their studies in H3: the economics historian Emma Rothschild and the Royal Astronomer Sir Martin Rees (Master of Trinity since 2004). Pokers are not required.

The Great Court that Gibbs designed was to contain three detached wings and not just this one. However, it was the old story – not enough money. Another century went by before the Front Court took on its present form. Between 1824 and 1828 William Wilkins, the most successful college architect of his day, designed the south wing with the hall crowned by two lanterns, and on the east side the gatehouse and screen, shutting out the street. This wall, with pinnacles balancing on its parapet as if they had climbed down from the roof of the chapel, is broken up by large Perpendicular windows, light and transparent, and it is low enough not to disturb the view of the chapel, acting almost like foothills to a great mountain, and constructed with elements that are exact copies of those on King's Chapel itself, which Wilkins had surveyed when he was a student. In the middle of the gate-house is a neo-Gothic fantasy, with dome and towers, Tudor roses, crowns and portcullises. Although there are more than 300 years separating the Perpendicular chapel from the Gothic Revival gatehouse, the whole thing seems so homogeneous and subtly balanced that one can only wonder at the ingenuity of the architect. We scarcely miss the cloister that Wilkins wanted to build on the inside.

For the last twenty years of his life, until he died in 1970, E. M. Forster lived in Front Court, on A Staircase, a college icon receiving visits and homage from dons and students, and no longer the 'pale cold chicken' that Virginia Woolf described. In James Ivory's film of his novel *Maurice*, a homosexual Cambridge love story, the Fellows still walk in procession to the high table in hall. But when I dined there myself, beneath the wooden beams of the neo-Gothic ceiling, it was all self-serv-ice, no one wore a gown, and there was no high table. 'We're proud of our egalitarianism,' said my companion, Hal Dixon, a retired Fellow. Looking down at us from the panelled walls were two old friends: England's first prime minister, Sir Robert Walpole, and his son Horace. The colleagues that Dr Dixon used to meet regularly here included Nobel laureates like the biochemist Frederick Sanger, historians like Noel Annan, the Marxist Eric Hobsbawm, and Tony Blair's guru, the sociologist Anthony Giddens. A young Fellow in shorts and a Hawaiian shirt was also to be seen here – the French tutor Andy Martin, known as the surf-ing don, who writes about surfing in much the same way as Roland Barthes wrote about the cultural myths of everyday life. My personal cicerone then led me through corridors and salons filled with the portraits of Kingsmen, many of them from the Bloomsbury Group (and apparently there are Indian miniatures in the ladies' lavatory), until we finally reached the college library.

King's Library, also designed by Wilkins, has some 130,000 books, specialist col-lections of medieval and oriental manuscripts, and the treasures of a bibliophile economist. When John Maynard Keynes died childless in 1946, he left the college first editions of Copernicus, Newton, Leibniz, Descartes, Voltaire, Milton and others – an exquisite library that encapsulates the history of European ideas. There are fifty 18th-century editions of Kant alone. For Keynes, reading was as natural as breathing, and he had been collecting books since his student days at King's. His Fellow's rooms in Webb's Court behind the library, on Staircase P, were decorated with naked dancers and grape-harvesters, later replaced by less provocative themes: eight lifesize allegories of the arts and sciences, painted in 1920–22 by his friends Duncan Grant and Vanessa Bell. They also provided the floral and still-life tiles in the corridors of the Garden Hostel, a hall of residence on the edge of the Fellows' Garden (1949). Perfectly preserved too are the painted doors and fireplace decorations with which in 1927 Dora Carrington and Douglas Davidson embellished the rooms of Keynes' protégé Dadie Rylands, who went on living there into the 1990s. Thousands of letters and photos of the Bloomsbury artists, the Charleston Papers, are kept in the Modern Archive Centre of the college library, together with manuscripts by Kingsmen such as Roger Fry and Alan Turing (see p. 266), and virtually the complete literary estate of E. M. Forster and Rupert Brooke. There must be at least a possibility that the former history student Salman Rushdie might one day entrust the typescripts of his novels to the Centre. In the reading room you will even find the painted doors from Keynes's London flat in Gordon Square.

Cows graze on Scholars' Piece, the King's meadows on the Cam. These cows are immortal, as we learn at the beginning of E. M. Forster's novel *The Longest Journey*, when some King's students are philosophizing: 'The cow is there…. Whether I'm in Cambridge or Iceland or dead, the cow will be there.' Only during the BSE crisis was the cow not there.

To get to the Backs, we must cross Wilkins's bridge over the Cam. A gently curving avenue of limes takes us through the meadows, where anemones, hyacinths, fritillaries, bluebells and narcissi blossom in colourful profusion, and the willows by the river are a shimmering green. But what is truly incomparable, even without these glorious spring colours, is the view from the Backs – unchanged since the 18th century – of King's College itself: the chapel, the Gibbs' Building, the Old Court of Clare, all rising majestically in the distance out of the green. This is the path taken every day by the choirboys of King's as they walk from their school to evensong in the chapel.

On 25 July 1446, St James' Day, Henry VI laid the foundation stone of a college chapel which must have seemed at the time even more grandiose than it does today. Only cathedrals and royal chapels were designed on such a scale. The chapel was meant to be a chantry for its founder, but it is really a monument to the church itself, in opposition to the Lollards and other heretics of his time. Seventy years and five monarchs later, King's College Chapel was completed, a landmark of Late English Gothic which, alongside St George's Chapel in Windsor, was the last great church to be built under royal patronage before the Reformation.

'The Shed' is what the porters call their chapel. Samuel Taylor Coleridge praised its 'transcendent beauty', J. M. W. Turner painted it, and William Wordsworth wrote three sonnets about it. Only John Ruskin, Oxford's architectural guru, quibbled about it and complained that it looked 'like tables upside down, with their four legs in the air'. For the climbers of the 1930s, there was no greater challenge than the Perpendicular cliff-face of the north-east tower. Far more prestigious than any academic title were the letters C.C. after one's name: Chapel Climber. And if anyone could fix an umbrella or a bicycle to one of the pinnacles to prove his triumph, his achievement was akin to that of the old stonemasons themselves on their rickety scaffolding.

At times there were more than 200 men working on the construction of the chapel, which was a lot in a town that numbered barely 5,000 inhabitants. Building began in 1446 under a Lancastrian king, was interrupted in 1461 by the Wars of the Roses, was resumed in 1477 by the Yorkist victors, was interrupted again in 1485, and was finally and gloriously completed by the Tudors in 1508–15. As was the custom, construction began from the east, with whitish grey magnesium limestone from Yorkshire. For the later, western part of the chapel they used the darker, cream-coloured Weldon stone from Northamptonshire. One can discern the break not only in the change of stone but also in the style. The western buttresses are richly decorated with Tudor roses, portcullises, fleurs-de-lys and heraldic beasts, unlike their eastern counterparts. And yet in spite of the differences, the long period of construction and the participation of at least four different architects, the overall effect could hardly be more harmonious.

'That Crystal Palace of stone and glass' is what John Betjeman called the chapel, where there seems to be no separation between load-bearing walls and windows, in a miraculous feat of structural engineering. The tracery that covers the windows, walls and ceiling is as delicate as a spider's web, binding them together in a vast and unified space. The walls are weightless, and seem to bear nothing but themselves. Light floods in from all sides. From the slender columns at the sides, the ribs grow upwards and over us, branching out into a vault whose reticulations again seem weightless as they create a phalanx of stone vortices. With a span of 12 metres and a length of 88 metres, this fan vault stretches without a break 24 metres above our heads – a feat of engineering that combines masterly tectonics with sublime aesthetics. The sheer size of the vault is breathtaking even now, and there is yet another daring feature: at the intersection of the fans, where the ribs come together to form a lozenge, there are keystones which themselves must weigh a ton – roses and portcullises as alternating Tudor emblems, carved from a single block of stone. The weight of this vault, measured at 1,875 metric tons, is diverted outwards onto four corner towers and 22 buttresses. A continuous series of side chapels conceals the depth of these massive buttresses, whose pinnacles soar like spears above the ridge of the roof and into the sky.

Thanks to one of the Fellows, I was given the privilege of entering the fan vault of the chapel. A spiral staircase in the north-west tower leads to a narrow passage that runs along the side walls, on which rest the mighty beams of oak that form the body of this lead-covered roof. Just below these beams is a dark room whose undulating floor is the reverse side of the fan vaulting. Caught between the oak ribs and the stone skin, I felt much like Jonah inside the whale. The genius who created the miraculous roof was John Wastell. This master mason was a member of the workshop of King's Chapel from 1485, and among the fan vaults attributed to him are those of the crossing tower in Canterbury Cathedral and the retrochoir in Peterborough Cathedral, but his undisputed masterpiece is King's College Chapel. Reginald Ely, Henry VI's architect, had originally planned lierne vaulting, but John Wastell completed the chapel in 1512–15 with this most royal of fan vaults, the biggest in England.

Wastell and his fellow master mason Thomas Stockton were also responsible for most of the vaults in the side chapels, the richly sculptured porches and corner towers, and the superbly carved heraldic emblems, comprising some 400 items including roses, crowns, portcullises, fleurs-de-lys, the greyhound of the Beauforts and the Welsh dragon of the Tudors. Henry VI would have profoundly disapproved of all these decorations. He wanted his whole chapel to be as simple as the eastern end, for it was to be the House of God. Henry VIII, however, made the ante-chapel into an heraldic showpiece for his own royal house: the majestic entrance of a state church, a Tudor hall of fame, for the still shaky foundations of the new dynasty needed propping up with an extravagant display of emblems. According to the art historian David Watkin, 'this architectural use of heraldry is characteristically Spanish and may be a consequence of Henry VIII's marriage to Catherine of Aragon in 1509.'

A magnificent screen of dark oak, a gift from the King, separates the ante-chapel from the choir. Here, at just the right moment, the great space of the interior is interrupted in the most eye-catching manner. The gates of the choir screen rise up like a triumphal Roman arch, with the organ (late 17th century) above it guarded by two angels blowing their shining trumpets. This is pure architectural theatre. The stylistic contrasts are also unusual and striking: amid the Gothic architecture are Renaissance wood-carvings on the screen and choir stalls; columns, pilasters, friezes, round arches and various classical forms divide up the almost Mannerist abundance of figures and decorations. In early Renaissance England, there is nothing to match this quality. Did the wood-carvers come from Italy, France or Holland? We do not know their names, but they did leave behind the royal initials HR and RA, Henricus Rex and Regina Anna, i.e. his second wife Anne Boleyn, whom he married in 1533 and had beheaded in 1536 – valuable evidence for the dating of the screen.

Unlike the carvers, the artists who created the windows are known to us because their contracts have survived. Bernard Flower, the King's glazier, was the first of six Flemish and English artists who made the stained glass between 1515 and 1547. It is the most complete cycle of church windows from the reign of Henry VIII. During the Second World War, they were removed piece by piece and stored in safety, and after the war it took five years to replace them. Stylistically they reflect the change from Gothic to Renaissance, whereas iconographically they follow faithfully in the tradition of the Middle Ages. The upper sections of the twenty-four side windows narrate tales from the Old Testament, while the lower sections contain corresponding scenes from the New Testament. The great east window, with the Passion and Crucifixion, balances the Last Judgment depicted on the west window (1879). It is immensely impressive, and a lesson in art history, but for direct emotional impact I recommend a picture in one of the side chapels: Craigie Aitchison's *Crucifixion* (1994), an image of timeless, endless forsakenness. There is a message scratched into the glass in the ante-chapel: 'John Blackmoor 1747 cleaned these windows.' A more recent engraver has added: 'They need cleaning again.'

The public's favourite is a magnificent Rubens, but when it arrived, it caused a storm of controversy. *The Adoration of the Magi* was painted in 1634 for a Flemish nunnery, later bought by the Duke of Westminster, auctioned in 1959 for the then record price of £275,000, and finally donated to the college by the new owner. However, it was too big for the space under the east window, and so the Fellows took down the historic high altar and also the panelling as far as the choir stalls. This vandalism by the art-lovers of King's might have been long since forgotten if the result had been convincing, but since then the Holy Family depicted in this showpiece of Baroque painting has clashed incessantly with the Tudor windows just above it. Let us, however, keep things in proportion: what has been done at the other end of the chapel is aesthetically a far worse catastrophe – a souvenir shop in the ante-chapel.

There is another problem. King's College Chapel needs money. The running costs alone come to more than £1,000 a day. Acid rain and exhaust fumes are constantly eating into the masonry, and every inch of erosion increases the problem of conservation and the cost of restoration. Years ago, when you could visit the chapel free of charge, people used to throw a voluntary contribution into an oak chest with metal fittings (now part of a chapel exhibition in the side chapels). This was the chest, it is said, in which Henry VII sent the gold and silver to Cambridge that was to pay for his chapel. Now there is another source of income – the golden voices of the choirboys.

King's Choir is older than the chapel itself. Six lay brothers and sixteen boys 'of sound condition and honest conversation', as stipulated by Henry VII in 1441, the year of the foundation, were to sing mass every day in the chapel. They have been doing so now for more than 560 years. Sixteen boys in Eton-style uniform – top hat and striped trousers – come to vespers every day at half past five, walking from their school on the other side of the Backs. King's College School, at 50 Grange Road, is a preparatory school for boys and girls between the ages of four and thirteen, and in addition to singing they are taught such old-fashioned virtues as self-discipline, loyalty and perseverance.

The Anglican Church has been admitting women to the priesthood for some years now, but there are no girls in King's College Choir. Out of the question. No soprano could ever match the vibrato of these boys' voices, with that inimitable timbre half way between angel and eunuch. These clear treble voices soar up into the fan vault of King's College Chapel with a magic sound that reaches its apogee just before the voice breaks. They incorporate the transience of pure beauty, the innocence of childhood, and they add incomparably to the enchantment as we gaze at the cherubim singing in the choir by the light of the smokeless Swedish candles. Charles Darwin recalled that when he was a student he often used to go to evensong at King's Chapel, and he was so enamoured of the sound that he 'sometimes hired the chorister boys to sing in my rooms.'

Ever since the Middle Ages, England's cathedrals and colleges have trained choirboys, and their voices have been used by composers for polyphonic church music, especially during the Tudor period. It is a musical culture that is peculiarly English, and is still current. The sound that was developed in those early days has reached its culmination here, and the 'King's sound' has a lucidity that is almost ethereal. During the term, you will always be able to find a seat for vespers, but once a year you will have to fight to get in. Indeed, the evening before the event you will see the first people in the queue with their sleeping bags outside the college gate. 'A Festival of Nine Lessons and Carols' is the name of the Christmas Eve concert at King's, and the listening audience is estimated at 190 million world wide, not including the 1,500 souls in the chapel itself. Every year since 1928, thanks to the BBC, people from as far away as Africa and New Zealand can tune in live to hear the silver tones of a solo voice that soars like a bird: 'Once in Royal David's City...' Carols from King's are as integral to an English Christmas as roast turkey and Christmas pudding.

Henry VI's choirboys have become a national treasure and a commercial commodity, managed and marketed just like the boy bands of the pop industry. Concerts at the weekends, overseas tours in the summer, three new CDs a year. In a secular society, church music has become surprisingly popular.

Many major musicians have begun their careers with this college choir: Orlando Gibbons, who sang here as a thirteen-year-old; the composer William Sterndale Bennett, who at the age of eight was already a chorister at King's and later became professor of music at Cambridge; the conductor John Eliot Gardiner; the composer Thomas Adès, now director of the Aldeburgh Music Festival; the countertenors David Cordier and Lawrence Zazzo. In May 1968 'six healthy Englishmen' (BBC), all former King's choirboys, formed an a cappella sextet which enjoyed huge success as The King's Singers and is now into its third generation.

Catz, a Dog and Two Queens

'Ah, the harbour bells of Cambridge! Whose fountains in moonlight and closed courts and cloisters, whose enduring beauty in its virtuous remote self-assurance... had once shone like a beacon out of the mysterious silence and solitude of the fens.'
Malcolm Lowry, *Under the Volcano*, 1947

In the third chapter of Malcolm Lowry's novel *Under the Volcano*, his drunken hero the Consul is in a street somewhere in Mexico, where he is rescued by a driver with a 'King's Parade voice' and a Trinity tie. Lowry himself was already a heavy drinker, as his biographers tell us, when he began his studies in the early 1930s at St Catharine's. On the wrought-iron railings that separate the open front court from Trumpington Street, you can see the instrument of torture that figures on the college coat of arms – the wheel of St Catharine, patron saint of learning.

Few scholars can have been more favoured by St Catharine than William Wotton. At six he could read Latin, Greek and Hebrew, was admitted to St Catharine's at nine, and by the age of twenty-one was a Fellow of the Royal Society. However, the career of this 17th-century prodigy fizzled out, and so too must our visit to his college, for we have already turned the corner into King's Lane.

This lane, between Catz and King's, is not exactly inviting, but it leads to a pure gem. Queens' College has everything to lift your heart: two royal foundresses, picturesque architecture and academic heroes. Despite its historical connection with King's and its proximity to the river, Queens' has a character all its own. This begins with the Master, who is called the President, and it extends as far as Sprite. Sprite is a Jack Russell terrier, but a statute of 1595 forbids all dogs to be kept at the university. Sprite has therefore been given 'honorary feline status', which in plain language means that he is to be regarded as a cat.

When Henry VI founded King's, his then eighteen-year-old wife Margaret also founded a college 'to laud and honneure of sexe feminine'. This happened in 1448, and it only took another 532 years for the 'sexe feminine' to be admitted to her college. After the defeat of the Lancastrians in the Wars of the Roses, Queen Margaret went home to Anjou, bitter and impoverished, and her foundation might well have died out had not a former lady-in-waiting of hers, Elizabeth Woodville, married Edward IV, become queen, and decided to carry on the work of her predecessor. That is why the college is called Queens' and not Queen's (as in Oxford). The driving force in the background, however, was a local clergyman named Andrew Dokett. He was the first President, and succeeded not only in surviving all the political upheavals, but also in attracting the patronage that would ensure the survival of his college. What would have become of Queens' without Dokett, and indeed what would the history of the university have been without its brilliant diplomats and mendicants?

Through the oak gate in Queens' Lane we enter one of the best-preserved college courts of the late Middle Ages. Old Court, begun in 1448, is as harmonious in its layout as in its construction: brick walls all round, windows with flat Tudor arches, a gatehouse with parapet and corner towers; opposite is the hall, in the north wing are chapel and library, and in the south wing accommodation – a beautifully symmetrical arrangement of functions. It is, we are always being told, later than you think, but seldom can there have been a more picturesque reminder than the sun and moon dial on the chapel wall (1733). The hall is even more colourful, since the Victorian architect G. F. Bodley gave it a permanent firework display with hundreds of gilded lead stars sparkling in a green and red sky of wooden beams (1873–75). A Pre-Raphaelite gem is the tile decoration over the mantelpiece, with figures designed by Ford Madox Brown and executed by William Morris, along with the stencilled walls. 'Floreat Domus' is the message over the high table at the neoclassical head of this hall, which in modern parlance apparently means: in such museum pieces let the conference business flourish. In March 1996, a washing machine firm hired the Old Hall for an evening to give awards to its best sales reps – in the manner of a degree ceremony, with gowns and mortarboards.

The passageway next to the hall leads to Cloister Court. This is so beautiful that you want to kneel down and kiss the lawn. Intimate, not so grandiose as Trinity, not a precise rectangle but filled with the charms of irregularity. Cloister Court, with its warm red Tudor bricks, was begun in around 1460 and was the first cloistered court in Cambridge – probably designed, like Old Court, by the local master mason Reginald Ely. Around 1540 the President's Lodge was extended with a long gallery – two timbered storeys over the north colonnades, with oriels on wooden columns. The President's Gallery is the only surviving timbered collegiate building in Cambridge, and provides an authentic Tudor setting for the Shakespeare productions which the students mount here in May Week.

In the south-west corner is the tiny Pump Court, where Erasmus of Rotterdam lived from 1511 till 1514, near Erasmus's Tower (see p. 259). 'The great civiliser of Europe', as Kenneth Clark called him, was a Fellow of Queens' and taught *arcanae litterae*, the secrets of Bible translation, in the new spirit of humanism, which entailed close and critical reading of the text. No Greek, no theology, he warned, and no good booze, no happy teacher. 'Cervisia hujus loci mihi nullo modo placet,' he wrote in 1511 to a friend in London – 'The beer in this place does not suit me at all and the wines are not very satisfactory either. If you are in a position to arrange for a cask of Greek wine, the best obtainable, to be shipped to me here, you will have done what will make your friend perfectly happy. (But I'd like it to be quite *dry* wine.)' This somewhat grumpy scholar, who spoke fluent Latin but no English, is also commemorated by Sir Basil Spence's Erasmus Building, a cube of brick and concrete (1959). Modern architecture on the Backs? The shocks of yesteryear seem very mild to us today.

One of the Fellows of Queens' was a famous expert on Sanskrit, Harold W. Bailey (1899–1996), who wrote a diary in a private language which he cobbled together out of Sarmatic inscriptions. Obscure? Not a bit of it. 'There's hardly a line that could not have been understood by any Persian of the fourth century.'

The Cam divides the two areas of Queens'. On the east bank lie the old buildings, and on the west are the new. They are linked by the legendary Mathematical Bridge. Apparently put together without any nails, this wooden bridge is so ingeniously constructed that it was attributed to Newton until a Victorian took it apart and then couldn't put it together again. It transpired that a student had designed this Chinese puzzle in 1749. Since then it has twice been rebuilt.

On the far side of the bridge is Cripps Court (1980), with white concrete pillars, a great deal of glass, and precious little feeling for its environment. Here some five hundred Queens' students have everything that an international conference centre needs: gym, squash courts, multimedia...Erasmus, where art thou now?

The Marlowe Mystery, The Parker Loot: Treasures of Corpus Christi

'Cambridge, wet, cold, abstract, formal as it is, is an excellent place to write, read and work.'
Sylvia Plath, 29 January 1956

On 28 February 1953, Francis Crick went for lunch at The Eagle in Bene't Street and announced that he and his colleague James Watson had just discovered the secret of life. This was the structure of DNA, the key to heredity. The two biogeneticists from the nearby Cavendish Institute were among the regulars who knew how to do justice to the draught beer served at The Eagle. In the yard of this inn of 1667, once a stopping place for stagecoaches, students and tourists now sit drinking their Greene King. The Eagle also has an Air Force bar, where English and American fighter pilots used to meet during the Second World War, some of them for the last time. Before going off on a mission, they would leave their names on the ceiling, burned on with candles or written with their girlfriends' lipstick.

When you leave The Eagle, you will see a somewhat angular, severe-looking tower opposite you, with louvres that seem to stare at you like an aged owl. This is St Bene't's (short for Benedict), and it was standing here even before the Normans conquered England. With the characteristic long and short work – alternating horizontal and vertical stones bonded into the walls – the Anglo-Saxon builders ensured that their towers would be stable and rectangular. The round arch under the tower rests on two wild beasts, maybe lions, in an echo of more violent, heathen times. St Bene't's has six bells, and just how many beautiful mathematical variations they could produce was discovered in the 17th century by a member of the parish named Fabian Stedman, a printer who has gone down in history as 'Father of English change-ringing'.

A little graveyard surrounds this, the oldest church in the city and indeed the county, erected in around 1040 though with later additions and alterations. Beyond its rubblework masonry, wall to wall with the dead, live the students of Corpus Christi. For centuries the main entrance was next to the church, which is why it was also known as Bene't College, but in 1827 it got a big neo-Gothic gatehouse of its own in Trumpington Street. Corpus Christi is the only college in Cambridge (and Oxford) to have been founded by two guilds and not by members of the Church or the aristocracy. This happened in 1352, for even then the merchant classes were well aware of the advantages of higher education. They were also anxious to have a college of their own so that they could exert some influence over the university, and not always be outsmarted in the battle between town and gown. But when the Peasants' Revolt spread to Cambridge in 1381, the middle-class origins of 'The College of Corpus Christi and the Blessed Virgin Mary' did not in any way protect it against the fury of the townspeople. One item that did escape the looting, however, was the silver-mounted drinking-horn from which the students still take their farewell drink after passing their exams.

If you turn left out of the stately first court, you will step straight from the 19th into the 14th century, into the modest, enclosed world of the Middle Ages. Cobblestones and an oval lawn surrounded by an obliquely angled square of low buildings – this is Old Court, built between 1352 and 1377, the oldest original court in Cambridge. Buttresses and attic storeys are 16th-century additions, as are the chimneys in the north wing, for until then the students had to live there without any heating. There would be several of them in one bedroom, around which would be grouped four cells for study, each with its own narrow window. You can still see some of these early windows, though the communal rooms have long since been converted into two-room apartments for students or Fellows (though they still don't have a WC of their own). The historical ecologist Oliver Rackham, Fellow of Corpus, has calculated that some 1,400 oak trees would have been used in the construction of Old Court, a total of around one hundred tons of wood for the floors and the timbered walls between the staircases. For more than two hundred years, the college used the neighbouring parish church of St Bene't as a chapel. It was on R Staircase of this Old Court, which was then the only one in Corpus, that in 1580 a shoemaker's son from Canterbury took up residence, having been granted a scholarship to Corpus. His name was Christopher Marlowe.

Here began the strange career of an Elizabethan dramatist who had all kinds of admirers, ranging from Goethe and Brecht through to Derek Jarman. Marlowe was a virtuoso of the masquerade. One of his many faces emerged in 1953 during restoration work behind a panelled wall in the Master's Lodge – all the more welcome for the fact that there is no known, authenticated portrait of him. It shows a twenty-one-year-old with gentle features, a mane of hair, a batiste collar, with arms folded over a black and red jabot – rather luxurious attire for a shoemaker's son. This unique portrait – although we cannot be certain of its identity – is dated 1585, one year after he had taken his degree, and it bears the motto 'Quod me nutrit me destruit' [what feeds me, destroys me]. It is as paradoxical as Marlowe himself, and the picture seems thus to embody the mystery of the man's life. It now hangs in the Old Combination Room, where the Fellows drink their port before dinner.

'Corpus is famous for its port.' Appropriately, it was the porter who told me this, as he showed me the Marlowe. 'When there's a good year, the Fellows buy thousands of bottles. The wine cellar is right next to the Masters' tomb.' William Wilkins also had himself buried in the college chapel, for of all his neo-Gothic creations, the architect of London's National Gallery most loved Corpus Christi's New Court (1823–27). Even if we may not be quite so enamoured as he was with tracery and crenellations, nevertheless this court harbours a treasure. It lies in the south wing, behind eight neo-Tudor windows, and its name is the Parker Library.

The Millennium Exhibition that I saw there could hardly have been simpler or more sensational. From their collection, they displayed one book for every century. The first was the 6th-century *Canterbury Gospels*, which the college only allows out for the enthronement of a new Archbishop of Canterbury, when it is guarded by two Fellows. One of the last was Thomas Moufet's *Insectorum sive minimorum animalium theatrum*, the first illustrated English book of insects, printed in 1634. The library owns early copies of works by Cicero, Ambrose, Augustine and the Venerable Bede, the magnificent Bury Bible (*c*. 1135) – illuminated by the first English artist to be known by name, Master Hugo – some 700 manuscripts, English, French and Flemish books of hours, and more than a hundred incunabula, masterpieces from the early days of printing. Only the British Library and the Bodleian have a larger collection of Anglo-Saxon manuscripts than the Parker Library. Most of this collection came from the son of a Norwich cloth maker named Matthew Parker. He was a student and Fellow of Corpus, became Master, Vice-Chancellor of the University, and finally Archbishop of

Canterbury. As an adviser to Henry VIII, he was able to rescue irreplaceable books and manuscripts from monastery and cathedral libraries before they were destroyed by fanatics. This ecclesiastic bibliophile then donated his loot to his old college, along with his collection of silver. Now Corpus is hunting for another such benefactor, for it needs £20 million for long overdue modernization of its library.

About 11,000 of the Parker books were printed before 1800. Alongside the classics, the bookshelves – designed by Wilkins – also hold works by famous Corpus alumni: Christopher Marlowe, John Fletcher, Christopher Isherwood. 'No first editions of John Cowper Powys,' complains the librarian. Powys himself, the most gargantuan of modern English novelists, had his eye on other attractions than the Parker Library when he was a student. The key to life lay not in books but in the moss and lichen that he found on a wall behind the Fitzwilliam Museum.

Two churches flank Corpus Christi: St Bene't's in the north and St Botolph's in the south. Botolph or Botulf was a 7th-century abbot, and an early patron saint of East Anglia. If as a tourist you want to avoid getting lost, robbed or crashed into, light a candle to him, for he is also a patron saint of travellers. This is why you will often find churches in his name at the entrance to towns, which was the case here, even though you can't see it now. In medieval Cambridge, St Botolph's stood at the south gate of the town, on the road to London. The Trumpington Gate has long since been demolished, but Botolph Lane, with its pastel plastered cottages, will take you past the cemetery and straight back into the Middle Ages.

Geniuses from the Bicycle Shed:
Old Cavendish

'Cambridge in my family was as axiomatic as porridge for breakfast,
eaten with salt, and any idea of Oxford would have seemed as
perversely heretical as sweetened bread-and-milk.'
Sir Clough Williams-Ellis, *Architect Errant*, 1971

Nowhere in Cambridge do the Middle Ages rub shoulders so nonchalantly with modern times as in Free School Lane. Running along the back of Corpus Christi, opposite the sooty college walls, this alley contains the entrance to the Mount Olympus of the natural sciences. The Nuclear Age and the Genetic Revolution began here at Old Cavendish Laboratory. When it was opened in 1873, there were nineteen students studying science at Cambridge. Today, the Cavendish alone can boast the names of some thirty Nobel laureates, from Ernest Rutherford to John Cockcroft. It was in the Cockcroft lecture hall that on 29 April 1980 a man in a wheelchair gave his inaugural lecture although he was unable to speak a word. This was Stephen Hawking, Lucasian Professor of Mathematics.

Not until the middle of the 19th century did Cambridge accord the same status to the natural sciences as to the arts. The new laboratories and lecture halls were built on the site of the former Botanic Gardens, east of Free School Lane. In the centre of this area was the physics laboratory founded by William Cavendish, then Chancellor of the University. Here James Clerk Maxwell studied the nature of light waves, and in 1897 Sir Joseph John Thomson discovered the existence of electrons. J. J. Thomson made the Cavendish into the world's leading centre for experimental physics. In 1919, his successor Ernest Rutherford split the atom, and until his death in 1937, he directed nuclear research in Cambridge. One of his closest colleagues, the Russian physicist Pyotr Kapitsa, had his own laboratory in the court opposite the Cavendish, the Mond Laboratory. On the clinker façade by the entrance to this institute, which today houses the department of aerial photography, is a crocodile with gaping jaws, a relief by Eric Gill (1936). 'Crocodile' was the nickname that Kapitsa gave Rutherford, because one could always hear his stentorian voice long before one saw him – a warning signal like the clock that was swallowed by the crocodile in *Peter Pan*. Rutherford, who believed in free access to knowledge, had no in-built clock to warn him against Kapitsa, for at the end of the 1920s, the Russian betrayed all their results to Moscow.

The now legendary Laboratory of Molecular Biology began in 1947 in a Cavendish bicycle shed. It has produced no less than thirteen Nobel laureates. It all started with an immigrant from Vienna, the chemist Max Perutz, and a Trinity graduate named John Kendrew. This team, which set out to study the molecular structure of biological systems, was joined by Francis Crick and James D. Watson – another unlikely couple: the Englishman Crick, thirty-five years old and trained as a physicist though still without a doctorate, and the twenty-three-year-old Watson from Chicago, originally an ornithologist. In February 1953, they succeeded in what Crick later called their 'mad pursuit': initially with pieces of cardboard, and then with rods and metal plates, they built a model that wound upwards like a kind of spiral staircase – the double helix of DNA, which contains the genetic information and hereditary characteristics of all living creatures. For this, the most far-reaching biological discovery of the 20th century, both men, together with the physicist Maurice Wilkins, received the Nobel Prize for medicine in 1962.

In the same year, when their colleagues Perutz and Kendrew also received the Nobel Prize for chemistry, the Laboratory of Molecular Biology moved into its present premises on the southern edge of the city, on the site of the New Addenbrooke's Hospital. Here the German immunologist Georges Köhler and the Argentinian César Milstein made another hugely significant biomedical discovery, the development of monoclonal antibodies, for which they received the Nobel Prize in 1984. The pioneers of xenotransplantation – by which organs may be transplanted from one species to another – are to be found in the research laboratories of Cambridge, which has become the thriving centre for the British biotech industry.

In 1973, a century after its foundation, the Cavendish moved into new laboratories on the western edge of the city, and in the meantime almost all the other labs have left their old home in Free School Lane. All that remained was a conglomerate of buildings, as desolate as a hospital backyard. What the university had built there since the 19th century for its scientists was aesthetically in reverse proportion to the astonishing achievements of those who worked within. Today, the area is euphemistically called the New Museums Site.

Do not be put off by the concrete mass that Sir Philip Dowson designed in the late 1960s for the zoology faculty. On a raised platform, the skeleton of a finback whale announces the entrance to the Zoology Museum, and here you can follow the whole course of creation – though only in glass cases – right back to the skeleton of a giant ground sloth that died out at the end of the Pleistocene epoch. There are even the remains of birds and fishes that Darwin brought back from his voyage on the *Beagle*. His microscope is one of the treasures that you can see at the neighbouring Whipple Museum of the History of Science, along with astrolabes, sundials, instruments for measuring and navigation, telescopes and spectroscopes – a fascinating collection of early scientific instruments and apparatus that was assembled by Robert Stewart Whipple, Chairman of the Cambridge Scientific Instrument Company, which is still flourishing today and which was co-founded by Darwin's youngest son Horace in 1878. Among other things, it produced the first seismographs in the world.

For its rapidly growing science departments, the university acquired land from Downing College in 1906, diagonally opposite the Cavendish complex. Within a few decades, the Downing Site was also packed with laboratories and institutes which were scarcely less diffuse and mediocre than the original laboratories. The Oxford architect T. G. Jackson designed the dominant brick building along Downing Street – an Edwardian pot-pourri (1904–11). Two university museums are housed there now: the Museum of Archaeology and Anthropology, and the Sedgwick Museum of Earth Sciences, which has one of the finest fossil collections in the world. Above one of the doorways is the personification of Alma Mater Cantabrigia – a stone relief of a naked woman with flowing milk, bearing a sun, a castle and a beaker, with the motto: 'Hinc Lucem et Pocula Sacra' – a symbolic exhortation to students to drink from the springs of light, wisdom and knowledge.

Nuclear and genetic research are far from being the only pioneering achievements of Cambridge's scientists. In the millennium year, a pair of physicists, Thomas Fink and Yong Mao, published a ground-breaking book that provided multiple and elegant mathematical solutions to another age-old problem: *The 85 Ways to Tie a Tie.*

Thomas Gray Moves House: From Peterhouse to Pembroke

'The Masters of Colleges are twelve grey-hair'd Gentlefolks, who are all mad with Pride; the Fellows are sleepy, drunken, dull, illiterate Things.'
Thomas Gray to Horace Walpole, 31 October 1734

On rainy days, two streams flow down Trumpington Street along broad stone gutters. They were laid in 1749 in order to channel water from the spring in the town centre. These gutters are called Pot and Pem, and they are much easier to distinguish than Tweedledum and Tweedledee: Pem flows on Pembroke's side, and Pot flows opposite, on Peterhouse's side (also known as Pothouse). That's how straightforward things are in Cambridge. When he was a student, Coleridge once came to the rescue of two drunken men who had fallen into the flowing gutters. 'S-save my fr-friend there,' mumbled one. 'N-never mind me – I can swim.'

Pembroke students' bicycles are also easy to distinguish, because they are marked with a 'V', which stands for Marie de Valence, Countess of Pembroke, who founded the college in 1347. You can't tell its age from its face, because the front was completely refashioned and modernized in the early 18th century with ashlar walls and crenellations. The natural sciences and Oriental studies are Pembroke's academic forte. The Victorian physicist George Gabriel Stokes taught here, and to him we owe Stokes' law for the force opposing a small sphere in its passage through a viscous fluid – which may not be everybody's cup of tea.

Pembroke is Cambridge's Poets' Corner. No other college has produced so many poets – Edmund Spenser, Richard Crashaw, Thomas Gray, Christopher Smart, Ted Hughes – that they can fill an anthology of their own, no less than fifty *Pembroke Poets*. And that's without including David Henry Wilson, whose *Jeremy James* stories have delighted children and parents all over the world, or Tom Sharpe, who immortalized the figure of the Head Porter: 'Skullion... as much a part of the college as the carved heraldic beasts on the tower above.'

In 1951, Ted Hughes came to Pembroke on a scholarship in order to study English. In his third year at Pembroke, when once again he was suffering from the weekly torment of producing an essay, he had a dream: a wounded fox limped into his room, put its bleeding human hand on his blank sheet of paper, and said, 'Stop this – you are destroying us.' It was against nature for a poet to study literature – that was how the young writer interpreted his dream, and so he switched faculties and studied anthropology and archaeology instead. His future problems would be less easy to solve, once he had taken his exams and met Sylvia Plath (see p. 244).

From the first court, you pass the hall and go into Ivy Court. In the south wing of this 17th century building, Thomas Gray found what he had been looking for – the peace and quiet of a Carthusian monastery. His *Elegy Written in a Country Churchyard* had made this shy don more popular than he wanted to be. Unlike Ted Hughes, he turned down the invitation to become Poet Laureate. From 1756, he lived on the first floor of the Hitcham Building, on I Staircase, so reclusive that it is said students would leave their meals and rush out to see him whenever he ventured forth. What exactly did he get up to, shut up there in his three rooms? He made notes for lectures that he never gave, collected material for a history of literature that he never wrote, studied genealogies and Chinese dynasties, and translated Linnaeus's insect categories into Latin hexameters. In short, he was a law unto himself, and no college – not even Pembroke – would tolerate such behaviour today. 'I am a sort of spider,' he said of himself, 'and have little else to do but spin my web over again, or creep to some other place and spin there.'

The manuscript of Gray's famous elegy is one of the treasures in the Old Library in the north-west corner of the first court. This was originally the college chapel. The present chapel was a gift from a former Fellow, Matthew Wren, Bishop of Ely, as a gesture of thanks for his rescue from the Tower after an eighteen-year incarceration by the Puritans. In 1663, Matthew Wren commissioned a complete beginner to build his chapel, his nephew in Oxford. It was a case of nepotism with the most felicitous consequences, for the name of the nephew was Christopher Wren. Pembroke Chapel marked his debut as an architect, and it was completed in 1665, before the Sheldonian Theatre in Oxford, which he had begun at the same time. It is a Roman temple, with a Baroque lantern, and its classical style was something quite new for Cambridge. The astonishing instinct for proportion and rhythm in this, Wren's very first commission, is evident from the west façade. The capitals of the Corinthian pilasters, the garlands and urns on the pediment – these fine examples of the stonemason's art were to become characteristic features of his later churches. Originally the chapel stood on its own, with no extensions, its ashlar front presented to Trumpington Street, and brick at the sides. The simple, rectangular interior, designed for a college community of just eighty people, was extended to the east in 1880; the new choir, with marble Corinthian columns, was designed by George Gilbert Scott the Younger.

In the chancel is what is believed to be a relic of a Protestant martyr: Ridley's Chair. Bishop Nicholas Ridley was a Fellow and then Master of Pembroke, and he was executed in Oxford in 1555 (see p. 137). In his last letter he spoke of the college gardens and 'the sweet smell thereof I trust I shall carry with me into heaven'; a fragrance that still wafts to the nostrils. In this garden the botanist William Turner, Ridley's contemporary, studied plants and gave them their first English names. Turner's *New Herball* (1551–68) marked the beginnings of the systematic study of botany in England. Behind a row of plane trees in the south-east corner of the garden stands Pembroke's newest student hall of residence, designed by the London firm of architects Eric Parry (1997) and providing a pleasant contrast to Alfred Waterhouse's dull Victorian buildings (1871–73).

At the tender age of fourteen, William Pitt the Younger arrived at Pembroke in 1773, and took up residence in Thomas Gray's rooms. Ten years later, he was prime minister, the youngest in British history. As the man who had saved Europe from Napoleon, Pitt returned to Pembroke in the form of a bronze statue, bigger than lifesize, in a Roman toga. So much money was donated for this monument, which stands outside the library, that there was enough to finance the Pitt Building of 1833 for the University Press in Trumpington Street. With its pinnacled tower, this neo-Tudor building looks like a church, and it was a favourite gag to send first-year students to attend mass in the 'Freshers' Church'. A much more mouth-watering prospect, however, is Fitzbillies, handily situated right next door to the college.

Here you can buy the stickiest Chelsea buns in the world. Fitzbillies is a bakery-cum-cakeshop-cum-patisserie, founded in 1922, and it is as much an institution as Pembroke itself, to which it belongs. Its chocolate cakes are sent all over the world, even as far as New Zealand, bringing back enchanted memories much like Proust's madeleines.

Opposite Wren's chapel is a little alleyway that branches off Trumpington Street, and it is as lovely as its name: Little St Mary's Lane. Whitewashed cottages on one side, and a little church with a graveyard on the other. We normally call such spots romantic, but this one has an extra dimension. Since 1925, the residents and other members of the community have tended a wild garden that was laid out in the churchyard by a Trinity don, with a network of winding paths; it's a picturesque landscape in miniature, and between the graves you will find a wonderful collection of herbaceous plants: laburnum, campanula, scented violets, the stinking *Helleborus foetidus*, monkshood, soapwort, cranesbill and goatsbeard, also known as Jack-go-to-bed-at-noon because it only opens in the morning sun. A botanist from the Wildlife Trust counted some two hundred different kinds of plant in this churchyard, and that's not including moss and lichen. Here you will also find the bright yellow *Rosa cantabrigiensis*, the Cambridge Rose. The gas lighting in Little St Mary's Lane, another Cambridge rarity, came from Arthur Peck, a classical philologist who filled his college rooms with Victorian gas lamps.

The little church to which this garden is attached is called St Mary the Less, though it's generally known as Little St Mary's. It has an east window with flamboyant Decorated tracery and a memorial plaque to an early 18th-century vicar named Godfrey Washington. The fact that the three stars and stripes in his family coat of arms became the Stars and Stripes of the American flag is part of heraldic history, and visitors from those former colonies are always intrigued to know the story. It's actually very simple: the vicar of Little St Mary's was a great-uncle of George Washington, the first President of the United States.

Next to this church, which until it was rebuilt in the mid-14th century was called St Peter's, lies the oldest college in Cambridge, Peterhouse. A Benedictine named Hugh de Balsham, Bishop of Ely, founded it in 1284, 'pro utilitate rei publicae' – for the use of the community. The House of St Peter was the first scholars' hall of residence in the town to put into practice the new statutes and non-monastic way of collegiate life. Great names encompass Peterhouse like the gilded bronze points of the railing that surround it. This is where the physicists Henry Cavendish and Lord Kelvin studied, the latter having prophesied the death of the planet from global warming; Charles Babbage, the genius of the calculating machine, was here,

as were the film star James Mason, the hapless Tory MP Michael Portillo, nicknamed 'Polly', the Elizabethan poet and composer Thomas Campion, who wrote
such wonderful songs for the lute, and the engineer Frank Whittle, who was still a
student when he took out a patent on his invention of the jet engine. The impact of
all these Petreans is out of all proportion to the size and intimacy of the college,
which with 250 students is still the smallest in Cambridge. For a long time it was a
centre of Royalist sympathies and High Church piety, so arch-conservative that it
did not admit women until 1985. Its reputation has suffered – not altogether unde-
servedly – from the 'Porterhouse' image reflected by Tom Sharpe's campus satire.
In order to break free from this, the college invited Madonna to give a lecture, but
she was cleverer than the dons expected – she didn't come.

From the street one can see the Elizabethan library on the left, a brick wing with
pointed roof and Gothic bay, and on the right a neoclassical residential block with
Venetian window; in the middle is the east end of the chapel, a cool mixture of Perpendicular and Renaissance, which already gives us a preview of the stylistic
pot-pourri that constitutes Peterhouse. There is a 13th-century hall, later decorated by the Pre-Raphaelites, and there is 18th-century Palladianism, 19th-century
Tudor-Gothic, and a 1960s tower block, but after more than 700 years, one can
hardly expect homogeneity.

Behind the colonnades of the first court shines the green rectangle of Old Court,
which is much older than its Georgian sash windows and ashlar façades suggest.
The hall in the south wing was built in 1286, the year when the Founder died, and it
is the oldest surviving college building in Cambridge. Through the centuries, this
dining hall has gone through many changes of taste, and it took on its present form
in 1870, when it was restored by George Gilbert Scott. It is now a brilliant example
of Victorian neo-Gothic, thanks to the Arts & Crafts contribution made by Morris & Co. Morris decorated the Tudor fireplace of 1501 with his enchanting daisy
tiles (1861) and the walls with floral stencilling. His Pre-Raphaelite friends Edward
Burne-Jones and Ford Madox Brown designed the stained glass, with idealized
portraits of Aristotle, Dante, Spenser – an Anglican cultural lesson in the spirit of
antiquity (1870–74). The Combination Room next door (1460) is also a Morris synthesis of the arts: oak-panelled walls, a shining tiled fireplace, and windows by
Brown and Burne-Jones, whose motifs combine a love of daisies with characters
from Chaucer's *Legend of Good Women*. It was in this darkly romantic room that
in 1997 the bursar of Peterhouse saw one of the two college ghosts – that of his
predecessor Francis Dawes, who hanged himself from a bell-rope in 1789. You will
be delighted to know that this rope is still in use today.

Not until 1632 did Peterhouse get a chapel of its own; before then, everyone had to go through a gallery into the neighbouring parish church of Little St Mary's. Open colonnades flank the chapel, whose architects are unknown. The mixture of styles is as unusual as the situation: the Perpendicular turrets and classical pediment of the eastern end rise up in the first court, while the western façade, with its curving Baroque gable, faces the Old Court. The dramatic Flemish Crucifixion in the east window (1639) was extended in 1855–58 through a stained glass cycle painted by the Munich artist Max Ainmiller – a remarkable alliance between Nazarene piety and the High Church.

The Palladian residential wing next to the chapel was designed by an amateur Cambridge architect, Sir James Burrough, Master of Caius. One of the first of the Petreans to move into the Burrough's Building in 1742 was Thomas Gray. He even stayed there after taking his degree in law, until finally he got so fed up with being bullied that he left. 'Miss Gray', as they used to call the shy young man, was so terrified of fire that he always had a rope ladder at the ready. One night, he was awoken by the cry of 'Fire!', climbed out of the window, and is said to have landed in a bucket of water. True or not, the factual basis of the story can be seen from Trumpington Street: the iron fixing on the top floor window to which Gray's rope ladder was attached. After this practical joke, in 1756, the poet moved across the street to Pembroke – the first and last move he ever made.

Thousands of narcissi bloom in the garden of Peterhouse. I walked along the edge of Coe Fen, through the park where the college kept a herd of red deer until the 1930s, and then round the back of the Fitzwilliam Museum to the William Stone Building. A high-rise block, here of all places? It was designed in 1964 by Sir Leslie Martin and Colin St John Wilson, both at one time professors of architecture here in Cambridge – an eight-storey residential tower of brick, with rigid, geometrical bands of windows, echoing Alvar Aalto. 'Absolute rubbish,' growled David Watkin, architectural historian and Fellow of Peterhouse. 'There's no point in having a tower, it destroys the whole Cambridge tradition of the community of the court – it's grotesquely planned, it's madness.'

A Home for All Arts:
Masterpieces in the Fitzwilliam Museum

'The exhibition of nude figures in a public gallery is always a matter of some embarrassment.'
William Whewell, Master of Trinity, 1855

Have you ever seen more arrogant lions than those in front of the Fitzwilliam Museum? They sit majestically on their pedestals, flanking the steps that rise from the depths of Trumpington Street to the monumental portico which leads into the ethereal regions of this temple of the arts. There could hardly be a greater contrast than the humble cottages opposite. And yet the attitudinal gap in the historical context is even greater than the gap between cottage and palace, for it was in the revolutionary year of 1848, when heads were falling bloodily all over Europe, that the Cantabrians opened the Fitzwilliam Museum. *Tu felix Cantabrigia.* As a university institution it was generally reserved for university members only, but on three days a week other visitors were allowed in, as long as they were 'respectably dressed'. Thus did the dress code take precedence over the class war.

For the foundation of the Fitzwilliam Museum we are indebted to a former student of Trinity Hall, the Irish Viscount Richard Fitzwilliam. He was a connoisseur and a music lover who spend his life collecting Italian and Flemish paintings, etchings, books and medieval illuminated manuscripts. Before he died a bachelor in 1816, he gave the university 144 paintings, including some by Titian, Veronese and Palma Vecchio, 10,000 books, and other items from his collection. He also gave them a fortune in South Sea annuities to build a museum. George Basevi, a pupil of Sir John Soane's, won the competition to design the museum, and construction began in 1837. It is one of the great neoclassical museums, conceived as a temple of the arts, along the same lines as Klenze's Glyptothek in Munich and Smirke's British Museum in London. But the way in which Basevi extended the classical portico to either side, opening up a massive front that recedes and then projects again, endows this neo-Grecian façade with a Baroque sense of movement. Basevi never saw the completion of his museum, as he fell to his death from scaffolding in Ely Cathedral. The stairs and entrance hall were given their final form by C. R. Cockerell and E. M. Barry (1846–75), with a grandiose display of marble and gold, that makes you feel you are entering a High Victorian manor house.

The Fitzwilliam Museum, or Fitz for short, is a miniature Louvre. Virtually every world culture and epoch is represented here by its finest works, but we are never overwhelmed by sheer quantity as we are, say, in the Metropolitan Museum. The range extends from painted Grecian urns to Japanese porcelain and Korean ceramics, from Renaissance sculptures, musical scores and writers' manuscripts to furniture, coins and majolica. In such treasure chambers, I like to emulate Alice and follow the advice of the King of Hearts ('Begin at the beginning'), and so on the ground floor, among the antiquities, I made the acquaintance of the *Unshaven Stonemason* from Egypt. This caricature, painted on a fragment of limestone in the 12th century BC, shows a stonemason at work – a slice of the everyday life that underpinned the stylized formal art of the ancient Egyptians. It is one of innumerable pieces to have come from Deir el Medineh, a village near Thebes, which was home to the craftsmen who decorated the tombs of the Valley of Kings.

The skylit central room in the old building is devoted to British art. Here and in the neighbouring rooms you will find a compact survey of the main and secondary figures, with portraits, landscapes and genre paintings by Hogarth, Gainsborough, Constable, the naturalized Flemings Anthony van Dyck and Hans Eworth, who was court painter to Mary Tudor, right through to Ben Nicholson, Henry Moore and the Pop art of the 1960s. Also in the Fitz is *The Last of England*, Ford Madox Brown's famous emigration scene of 1855, in which he used himself and his family as models (replica of 1860). Sometimes a single picture can encapsulate the spirit of a place or the history of a passion. *Gimcrack* is one such work, painted by George Stubbs (*c.* 1765). It is an everyday scene on Newmarket Heath: a jockey on his grey horse, with a post on the left-hand side of the picture, and on the right the brick house where the sweating horses are rubbed down after their training run. There is enormous subtlety in the geometry of the lines and spaces, and in the balance of the composition. Gimcrack was a superstar of his time, and he earned a fortune for his owners and for the bookmakers. Today, Stubbs' horses are superstars on the art market.

In addition to these icons of English art history, there is a section which because of its format you might easily overlook: miniature portraits painted on parchment, enamel or ivory. Along with the collection at the Victoria & Albert Museum, this is the most important in the country. From the early 16th to well into the 19th century, the English developed their miniature painting into the finest of arts, particularly during the Tudor and Stuart periods. In the Fitzwilliam Museum you can follow its history from start to finish. The specialists are represented by virtuoso pieces, with Nicholas Hilliard and his pupil Isaac Oliver well to the fore. As a royal miniature painter, an artist from Tübingen made his career at the court of George III: Jeremiah Meyer, who was a founder member of the Royal Academy. The jewel in this collection of rarities is provided, as so often, by Henry VIII, who was painted in around 1526 by Holbein's teacher Lucas Hornebolte on a surface the size of a postage stamp – 53 x 48 millimetres. It is one of the earliest surviving miniature portraits, and it demonstrates beautifully the origins of this exquisite technique, which developed out of medieval illumination. Indeed there are also illuminated manuscripts on show in the Fitz, and you must see at least two outstanding and rare examples: the Breton gospel (9–10th century) and the Grey-Fitzpayn Hours (c. 1300), a book of hours decorated with fantastic beasts and grotesques, which William Morris sold to the museum.

One of the attractions here is the Italians in the Courtauld Gallery: Titian's *Venus and Cupid with a Lute Player* is right next to Palma Vecchio's *Venus and Cupid* reclining in a landscape – enchanting and highly seductive nudes. It is scarcely surprising that the Victorian Master William Whewell wanted them taken down. These pictures ask: What is beauty? And the answer comes with an act of violence: *Tarquin and Lucretia*, a late Titian depiction of the rape scene, painted for his royal patron Philip II. As grey as a corpse beneath his crown of thorns, and utterly forsaken – this is how Guido Reni painted his *Man of Sorrows* (c. 1639), a truly moving depiction of Christ's Passion, and just one of the many masterpieces in this gallery.

With some 250,000 drawings, etchings and engravings, the Fitzwilliam is one of England's greatest treasure houses. It is particularly rich in English watercolours, Indian miniatures, Rembrandt etchings, and drawings by 17th-century Dutch masters. There are some outstanding watercolours and colour prints by William Blake, that apocalyptic visionary, with illustrations of the Bible and Dante from the Geoffrey Keynes collection. It was his brother, the great economist Maynard Keynes, whose championship of Cézanne, Picasso, Braque and Matisse ensured that the Fitzwilliam had at least a smattering of modern art. New acquisitions of contemporary work include pieces by Damien Hirst and Marc Quinn, who studied at Robinson College. Quinn caused something of a furore with unusual concepts such as sculptures made from his own frozen blood or, more recently, his Trafalgar Square project *Alison Lapper*.

Again and again, private collectors have enriched the museum with the individuality and quality of their gifts. They include the Courtaulds and the Rothschilds, and Henry Broughton, who in 1973 donated more than 1,000 floral paintings, including Dutch and Flemish masters of the 17th and 18th centuries – a collection within a collection. There is even a gallery here for painted and printed fans. This sort of eccentricity makes the Fitz even more attractive. Everything is presented in the traditional, academic manner of a university museum which, compared to the current trend of an ever-changing, let's-have-a-bit-of-fun culture, seems almost revolutionary. Lord Fitzwilliam took strict precautions to prevent wear-and-tear on his pictures through global lending: a far-sighted clause in his deed of gift specifies that no work from his collection can ever be let out on loan.

The American millionaire art collector Paul Mellon was one of the great modern benefactors. When he died in 1999, this former student of Clare left the Fitzwilliam some $8 million for the relaunch and expansion of the museum, the Courtyard Development and the new Mellon Gallery of 2004.

I can never leave this place without being smiled at by the Madonnas. There is one particularly heavenly smile, painted by Joos van Cleve – quite down-to-earth, with a Flemish lust for life.

Heading for the Botanic Garden

> 'Oh! he was a wise man...he woulde have tolde by a cowe's water
> how manie gallons of milke shee would have given, foretolde by the
> motion of his dun horse's taile the change of the weather.'
> Student satire on the 'University carrier' Thomas Hobson (1544–1631)

If the sight of the Chelsea porcelain carp tureen in the Fitzwilliam has whetted your appetite, just opposite the museum is the best fish restaurant in town. In a Tudor cottage on Trumpington Street, the Loch Fyne Oyster Company from Argyll has set up a branch where you can sit down to a gastronomic treat, from a salmon breakfast to an oyster dinner.

If you should happen to have eaten a bad one, until a few years ago you could have rushed next door for treatment at Addenbrooke's Hospital. Just like the Fitz, the university hospital grew out of a gift from a former student, the Fellow John Addenbrooke. After opening in 1740, it was extended several times, until the Victorian architect Matthew Digby Wyatt designed the bulk of the present façade in 1863, with arcades, loggias and long rows of blind arches. A hundred years later, all scope for further expansion was exhausted. The new hospital on the southern edge of the city is one of the largest university clinics in Europe, and is a major centre for medical research and teaching. Meanwhile, Old Addenbrooke's has enjoyed an

amazing renaissance. In 1996, it was reopened by Queen Elizabeth as the Judge
Institute of Management Studies, named after its main sponsor, the entrepreneur
Sir Paul Judge, a Trinity graduate. A link between university and commerce, this
business school is totally in keeping with the times, and so is its architecture.

With red, green and blue colours and a central pediment, John Outram post-
modernized the Victorian front, with a colouristic show of strength that preserves
the outer appearance of the building but gives a radical shake-up and a new structure to the interior. From the marble floor right up to the roof, the light and airy
atrium is like a set from Fritz Lang's Metropolis with Disney colouring. Flying
staircases swing from mighty columns, zig-zagging from one floor to the next past
bending gangways and balconies in blue, red and ochre – a mixture of Legoland
and Karnak temple. One finds oneself in a state of polychromatic confusion. And
this is where the potential business elite learn to organize and maximize and capi-
talize, emerging from their gigantic playpen as the global players of the future.

A word about John Outram's building materials. 'Blitzcrete' is the name he
gives to his special mixture of crushed brick and concrete, and the variation with
patterns of contrasting colours he calls 'doodlecrete'. He has replaced the classical
order of columns with a 'robot order' of hi-tech monsters which contain the venti-
lation and cables for the utilities and are crowned by Egyptian style capitals – a
light-hearted comeback for ornamentation. The tradesmen's entrance to the Judge
Institute is in Tennis Court Road, and Outram has made it into a completely new
wing. As massive as Milan's Castello Sforzesco, which was its inspiration, this
'castle block' unfolds more of Outram's repertoire: powerful cylindrical forms,
weighty cornices and 'geological' strata of masonry. This is eccentric architectural
entertainment, street theatre in technicolor. It is the first major public work by an
outsider among English architects, who had previously built mainly private
houses, including the Sussex country home of the Swedish Tetra-Pak billionaire
Hans Rausing.

If you follow the Trumpington Street gutters further out of town, at the corner
of Lensfield Road you will come to Hobson's Conduit. A gold pineapple crowns
this hexagonal Baroque fountain, which stood in the market place until 1856. There
for 240 years it had supplied the townsfolk of Cambridge with pure spring water
from the nearby Gog Magog Hills. Two early 17th-century college Masters had
thought up the idea of piping the water, and university and town had got together
to execute the plan; the fountain itself, however, was named after Thomas Hobson, who paid for it in 1614. The other men were just clever, but Hobson was clever
and popular. John Milton wrote his epitaph, and his name became a household

phrase. If anyone, student or don, wanted to borrow a horse from him, it would have to be the one standing nearest the stable door, because that was the one that had been longest in the stable and had had the most rest. You did not have a choice, and hence the expression 'Hobson's choice'.

In Lensfield Road is a little museum which is devoted to great adventures on ice. *QUAESIVIT ARCANA POLI VIDET DEI* is the inscription on the cornice – 'he explored the secrets of the Poles and now he sees the secrets of God'. The Scott Polar Research Institute, named after the Antarctic explorer Robert Falcon Scott, was founded in 1934 by a member of his 'Terra Nova' expedition who later became a geography professor in Cambridge: Frank Debenham. On the walls are Scott's skis and Shackleton's sledge, and in the display cabinets are photographs, letters, and the last diary entries. The relics you see in this institute, which is run by the geography and geology faculty, bring to vivid life the history of polar exploration: compasses, ice picks, a piece of biscuit, and a fragment of silk from Amundsen's tent, left behind at the South Pole in 1911.

What is good architecture? Just go round the corner, and you'll see it: the Crystallographic Data Centre in Union Road. Thin, handmade bricks – that's the start of it. Then strict, clear forms, a cube that is not monotonous. The brick wall next to the entrance is artificially broken up by a flint wall that is exposed like a vein in crystal – a playful allusion to the world of the crystallographer. The databank of 1993 was designed by the Danish architect Erik Sørensen, as were the interiors: mahogany furniture, *trompe-l'oeil* marble floors. Sørensen and his wife Cornelia Zibrandtsen were also responsible for the neighbouring Unilever Centre for Molecular Informatics, part of the University's Chemistry Department (2001).

A few streets further on, and at last we're back in the green – in the Botanic Garden, to be precise. When it was opened in 1846, on the initiative of Darwin's mentor, the botany professor John Henslow, it lay in the middle of open fields, just like the nearby railway station, which had begun operations the year before. To mark the opening, a Dutch lime tree was planted, and it is still to be seen on the western edge of the garden, next to the Trumpington Gate. This wrought-iron gate was the entrance to the old Botanic Garden in Free School Lane, where in 1762 – long after its Oxford counterpart – the university had laid out a physic garden, which was meant simply for the study of medicinal herbs, but was open to everyone. What in those days would have been dismissed as mere pleasure, i.e. flowers and trees, are now available in abundance.

In the western half of the 16-hectare site, the Victorian layout is largely preserved: the central avenue, broad expanses of lawn, the lake, which is fed by

Hobson's water pipes, and the 'systematic beds', in which about 1,600 hardy herbaceous plants display their family credentials – euphorbia and ranunculus and more, precisely labelled, so that all we have to do is bend down and profit from other people's knowledge and research, until our backs ache like botany students doing their first term's assignments. In the 'chronological beds' you will see some two hundred plants from overseas, arranged according to the date when they were first imported into Britain; in the 'genetics garden', we are shown the effect of genetic factors on wild and on cultivated plants. One of the main attractions of the Botanic Garden is the National Collections of tulips, bergenias, fritillaries, alchemilla, saxifrage, honeysuckle and geraniums.

Like all good gardens, this one also has its winter attractions, including spectacular dogwoods, with their green, red, black and brownish-yellow trunks. Tree lovers will find special collections of willows, poplars and junipers, as well as exotic rarities like the single-needled pine (*Pinus cembroides var. monophylla*), the Californian *Umbellularia* laurel, also known as the headache tree, and the conical *Metasequoia glyptostroboides*, the dawn redwood – a prehistoric tree which had long been known only through fossils until in 1941 it was rediscovered in the grounds of a Chinese temple. Some of the botanical wonders of the world are to be seen in this garden, which contains about 8,000 different varieties of plant. In the greenhouses, to the disgust of vegetarians, you will also find a collection of carnivorous plants. At the time of writing, a new visitors' centre is being planned, with a roof of cedarwood shingles and solar cells, designed by the London architect Edward Cullinan.

Two of England's foremost gardeners today are Cambridge graduates: Penelope Hobhouse (Girton) and Christopher Lloyd (King's). In 1660, long before the Botanic Garden came into being, John Ray published the *Catalogus Plantarum circa Cantabrigiam nascentium*. Ray taught Greek and maths at Trinity, but this did not stop him from cataloguing every plant that grew in and around Cambridge at that time. One is tempted to look for all the places and plants he describes: notchweed, for example, or stinking goosefoot, which Ray found on the walls of Peterhouse. Is it still there? More reports, please.

Noble Entry and Gay Exit:
Downing and Emmanuel

'My father...sent me to Emmanuel College in Cambridge at fourteen years old, where I resided three years, and applied myself close to my studies.'
Jonathan Swift, *Gulliver's Travels*, 1726

When the Monty Python star John Cleese was studying at Downing College in the early 1960s, the brave new college library was not yet ensconced by the entrance. It looks as if it has been designed by someone from the Ministry of Silly Walks, taking a stroll through the history of styles. The Athenian Tower of the Winds rises up over a Palladian villa, while the Doric portico recalls the glories of ancient temples. This 1992 anachronism shows a little more subtlety in the metopes of the frieze running below the pediment. Symbols carved in the stone denote the subjects that can be studied here: the double helix for biology, the radio telescope for astronomy, the hourglass for history, the laurel wreath for English literature, and the Tower of Babel for foreign languages. The scales of justice indicate a traditional domain in this college, where legal historian Frederic William Maitland once taught. Another Fellow of Downing was a literary guru of his time, 'a magnificent, acid, malevolently humorous little man who looks exactly like a bandy-legged leprechaun', as Sylvia Plath described F. R. Leavis in October 1955.

After just a few steps you will get a physical sensation of what makes Downing special. Coming from the bustle of Regent Street, you don't step into one of those familiar, monastic inner courts, but straight into a park, bordered by temple-like wings that remain open to the south and offer a view over sweeping lawns as far as the pointed spire of St Mary's on Hills Road. No other college in Cambridge conveys such an impression of space, such an Arcadian illusion of noble research and serene study.

Downing was the gift of a property speculator named Sir George Downing. London's Downing Street is named after his grandfather. Sir George died in 1749, whereupon there was a protracted and complicated battle over his estate, as a result of which Downing did not receive its charter until 1800. It was the first new foundation for more than 200 years, and even the king, George III, took an interest in the architecture. It was to be classical – not Gothic – and the competition was won by a twenty-eight-year-old student architect, William Wilkins, Fellow of Caius. His design (1806) made architectural history.

Instead of the traditional inner courts of the medieval colleges, Wilkins planned a group of separate pavilions which would surround a park-like area of lawn in an open rectangle. Downing was the first campus-style college, even before the University of Virginia, which was the first American campus (co-founded by Thomas Jefferson). Furthermore, Downing marks a turning point in English classicism, with Roman-Palladian giving way to Greek forms, known as the Greek Revival. The simplicity and dignity of Greek architecture corresponded exactly to the new taste of the Graecophiles, of whom Lord Byron was one. Inlaid in the floor of the college chapel, near the altar, is a piece of marble excavated from a church in Sparta by one of the college tutors – a cultic link between religion and the new love of all things Greek. It is no coincidence that even today there is a triennial 'Cambridge Greek Play', which is performed in the original language and began in 1882 with Sophocles' *Ajax*.

Wilkins was only able to realize part of his temple of learning. The Master's Lodge at the end of the east wing was the first building to be completed (1807–10), and on the other side of the lawn was its counterpart, the hall, with its Ionic portico; these were followed by the houses of the Fellows and students, simple and plain, but with elegant doorcases and cornices and elaborate, creamy brown limestone. The Doric propylaea that Wilkins had planned for the north side never came to fruition; nor did the monumental south wing. Instead, E. M. Barry watered down the plans by linking the pavilions together into continuous wings (1873). Sir Herbert Baker sealed off the north side, and his modern successor built a chapel in the centre of it, with a portico and pediment – Greek Survival, anno 1953.

What can be achieved by top-class modern architecture in such surroundings can be seen with the Senior Combination Room west of the hall. With slender concrete pillars and broken pediments, Bill Howell's pavilion (1970) quotes Wilkins' motifs as a structural echo in a bold geometrical abstraction of the ancient style. This gave the Fellows of Downing such a shock that for further college extensions they commissioned Quinlan Terry. He designed the Howard Building in 1987, a conference centre in retro-chic, its façade decked out with Corinthian columns, pilasters, pediments and urns. In the adjacent residential block, the Howard Court of 1994, there are more nostalgic Doric colonnades of yesteryear, going as far as the library at the entrance – the pretentious, postmodern jumble of styles already described. With Quinlan Terry's historical resurrections, Downing's classicism is beginning to take on a haunted look.

Parker's Piece is the name of the large common on the other side of Regent Street – a stretch of land that was leased from 1587 to a certain Edward Parker, who was the cook at Trinity. In 1613, town and gown agreed to exchange some land: Trinity gave Parker's Piece to the town, and for these ten hectares the town gave the college a much smaller but central piece of land in the Backs, where Trinity Library stands today. Thus both sides were happy, and so are we because Parker's Piece has remained common land ever since, uncultivated, and open to everyone to enjoy. This is where the hero of Ian Buruma's novel *Playing the Game* – the Indian prince Ranji, who studies at Trinity to complete his education as a gentleman – enjoys his first triumphs as a cricketer. The elegance of his stroke play, which makes him the darling of Parker's Piece, is not always matched next door, where behind the youth hostel is Fenner's, one of the country's most venerable cricket grounds.

Don't be put off by yet more classical fronts in St Andrew's Street, for you should visit Emmanuel College. When I entered the first court, there was a duck crossing the lawn with its ducklings, which the likes of us would never be allowed to do. Emmanuel, I was told, is the only college in Cambridge with its own ducks. Their home is the pond in the garden behind the chapel, where once the Dominicans kept their fish. It was on the site of the dissolved Black Friars' monastery that Emmanuel was founded in 1584 by Sir Walter Mildmay, Elizabeth I's Chancellor of the Exchequer. This was the first new foundation after the Reformation, and Mildmay wished to provide training for Protestant priests. 'Sir Walter,' said the Queen, 'I hear you have erected a Puritan foundation.' 'No, madam, far be it from me to countenance anything contrary to your establishment laws,' replied Sir Walter, 'but I have set an acorn, which when it becomes an oak, God alone knows what will be the fruit thereof.' Emmanuel became a bastion of Puritanism, and theology is still one of its strong subjects. It produced many of the Cambridge Platonists – philosophers of sober piety who sought to link reason and faith in the spirit of a Platonic humanism.

In the 17th century, Archbishop Laud's orthodox reforms of the Church drove many Puritans to emigrate. Of the 140 Oxbridge men who for reasons of conscience went to America before 1645, 104 came from Cambridge, and a third of these were from Emmanuel, which was more than all the Oxonians put together. It used to be said that New England was 'Emmanuel's Land'. One of these Emmanuel emigrants was John Harvard. When he died in the New World in 1638, at the age of thirty, he left half his fortune and his entire library of some 400 books to the college which had recently been founded by the Massachusetts Bay Company on the outskirts of Boston. His collection consisted mainly of biblical commentaries and sermons, but there were also classics like Homer, Seneca and Cicero – the working library of a Puritan priest. Harvard University is named after him. Every year Harvard and Emmanuel send an exchange student to Cambridge (England) and Cambridge (Massachusetts) respectively. This programme is financed by a gift from a former Emmanuel student, the chemist Herchel Smith, who earned so much from developing the contraceptive pill that he left over £45 million to his Alma Mater.

Emmanuel College, known as Emma, has a much photographed beauty spot which nestles amid the arcades in the first court: Christopher Wren's chapel. It was designed in 1666, when he was not yet famous as an architect, and it was completed in 1674, together with the colonnades on either side. The balance between round and rectangular forms is masterly, as is the quality of the stone decorations. He used Ketton stone, which in a certain light glows pale pink. This chapel is different from Wren's first work in Cambridge, the classically disciplined Pembroke chapel, as it has a number of Baroque features. The pediment is broken up by a clock, above which is a tall lantern. There are festive garlands and fruits between the Corinthian capitals of the half columns and pilasters. The most Baroque element of all is the illusory layout, for the chapel itself does not begin until some way behind the façade. Above the open arcades is a long gallery which runs the entire length of the wing – a Tudor motif which Wren took up again so that the Master could be on a par with his colleague at Queens'. The interior of the chapel itself is simple, though there are some fine details in plaster and wood. The stained-glass windows are a Victorian celebration of Emma's past, with John Harvard taking his place alongside Cranmer, Tyndale and other heroes of Protestant church history.

There are some wonderful trees in the college garden: a Caucasian wing nut and an Oriental plane tree. In New Court is a herb garden for the college kitchen, a box parterre in Tudor style, as geometrical as a Mondrian in green and grey. Next to this court is a theatre and concert hall which Michael Hopkins built for the college in 1995 – a miniature masterpiece of Ketton stone, like Wren's chapel. Queen's Building is the name of this gem, which of course allows for a certain amount of lewd punning by the students. Among things not to do at your interview: 'Ask if the Queen's Building really is a gay disco.'

On the Far Side of the Cam

'In my life I never spent so many pleasant hours together as
I did at Cambridge. We were walking the whole time –
out of one College into the other... I liked them all best.'
Mary Lamb, 1815

N ot another college!' This was the cry I heard from an exhausted tourist as I
walked across Silver Street Bridge. You would certainly expect to have seen
the best once you've been to the centre, so why bother to cross the river? But if we
left out West Cambridge, we would miss all the developments of the last 130 years.
It was on the far side of the Cam that in the late 19th century the first women's colleges were established, Girton and Newnham, and after 1960 the first graduate
colleges, because after the war the number of graduates rose so steeply that the
colleges could no longer cope. The great new foundations of the post-war era,
Churchill and Robinson, also went to West Cambridge, where there was still some
space between the Victorian villas and the sports grounds. In 1934, the towering
University Library had already paved the way for expansion beyond the Backs,
and for the establishment of a new campus at the intersection between the historical and the modern.

There are long rows of punts lying at the foot of Silver Street Bridge. Generations of students have drunk their pints there at the Anchor Inn or The Mill, or
outside on the little Mill Pond island. This meadow is called Laundress Green,
because it was here that the colleges used to bleach their linen. Sheep's Green,
Lammas Land, Coe Fen – not just the names but also the water meadows themselves are relics of medieval Cambridge. These are the remains of the Fens, whose
white willows and dark ditches reach right into the town, though they are not so
domesticated as the Backs. Cows, horses and sheep graze in these water meadows,
which for centuries have been common land, untouched by herbicides and pesti-
cides. The Coe Fen is full of wild flowers, such as lady's smock and gipsywort, and
there are dragonflies humming over the irises. There is a path along the river from
here to Grantchester Meadows, and then on to Grantchester itself.

Building for Bluestockings:
Darwin and Newnham

'What would I not give to see colleges for women like this in my own country.'
Ivan Turgenev, visiting Newnham in 1878

On a long and narrow strip of land between Silver Street and a branch of the Cam stands Darwin College, founded in 1964. It was the first purely graduate college in Cambridge, and the initiative and money came from three colleges – Caius, St John's and Trinity. The choice of name, in homage to the great naturalist, ties in with a piece of Cambridge family history. The Hermitage, Newnham Grange and Old Granary are three early 19th-century houses where the college was established, and they belonged to Charles Darwin's descendants. His son George, a Cambridge professor of astronomy, bought Newnham Grange in 1885, and until 1962 it was the home of Darwin's grandson Sir Charles Galton, Master of Christ's. Darwin College is not open to visitors, but the *genius loci* is vividly captured in the memoirs of Darwin's granddaughter, the woodcarver Gwen Raverat, who grew up in Newnham Grange. Her *Period Piece* describes the lost Cambridge of her youth, the Victorian customs and rituals, her uncles, aunts and great-uncles and the extraordinary academic clan that grew up in the great man's shadow.

A brick wing links the three Darwin houses into a continuous building, and there are idyllic riverside gardens as well as a landing stage for punts. From the opposite side of the river you can see the architectural originality of the extension by Jeremy Dixon and Edward Jones (1994). The Darwin Study Centre lies like a houseboat on the millpond, with a wooden deck on top of the bright brick hull, balconies on consoles, and seminar and lecture rooms at the back. The first chair jointly financed by the universities of Cambridge and Hamburg is based here – the Darwin professorship, by means of which a geologist alternates his teaching and research between the two cities.

When the Darwins were still in residence here, Gwen Raverat recalls the 'dowdy Newnham students of those days passing our house', and Uncle William gloomily commenting, 'Why do those young women always wear dung-coloured coats?' But underneath the coats Mr Darwin would have discovered the Pre-Raphaelite look of a thoroughly fashion-conscious generation of students, who would have decorated their college rooms with Morris wallpaper. They were the avant-garde of the university – not the men, who were stuck in their centuries-old traditions.

Cambridge's second women's college was founded in 1871, two years after Girton, and began in rented accommodation at 74 Regent Street. There were five students and a principal, Anne Jemima Clough. She was the driving force behind the whole enterprise and was, incidentally, the sister of the poet Arthur Hugh Clough, best remembered for his famous line 'Say not the struggle nought availeth'. Anne Jemima's struggle availed a good deal, for just four years later her students moved into their own rooms in Newnham, the village on the outskirts which gave the college its name.

Among the early Newnhamites that passed by the Darwins' windows on their way to lectures were such eminent suffragettes as Lytton Strachey's sister Pernel, later Principal of Newnham, and the flamboyant Jane Harrison, Hellenist, chain-smoker, queen of fashion, and one of the most glamorous figures in the history of classical studies. With her books on the origins of Greek religion, Jane Harrison wrote her way to the very head of the so-called Cambridge Ritualists – an academic superwoman whose lectures were as dazzling as her appearances in Sapphic pose at the Bloomsbury parties. Also among the first students at Newnham were Helen Gladstone, daughter of the prime minister, and Eleanor Balfour, sister of a later premier, and these were by no means the only well-connected ladies to demonstrate the interest of the liberal upper classes in the new foundation. Eleanor Balfour married a Trinity don, the moral philosopher Henry Sidgwick, who was passionate about Newnham for more than just romantic reasons. Named after him is the avenue of plane trees on the sunny side of which the college lies.

Red brick, large white wooden windows, Dutch gables – Newnham abounds with the charm of the Queen Anne style, best seen from the gardens. The decorative delights of this brickwork art are unfolded in a wealth of delicately crafted garlands, masks and pilasters. 'Domestic Collegiate' was the term used by Basil Champneys to describe his design for the women of Newnham. He wanted to give these pioneering female academics a feeling of privacy and security, with the cosy family atmosphere one finds in Dutch houses. The then popular 'Dutch redbrick style' was quite new to college architecture, and was very different from the Tudor and Gothic styles of the men's colleges, though no less conservative in its way. 'Building for Bluestockings' was how Margaret Birney Vickery described it – a little bit of feminist understatement in late Victorian England.

Instead of enclosed courts, Basil Champneys designed a row of houses along Sidgwick Avenue. Each student was to be part of a little family unit as well as belonging to the wider college community. Champneys worked on the Newnham project for thirty-five years, until 1910. He built the Old Hall, the original gatehouse

next to it – a monumental example of Edwardian architecture – and Clough Hall
with its elegant refectory and two large, round bay windows. As the students at
the time were not allowed to attend physics or chemistry practicals with their male
counterparts, the Newnhamites had their own laboratories. There were no plans
at all for a chapel, unlike Girton, but to make up for that, there was an extensive
library, not least because women were still not allowed to use the University
Library. For the rare books and incunabula printed before 1800, including Hart-
mann Schedel's *Nuremberg World Chronicle* of 1493, the London-based architect
Joanna van Heyningen designed a fireproof, air-conditioned architectural gem in
1981. It stands like a little Lego treasure-chest right on the street, with horizontally
striped brick walls and a lead-covered barrel vault.

Newnham's most recent and very successful piece of modern architecture is the
Rosalind Franklin Building by Bob Allies. This is a graduate hall of residence
(1995) named after the crystallographer Rosalind Franklin, a Newnham graduate
who died tragically young and whose work in the field of molecular biology was
of major importance in paving the way for Crick and Watson's discovery of DNA.

They were not 'destined to become schoolmistresses in shoals', as Virginia
Woolf observed mockingly when in 1928 she unfolded her vision of 'Shakespeare's
sister' to the female students of Cambridge ('nobody respected me'). The famous
Newnhamites include Sylvia Plath, who described her women tutors as 'grotesque
bluestockings who only know life second-hand', A. S. Byatt and her sister Margaret Drabble, the actress Emma Thompson, Fiona Reynolds – the present
General Director of the National Trust –, the feminist author and academic Germaine Greer, and Mary Archer, an expert on solar energy and Jeffrey. Among the
wonderwomen of Newnham are also Julia Neuberger, England's first female
rabbi, and Cecilia Gaposchkin, the first woman to be made a professor (of astronomy) at Harvard in 1956.

Oracular Bones and Incunabula:
A Noah's Ark of Books

'Not once during my three years of Cambridge – repeat: not once –
did I visit the University Library, or even bother to locate it.'
Vladimir Nabokov, *Speak, Memory: An Autobiography Revisited*, 1966

One spring morning I walked along the avenue of blossoming cherry trees in the garden of Selwyn College, and I thought of John Selwyn Gummer, who had studied here. In 1990, at the height of the BSE crisis, this Minister for Madness had stood in front of the TV cameras with his daughter Cordelia and had made her eat a beefburger, in order to reassure the British public that beef was safe. Perhaps one day they will erect a monument to this great champion of the British meat industry: a monumental beefburger designed by Claes Oldenburg.

Selwyn College was founded in 1882 as a bulwark of Anglicanism, and that is how it looks. Tudor neo-Gothic, redbrick like Keble in Oxford, whose statutes served as its model. The Greek inscription on the gate invokes the Victorian ideal of 'muscular Christianity', impressively embodied by the man who gave the college its name: George Augustus Selwyn. When he was a student in 1829, he was a member of the Cambridge crew that lost the first Boat Race against Oxford, and so he went off and became Bishop of New Zealand.

If Selwyn's Fellows had not rejected James Stirling's design for a student hall of residence in 1959, we might have had reason to spend more time here, but instead we shall take ourselves off to Sidgwick Site. Here in 1964–68, the Scottish architect constructed a building for the Faculty of History that brought an equal measure of fame and fury. It consists of two seven-storeyed, right-angled wings with rooms for administration and lectures, and between them a fan-shaped glass dome for the library and reading-room. 'Shocking!' was the cry. Industrial red bricks, patent glazing – you could build an engineering faculty like this, but not a history library! And indeed, Stirling did use materials which had previously been confined to greenhouses and warehouses, but he did it with a sculptural power that made his Cambridge design into a pioneering work. This, whether you like it or not, is one of the sources of the inflated glass atria that are now so common in shopping malls and office blocks.

For years after it had been opened, Stirling's building was encased in scaffolding. Water damage, poor sound insulation, hothouse temperatures – considering the horrendous cost of repairs, the university authorities would have preferred to demolish its unpopular faculty building. But since spring 2000, it has been under a preservation order. Such is the narrow borderline between the aesthetic shocker and the museum piece. Star architects simply line up next to one another in Cambridge. Right beside Stirling is Sir Norman Foster. His building for the law faculty (1995) opens with a wedge-shaped atrium, and it unfolds with the clarity and sharpness of a good summation. The north side has a curved, steel-framed front of silicon glass, while the south front is smoothly vertical, half Portland stone and half glass, and the streamlined shape of the whole draws its inspiration from airship design. The Faculty of Law adds a degree of elegance to the architecturally diffuse area between Sidgwick Avenue and West Road. On this windy, unloved site, which is now at last being redeveloped, the university set up its arts faculties in the 1950s, together with the West Road Concert Hall designed by Sir Leslie Martin, the architect of the Royal Festival Hall in London. There are regular performances given here by the Academy of Ancient Music, an ensemble that specializes in period music and was founded in Cambridge by Chris Hogwood in 1973. Well worth seeing is the Museum of Classical Archaeology, with its collection of more than 600 plaster casts of ancient masterpieces.

In Cambridge, this 'storehouse of knowledge' as Goethe once called Jena, there are more than a hundred college and faculty libraries, but there is only one University Library. Its almost 50-metre tower is an unmistakable landmark as well as being a symbol for the whole campus that has grown up in the shadow of the book-tower on the far side of the river. With this, its third new home, the university's library left its historical place in the centre of the town. It was built in 1931–34 by the architect who was also responsible for Oxford's New Bodleian, Sir Giles Gilbert Scott. Rust-brown bricks, a strict symmetry, rows of windows that extend vertically over six storeys – it's a monumental mixture of warehouse and Assyrian palace. It has a certain brusqueness about it, and is certainly not as inviting as the red telephone booths that we owe to the same designer. But its users reckon that with its seven million books and journals, the UL is one of the finest working libraries in Europe, thanks to the direct accessibility of its vast collection. There are 60,000 reference books alone in the main reading-room, which is as massive as a London railway station.

Before it took on these Alexandrian proportions, the University Library was a very modest affair. In the beginning a few chests sufficed to keep the books, at first in the university's treasure chamber, and then in a room in the east wing of Old Schools. At a time when the Peterhouse library contained more than 300 books, the university catalogue of 1424 showed that its own library possessed just 122. These were mainly religious works of theology and canon law, but there was also the classic medieval comforter, Boethius's *De consolatione philosophiae*, an illuminated manuscript (*c.* 1400) with Chaucer's translation. It is one of only three works that have survived from the original collection. The turbulence of the Reformation resulted in further shrinkage, but at the same time the library acquired some of its most valuable manuscripts, which Matthew Parker, Archbishop of Canterbury, gave to his Alma Mater, including some key Anglo-Saxon texts such as Aelfric's *Homilies* and King Alfred's translation of Pope Gregory the Great's *Cura pastoralis*. In 1709, the library had a collection of 15,693 books and 658 manuscripts. In the same year, it became one of the five copyright libraries, which meant that by law it had to be given a copy of every single book published in Great Britain. It was a privilege that brought with it inflationary consequences. The most valuable additions, however, came from different sources.

In 1715, George I gave the university some 30,000 books as a thank you for Cambridge's loyalty to the House of Hanover during the Jacobite Rebellion; to the rebellious Oxford he sent his soldiers. This Royal Library, whose oak bookcases are still in use, had belonged to the recently deceased Bishop of Ely, John Moore, who in addition to many medical and legal books, had collected first editions of Palladio, Newton and Shakespeare, medieval reference works like the Venerable Bede's *Historia Ecclesiastica* (8th century), and illuminated treasures such as the *Book of Cerne* and the *Book of Deer* (9th century). This ecclesiastical bibliophile was particularly fond of William Caxton, the English Gutenberg, and he had collected more than forty editions of his work, including the very first book to be printed in English: *Recuyell of the Histories of Troy* (1475–76). Cicero's essay on duty *De officiis*, printed in Mainz in 1466, also came with the collection – the first printed copy of an ancient classic, and also the oldest surviving copy of a printed work in England. This single royal gift tripled the number of books in the library, and some of these treasures can be seen in special exhibitions.

The scholars sit in the Rare Books Reading Room, doing their research, bent over Henry III's bestiary, absorbed in the sumptuous Flemish books of hours. With more than 4,500 incunabula, this is the third biggest collection in the country, next to the British Library and the Bodleian. One of its priceless manuscripts is the *Codex Bezae Cantabrigiensis*, 1,600 years old, with the gospels and the story of the apostles written in uncial script. The earliest documents are more than twice as old, including 800 Chinese oracles scratched into bones (*c.* 1200 BC). Another priceless treasure is the Genizah Collection: some 140,000 fragments of Hebrew texts from seven centuries, discovered in the backroom of a synagogue in Cairo – an invaluable source of information about the everyday lives of the Jews in the Mediterranean region since the 9th century.

When Queen Victoria visited Cambridge in 1843, her sightseeing tour included the University Library, where Prince Albert remarked that it contained some interesting manuscripts. 'Yes, my dear,' replied the Queen, 'but don't stay.' The shelves of books cover almost 180 kilometres, and visitors might think that they are orbiting the mind of the world as they wander through the corridors of book-shelves, like Büchner's Lenz wandering through the mountains: 'He did not feel tired, but at times it bothered him that he could not walk on his head.' This is a library that consists of many libraries. It has absorbed the collections of church-men, scholars and institutions, as well as 17th-century Japanese recipe books, prime minister Robert Walpole's archives, the libraries of Peterborough Cathedral and the Royal Commonwealth Society, and the private library of Geoffrey Keynes. The Darwin archive alone contains hundreds of manuscripts and more than 14,000 letters, many of them unpublished.

The fact that the Old Library was bursting at the seams and it was necessary to build a new one was due not least to the 70,000 volumes that it inherited from the library of Lord Acton, the historian, who died in 1902 at Tegernsee in Bavaria. He was a diplomat, a friend of Gladstone's, and the first Catholic Regius professor in Cambridge. He was related to Italian dukes and Bavarian counts, and for a while he was chamberlain to Queen Victoria, who admired him because he was the only man in her Empire 'who can go to foreign courts and condole with my relations in their own languages, in case of funerals.' In 1992, the East Berlin author Stefan Heym gave his private archive to Cambridge University, and not to any German library: diaries, letters and all his manuscripts. Whoever wants to do research on Heym in the future will therefore have to go to Cambridge.

Opposite the University Library, and on the same axis, stands Memorial Court, designed in 1923 for Clare College by the same architect, Sir Giles Gilbert Scott. This neo-Georgian student hall of residence was the first college extension to the west across the Backs, which was a very controversial step. This open, winged building has been linked since 1986 to the new college library, a silver-grey brick octagon by Sir Philip Dowson. Henry Moore's *Falling Warrior* (1956) reminds us not only of the fallen from this college, for it is the modern archetype of all those who die in war. Next to it grows a mighty pine tree – a combination of nature and art which is as native to this town as the interweaving of life, learning and death.

New Founders, New Ideas:
Robinson and Churchill

'A university that is worthwhile is quite simply one in which the student
is brought into personal contact with the aura and with the
threat of the first class, in which he will be made susceptible to that.'
George Steiner, *Errata*, 1997

Y ou too can found a college. David Robinson, for instance, left school at fifteen, and worked in his parents' bicycle shop in Cambridge, until he realized
that he could earn more by renting out television sets. He finished up owning one
of the most successful racing stables in England, and making a name for himself in
his home town by giving it £18 million to build a college. Queen Elizabeth came
and opened it in 1981, and David Robinson, son of a bicycle dealer, became Sir
David. Just like a fairy tale. And just like a medieval college, this newest one of all
has everything a college should have: a gatehouse, a chapel, a hall, a library and
rooms for some 400 students.

A brick ramp leads from Grange Road to the entrance. The gatehouse rises up
rather abruptly, and is as inviting as an archer aiming at you from the top of the
tower. The trellises and grilles on the long outer walls are like portcullises, and
indeed the college seems to be shutting itself off from the outside world like a
fortress. On their ground plan of an inverted 'L', the Glasgow architects Andrew
MacMillan and Isy Metzstein designed two rings of buildings: in the outer ring are
the offices, chapel and library, while the inner wings hold the student halls of residence and the hall; between them is a narrow gorge of somewhat claustrophobic
little courts that give access to the staircases. The reinforced concrete frame is
clothed in brick – to be precise, 1.25 million handmade Dorset bricks in varying
shades of red. Just how superbly the brick tradition has been carried on here can be
seen from the entrance to the chapel, with its geometrically abstract stepped portal. The chapel itself is also resplendent, with two John Piper windows depicting
The Light of the World - an epiphany of colour. Behind the two bands of buildings
lies one of the most beautiful college gardens in Cambridge, with old trees and a
little lake. There is also a Weeping Wellingtonia here, a giant sequoia which lowers
its head in elegant mourning, like one of Mary Wigman's dancers.

Robinson is the first college in Cambridge to have been founded specifically for
both men and women, and with all the facilities for a double academic life, as it

functions as a conference centre in the vacations. At the time of writing, only two-thirds of the college has been built, and a north wing is still at the planning stage. Opposite, on Herschel Road, Clare built its own graduate college in 1966, Clare Hall, designed by an English architect who lived in Stockholm, Ralph Erskine. In contrast to the traditional large-scale concept of a college, he built an academic village: a group of houses, apartments and common rooms, linked by small courts, creating an informal, family atmosphere unlike that of any other college. Expressive, original shapes, natural materials, surprising changes of level – this is a contemporary continuation of the Victorian West End of Cambridge, where the dons once had their villas and gardens.

'And now for something completely different.' In 1955, Sir Winston Churchill stepped down as prime minister and exposed himself to a boring old age. A group of influential friends exploited the opportunity to mobilize the grand old man for a political and educational project that would also be a monument to him: the founding of Churchill College (1960). This, the first college to be named after a living person, was the culmination of the Churchill cult that dominated the post-war era. Gifts flooded in from all over the Empire to make the project possible: copper from Rhodesia, carpets from India, wood from Australia, New Zealand and Nigeria. The college scarf and rowing boats bear Churchill's racing colours: chocolate brown and pink. 'Forward' is the college motto, the key word in his famous 'blood, sweat and tears' speech of May 1940 ('Let us go forward together') – a rallying cry that found a new application in the rhetoric of the new college: it was the end of the 1950s, when the Cold War was at its peak, and Churchill College was to support the new technological elite who would ensure that Britain led the way forward into the future.

Inspired by the Massachusetts Institute of Technology, this new college focuses mainly on the natural sciences. According to its statutes, 70 per cent of the students and teachers must be engaged in the study of mathematics, engineering or science. The first Master, at Churchill's own invitation, was nuclear physicist and winner of the Nobel Prize for physics, Sir John Cockcroft. But, in good classical Cambridge tradition, the motto at the entrance is a Virgil hexameter: 'Felix qui potuit rerum cognoscere causas' – happy the man who can learn the causes of the world (*Georgics* II, 490).

As we have seen, the foundation was financed not by the State but by industry and private means. It was all done on a princely scale in terms of both space and staff, originally meant for 60 Fellows – now 140 – and 540 students. One goes between two brick pylons, a minimalist abstract form of gatehouse, into a complex of buildings and lawns which is so broad and spacious that one gets the feeling this 17-hectare site is just the beginning of an infinite expanse. Between 1959 and 1968, Richard Sheppard, Robson & Partners constructed a series of ten inner courts, containing student accommodation of brown brick and exposed concrete with large bay windows. Like satellites, these courts orbit the central area of common rooms, hall, auditorium and library. This gives a completely new twist to the traditional combination of court and campus landscaping. It is functional architecture of the 1960s, with flat roofs, teak window frames, and a dash of brutalism. With the grim determination of one of Churchill's war speeches, the hall towers over the rest of the complex, with its three barrel vaults of concrete.

On the lawn a Barbara Hepworth sculpture displays the abstract charm of the 1960s – *Four-Square Walk Through*, four slices of Emmenthal cheese made of bronze. Meanwhile, another 'period piece' of that time has left the college: the literary historian George Steiner. Instead of lecturing on Dryden's Middle Period, he would interpret poetry through the eyes of Marx and Freud, and he would talk to packed audiences about structuralism, culture and barbarism, and other unorthodox subjects that made him unpopular with the academic Establishment and all the more popular with the students, especially during the Vietnam War. Steiner was a Churchillian literary guru, but he did not get a chair until he left Cambridge in 1974 (see p. 266).

If you want to visit the chapel, you will have to go to the far end of the campus. Originally, it was meant to be built near the entrance, and then it was not meant to be built at all. Francis Crick protested that a chapel was an anachronism, especially in a community of scientists: 'The churches in town, it has been said, are half empty. Let them go there,' he wrote to Churchill on 12 October 1961. Along with his letter, the famous molecular biologist and Fellow of Churchill enclosed ten guineas to help finance a college brothel. This, he said, would be a useful institution, and in time the ladies concerned could be given college dining rights, like college chaplains. But in 1967, the college got a chapel after all, privately financed and maintained, and built so close to the sports grounds that it might be taken for a somewhat eccentric public convenience. Nevertheless, behind the off-putting walls is an interior of striking intensity, following the ground plan of a Greek cross and containing windows by John Piper (1970).

On the grassy slopes between college and chapel, the Møller Centre was opened in 1992, a long, light brown brick building with bands of sandstone and a barrel roof which according to *The Observer* looked as if it had been squeezed out of a tube of toothpaste. Off-centre is an octagonal belvedere with a pyramidal glass dome. This conference centre *à la mode*, which is also a seventy-room hotel, was designed by the Danish architect Henning Larsen, and was a gift from his fellow countryman Maersk McKinney Møller, a shipping and oil magnate and an admirer of Churchill. Sir Winston himself left to his college not only an oak and a mulberry tree, both of which he planted with his own hands, but also literary, political and private documents and records which are of immense historical importance. The Churchill Archives Centre now holds the archives of some three hundred politicians, members of the armed forces, and scientists, including those of prime minister Clement Attlee, the immigrant atomic physicist Lise Meitner, and the Oxford graduate Margaret Thatcher, who preferred to give them to Churchill rather than the Bodleian Library – a little act of revenge, since Oxford had refused to give her an honorary doctorate.

When you leave the college, it's worth going round the corner to Storey's Way. On the south side of the street are some Arts & Crafts houses from the turn of the last century – five of them were designed by Mackay Hugh Baillie Scott (nos. 29, 30, 48, 54 and 56). The most striking of these, no. 48, was sold in 2000 for no less than £1 million. This part of West Cambridge has a very different attraction for natural scientists: the new Cavendish Laboratories south of Madingley Road. In the fields just before you reach the M11, you will see a giant tent with eight masts. It's not Chipperfield's Circus, but the Schlumberger Building. Sir Michael Hopkins designed this research laboratory for a multinational oil and electronics company in 1985. It was seen as a shining, hi-tech emblem of innovation, symbol of the Cambridge Phenomenon, a high profile, much photographed modern counterpart to King's College Chapel. But some icons last for ever, while others quickly fade.

Life, Art and Pebbles:
Kettle's Yard

'There should be a Kettle's Yard in every university.'
Jim Ede, 1970

K ettle's Yard lies on Honey Hill, and what awaits us there is a sweet experience indeed. It's just a few cottages with hipped roofs on a grassy slope, with
the church tower of St Peter's behind the trees, and it was the home of a man
named Jim Ede, who lived in this rural corner of Cambridge with his art collection
and wanted to share his love of life and art with other people. It's a house full of art,
but it's not a museum. As you would on a private visit, you have to ring the door-
bell to be let in. You write your name in a visitors' book, and one of the friendly
housekeepers tells you, 'You may sit on any chair.' You are made to feel at home,
like a guest of the owner who, unfortunately, is not able to welcome you in person.
Jim Ede may no longer be with us, but everything is just as he left it.

There are round pebbles on a table, a spiral of white, grey and black stone balls,
monochromes of a beachcomber. The wooden floorboards are bare, and the walls
are white, hung with pictures by Ben Nicholson and his wife Winifred, Christopher Wood, Alfred Wallis, Joan Miró. On tables and chests of drawers there are
sculptures and ceramics by Bernard Leach and Lucie Rie, and on the grand piano
is Constantin Brancusi's *Prometheus*, a stone head (1912). Among all these are natural objects – shells, stones, dried flowers, bird feathers in a glass. Ede did not
search for individual masterpieces but for links between nature and art, and
between art and everyday life. From the world of appearances he brought a selection back to his home. But who was Jim Ede?

Harold Stanley Ede came from a family of Welsh Methodists. He went to school
in Cambridge, but spent most of his time in the Fitzwilliam Museum. He wanted
to be a painter, like those of the quattrocento, whom he particularly admired.
After studying at the Slade in London, he became an assistant in the Tate Gallery
in 1920. A little later he got to know the Nicholsons, who opened his eyes to contemporary art – Picasso, Braque, Brancusi – and Ben sold him some pictures for
the price of the materials at a time when hardly anyone showed any interest in
them. Today there are more than forty of Nicholson's works in Kettle's Yard,
ranging from a still life of fruit painted in the 1920s to the geometrical abstractions
of the 1960s. Jim Ede was one of the first to collect pictures by Alfred Wallis, the

great naive painter of St Ives, of whose works he collected about a hundred. And when the sculptures of the Frenchman Henri Gaudier-Brzeska came to the Tate and nobody wanted them, Ede bought as many as he could. Kettle's Yard has more works by this Vorticist than most museums.

In 1936, Jim Ede left the Tate and went to Tangier – a dropout who, however, never let himself be dragged down by the enclave of hedonists and adventurers. He wrote, travelled, and gave lectures on art. In 1956 he returned to Cambridge with his wife Helen, and next to St Peter's churchyard they found four dilapidated 17th- and 18th-century cottages which they restored and moved into with all their treasures. Before long, they were opening their home up to visitors during term-time, and there were many students who enjoyed their first experience of modern art over a cup of tea. Ede would even lend them original works to put up in their college rooms, because for him art was *A Way of Life*, as he called his autobiography. 'He was deeply religious, a kind of mystic,' I was told by one of his former colleagues. Kettle's Yard is a spiritual place, where objects, light and space are sublimely balanced. Despite the abundance of things, you never feel overwhelmed, for everything is simple, quiet and harmonious. What Ede set out to do here was, in his own words, 'to make manifest the underlying stability which more and more we need to recognise if we are not to be swamped by all that is so rapidly opening up before us.'

In 1966 the Edes gave their house and collection to the university. For a while they went on living there, but then they moved to Edinburgh, where Jim died in 1990 at the age of ninety-four. To prevent Kettle's Yard from becoming a mausoleum, and to ensure that its classic modern collection should not lose touch with contemporary art, the collector himself took the necessary precautions well in advance: there is an annexe for chamber concerts, an innovative forum for contemporary music, and a separate gallery for temporary exhibitions, designed by Sir Leslie Martin (1970). Jim Ede's house, however, remains a singularly personal testimony to the pre-war British avant-garde and to the enterprise of an enthusiast. The Romantic idea of a union between art and nature is staged here as a form of life, and it will go on resonating for as long as Kettle's Yard is there to welcome its visitors.

The little church of St Peter's stands on the hill behind Kettle's Yard, in the shade of maple and chestnut trees. It is all that remains of what was once a bigger 12th-century church. In the masonry of the tower are Roman bricks which may have come from the old town walls. When there were only fourteen households in the parish, at the beginning of the 17th century, the church fell into disrepair. It was rebuilt on a smaller scale, but when there were not enough people to fill even this tiny space (barely 11 metres long), St Peter's became a case for tender loving care – in other words, redundant. Sometimes the gallery uses it for exhibitions, which is thoroughly in keeping with the spirit of Jim Ede, to whom there is a memorial stone with lines from John Donne. But this space is at its most beautiful when there are no pictures, and it is devoted to pure stillness.

One thing that has been left in the church is a Norman font, and if I were a baby, I'm not sure whether I would scream in terror or gurgle with delight on being dipped in such a basin. Leaning forward from each of the four corners of this stone block is a triton who is grasping both ends of his fish tail and bending it upwards to the edge of the font. It is rare enough to see Poseidon's sons practising their yoga, but it is equally rare to find such hybrid creatures from heathen mythology associated with Christian symbolism. The fish, however, was an early emblem for Christ, and the baptismal water is a basic element of life for his followers. This is the message carved in the stone with a magical, living power that has survived long after the priests have fallen silent. The symmetry of the decorations, the geometry of the form, the circular basin and the square block – these all combine to create the special aesthetic enchantment of this extraordinary piece of medieval art.

The weathercock on the spire of St Peter's bears the letters A.P., the initials of Andrew Perne. He was Master of Peterhouse from 1553 to 1589, and in these turbulent times proved to be so adaptable that his weathercock could be read as a symbol of his character: A.P. could mean 'A Protestant', 'A Papist', or 'A Puritan', whichever way the political wind was blowing.

The corner house on Castle Street, a former 16th-century inn, is now the home of the Cambridge & County Folk Museum, filled to the brim with generations of household goods from the history of town and county. An old poster in this domestic museum offers an invitation to the public execution of Elias Lucas and Mary Reader on Castle Hill in 1850.

There is grass growing on the hill diagonally opposite, which William the Conqueror had built in 1068 as part of a castle, initially of wood and later of stone, with a gatehouse and towers – a useful quarry in later years for the college builders. Today, there is not even a ruin on Castle Hill, or a gallows – just a beautiful view.

Three Colleges and a Grave:
Wittgenstein's Neighbours

'It is strange when two different worlds can live in two rooms one beneath
the other. This happens when I live below the two students who make noise
above me. These are really two worlds & no communication is possible.'
Ludwig Wittgenstein, 7 November 1931

In her novel *An Unsuitable Job For a Woman*, P. D. James has her private detective Cordelia Gray investigating her first case in Cambridge. The death of a history student takes her into a college on the outskirts of the city: 'New Hall, with its Byzantine air, its sunken court and its shining domed hall like a peeled orange, reminded Cordelia of a harem; admittedly one owned by a sultan with liberal views and an odd predilection for clever girls, but a harem nonetheless.'

New Hall was founded in 1954, and was the third women's college after Girton and Newnham. The students are all female, but male Fellows are tolerated as a concession to post-feminism. The buildings shine brightly behind the trees in Huntingdon Road – white brick and white exposed concrete. The firm of Chamberlin, Powell & Bon built the college in 1962–66 with a good deal more sensitivity than their London Barbican complex. The hall towers up, rather like an observatory with its segmented dome, on a ground plan in the shape of a Greek cross, surrounded by four round towers with staircases and smaller domes. The Byzantine style of the hall is offset by a certain prefabricated aesthetic, with blocks of concrete so huge that the cranes could hardly lift them – an economical use of materials essential when there is a limited budget. Opposite the dining hall is the barrel-vaulted library, and in between is a court with a splashing fountain. For purists like Pevsner, such 'easy beauty' was suspect – the virgin white, the voluptuous curves, as if the architects were trying to suck up to their female clients with markedly feminine architecture. But this would be totally unfair in view of the sober objectivity of the other wings.

The Fellows of New Hall soon realized that the white brick walls provided perfect conditions for displaying works of contemporary art. In the long and well-lit corridors of the central Fountain Court, in the common rooms and in the hall as well as outside on the lawn, art is everywhere. From batik to steel sculpture, there are all kinds of media and techniques – paintings, photographs, woodcuts by Gwen Raverat, a bronze head by Elisabeth Frink, a Gulf War picture by Maggi

Hambling. Well over 230 works by more than 190 women artists now make up this college collection, and they include famous names like Paula Rego and Barbara Hepworth, as well as the work of former students. Women's art in a women's college provides what even today is a programmatic alternative to the mixed but still predominantly male culture of Cambridge. *The Obstacle Race* was the title of Germaine Greer's feminist history of art (1979), and the aesthetic sequel to this classic is now visible in solid form before the very eyes of New Hall's students – not the worst preparation for the obstacle courses that they will later face in the outside world. Anne Lonsdale, President of New Hall, argues convincingly for the lasting efficacy of the college system: 'The crucial global issues like environmental climate change that now confront us require the sort of interdisciplinary thinking college life promotes.'

The neighbouring Fitzwilliam College was built at about the same time as New Hall. It was in fact the rebuilding of an 1869 foundation that was originally meant for students who did not belong to any of the established colleges. As its first premises were in Trumpington Street opposite the Fitzwilliam Museum, it took on the same name, 'Fitz' for short. Today about 70 per cent of its students come from state schools, which is well above the average, as befits the social roots of this Victorian initiative. The college motto runs: 'Ex Antiquis et Novissimis Optima' – from the old and from the newest, the best. Unfortunately, Denys Lasdun took no notice of the motto.

What this once-celebrated architect of the National Theatre in London built in Huntingdon Road between 1961 and 1967 has all the charm of a motel. Façades of engineering brick, a miserable brown, and floors in stripes of concrete. The residential wings are monotonous, and the hall is literally over the top with its baldachin roof: tall windows over which there are projecting bonnets of concrete which look for all the world like a phalanx of excited nuns. Luckily the Fitz ran out of money. The chapel was designed in 1992 by Richard MacCormac, who put a round building at the end of one Lasdun wing and within this rotunda set a cube, which is the chapel on the first floor. The altar wall is entirely glass – an east window that does not require any decoration because above and beyond the altar you can see a huge plane tree. This pure clear space opens itself up both inwards and outwards. Natural light becomes a revelation, and the Word evokes the images. It is as if Cambridge's Puritan tradition had found an echo here in a modern purism. This chapel alone makes a visit to Fitz worthwhile.

Some way out of town, on the dead straight Roman road to Huntingdon, lies Girton College. It is blessedly far from the tourists' beaten track. There is, to be honest, not much to see, though there is plenty to admire. Girton was Britain's first women's college. With the support of the National Society for Women's Suffrage, Emily Davies founded a domestic community with five students in 1869, initially in Hitchin, Hertfordshire, but from 1873 onwards at the present location. Like Newnham, the college adopted the name of the village. 'That infidel place' was the scornful epithet used by a Cambridge cleric at the time. Today the college has about 650 students, but only half of these are women, as men have been admitted to Girton since 1979.

The buildings that Sir Alfred Waterhouse designed for the ladies of Girton in 1873 were routine Victorian, like his buildings for Jesus and Pembroke: neo-Tudor, red brick and terracotta, with all the traditional features from gatehouse to chapel, which signified parity with the men's colleges. The only feature that Waterhouse did not adopt was the prevalent staircase principle. Corridors and neighbourliness were the key to making the female community feel more comfortable and more secure. No Cambridge college has longer corridors than Girton's, and none of them have a heated swimming pool either. The Fellows' Garden was designed by a former maths student, Penelope Hobhouse, the doyenne of English gardening.

From Girton back into town takes ten minutes by bike. At the halfway mark, All Souls Lane branches off from the main road. On the other side of the yew trees lies a shining green expanse of fields and meadows, which makes you feel that the real end of All Souls Lane must be the countryside and not St Giles's Cemetery. Here in the graves, town and gown lie peacefully side by side – the Masters and the mayors, the professors and the professionals, the clerics and the clerks, and even the Fellows of Trinity and the Fellows of King's, no longer at each other's throats. Quiet rests the don, and if he was important enough, you will see his (provisionally) last address on the blackboard by the cemetery chapel.

A Who's Who of St Giles's Cemetery: the economist Alfred Marshall, the moral philosopher George Edward Moore, the Latinist Charles Oscar Brink, who emigrated from Berlin, Sir James George Frazer, who wrote *The Golden Bough*, and William Heffer, who founded the much loved bookshop. There are many great names on these graves, and even more great names that have been forgotten. The Darwins are also represented here, in the persons of Sir Francis, an orchid expert and biographer of his father, and Darwin's granddaughter, Frances Cornford, whose fame as a poetess has been reduced to three lines:

> 'O why do you walk through the fields in gloves,
> Missing so much and so much?
> O fat white woman whom nobody loves.'

On 1 May 1951, Ludwig Wittgenstein was buried in St Giles's Cemetery, beneath a Scots pine with spreading branches (Plot 5). His story ended like a bad pun at Storey's End, in the house of a doctor friend. It is clear from his notes that he was preoccupied right to the end with problems of certainty, evidence and error. He was sixty-two when he died from cancer of the prostate. His last words, if report is to be believed, were: 'Tell them I've had a wonderful life.' On his gravestone stands the only thing that can be said with certainty: Ludwig Wittgenstein 1889–1951. But life had one last little joke to play on the great philosopher of language. His neighbour in the graveyard was called James Eadie Tod. And 'Tod' is the German for 'death'.

'Grantchester! ah, Grantchester!':
Honey for the Patriot's Tea

'See the splashing of the kingfisher flashing to the water.
And a river of green is sliding unseen beneath the trees
Laughing as it passes through the endless summer
Making for the sea.
In the lazy water meadow I lay me down.'
Pink Floyd, *Grantchester Meadows*, 1969

There is really only one way to get from Cambridge to Grantchester in style, and that is punting up the River Granta. For generations of students this trip with girlfriend and picnic basket has been as integral a feature of Cambridge life as supervisions and the May Ball. But the path along the river, through Grantchester Meadows, is just as beautiful – so beautiful in fact that the rock band Pink Floyd, who are not exactly famous for being nature lovers, wrote a song about it. 'Welcome to Paradise' says the sign for a nature reserve where kingfishers and water rats, grass snakes and garden warblers live together more or less in peace. 'In the lazy water meadow I lay me down.' When we have squeezed through the kissing gate, and kissed each other in accordance with the cunning custom devised by the cattle farmers, we can wander along the river all the way to Grantchester.

Thatched cottages, flower-show gardens, a church and three pubs. It's a village like hundreds of others in England, even today. So what's special about it? 'Our village has about 600 inhabitants, three Nobel laureates, five members of the Royal Society, and eight Cambridge professors,' I was told by one of them – the best-selling novelist Jeffrey Archer. He would like to be as romantic a figure as Rupert Brooke. Brooke is one of the few poets to have made it onto a pub sign, and in England that is a far greater measure of popularity than even a spot in Poets' Corner. Without Brooke, Grantchester would just be one of many academic villages around Cambridge. But without Grantchester, Brooke would not have written his most popular poem. He wrote it in May 1912 in the Café des Westens in Berlin, the meeting place of the intellectual Bohemians. '*Temperamentvoll* German Jews / Drink beer around,' he observed, and recalled the meadows at 'Haslington and Coton / Where *das Betreten*'s not *verboten*'. Homesick, he penned his hymn to England, 'The Sentimental Exile' as it was originally called, a homage to the lost scenes of his youth, now famous under the title 'The Old Vicarage, Grantchester':

> Oh, is the Water sweet and cool,
> Gentle and brown, above the pool?
> And laughs the immortal river still
> Under the mill, under the mill?
> Say, is there Beauty yet to find?
> And Certainty? and Quiet kind?
> Deep meadows yet, for to forget
> The lies, and truths, and pain?

And then the much-quoted closing lines that have passed into the realms of the proverbial: 'Stands the Church clock at ten to three? / And is there honey still for tea?' Brooke's Grantchester is a place where time stands still. Prosaically, however, the vicar turned down the suggestion that in the poet's memory the hands of the church clock should be stopped forever at ten to three.

Rupert Brooke was the son of a teacher at Rugby. He lived first of all at King's College and then moved to Grantchester in June 1909 in order to write his dissertation on the Elizabethan dramatist John Webster. He rented a room in the Orchard, which really is an orchard and since 1897 has also been a tea garden on the River Granta. The customers used to sweeten their tea with honey from the hosts' beehives, and when the students had danced through the nights of May Week, they would come here at six o'clock and have breakfast in the Orchard Tea Garden. And now we can sit there in green deckchairs scattered among the apple and pear trees, and drink our tea, which is no longer sweetened with honey but with Brooke's verses quoted in the brochure and with the knowledge that we are in one of the nation's holiest groves, 'where more famous people have taken tea than anywhere else in the world'.

In summer 1911 Virginia Woolf, who at the time was still called Virginia Stephen, visited Brooke in Grantchester. She was less impressed by his poetry than by his personality ('I thought he would be Prime Minister'), and on a warm, moonlit night ('let's go swimming, quite naked') they dived into Byron's Pool, which is a little weir on the edge of the village. This was where, as a student, Lord Byron got himself fit for his crossing of the Hellespont. The 'Neo-Pagans', as Virginia Woolf called the fresh-air fiends gathered around Brooke, celebrated the simple life with poetry and excursions into the country, far from the madding, urban world of modern times. Love of nature, socialist ideals, sexual freedom – these all came effortlessly together in the Arcadian idyll of the Cambridge intellectuals. And shining brightly at the centre of this circle was Rupert Brooke: barefoot, open-neck shirt, flowing nut-brown locks parted in the centre, a kind of Edwardian Hugh Grant, surrounded by a swarm of men and women oscillating between the bisexual and the homosexual, a flirt, a charmer, a born winner.

Sharing the enthusiasm of most of his generation, he went to war in 1914: 'The thing God wants of me is to get good at beating Germans.' Just one year later, he died at the age of twenty-seven, on a hospital ship in the Mediterranean. The fact that he did not die in action but from an insect bite did not quite fit in with the image of a national hero, but Churchill, who was then First Lord of the Admiralty, nevertheless wrote a glowing obituary of the 'poet soldier' in *The Times*. And in his Easter sermon of 1915, shortly after the poet's death, the Dean of St Paul's quoted lines from the sonnet 'The Soldier': 'If I should die, think only this of me: / That there's some corner of a foreign field / That is for ever England.' Rupert Brooke was buried in an olive grove on the Aegean island of Skyros. The aura of golden youth and his early death made him into a romantic legend, a symbol of the lost generation of the First World War, but also regrettably the mouthpiece of a deep-rooted English hostility towards the Germans.

More recent biographers have stripped much of the glamour from the golden-boy image, and yet his weaknesses and the narrow range and creaking technique of his poetry all seem to dissolve like honey in tea, and the myth of Grantchester remains untouched. The poet's village has long since become a Mecca for tourists, as the very embodiment of romanticized Englishness. Grantchester, as the Orchard brochure tells us, is 'Forever England', an idyllic retreat in which the old imperial glory is encapsulated in a little corner beyond the reach even of Brussels. And so when we lie in our green deckchairs, sipping our tea beneath the blossoming apple trees of the Orchard, we are lying in the trenches of the English soul. This alone explains the vehemence with which Prince Charles and other Old Cantabrigians leapt to the defence of the tea garden when property speculators proposed to build on it.

'But Grantchester! ah, Grantchester! / There's peace and holy quiet there.' Yes, but only in winter. From the Orchard, the line of literary pilgrims moves on to the pub with the garish portrait of the poet, and then to the church whose clock unfortunately does not register the photogenic ten to three, and from there to the Old Vicarage, where he had his last lodgings near the river and where 'The chestnuts shade, in reverend dream, / The still unacademic stream.' But since 1980 – and this is pure sacrilege for the fans of Rupert Brooke – the occupant of the Old Vicarage has been none other than the novelist, ex-politician, ex-jailbird Jeffrey Archer. On his desk stands an hourglass made specially to drain itself in two hours. This is the timer by which he writes his record-breaking best-sellers. The locals have changed the ethereal line of Brooke's poem at Archer's expense: 'And is there money still for me?' Archer was the Conservatives' golden boy, 'Mrs Thatcher's best-seller', her loyal defender, her favourite author, a man of many careers and affairs, dubbed 'Lord of the Lies' by the English press, a bankrupt, a millionaire, who entertained the House of Commons, went up into the House of Lords, then went down again in a sensational tangle of sex, bribery and perjury, served his prison sentence, and is now just a little Gatsby skulking away in Grantchester. He was seldom to be seen in the Rupert Brooke, but he did go to church on Sunday, where his immortally 'fragrant' wife Mary conducts the choir.

Ever since the 14th century, Grantchester Church has been part of the living of Corpus Christi, although the land actually belongs to King's. Farmers and dons, 'men with splendid hearts' as Brooke called them, have gone to their final rest in the old walled churchyard. Its status as an academic cemetery was greatly enhanced in 1986, when two lichenologists made a remarkable discovery: it contains 16 different kinds of snail, 44 kinds of lichen, and 36 kinds of moss, including the rare *Tortula papillosa*.

'After Cambridge, blank, blank, blank.'
Lytton Strachey (1880–1932)

A Short Oxbridge Glossary

'Were you at Oxford, James?'
'Yes, sir. The House.'
'The House?' queried Harvey.
'Christ Church, sir.'
'I'll never understand Oxford.'
'No, sir.'
Jeffrey Archer, *Not a Penny More, Not a Penny Less*, 1976

The Backs The park behind the colleges on the River Cam.

Bedder A cleaner in a Cambridge college (= bedmaker). See **scout**.

Bedels University heralds; a position recorded in Oxford since the 13th century.

Blue Sporting colours awarded to those who play in an official match between Oxford (dark blue) and Cambridge (light blue). There is a distinction between Full Blue and Half Blue (see p. 23).

Boat Race Rowing race between both universities. Takes place on the Thames every year, usually at the end of March.

The Bod Bodleian Library, Oxford.

Bulldog Also known as 'buller', the oldest private police at a British university (Oxford), abolished in 2002.

Bumps Boat race between college crews to decide 'Head of the River'. Each boat tries to bump the boat ahead of it. Known as 'Torpids' in the spring term and 'Eights' ('Mays' in Cambridge) in the summer.

Cantab From Latin *Cantabrigium*, placed after a Cambridge graduate's degree.

Cap and gown Traditional student uniform, see also **subfusc**.

Chancellor An honorary, lifetime title, elected by members of Convocation (Oxford) or the Senate (Cambridge). From the Middle Ages until the Restoration the Chancellor was the leading authority at the university, but is now mainly a figurehead and a fundraiser.

Commemoration Celebrations at the end of the summer term, with Encaenia, boat races and balls, in memory of founders and benefactors of the university.

Common Rooms Known as 'Combination Rooms' in Cambridge. The Junior Common Room (JCR) is for students, and the Senior Common Room (SCR) for Fellows; many colleges also have a Middle Common Room (MCR) for Fellows and graduates.

Congregation The university parliament; in Cambridge the Regent House meets at the Senate House for elections or conferral of degrees; in Oxford the resident Masters of Arts meet at the Sheldonian Theatre.

Convocation A meeting of all Oxford graduates, including those not resident, to elect the Chancellor or the Professor of Poetry.

Council Executive body in Cambridge, elected by the Regent House. The Council is the official link between the university and the colleges, and is responsible for planning, finance, etc.

Court Inner courtyard in Cambridge, known as a 'quad' in Oxford.

Cuppers Annual sporting contests between colleges.

Dean Usually in charge of the chapel and the religious life of the college. In some colleges he is the Fellow responsible for discipline and counselling. In Christ Church, the Master is called the Dean, and he is also Dean of the Cathedral.

Degrees Academic titles: the Bachelor of Arts (BA) is awarded at both universities for subjects in the arts and sciences, and the Bachelor of Science (BSc) for outstanding research. Higher degrees: Master and Doctor. Titles are generally written in abbreviated form after the name, with an added distinction for Oxbridge graduates, e.g. Doctor of Philosophy: D.Phil. (Oxon), or Ph.D. (Cantab).

Don From the Latin *dominus*, master of learning – a colloquial term for academics engaged in teaching or research.

Eights Week A week of celebrations in June, called 'May Week' in Cambridge, with college boat races ('eights'), balls, concerts, theatre, etc.

Encaenia From the Greek *egkainia*, festival of renewal at the end of the university year, in the 9th week of Trinity Term (in June), with conferral of honorary doctorates at the Sheldonian Theatre (Oxford).

Essay Short piece of writing on a given subject, to be handed in for the weekly tutorial or supervision, hence precipitating the weekly 'essay crisis'.

Fellow Loan translation from the Latin (*socius* = companion). Member of the governing body of a college, for a limited period as a Junior Fellow but with life tenure as a Senior Fellow, with various privileges including the right of residence in the college. There are also Research Fellows, Visiting Fellows, Tutorial Fellows, Honorary Fellows and Emeritus Fellows, all of different status. Fellows can (but need not) hold teaching and administrative posts in the college.

Finals Examinations after three or four years of study to obtain a degree.

First This is the top grade of degree, followed by Upper Second, Lower Second (II.1 and II.2) and Third. These are called honours degrees, but it is also possible to pass (without honours) and, of course, to fail (positively dishonourable).

Fresher Undergraduate in his or her first year.

Gaudy From the Latin *gaudium*, a college festival, particularly a reunion for former students (Oxford).

Going up, coming up To go/come and study at Oxbridge, no matter which direction or country you have travelled from. The adverb 'up' indicates the loftiness of Oxbridge compared to all other places. Consequently, leaving Oxbridge entails 'going down'. However, according to the Alternative Prospectus of Jesus College, 'Oxford is up, everywhere else is down and Cambridge is nowhere'.

Grads Short for graduates; these are students who have passed their final examinations.

Greats The Oxford name for the classical subjects – Latin, Greek, literature, history, philosophy (*litterae humaniores*). The Oxford 'Greats' examination is called 'Mays' in Cambridge. Since 1920 there have also been 'Modern Greats', combining philosophy, politics and economics, shortened to PPE.

Hall Dining hall, but originally applied to student accommodation in general. 'Formal hall' is a college meal at which students wear gowns and are waited on, instead of the usual self-service.

Heads of Houses The Masters of the colleges, elected by the Fellows, except at Trinity, Cambridge, where the Master is appointed by the Crown. The individual colleges sometimes like to give their Masters different titles. Only Christ Church, Oxford, has a Dean; some have a Master (Balliol) or a Mistress (Girton); Magdalen, Queens' and some others have a President; Brasenose, Somerville and others have a Principal; Oriel and King's have a Provost; Exeter has a Rector, and All Souls and Merton have a Warden.

Hebdomadal Council Responsible for university administration, and consists of college Masters, professors and MAs, elected by **Congregation**. This University Council, as it is now called, meets once a week during the term (Oxford).

High Table Dining table for the Master, Fellows and guests; in the older colleges, it is usually on a raised platform at the end of the **hall**, at right-angles to the students' tables. An essential talent at Oxbridge is 'to be amusing at high table'.

Hilary Spring term at Oxford, named after the Feast of St Hilarius (13 January); see also **Lent** and **Terms**.

Isis Name of the Thames in Oxford (and the name of a student magazine).

Lent Spring term at Cambridge.

MA Anyone who has passed a Bachelor degree (BA) is awarded the Master of Arts degree without any further examinations on payment of a small fee; in

Oxford alumni can pick up their MA seven years after matriculation, and in Cambridge after six.

Matriculation From the Latin *matricula* (little list); it denotes registration at the beginning of the academic year, which is early in October.

May Week see **Eights Week**.

Michaelmas Autumn term, beginning after St Michael's Day (29 September); see **Terms**.

Mods Short for 'Moderations', first examination at the end of the first or second year.

Moral tutor Deals with any personal problems a student may have (Oxford).

Norrington Table Annual ranking of Oxford colleges, named after Sir Arthur Norrington, former President of Trinity, who in 1963 developed a system of examination points for an academic league table. Its Cambridge equivalent is the **Tomkins Table**.

OUSU Oxford University Student Union. The Cambridge equivalent is CUSU.

Oxon From the Latin *Oxoniensis*, added to the degree after the name of Oxford graduates (Oxonians). Also an abbreviation for the county of Oxfordshire.

The Parks Always plural, and refers to Oxford's university park, named after the 'gun parks' installed there during the Civil War.

Porter College porters do not carry luggage; they take care of keys, post and students, and know all there is to know about the weather, the college, politics and life. They are correspondingly authoritative: 'The Head Porter comes directly under the Master.' (Donald Thomkins, Acting but now retired Head Porter at St John's, Cambridge).

Prelims Short for 'Preliminaries', meaning the first examinations held in some faculties at the end of the first or second term.

Proctors From the Latin *procurator academiae*. These are two university officials appointed each year by the colleges from among the Fellows, nowadays more for representative duties than for matters of discipline; first mentioned in Oxford in 1248.

Professor Either the occupant of a chair in a specific subject, or the head of a faculty. Other teachers in order of seniority are readers and lecturers.

Quad Short for quadrangle – the inner court of a college in Oxford; see **Court**.

Rad Cam The Radcliffe Camera, part of the Bodleian Library.

Regent House All the teaching and administrative staff of Cambridge University and its colleges, a total of some 3,000 people. They elect a Council, which is the administrative authority of the university.

Regius Professor Occupant of a chair endowed by and generally also appointed by the Crown. The first Regius Professorships were established by Henry VIII in 1540 for Cambridge (divinity, civil law, medicine, Greek and Hebrew), with five more in 1546 for Oxford.

Residence It is compulsory for Cambridge students to be 'in residence', i.e. to be accommodated within the university boundaries, which means within a three-mile radius of Great St Mary's.

Rusticated From the Latin *rusticari*, to live on the land; it means to be excluded from the university for a specific period, in contrast to being 'sent down', which means to be expelled for good.

Scarlet Day A special occasion when the doctors have to wear their scarlet gowns in public.

Schools The various faculties and their examinations (= taking schools) in the Examination Schools in Oxford High Street. Cambridge students simply 'take exams'; see **Tripos**.

Scout Cleaner in an Oxford college; known as a **bedder** in Cambridge. In the 18th century scouts were exclusively men who kept the gentlemen students' rooms clean and tidy; known as 'gyps' in Cambridge (and Durham).

Senate As Cambridge University's highest authority, it is now largely separate from the Council, and is composed of graduates with an MA or higher degree. 'A body designed to teach men the mortification of the spirit' (Geoffrey Elton).

Sporting the oak The equivalent of 'Do not disturb', referring to anyone who closes the oak door of his or her room – the term has become obsolete with the installation of double doors.

Subfusc From the Latin *subfuscus* (dark): Oxford term for the academic dress which is compulsory at matriculation, examinations and degree award ceremonies: a dark suit with white shirt and white bow tie for male students; a black dress, white blouse and black bow tie for female students; they must also wear a black gown and mortar board. 'This is positively the silliest outfit you will ever be expected to wear.' (*Oxford Handbook*, 1998)

Supervisor see **Tutor**

Target Schools Oxbridge campaign in state schools with a view to combining equal opportunities with elitist aspirations.

Terms The academic year has three terms, each of which lasts for eight weeks: Michaelmas, October – early December; Hilary (O), Lent (C), January – mid-March; Trinity (O), Easter Term (C), April – mid-June. The holidays are called 'vacations', and the summer holiday is known as the 'long vac'.

Tomkins Table League table of Cambridge colleges according to examination results, devised in 1980 by Peter Tomkins, examiner in economics, and based on the Oxford **Norrington Table**.

Torpids see **Bumps**

Town and gown Distinction between town and university going back to the Middle Ages and frequently involving conflict (less frequently cooperation).

Trinity Summer term in Oxford, named after *Trinitatis*, the Sunday after Whitsun; called 'Easter Term' in Cambridge.

Tripos Cambridge Bachelor of Arts examinations, named after the three-legged stool on which 'Mr Tripos' (the speaker at 'Commencement') used to sit declaiming humorous verses.

Tutor Teacher responsible for a small group of students, whom he/she meets once a week for about an hour; in Oxford the meeting is called a tutorial or 'tute'. In Cambridge it is called a supervision (though 'tutorial' is also used) and the teacher is known as a supervisor.

The UL Cambridge University Library.

Undergraduate Traditional term for Oxbridge students. Only the Fellows of Christ Church are called 'students'. After the BA, one can do further studies or a doctorate as a postgraduate.

The Union University debating society, not to be confused with a trade union or with the Student Union.

Varsity Cambridge student newspaper.

Varsity Match Sporting contest between the two universities, e.g. the rugby match at Twickenham (held on the second Tuesday in December).

Vice-Chancellor The administrative head of the university, formerly elected for two years from among the college Masters, but now appointed for seven years by the Council.

A College Who's Who

The following list contains only a small selection of prominent college alumni and Fellows. A few names are duplicated as they were students at one college and Fellows at another.

OXFORD

All Souls College

Sir Isaiah Berlin, historian of ideas; Sir William Blackstone, jurist; Geoffrey Faber, publisher; Sir John Hicks, winner of the Nobel Prize for economics; Sir Michael Howard, military historian; Leszek Kolakowski, philosopher; T. E. Lawrence ('Lawrence of Arabia'), writer; Thomas Linacre, physician; Sir Sarvapali Radhakrishnan, President of India; A. L. Rowse, historian; Thomas Sydenham, physician; Sir Christopher Wren, architect; Edward Young, poet

Balliol College

Thomas Bradwardine, philosopher; Richard Dawkins, ethologist; Reginald Farrer, gardener and plant collector; Christopher Hill, social historian; Sir Cyril Hinshelwood, Nobel Prizewinner for chemistry; Benjamin Jowett, classical philologist; Sir Anthony Kenny, philosopher; Anthony Leggett, Nobel Prizewinner for physics; H. E. Manning, Cardinal; Olaf V, King of Norway; Sir John Pope-Hennessy, art historian; Christopher Ricks, literary critic; John Schlesinger, film director; Adam von Trott zu Solz, resistance fighter; Sir Bernard Williams, philosopher; Michael Winterbottom, film director; John Wyclif, theologian

Prime ministers: Herbert Asquith, Sir Edward Heath, Harold Macmillan

Politicians: Lord Curzon, Denis Healey, Roy Jenkins, Boris Johnson, Chris Patten

Writers: Matthew Arnold, Hilaire Belloc, John Evelyn, Graham Greene, L. P. Hartley, Gerard Manley Hopkins, Aldous Huxley, Ved Mehta, Harold and Nigel Nicolson, Anthony Powell, Robert Southey, A. C. Swinburne

Journalists: David Astor, Cyril Connolly, Christopher Hitchens, Richard Ingrams, Lord William Rees-Mogg, Hugo Young

Brasenose College
Elias Ashmole, collector and benefactor; Vernon Bogdanor, specialist in public law; Colin Cowdrey, cricketer; Sir Arthur Evans, archaeologist; Earl Haig, field marshal; H. L. A. Hart, legal philosopher; John Middleton Murry, critic and editor; Michael Palin, comedian; Robert Runcie, Archbishop; Viscount Sidmouth, prime minister

Writers: John Buchan, William Golding, John Mortimer, Walter Pater

Christ Church
Sir Harold Acton, connoisseur; Sir Alfred J. Ayer, philosopher; Sir Joseph Banks, botanist; Sir Adrian Boult, conductor; William Buckland, palaeontologist; Alan Clark, politician; Peter Conrad, literary historian; David Dimbleby, journalist and TV presenter; Edward VII, King of England; Kurt Hahn, educationist; Robert Hooke, physicist; Edward James, art collector and patron; Frederick Lindemann, physicist; Lord Longford, historian and politician; Peter Moores, entrepreneur and collector; Ferdinand Mount, journalist and novelist; David Ogilvy, advertising guru; Sir Philip Sassoon, politician and socialite; John Taverner, composer; Hugh Trevor-Roper, historian; Jakob von Uexkull, founder of the alternative Nobel Prize; Sir William Walton, composer

Prime ministers: Sir Anthony Eden, William Gladstone

Writers: W. H. Auden, Robert Burton, Lewis Carroll, Michael Hamburger, Jan (James) Morris, John Ruskin, Sir Philip Sidney, Richard Steele, Anthony Thwaite

Corpus Christi College
Al Alvarez, poet and poker player; Ian Bostridge, opera singer; Eduard Fraenkel, classical philologist; Richard Hooker, theologian; John Keble, churchman; Nicholas Kratzer, mathematician and astronomer; Sir Keith Thomas, historian; William Waldegrave, politician

Exeter College
Sir Roger Bannister, athlete; Sir Edward Burne-Jones, painter; Richard Burton,

actor; William Morris, artist; Sir Hubert Parry, composer; Anthony Ashley-Cooper, 1st Earl of Shaftesbury, politician

Writers: Martin Amis, Alan Bennett, R. D. Blackmore, Salvador de Madariaga, Philip Pullman, Craig Raine, J. R. R. Tolkien

Harris Manchester College
John Dalton, physicist and chemist; Joseph Priestley, discoverer of oxygen

Hertford College
Edward Hyde, 1st Earl of Clarendon, politician and historian; Charles James Fox, politician; Thomas Hobbes, philosopher; Dom Mintoff, prime minister of Malta; Henry Pelham, prime minister; William Tyndale, Bible translator

Writers: John Donne, Tom Paulin, Jonathan Swift, Evelyn Waugh

Jesus College
John Cornwell, historian; Gwynfor Evans, politician; T. E. Lawrence ('Lawrence of Arabia'), writer; Beau Nash, dandy; Will Self, writer; Lord Harold Wilson, prime minister

Keble College
Ian Hamilton, literary critic; Walter Hussey, art collector; Imran Khan, cricketer; Sir Peter Pears, tenor; Andreas Whittam Smith, journalist

Lady Margaret Hall
Astrid of Norway, princess; Gertrude Bell, archaeologist and travel writer; Benazir Bhutto, prime minister of Pakistan; Caryl Churchill, playwright; Vivien Duffield, philanthropist; Lady Antonia Fraser, writer; Dame Helen Gardner, Anglicist; Nigella Lawson, cookery writer; Elizabeth, Countess of Longford, historian; Dame Pauline Neville-Jones, former Chairman of the JIC and BBC Governor; Marina Warner, writer; Baroness Mary Warnock, philosopher

Lincoln College
Howard Florey, winner of the Nobel Prize for medicine; Sir Osbert Lancaster, writer and cartoonist; John Le Carré, writer; Edward Thomas, poet; Egon Wellesz, composer and musicologist; John Wesley, Methodist

Magdalen College

Sir Richard Attenborough, actor and film director; Peter Brook, theatre director; Edmund Cartwright, inventor; Wesley K. Clark, NATO Supreme Commander; Lord Denning, Master of the Rolls; Sir John C. Eccles, winner of the Nobel Prize for medicine; Edward VIII, King of England; Niall Ferguson, historian; Edward Gibbon, historian; William Hague, politician; Ian Hislop, journalist; Michael Hofmann, poet and translator; Paul Johnson, journalist and historian; James Lees-Milne, diarist; Desmond Morris, zoologist; Lord Arthur E. Porritt, physician; Martin Routh, theologian; Erwin Schrödinger, winner of the Nobel Prize for physics; Sir Wilfred Thesiger, explorer

Writers: Joseph Addison, Sir John Betjeman, Henry Green, James Fenton, John Fuller, Alan Hollinghurst, C. S. Lewis, Sir Compton Mackenzie, Ernst Stadler, Oscar Wilde

Merton College

Theodor W. Adorno, philosopher; Sir Basil Blackwell, bookseller; Sir Thomas Bodley, classical philologist; Robert Byron, writer; John Carey, literary historian; Earl of Elgin, connoisseur; Martin Gilbert, historian; Jeremy Isaacs, film director; P. J. Kavanagh, poet; Kris Kristofferson, actor and singer; Robert May, biologist; Naruhito, Crown Prince of Japan; Sir Henry Savile, scholar; Mark Thompson, Director General of the BBC; Nikolaas Tinbergen, winner of the Nobel Prize for medicine; J. R. R. Tolkien, Anglicist and writer; Sir Angus Wilson, writer; John Wyclif, theologian

New College

Kate Beckinsale, actress; Tony Benn, politician; Richard Dawkins, ethologist; Richard Ellmann, literary critic; Robin Lane Fox, classical philologist and garden columnist; Hugh Gaitskell, politician; Hugh Grant, actor; Sir Julian Huxley, biologist; Brian Johnston, cricket commentator; Hermione Lee, literary historian; Lord Longford, politician; Neil MacGregor, museum director; Gilbert Murray, Hellenist; E. F. Schumacher, economist; W. A. Spooner, scholar; Naomi Wolf, feminist; James Woodforde, diarist

Writers: John Fowles, John Galsworthy, Dennis Potter, Craig Raine, Sydney Smith, Adam Thirlwell, D. M. Thomas, A. N. Wilson

Nuffield College
Lord Max Beloff, historian; James Mirrlees, Nobel Prizewinner for economics

Oriel College
Thomas Arnold, headmaster; Beau Brummel, dandy; Raymond Klibansky, philosopher; Sir Thomas More, humanist; John Henry Newman, theologian; Sir Walter Raleigh, courtier and navigator; Stefan von Ratibor, manager of Christie's; Cecil Rhodes, entrepreneur and politician; Felix Graf von Schwerin, diplomat and resistance fighter; A. J. P. Taylor, historian; Sir Alexander Todd, winner of the Nobel Prize for chemistry; Gilbert White, nature writer

Pembroke College
Francis Beaumont, playwright; Sir Thomas Browne, physician and essayist; Sir Rocco Forte, hotelier; J. William Fulbright, US Senator; Michael Heseltine, politician; Samuel Johnson, writer and lexicographer; James Smithson, founder of the Smithsonian Institute; George Whitefield, Methodist

The Queen's College
Rowan Atkinson, comedian; Jeremy Bentham, philosopher; Tim Berners-Lee, inventor of the World Wide Web; Alec Clifton-Taylor, architectural historian; William Gilpin, writer; Edmund Halley, astronomer; Edwin Hubble, astronomer; Ruth Kelly, politician; Michael Naumann, journalist; Walter Pater, art critic and essayist; Leopold Stokowski, conductor

Ruskin College
John Prescott, politician; Raphael Samuel, historian; Norman Willis, union leader

St Anne's College
Mary Archer, chemist; Karen Armstrong, writer; Sister Wendy Beckett, Carmelite nun and art critic; Tina Brown, journalist; Edwina Currie, politician; Helen Fielding, writer; Zoë Heller, journalist; Elizabeth Jennings, poet; Penelope Lively, writer; Naomi Mitchison, writer; Polly Toynbee, journalist; Baroness Young, politician

St Antony's College
Lord Ralf Dahrendorf, sociologist; Timothy Garton Ash, historian; Albert Hourani, Arabist; Theodore Zeldin, historian and anthropologist

St Catherine's College

J. Paul Getty, philanthropist; Peter Levi, literary historian and poet; Peter Mandelson, politician; Tom Phillips, artist; Matthew Pinsent, rower and Olympic gold medallist; Sir John Walker, winner of the Nobel Prize for chemistry; Simon Winchester, journalist; Jeanette Winterson, writer

St Edmund Hall

Sir Richard Blackmore, physician; Sir Robin Day, journalist; Terry Jones, comedian; Sir Michael Rose, General; John Wells, satirist

St Hilda's College

Wendy Cope, poet; Jenny Joseph, poet and children's author; Hermione Lee, literary historian; Val McDermid, thriller-writer; Kate Millett, feminist; Jacqueline du Pré, cellist; Barbara Pym, writer; Gillian Shephard, politician; Ann Thwaite, writer

St Hugh's College

Elizabeth Anscombe, philosopher; Barbara Castle, politician; Ann Pellew, RAF pilot; Aung San Suu Kyi, winner of the Nobel Prize for peace

St John's College

Tony Blair, prime minister; Edmund Campion, martyr; Inspector Morse, fictional detective; Lester Pearson, prime minister of Canada; Dean Rusk, US Secretary of State; Jethro Tull, agriculturalist; Peter Zadek, theatre director

Writers: Sir Kingsley Amis, Robert Graves, A. E. Housman, John Lanchester, Philip Larkin

St Peter's College

Edward Akufo-Addo, President of Ghana; Ken Loach, film director; Sir Paul Reeves, Governor-General of New Zealand

Somerville College

Katherine Duncan-Jones, literary historian; Philippa Foot, philosopher; Indira Gandhi, prime minister of India; Dorothy Hodgkin, winner of the Nobel Prize for chemistry; Emma Kirkby, soprano; Esther Rantzen, TV presenter; Margaret Thatcher, prime minister; Dame Janet Vaughan, pathologist; Shirley Williams, politician

Writers: Nina Bawden, Vera Brittain, Penelope Fitzgerald, Margaret Forster, Victoria Glendinning, Liz Jensen, Margaret Kennedy, Dame Rose Macaulay, Dame Iris Murdoch, Dorothy L. Sayers

Trinity College
Count Albrecht von Bernstorff, diplomat and resistance fighter; Lord Kenneth Clark, politician; Anthony Crosland, politician; Francis Haskell, art historian; Miles Kington, columnist; Sir Hans Krebs, winner of the Nobel Prize for medicine; John Henry Newman, Cardinal; Lord North, prime minister; William Pitt the Elder, statesman; Peter Stothard, journalist; Ronald Syme, historian;

Writers: John Aubrey, Justin Cartwright, James Elroy Flecker, Walter Savage Landor, Sir Arthur Quiller-Couch, Sir Terence Rattigan, Thomas Warton

University College
Clement Attlee, prime minister; Bill Clinton, US President; Max Hastings, journalist; Bob Hawke, prime minister of Australia; Stephen Hawking, astrophysicist; Sir William Jones, Orientalist and jurist; Sir Thomas Phillipps, bibliomaniac; John Radcliffe, physician; Peter Snow, journalist

Writers: C. S. Lewis, Andrew Motion, Sir V. S. Naipaul, Percy Bysshe Shelley, Sir Stephen Spender

Wadham College
Lindsay Anderson, film director; Sir Thomas Beecham, conductor; John Birt, Director-General of the BBC; Sir Robert Blake, Admiral; Melvyn Bragg, writer and journalist; Lord Alan Bullock, historian; Cecil Day-Lewis, Poet Laureate; Sir Michael Foot, politician; C. B. Fry, cricketer and all-round sportsman; Bernard O'Donoghue, poet and Anglicist; Earl of Rochester, poet; Nathaniel Rothschild, heir; Sir Christopher Wren, architect

Wolfson College
Sir Isaiah Berlin, historian of ideas; Norman Davies, historian; Dorothy Hodgkin, winner of the Nobel Prize for chemistry; Raymond Klibansky, philosopher; Erich Segal, writer and literary historian

Worcester College

Patrick Bahners, journalist; Thomas de Quincey, writer; Florian Illies, journalist; Rupert Murdoch, media tycoon; Sir Peter Palumbo, property tycoon; Ben Pimlott, historian and journalist; Sir Timothy Sainsbury, entrepreneur; Norman Stone, historian; Woodrow Wyatt, politician and diarist

CAMBRIDGE

Christ's College

Ali G, aka Sacha Baron Cohen, comedian; Sir Anthony Caro, sculptor; Charles Darwin, biologist; Sir Frank Kermode, literary historian; Phillip King, sculptor; Frank Kingdon-Ward, botanist; James E. Meade, winner of the Nobel Prize for economics; John Milton, poet; Lord Mountbatten, Admiral; Roy Porter, historian; Simon Schama, cultural historian; C. P. Snow, physicist and novelist; Sir Alexander Todd, winner of the Nobel Prize for chemistry; Rowan Williams, Archbishop of Canterbury

Churchill College

Sir Alec Broers, nanotechnologist; Sir John Cockcroft, winner of the Nobel Prize for physics; Francis Crick, winner of the Nobel Prize for medicine; Sir William Hawthorne, engineer; George Steiner, specialist in comparative literature; Michael Young, sociologist

Clare College

Peter Ackroyd, writer; Sir David Attenborough, naturalist; David Cannadine, historian; Sir Philip Dowson, architect; Nicholas Ferrar, theologian; Hugh Latimer, Reformer and martyr; Andrew Manze, Baroque violinist; Paul Mellon, millionaire and patron of the arts; Sir Roger Norrington, conductor; Siegfried Sassoon, poet; Frank Schirrmacher, journalist; William Whitehead, Poet Laureate

Corpus Christi College

Robert Browne, Nonconformist; Thomas Cavendish, round-the-world yachtsman; John Fletcher, playwright; Christopher Isherwood, writer; Christopher Marlowe, playwright; Robert McCrum, journalist; John Cowper Powys, writer;

Oliver Rackham, eco-historian; Sir George Thomson, winner of the Nobel Prize for physics

Downing College

Mike Atherton, cricketer; Quentin Blake, children's author and illustrator; John Cleese, comedian; Lord Goodman, jurist; F. R. Leavis, literary historian; F. W. Maitland, legal historian; Sir Trevor Nunn, theatre director; Michael Winner, film director

Emmanuel College

Peter Burke, cultural historian; Graham Chapman, comedian; Sebastian Faulks, writer; Michael Frayn, writer; Eddie George, banker; John Harvard, Puritan; Geoffrey Hill, poet and Anglicist; Sir F. G. Hopkins, winner of the Nobel Prize for medicine; William Law, Methodist; F. R. Leavis, literary historian; Herchel Smith, chemist; Sir William Temple, Swift's mentor

Fitzwilliam College

John Costello, historian; Lee Kuan Yew, prime minister of Singapore; David Starkey, historian

Girton College

Sally Beauman, writer; Dame Mary Lucy Cartwright, mathematician; Valerie Grove, journalist; Penelope Hobhouse, gardener; Jennifer Jenkins, Director General of the National Trust; Rosamond Lehmann, writer; Kathleen Raine, poet; Eugénie Sellers Strong, archaeologist; Baroness Mary Warnock, philosopher; Helen Waterhouse, archaeologist

Gonville and Caius College

Alain de Botton, writer; Alastair Campbell, spin doctor; Sir James Chadwick, winner of the Nobel Prize for physics; Kenneth Clarke, politician; David Frost, TV personality; Sir Thomas Gresham, financier and philanthropist; Hamish Hamilton, publisher; William Harvey, physician; Stephen Hawking, astrophysicist; Norman Lamont, politician; Joseph Needham, Sinologist; Michael J. Oakeshott, philosopher; E. S. Prior, architect; Jeremy Prynne, poet; Jonathan Sacks, rabbi; Norman Stone, historian; William Wilkins, architect; John Dover Wilson, Shakespearean scholar

Jesus College

Samuel Taylor Coleridge, poet; Alistair Cooke, journalist; John Cornwell, historian of ideas; Thomas Cranmer, Archbishop and martyr; Ted Dexter, cricketer; Terry Eagleton, literary historian; John Flamsteed, astronomer; David Hare, playwright; Nick Hornby, writer; Sir Leslie Martin, architect; Sir Arthur Quiller-Couch, literary historian; Roger Scruton, journalist; Lord Snowdon, photographer; Laurence Sterne, writer; Prince Edward, Earl of Wessex

King's College

Thomas Adès, composer; Noel Annan, historian; Neal Ascherson, journalist; C. R. Ashbee, architect; Patrick Bateson, behavioural scientist; Mark Boxer, cartoonist; Rupert Brooke, poet; Bill Buford, journalist; Charles Clarke, politician; Tam Dalyell, politician; E. M. Forster, writer; Roger Fry, art critic and painter; Sir John Eliot Gardiner, conductor; Anthony Giddens, sociologist; Sir John Harington, inventor of the flushing lavatory; Eric Hobsbawm, historian; Simon Hoggart, journalist; Michael Ignatieff, journalist; M. R. James, medievalist and author; John Maynard Keynes, economist; Arthur Cecil Pigou, political economist; Stephen Poliakoff, playwright; Sir Martin Rees, astronomer; Salman Rushdie, writer; George Rylands, Anglicist; David Sainsbury, politician; Frederick Sanger, winner of the Nobel Prize for chemistry; Charles Saumarez Smith, museum director; Zadie Smith, writer; Susan Tomes, pianist; Alan Turing, mathematician; Horace Walpole, writer; Sir Robert Walpole, prime minister; Judith Weir, composer; Patrick White, winner of the Nobel Prize for literature

Magdalene College

Nicholas Boyle, Germanist; Monty Don, gardener; Sir William Empson, poet and literary historian; Bamber Gascoigne, writer and TV presenter; Michael Hofmann, poet and translator; Charles Kingsley, writer; C. S. Lewis, writer; George Mallory, mountaineer; Samuel Pepys, diarist; Michael Redgrave, actor; Nicholas Shakespeare, writer; John Simpson, journalist

New Hall

Elizabeth Anscombe, philosopher; Anita Brookner, writer and art historian; Dame Rosemary Murray, chemist; Maggie O'Farrell, writer; Tilda Swinton, actress

Newnham College

Mary Archer, chemist; Joan Bakewell, journalist; Antonia S. Byatt, writer;

Margaret Drabble, writer; Jane Goodall, primatologist; Germaine Greer, literary historian and feminist; Jane Harrison, Hellenist; Dorothy Hodgkin, winner of the Nobel Prize for chemistry; Lisa Jardine, historian and biographer; Julia Neuberger, rabbi; Frances Partridge, diarist; Sylvia Plath, poet; Fiona Reynolds, Director General of the National Trust; Pernel Strachey, literary historian; Emma Thompson, actress; Claire Tomalin, literary critic and biographer

Pembroke College
Richard A. Butler, politician; Peter Cook, comedian; Stephen Greenblatt, literary critic; Christopher Hogwood, musician; Eric Idle, comedian; Peter May, cricketer; William Pitt the Younger, prime minister; Rodney R. Porter, winner of the Nobel Prize for medicine; Nicholas Ridley, Reformer and martyr; Chris Smith, politician; Sir George Gabriel Stokes, mathematician and physicist; William Turner, botanist

Writers: Richard Crashaw, Thomas Gray, Ted Hughes, Clive James, Tom Sharpe, Christopher Smart, Edmund Spenser, David Henry Wilson

Peterhouse
Charles Babbage, mathematician; Thomas Campion, poet and composer; Sir Christopher Cockerell, engineer and inventor; Sir Richard Eyre, theatre director; Thomas Gray, poet; Colin Greenwood, musician; Michael Howard, politician; Lord William Kelvin, physicist; Sir John Kendrew and Sir Aaron Klug, molecular biologists and Nobel laureates; James Mason, actor; Max Perutz, winner of the Nobel Prize for chemistry; Michael Portillo, politician; Arthur M. Schlesinger Jr, journalist; John Skelton, poet; David Watkin, art historian; Sir Frank Whittle, engineer and inventor; Sir Peregrine Worsthorne, journalist

Queens' College
Harold W. Bailey, Sanskrit expert; Edward Cullinan, architect; Erasmus of Rotterdam, humanist; Lord Falconer, politician; Stephen Fry, actor and writer; Thomas Fuller, historian; Roland Penrose, painter and writer; Charles Villiers Stanford, composer; Graham Swift, writer; Charles Tomlinson, poet; T. H. White, writer

St Catharine's College
Howard Brenton, playwright; Donald Davie, poet and critic; Sir Peter Hall, theatre director; Malcolm Lowry, writer; Sir Ian McKellen, actor; Tim Parks, writer; Jeremy Paxman, journalist

St John's College

Roger Ascham, humanist; Sir Cecil Beaton, photographer; Mike Brearley, cricketer; Sir Hugh Casson, architect; John Dee, mathematician and astrologer; Sir Vivian Fuchs, explorer; Sir John Herschel, astronomer; Sir Harry Hinsley, historian; Philip Howard, Saint; Sir Derek Jacobi, actor; Alfred Marshall, economist; Jonathan Miller, stage and opera director and author; Sir Nikolaus Pevsner, art historian; Henry Wriothesley, 3rd Earl of Southampton, patron of Shakespeare; Lord Thomson of Fleet, press baron; William Wilberforce, politician

Writers: Douglas Adams, William Barnes, Samuel Butler, Robert Herrick, Frederic Raphael, William Wordsworth, Sir Thomas Wyatt

Selwyn College

John Selwyn Gummer, politician; Robert Harris, writer; Howard Jacobson, novelist and columnist; Hugh Laurie, actor; Malcolm Muggeridge, journalist

Sidney Sussex College

Oliver Cromwell, statesman; Earl of Manchester, General; David Owen, politician; Charles Thomson Rees Wilson, winner of the Nobel Prize for physics; Sir John Walker, winner of the Nobel Prize for chemistry

Trinity College

Charles Babbage, mathematician; Lord Carnarvon, Egyptologist; James George Frazer, anthropologist; Antony Gormley, sculptor; Michael Hofmann, poet and translator; Richard MacCormac, architect; Charles Rolls, co-founder of Rolls Royce; John Montagu, 4th Earl of Sandwich, inventor of the sandwich; W. H. Fox Talbot, pioneer of photography; Ralph Vaughan Williams, composer; Sir Clough Williams-Ellis, architect

Writers: Lord Byron, John Dryden, Edward Fitzgerald, Simon Gray, George Herbert, A. E. Housman, Andrew Marvell, A. A. Milne, Vladimir Nabokov, Peter Shaffer, Lytton Strachey, Lord Alfred Tennyson, William Thackeray

Prime ministers: Stanley Baldwin, Arthur Balfour, Rajiv Gandhi, Earl Grey, Viscount Melbourne, Jawaharlal Nehru

Politicians: Leon Brittan, Douglas Hurd, Enoch Powell

Kings and Princes: Edward VII, George VI, Charles Windsor

Spies: Anthony Blunt, Guy Burgess, John Cairncross, Kim Philby

Philosophers: Francis Bacon, G. E. Moore, Bertrand Russell, Henry Sidgwick, A. N. Whitehead, Ludwig Wittgenstein

Historians: Lord Acton, E. H. Carr, Richard J. Evans, Orlando Figes, Thomas Babington Macaulay, Steven Runciman, G. M. Trevelyan

Natural scientists: James Clerk Maxwell, Isaac Newton, John Ray, Victor Rothschild, Ernest Rutherford

Nobel laureates: Lord Adrian, William and Lawrence Bragg, Alan Hodgkin, Brian Josephson, Sir John Kendrew, Amartya Sen, J. J. Thomson

Trinity Hall
Hans Blix, UN chief weapons inspector; Edward Bulwer-Lytton, writer; Ronald Firbank, writer; Viscount Fitzwilliam, art collector and benefactor; Sir Norman Fowler, politician; Stephen Gardiner, Lord Chancellor; Robert Herrick, poet; Lord Howard of Effingham, Admiral; Sir Geoffrey Howe, politician; Donald MacLean, spy; J. B. Priestley, writer; Sir Leslie Stephen, literary historian; Edmund de Waal, potter

Museums and Other Sights to See in Oxford

'For an hour [Morse] wandered contentedly around the Ashmolean, where amongst other delights he stood for many minutes in front of the Giorgione and the Tiepolo.'
Colin Dexter, *Service of All the Dead*, 1979

Dialling code for Oxford: 01865

Ashmolean Museum
Beaumont St
Tel. 278000
www.ashmol.ox.ac.uk
Tue–Sat 10 am–5 pm; Thu until 7 pm in summer months; Sun 12–5 pm

Bate Collection of Musical Instruments
Faculty of Music, St Aldate's St
Tel. 276139
Based on the collection of the BBC producer Philip Bate (1909–99)
Mon–Fri 2–5 pm; Sat 10 am–12 pm

Bodleian Library
Broad St
Tel. 277216
www.bodley.ox.ac.uk
Mon–Fri 9 am–5 pm; Sat 9 am–12.30 pm
Only Convocation House, Divinity School and Duke Humfrey's Library are open to visitors.

The Burton Taylor Theatre
Gloucester St
Tel. 798600
www.oxfordplayhouse.burtontaylor.com
Studio theatre of the Oxford Playhouse with many student productions.

Christ Church Picture Gallery
Oriel Square
Tel. 276172
www.chch.ox.ac.uk
College collection of old masters, with changing exhibitions.
Oct–Mar: Mon–Sat 10.30 am–1 pm, 2–4.30 pm; Sun 2–4.30 pm
April–Sept: Mon–Sat 10.30 am–5 pm; Sun 2–5 pm

Covered Market
Between High St and Market St
Victorian market, a favourite with both town and gown.
Mon–Sat 8.30 am–5.30 pm

Jacqueline du Pré Music Building
St Hilda's College
Cowley Place
Tel. 276821
www.sthildas.ox.ac.uk
College concert hall with chamber concerts open to public.

Modern Art Oxford
30 Pembroke St
Tel. 722733
www.modernartoxford.org.uk
Tue–Sat 10 am–5 pm; Sun 12–5 pm

Museum of the History of Science
Broad St
Tel. 277280
www.mhs.ox.ac.uk
Tue–Sat 12–4 pm; Sun 2–5 pm

Museum of Oxford
St Aldgate's
Tel. 252761
www.oxford.gov.uk/tourism/museum.cfm
History of city and university
Tue–Fri 10 am–4 pm; Sat 10 am–5 pm; Sun
12–4 pm

The Old Fire Station
40 George St
Tel. 794490
Studio theatre next to Apollo Theatre
(opened 1934); touring companies and
student productions.

Oxford Playhouse
Beaumont St
Tel. 798600
www.oxfordplayhouse.com
Built in 1938; many productions go on to
the West End.

The Oxford Story
6 Broad St
Tel. 728822
www.oxfordstory.co.uk
History of the city and university, jazzed
up for tourists ('From DON to DNA').
Mon–Sat 10 am–4.30 pm; Sun
11 am–4.30 pm

The Painted Room
3 Cornmarket
Tel. 791017
Renaissance wall paintings. By
appointment only.

The Pasternak Trust
Paintings and drawings by Leonid
Pasternak.
Tel. 515994
1st Sunday of the month, 2–4 pm, by
appointment only.

Pitt Rivers Museum
Parks Rd
Tel. 270927
www.prm.ox.ac.uk
Archaeology and anthropology museum
Daily 12–4.30 pm

Sheldonian Theatre
Broad St
Tel. 277299
www.sheldon.ox.ac.uk
For official university functions, academic
ceremonies, concerts and lectures.
Mon–Sat 10 am–12.30pm and 2–4.30 pm

St Michael at the North Gate
Cornmarket St
Tel. 240940
www.oxmust.co.uk/stmichael/
Church tower, Oxford's oldest building.
Daily 10 am–5 pm

University Church of St Mary the Virgin
High St
Tel. 243806
www.university-church.ox.ac.uk
Church with fine view from tower.
Mon–Sat 9 am–5 pm; Sun 12–5 pm

University Museum of Natural History
Parks Rd
Tel. 272950
www.oum.ox.ac.uk
Daily 12–5 pm

University of Oxford Botanic Garden
Rose Lane
Tel. 286690
www.botanic-garden.ox.ac.uk
Daily 9 am–4.30 pm (6 pm May to August)
Harcourt Arboretum in Nuneham
Courtenay (10 km south, A423):
23 hectares, laid out in 1835.
Daily 10 am–4.30 pm

University and Colleges: Oxford

'Undergraduates owe their happiness chiefly to the consciousness that they are no longer at school. The nonsense which was knocked out of them at school is all put gently back at Oxford or Cambridge.'
Sir Max Beerbohm, 1899

University of Oxford
University Offices
Wellington Square
OX1 2JD
Tel. 280545
www.ox.ac.uk

Oxford Colleges Admissions Office
Tel. 270207

Oxford University Student Union
28 Little Clarendon St
OX1 2HU
Tel. 270777
www.ousu.ac.uk

The Oxford Union
Frewin Court
OX1 3JB
Tel. 241353
www.oxfordunion.org

Oxford University Press
Great Clarendon St
OX 2 6DP
Tel. 267268
ww.oup.co.uk

Homepage of the Oxford English Dictionary:
www.oed.com
Small OUP museum, open Mon–Fri 10 am–4 pm, by appointment only.
Tel. 353527

Oxford University Society
Oxenford House
OX1 3AB
Tel. 288088
www.alumni.ox.ac.uk
Oxford alumni office; the homepage includes information about more than 40 Oxford societies all over the world.

Rhodes House
South Parks Rd
OX1 3RG
Tel. 270909

Colleges

Colleges are private institutions for residence and study; they are not museums. Opening times are therefore restricted, especially during examinations. In order to avoid disappointment, you should telephone before visiting, or ask the porter. The following list includes some fixed opening times, plus addresses and websites; in brackets, the date when each college was founded.

All Souls College (1438)
High St
OX1 4AL
Tel. 279379
www.all-souls.ox.ac.uk
Mon–Fri 2–4.30 pm

Balliol College (1263/68)
Broad St
OX1 3BJ
Tel. 277777
www.balliol.ox.ac.uk

Brasenose College (1509)
Radcliffe Square
OX1 4AJ
Tel. 277830
www.bnc.ox.ac.uk

Christ Church (1546)
St Aldgate's St
OX1 1DP
Tel. 276150
www.chch.ox.ac.uk
Picture Gallery: Mon–Sat 10.30 am–1 pm,
2–4.30 pm; Sun 2–4.30 pm

Corpus Christi College (1517)
Merton St
OX1 4JF
Tel. 276700
www.ccc.ox.ac.uk

Exeter College (1314)
Turl St
OX1 3DP
Tel. 279600
www.exeter.ox.ac.uk
Open daily 2–5 pm

Green College (1979)
Woodstock Rd
OX2 6HG
Tel. 274770
www.green.ox.ac.uk

Harris Manchester College (1786)
Mansfield Rd
OX1 3TD
Tel. 271006
www.hmc.ox.ac.uk

Hertford College (1740)
Catte St
OX1 3BW
Tel. 279400
www.hertford.ox.ac.uk

Jesus College (1571)
Turl St
OX1 3DW
Tel. 279700
www.jesus.ox.ac.uk

Keble College (1870)
Parks Rd
OX1 3PG
Tel. 272727
www.keble.ox.ac.uk

Kellogg College (1990)
Wellington Square
OX1 2JA
Tel. 270383
www.kellogg.ox.ac.uk

Lady Margaret Hall (1878)
Norham Gardens
OX2 6QA
Tel. 274300
www.lmh.ox.ac.uk

Linacre College (1962)
St Cross Rd
OX1 3JA
Tel. 271650
www.linacre.ox.ac.uk

Lincoln College (1427)
Turl St
OX1 3DR
Tel. 279800
www.lincoln.ox.ac.uk
Mon–Sat 11 am–5 pm; Sun 2–5 pm

Magdalen College (1458)
High St
OX1 4AU
Tel. 276000
www.magd.ox.ac.uk
Daily 1–6 pm

Mansfield College (1886)
Mansfield Rd
OX1 3TF
Tel. 270999
www.mansfield.ox.ac.uk

Merton College (1264)
Merton St
OX1 4JD
Tel. 276310
www.merton.ox.ac.uk
Mon–Fri 2–4 pm; Sat–Sun 10 am–4 pm

New College (1379)
Holywell St
OX1 3BN
Tel. 279555
www.new.ox.ac.uk
April–October daily 11 am–5 pm; winter
2–4 pm

Nuffield College (1937)
New Road
OX1 1NF
Tel. 278500
www.nuff.ox.ac.uk

Oriel College (1326)
Oriel Square
OX1 4EW
Tel. 276555
www.oriel.ox.ac.uk

Pembroke College (1624)
Pembroke Square
OX1 1DW
Tel. 276444
www.pmb.ox.ac.uk

The Queen's College (1341)
High St
OX1 4AW
Tel. 279120
www.queens.ox.ac.uk

St Anne's College (1879)
Woodstock Rd
OX2 6HS
Tel. 274800
www.st-annes.ox.ac.uk

St Antony's College (1950)
62 Woodstock Rd
OX2 6JF
Tel. 284700
www.sant.ox.ac.uk

St Catherine's College (1963)
Manor Rd
OX1 3UJ
Tel. 271700
www.stcatz.ox.ac.uk

St Cross College (1965)
St Giles'
OX1 3LZ
Tel. 278458
www.stx.ox.ac.uk

St Edmund Hall (1278)
Queen's Lane
OX1 4AR
Tel. 279000
www.seh.ox.ac.uk

St Hilda's College (1893)
Cowley Place
OX4 1DY
Tel. 276884
www.sthildas.ox.ac.uk

St Hugh's College (1886)
St Margaret's Rd
OX2 6LE
Tel. 274900
www.st-hughs.ox.ac.uk

St John's College (1555)
St Giles'
OX1 3JP
Tel. 277300
www.sjc.ox.ac.uk

St Peter's College (1929)
New Inn Hall St
OX1 2DL
Tel. 278900
www.spc.ox.ac.uk

Somerville College (1879)
Woodstock Rd
OX2 6HD
Tel. 270600
www.some.ox.ac.uk

Templeton College (1965)
Kennington Rd
OX1 5NY
Tel. 422500
www.templeton.ox.ac.uk

Trinity College (1555)
Broad St
OX1 3BH
Tel. 279900
www.trinity.ox.ac.uk

University College (1249)
High St
OX1 4BH
Tel. 276602
www.univ.ox.ac.uk

Wadham College (1610)
Parks Rd
OX1 3PN
Tel. 277900
www.wadham.ox.ac.uk
In termtime, daily 1–4.15 pm;
out of term 10.30–11.45 am, 1–4.15 pm

Wolfson College (1964)
Lintons Rd
OX2 6UD
Tel. 274100
www.wolfson.ox.ac.uk

Worcester College (1714)
Worcester St
OX1 1DW
Tel. 278300
www.worcester.ox.ac.uk

Museums and Other Sights to See in Cambridge

Dialling code for Cambridge: 01223

ADC Theatre
Park St
Tel. 300085 & 359547
www.adc-theatre.cam.ac.uk
ADC stands for Amateur Dramatic Club,
England's oldest university theatre.
Footlights revue in June.

Cambridge Arts Theatre
6 St Edward's Passage
(Entrance: Peas Hill)
Tel. 503333
www.cambridgeartstheatre.com
Founded in 1936 by Maynard Keynes,
known as The Arts. Touring productions
of theatre, musicals and ballet.

Cambridge Corn Exchange
Wheeler St
Tel. 357851
www.cornex.co.uk
Former Victorian corn exchange, built
1875. Now a venue for concerts and other
events.

Cambridge & County Folk Museum
2 Castle St
Tel. 355159
www.folkmuseum.org.uk
Tues–Sat 10.30 am–5 pm; Sun 2–5 pm

**Cambridge Shakespeare Festival
Company**
Tel. 511139
Founded in 1988 by David Crilly.
Holds Shakespeare productions in
college gardens.
www.cambridgeshakespeare.com

Cambridge University Botanic Garden
Bateman St
Tel. 336265
www.botanic.cam.ac.uk
Apr–Sep 10 am–6 pm; Feb, Mar & Oct
10 am–5 pm; Nov–Jan 10 am–4 pm

Cambridge University Library
West Rd
Tel. 333000
www.lib.cam.ac.uk
Mon–Fri 9 am–7.15 pm; Sat 9 am–5 pm

Cambridge University Press
Shaftesbury Rd
Tel. 358331
Bookshop: 1 Trinity St
Tel. 333333
www.cup.cam.ac.uk
Mon–Sat 9 am–5.30 pm; Sun 11 am–5 pm

Fitzwilliam Museum
Trumpington St
Tel. 332900
www.fitzmuseum.cam.ac.uk
Large collections, small café
and museum shop.
Tue–Sat 10 am–5 pm; Sun 12–5pm

The Junction
Clifton Road
Tel. 511511
www.junction.co.uk
Arts centre, theatre and music venue.

Kettle's Yard
Castle St
Tel. 352124
www.kettlesyard.co.uk
House of art collector Jim Ede, gallery
with changing exhibitions.
Summer: Tue–Sun 1.30–4.30 pm
Winter: Tue–Sun 2–4 pm

**Museum of Archaeology and
Anthropology**
Downing St
Tel. 333516
http://museum-server.archanth.cam.ac.uk
The Oceania collection is a particular
highlight.
Tue–Sat 2–4.30 pm

Museum of Classical Archaeology
Sidgwick Avenue
Tel. 335153
www.classics.cam.ac.uk
Mon–Fri 2–5 pm; Sat 10 am–1 pm

Museum of Zoology
Downing St
Tel. 336650
www.zoo.cam.ac.uk
Mon–Fri 10 am–4.45 pm

Primavera
10 King's Parade
Tel. 357708
www.primaverauk.com
Founded 1946. Gallery of contemporary
British crafts.

Scott Polar Research Institute
Lensfield Rd
Tel. 336540
www.spri.cam.ac.uk
Founded 1934, with small museum on the
history of British expeditions to the
Arctic and Antarctic.
Tue–Sat 2.30–4 pm

Sedgwick Museum of Earth Sciences
Downing St
Tel. 333456
www.sedgwickmuseum.org
Large collections of fossils and minerals.
Mon–Fri 9 am–1 pm, 2–5 pm; Sat
10 am–4 pm

**Whipple Museum of the
History of Science**
Free School Lane
Tel. 330906
www.hps.cam.ac.uk/whipple/
Mon–Fri 12.30–4.30 pm

University and Colleges: Cambridge

In Thomas Bernhard's novel *Korrektur* (*Correction*), Roithamer, an Austrian professor in Cambridge, comments, 'It is always astonishing how many people, while they are still young and very often at just the right moment, go to England in order to be able to develop, and almost all of those who have been to England have got on in life.'

Below are the important addresses:

University of Cambridge
The Old Schools
Trinity Lane
CB2 1TN
Tel. 337733
www.cam.ac.uk

Cambridge Admissions Office
Fitzwilliam House
32 Trumpington St
CB2 1QY
Tel. 333308
www.cam.ac.uk/admissions

Cambridge University Student's Union
11–12 Trumpington St
CB2 1QA
Tel. 356454
www.cusu.cam.ac.uk

Cambridge Alumni Office
1 Quayside
Bridge St
CB5 8AB
Tel. 332288
www.foundation.cam.ac.uk

Colleges
(foundation date in brackets)

'Know the Master of Jesus
Does hugely displease us.'
Thomas Gray (1716–71),
'Satire on the Heads of Houses'

Christ's College (1505)
St Andrew's St
CB2 3BU
Tel. 334900
www.christs.cam.ac.uk

Churchill College (1960)
Storey's Way
CB3 0DS
Tel. 336000
www.chu.cam.ac.uk

Clare College (1326)
Trinity Lane
CB2 1TL
Tel. 333200
www.clare.cam.ac.uk

Clare Hall (1966)
Herschel Rd
CB3 9AL
Tel. 332360
www.clarehall.cam.ac.uk

Corpus Christi College (1352)
Trumpington St
CB2 1RH
Tel. 338000
www.corpus.cam.ac.uk

Darwin College (1964)
Silver St
CB3 9EU
Tel. 335660
www.dar.cam.ac.uk

Downing College (1800)
Regent St
CB2 1DQ
Tel. 334800
www.dow.cam.ac.uk

Emmanuel College (1584)
St Andrew's St
CB2 3AP
Tel. 334200
www.emma.cam.ac.uk

Fitzwilliam College (1869)
Huntingdon Rd
CB3 0DG
Tel. 332000
www.fitz.cam.ac.uk

Girton College (1869)
Huntingdon Rd
CB3 0JG
Tel. 338999
www.girton.cam.ac.uk

Gonville and Caius College (1348/1557)
Trinity St
CB2 1TA
Tel. 332400
www.cai.cam.ac.uk

Homerton College (1768)
Hills Rd
CB2 2PH
Tel. 507111
www.homerton.cam.ac.uk

Hughes Hall (1885)
Mortimer Rd
CB1 2EW
Tel. 334898
www.hughes.cam.ac.uk

Jesus College (1496)
Jesus Lane
CB5 8BL
Tel. 339339
www.jesus.cam.ac.uk

King's College (1441)
King's Parade
CB2 1ST
Tel. 331100
www.kings.cam.ac.uk

Lucy Cavendish College (1965)
Lady Margaret Rd
CB3 0BU
Tel. 332190
www.lucy-cav.cam.ac.uk

Magdalene College (1542)
Magdalene St
CB3 0AG
Tel. 332100
www.magd.cam.ac.uk

New Hall (1954)
Huntingdon Rd
CB3 0DF
Tel. 762100
www.newhall.cam.ac.uk

Newnham College (1871)
Sidgwick Avenue
CB3 9DF
Tel. 335700
www.newn.cam.ac.uk

Pembroke College (1347)
Trumpington St
CB2 1RF
Tel. 338100
www.pem.cam.ac.uk

Peterhouse (1280–84)
Trumpington St
CB2 1RD
Tel. 338200
www.pet.cam.ac.uk

Queens' College (1448)
Queen's Lane
CB3 9ET
Tel. 335511
www.quns.cam.ac.uk

Robinson College (1979)
Grange Rd
CB3 9AN
Tel. 339100
www.robinson.cam.ac.uk

St Catharine's College (1473)
Trumpington St
CB2 1RL
Tel. 338300
www.caths.cam.ac.uk

St Edmund's College (1896)
Mount Pleasant
CB3 OBN
Tel. 336250
www.st-edmunds.cam.ac.uk

St John's College (1511)
St John's St
CB2 1TP
Tel. 338600
www.joh.cam.ac.uk

Selwyn College (1882)
Grange Rd
CB3 9DQ
Tel. 335846
www.sel.cam.ac.uk

Sidney Sussex College (1596)
Sidney St
CB2 3HU
Tel. 338800
www.sid.cam.ac.uk

Trinity College (1546)
Trinity St
CB2 1TQ
Tel. 338400
www.trin.cam.ac.uk

Trinity Hall (1350)
Trinity Lane
CB2 1TJ
Tel. 332500
www.trinhall.cam.ac.uk

Wolfson College (1965)
Barton Rd
CB3 9BB
Tel. 335900
www.wolfson.cam.ac.uk

Festivals and Events

'Miss Dobson, we have an institution in Cambridge, known as May Week. It isn't exactly a week and it isn't in May, but it can be quite pleasant.'
S. C. Roberts, *Zuleika in Cambridge* (1941)

A somewhat eccentric measurement of time is part of the Oxbridge academic tradition. Otherwise, the Gregorian calendar is generally applicable.

JANUARY
Needle and Thread Dinner: New Year celebration at Queen's, Oxford

MARCH
Torpids (Oxford) and **Bumps** (Cambridge): college boat races
The Boat Race, Oxford v Cambridge

APRIL
Fritillary Walk, Iffley Meadows, Oxford

MAY
Choral singing from Magdalen Tower, Oxford (1 May, 6 am)
Beating the Bounds: walk around the parish boundaries from St Michael's at the Northgate to Lincoln College, Oxford (Ascension Day)
Eights Week: boat races in Oxford, balls, theatre etc. (in 5th week of Trinity term)

JUNE
May Week: boat races in Cambridge, balls etc. (end of Easter term)

Strawberry Fair: music and arts festival on Midsummer Common, Cambridge
Encaenia (Oxford) and **Honorary Degree Day** (Cambridge), conferral of honorary doctorates

JULY
Cambridge Shakespeare Festival (till end August)
Cambridge Folk Festival

SEPTEMBER
St Giles' Fair, Oxford (Mon & Tues after St Giles' Day, 1 September)

OCTOBER
St Frideswide's Day, Festival service in Christ Church Cathedral, in honour of Oxford's patron saint (19 October)
Restoration Dinner, at Magdalen College, Oxford (25 October)

NOVEMBER
All Souls Day: celebration at All Souls College, Oxford, with the 'Mallard Song' in memory of the legendary duck found when the college was under construction (2 November). Takes place only once every hundred years.

DECEMBER
Boar's Head Dinner, at Queen's College, Oxford (the Saturday before Christmas)
Festival of Nine Lessons and Carols, at King's College, Cambridge (3 pm, 24 December)

Bibliography

Noel Annan, *The Dons: Mentors, Eccentrics and Geniuses*, London: HarperCollins, 1999

Philip Atkins and Michael Johnson, *A New Guidebook to the Heart of Oxford*, Stonesfield: Dodo, 1999

Nicolas Barker, *The Oxford University Press and the Spread of Learning, 1478–1978: An Illustrated History*, Oxford: Clarendon Press, 1978

Brian Bell (ed.), *Oxford*, Singapore: APA Publications, 1990

John Betjeman, *An Oxford University Chest*, London: John Miles, 1938

Richard Bird, *The Gardens of Cambridge*, photographs by Dona Haycraft, Cambridge: Covent Garden, 1994

Andrew Boyle, *The Climate of Treason: Five Who Spied For Russia*, London: Hutchinson, 1979

Christopher Brooke and Roger Highfield, *Oxford and Cambridge*, photographs by Wim Swaan, Cambridge: CUP, 1988

Christopher Brooke (ed.), *History of the University of Cambridge*, Cambridge: CUP, 2004

Hugh Casson, *Hugh Casson's Cambridge*, London: Phaidon, 1992

Graham Chainey, *A Literary History of Cambridge*, Cambridge: Pevensey, 1985

Alec Clifton-Taylor, *The Pattern of English Building*, 4th ed., London: Faber & Faber, 1987

Alan B. Cobban, *The Medieval English Universities: Oxford and Cambridge to c.1500*, Aldershot: Scolar, 1988

John Costello, *Mask of Treachery*, London: Collins, 1988

Jon Davison, *Oxford: Images & Recollections*, Oxford: Jon Davison Publications, 1995

Richard Deacon, *The Cambridge Apostles: A History of Cambridge University's Elite Intellectual Secret Society*, London: Royce, 1985

Alexander Demandt (ed.), *Stätten des Geistes: grosse Universitäten Europas von der Antike bis zur Gegenwart*, Cologne: Böhlau, 1999

Christopher Dodd, *The Oxford & Cambridge Boat Race*, London: Stanley Paul, 1983

John Dougill, *Oxford in English Literature: The Making, and Undoing, of 'the English Athens'*, Ann Arbor: University of Michigan Press, 1998

David Edmonds and John Eidinow, *Wittgenstein's Poker: The Story of a Ten-Minute Argument Between Two Great Philosophers*, London: Faber & Faber, 2001

Walter Ellis, *The Oxbridge Conspiracy: How the Ancient Universities Have Kept Their Stranglehold on the Establishment*, London: Michael Joseph, 1994

Laurence and Helen Fowler (eds), *Cambridge Commemorated: An Anthology of University Life*, Cambridge: CUP, 1984

Peter Fox (ed.), *Cambridge University Library: The Great Collections*, Cambridge: CUP, 1998

Martin Garrett, *Cambridge: A Cultural and Literary History*, Oxford: Signal, 2005

Ronald Gray, *Oxford Gardens*, photographs by Ernest Frankl, Cambridge: Pevensey Press, 1987

A. H. Halsey, *The Decline of Donnish Dominion: The British Academic Professions in the Twentieth Century*, Oxford: Clarendon Press, 1992

Christopher Hibbert, *The Encyclopaedia of Oxford*, London: Macmillan, 1988

Tanis Hinchcliffe, *North Oxford*, New Haven and London: Yale University Press, 1992

David Horan, *Oxford: A Cultural and Literary Companion*, Oxford: Signal, 1999

Clive James, *May Week Was In June*, London: Cape, 1990

Tony Jedrej, *Cambridge Cats*, text by John Gaskell, London: Duckworth, 1994

Anthony Kenny (ed.), *The History of the Rhodes Trust, 1902–1999*, Oxford: OUP, 2001

Margaret Elizabeth Keynes, *A House by the River: Newnham Grange to Darwin College*, Cambridge: Darwin College, 1976

Elisabeth Leedham-Green, *A Concise History of the University of Cambridge*, Cambridge: CUP, 1996

W. C. Lubenow, *The Cambridge Apostles, 1820–1914: Liberalism, Imagination, and Friendship in British Intellectual and Professional Life*, Cambridge: CUP, 1998

Rita McWilliams Tullberg, *Women at Cambridge*, 2nd ed., Cambridge and New York: CUP, 1998

James Morris, *Oxford*, London: Faber & Faber, 1965

Jan Morris, *The Oxford Book of Oxford*, Oxford: OUP, 1978

Richard Ollard (ed.), *The Diaries of A. L. Rowse*, London: Allen Lane, 2003

Nikolaus Pevsner, *Cambridgeshire*, 'The Buildings of England', 2nd ed., Harmondsworth: Penguin, 1970

David Piper, *The Treasures of Oxford*, New York and London: Paddington Press, 1977

David Piper, *Treasures of the Ashmolean Museum*, Oxford: Ashmolean Museum, 1995

John Prest (ed.), *The Illustrated History of Oxford University*, Oxford and New York: OUP, 1993

Gwen Raverat, *Period Piece: A Cambridge Childhood*, London: Faber & Faber, 1952

Tim Rawle, *Cambridge Architecture*, London: Trefoil, 1985

Nicholas Ray, *Cambridge Architecture: A Concise Guide*, Cambridge: CUP, 1994

Robert T. Rivington, *Punting: Its History and Techniques*, Oxford: R.T. Rivington, 1993

Lisa Sargood, *Literary Cambridge*, Stroud, Glos.: Sutton Publishing, 2004

Norman Scarfe, *Cambridgeshire*, London: Faber & Faber, 1983

Jennifer Sherwood and Nikolaus Pevsner, *Oxfordshire*, 'The Buildings of England', Harmondsworth: Penguin, 1974

Andrew Sinclair, *The Red and the Blue: Intelligence, Treason and the Universities*, London: Weidenfeld and Nicolson, 1986

Peter Snow, *Oxford Observed: Town and Gown*, London: Murray, 1991

Richard Surman, *College Cats of Oxford and Cambridge*, London: HarperCollins, 1994

Ted Tapper and Brian Salter, *Oxford, Cambridge and the Changing Idea of the University*, Buckingham: Open University Press, 1992

Alison Taylor, *Cambridge: The Hidden History*, Stroud, Glos.: Tempus, 1999

Ann Thwaite (ed.), *My Oxford*, London: Robson, 1977

Geoffrey Tyack, *Oxford and Cambridge*, 'Blue Guide', London: A & C Black, 1995

David Walter, *The Oxford Union: Playground of Power*, London: Macdonald & Co., 1984
Sydney Waterlow (ed.), *In Praise of Cambridge*, London: Constable & Co., 1912
Whipplesnaith (Noël Howard Symington), *The Night-Climbers of Cambridge*, London: Chatto & Windus, 1937
Jon Whiteley, *Oxford and the Pre-Raphaelites*, Oxford: Ashmolean Museum, 1989
Simon Winchester, *The Surgeon of Crowthorne*, London: Viking, 1998
Simon Winchester, *The Meaning of Everything: The Story of the Oxford English Dictionary*, Oxford: OUP, 2003
Francis Woodman, *The Architectural History of King's College Chapel*, London: Routledge & Kegan Paul, 1986
A. R. Woolley, *The Clarendon Guide to Oxford*, 4th ed., Oxford: OUP, 1979

Picture Credits

Oxford

pp. 1–7   Photographs by Peter Sager
p. 8   John Ruskin from *A Reader's Guide to Writer's Britain* by Sally Varlow
           A. E. Housman: The Housman Society
           Thomas Hardy: Thomas Hardy Image Gallery
           Oscar Wilde and Bosie: The Oscar Wilde Society
           John Betjeman: The Estate of John Betjeman
p. 9   Dorothy L. Sayers: The Dorothy L. Sayers Collection
           Lewis Carroll: The Lewis Carroll Society
           J. R. R. Tolkien: The J. R. R. Tolkien Society
           W. H. Auden, Cecil Day-Lewis and Stephen Spender from *A Reader's Guide to Writer's Britain* by Sally Varlow
pp. 10–16 Photographs by Peter Sager

Cambridge

pp. 1–7   Photographs by Peter Sager
p. 8   Alfred Lord Tennyson: The Tennyson Society
           Christopher Marlowe: The Marlowe Society
           E. M. Forster: E. M. Forster Collection
           Thomas Gray: The Thomas Gray Archive
p. 9   William Wordsworth: The Wordsworth Trust
           Bertrand Russell: The Bertrand Russell Archives
           Ludwig Wittgenstein: The Wittgenstein Archives
           Sylvia Plath and Ted Hughes: Rollie McKenna
pp. 10–16 Photographs by Peter Sager

Index of People

Page numbers in **bold** type indicate primary entries.

Index of Places and Themes

Page numbers in **bold** type indicate primary entries.
(O) = Oxford, (C) = Cambridge